The Wars of the Roses

The Wars of the Roses
Military Activity and English Society, 1452–97

Anthony Goodman

Dorset Press
New York

To the memory of my mother

This edition published by Dorset Press
a division of Marboro Books Corporation,
by arrangement with Routledge
1990 Dorset Press

ISBN 0-88029-484-1

Printed in the United States of America
M 9 8 7 6 5 4 3 2 1

Contents

Illustrations

Preface

Yet another book about the Wars of the Roses needs to start with an apology. For the battles have often been refought, and in recent years historians have gone far in reweaving the fabric of the political backcloths. Nevertheless, I felt it might be worthwhile to review in particular strategic, technical and logistic aspects of the wars which were important factors in them and in the evolution of English military skills. I have, besides, examined the tangled subject of the effects of the wars on society: I suspect that one important effect was to intensify feelings of regional particularism, facilitating Tudor rule over communities which found it hard to combine against the crown.

I owe especial thanks to Professor Kenneth Fowler for his comments on chapter 8, and to Dr Angus MacKay for introducing me to Mosén Diego de Valera's and Andres Bernaldez's lively reactions to the turbulent and ferocious English. I hope that my incidental remarks about institutions and society adequately reflect the stimulating teaching of my former colleagues Professor Ted Cowan and Professor Alan Harding, with whom I taught a senior course on such aspects of late medieval British society for several years. I am grateful to the officers of county record offices who have helpfully answered my inquiries about urban financial accounts – particularly to Jennifer Hofmann, Senior Assistant Archivist at the Dorset County Record Office, who brought the Bridport Muster Roll to my attention. Anna P. Campbell typed the manuscript with her customary skill.

But, above all, I owe thanks to the encouragement of my wife, Jacqueline, and to the patience of my daughter, Emma. Regrettably, my mother, Ethel Lilly Eels, did not live to see this book, to whose completion she looked forward eagerly.

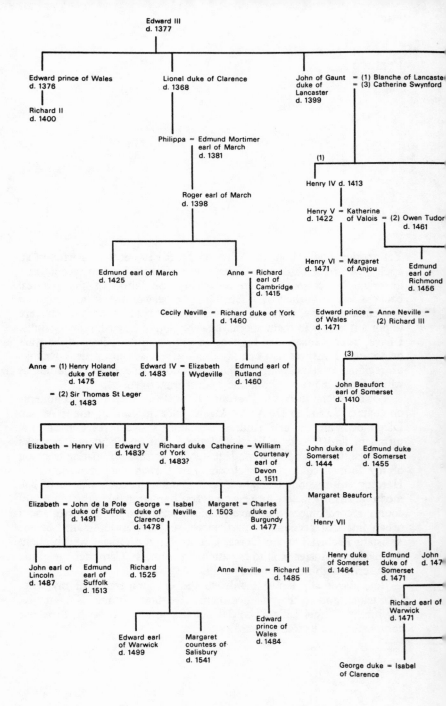

The succession to the English throne in the later fifteenth century

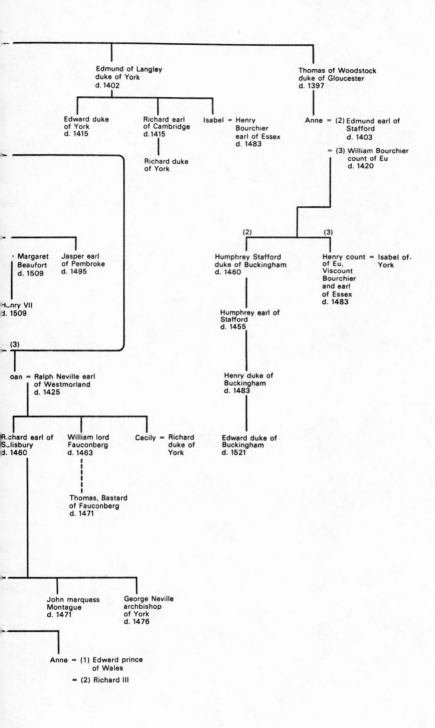

The Wars of the Roses

Introduction

'The Wars of the Roses' is the name commonly given by modern historians to campaigns in the second half of the fifteenth century which were fought mainly in England and Wales, but also spilled over on to Irish, French and Scottish soil, and had important international repercussions and involvements. Their starting-point has usually been taken to be the brief revolt in May 1455 headed by the richest secular magnate in the realm, Richard duke of York, a great lord in that part of Wales known as the Marches as well as in northern England. York was protesting against the enmity shown to him by those favoured by Henry VI, notably Edmund Beaufort, duke of Somerset.

Henry's grandfather, Henry of Bolingbroke, duke of Lancaster, had gained the throne in 1399 as Henry IV, by procuring the deposition of Richard II. The claim to the succession of York's uncle Edmund Mortimer, earl of March (whose heir York was), was passed over then. In 1459 and 1460 York again headed rebellions against courtiers and councillors whose hostility towards him was strongly sustained by the forceful queen, Margaret of Anjou. The wars began as a lengthy political, and eventually armed, struggle, predominantly for influence at court and in the localities, between alliances of magnates and gentlefolk. But after the success of the 1460 revolt York gave primacy to the dynastic issue. He laid claim to the throne in right of his Mortimer descent before parliament, which recognized that he should succeed Henry, displacing as heir the latter's son, the young Edward prince of Wales. Soon afterwards, however, York died fighting against the queen's and prince's supporters who opposed the parliamentary compromise.

In March 1461 York's eldest son, the earl of March, was acclaimed in London by his supporters as Edward IV. Though the young king speedily drove Henry and Margaret from the realm, it was not until 1464 that the last serious Lancastrian stir was defeated. Thereafter the queen and her son maintained a threadbare court over the water, a centre for intrigue, and Henry's standard was still on occasion defiantly raised in Wales.

The strenuous military and financial demands which Edward made on his subjects in order to oust the Lancastrians in the early 1460s disillusioned them with his rule, which consequently remained vulnerable. In the late 1460s Richard Neville, earl of Warwick, head of the magnate family which since 1455 had given the most notable support to the Yorkist cause, became alienated from Edward, whose favour to some other leading supporters – such as the kinsmen of his queen, Elizabeth Wydeville – provoked tensions. Warwick, like York in the 1450s, used his formidable prestige, wealth and local influence to instigate rebellions in 1469 and in March 1470, with the aim of establishing his primacy at court, in alliance with Edward's brother George duke of Clarence, who married the earl's daughter Isabel. Like York, but more quickly, the pair were driven to dynastic plotting, since their ostensibly 'reformist' agitation, with its aim of personal domination of the crown, received enthusiastic support widely only from the commons. In October 1470 Clarence and Warwick succeeded in driving Edward into exile and in restoring the passive Henry VI, who had been a prisoner in the Tower since 1465. This 'Readeption' of Henry, inspired by Louis XI of France, turned out disastrously for Warwick and his uncomfortable Lancastrian bedfellows. In 1471 Edward resolutely reconquered the realm, slaying in battle Warwick, his brother Marquess Montague, Henry's son Prince Edward, executing the last male Beaufort, Edmund duke of Somerset, imprisoning Margaret of Anjou and apparently having Henry murdered in the Tower.

For the rest of his life Edward's rule was not seriously challenged, but soon after his twelve-year-old son succeeded him as Edward V in 1483, Edward IV's surviving brother, Richard duke of Gloucester, usurped the throne. Within months Richard III faced and convincingly crushed a major rebellion, whose public aim was to put an obscure exile, Henry Tudor, on the throne. Henry claimed it in right of his mother, Margaret Beaufort, as the surviving male representative of the house of Lancaster. In 1485 he defeated and killed Richard at the battle of Bosworth, assumed the crown, and in January 1486 married Edward IV's eldest child, Elizabeth. Bosworth has often been taken by historians as marking the end of the Wars of the Roses, and the beginnings of a new era of relative Tudor political stability and internal peace.

Implicit in the phrase 'the Wars of the Roses' are the propositions that a number of campaigns occurring in a thirty-year period had a causal link, and that this link was the enmity between the houses of

Lancaster and York, symbolized respectively by red and white roses. In fact the white rose was only one of several badges used by the Yorkist family, and was to become the prime emblem of the distinctive dynastic links of some of their sixteenth-century descendants.[1] There is no definite evidence that Lancastrian princes and their supporters displayed a red rose. A mixed red and white one was invented for Henry VII and Elizabeth of York to symbolize the intention of their marriage to reconcile the two warring families. The mixed rose became a favourite Tudor emblem.[2]

Contemporaries have left few direct analytical comments about the wars as a whole, since a total concept of them was embryonic. A connection between troubles was perceived because of their relevance to disputes over the crown, whose rightful tenure was widely regarded as being of vital importance. Calamities were regarded as the inevitable corollaries of attempts to dethrone lawful kings and of rule by usurping ones. Also literary criticism and satire about the state of the polity – such as that in surviving English verses – shows the strength of contemporary convictions that there were other current disintegrative social trends: persistent royal failures to provide justice, burdensome royal financial demands, and the protection which nobles gave to law-breakers.[3] Some became concerned at the commons' propensity to rebel.[4]

One of the origins of later dynastic interpretations of the wars is to be found in the declaration of Edward IV's title to the throne in parliament (November 1461), where the usurpation of Henry IV was cloudily linked with all the troubles which the realm had experienced since 1399:

> whereof the heavy explanation in the doom of every Christian man
> soundeth into God's hearing in heaven, not forgotten in the earth,
> specially in this Realm of England, which therefore hath suffered the
> charge of intolerable persecution, punition and tribulation, whereof
> the like hath not been seen or heard in any other Christian Realm, by
> any memory or record.[5]

But to help justify Henry VII's rule, a non-dynastic explanation was put forward more specifically for the troubles in the thirty or so years before 1485 – an explanation providing the tenacious idea that Tudor rule had then ushered in, as pre-ordained, a new era of lasting domestic peace. Henry, born in 1456, the year after the first battle of St Albans, was of mixed Welsh and English parentage, with a strain of French royal blood from his grandmother Katherine of Valois, which he was to value highly.[6] In the 1460s he was brought up in the household of Edward's leading Welsh supporter, Lord Herbert. Henry's alleged

descent from Cadwalader (who according to Geoffrey of Monmouth was
the last king of Great Britain, driven out by the Saxons) may have made
him especially aware of Welsh beliefs, based on prophecies, that a
native prince would arise to crush the Saxons – predictions which some
people associated with Edward IV's accession, and some, more briefly,
with the Herberts' invasion of England in 1469.[7]

Henry's residence in Brittany (1471–84) and in France (1484–5),
as a dependant of their respective courts, may have confirmed a
tendency to view English history and politics in an alien interpretative
and critical spirit. At the Breton court the legendary British history
embodied in Geoffrey of Monmouth's *Historia Regum Britanniae* was
cherished as a glorification of ancient Breton independence and
greatness. In the definitive history of Brittany written in the late 1490s
by Alain Bouchard with the encouragement of Charles VIII's queen,
Anne duchess of Brittany, the struggles of the kings of Great Britain
against the restless, perfidious Saxons were outlined, with the fall of
Cadwalader.[8]

The British history also provided material for the French court's
current interpretation of English history, which emphasized the violence
and perfidy with which kings were habitually overthrown. This received
new publicity in January 1484, when Charles VIII's chancellor, at the
estates general of Tours, contrasted his happy accession with Richard
III's murder of his nephews.[9] Henry Tudor's princely foreign patrons
firmly believed in the ingrained political viciousness of the English, once
more exposed in recent dissensions and usurpations. In this context he
and they are likely to have been excited by the possible significance of
his descent from Cadwalader, a sign that he was intended to restore the
more Christian, more glorious polity of Great Britain.

The panegyric biography written for Henry the mature ruler by the
French Augustinian friar Bernard André related the downfall of
Cadwalader and emphasized Henry's descent from him. André also
emphasized that Henry's destiny had been to calm the deep-rooted
saevitia Anglorum, to block the influence of that *malignus spiritus*
which had brought Britons and Saxons into collision, which had shown
itself once more in the rage against Henry VI, and which Henry VII's
English 'Juno', Edward IV's sister Margaret, dowager duchess of
Burgundy, attempted to kindle against him.[10]

Henry's likely conviction that he had been divinely ordained to
destroy the ancient vice, whose recurrence since Henry VI's accession
had filled the realm with turbulence, is probably reflected in court
verses celebrating a new era of peace, such as those written by Pietro
Carmeliano and Giovanni de' Giglis, and in the florid address to Henry
by Walter Ogilvie, written soon after James IV's marriage in 1502 to
Henry's daughter.[11]

Thus the foreign elements in Henry's upbringing provided him with a novel sort of justification for his rule, focusing on the dissidence of the previous thirty years, and treating it as a distinct phenomenon terminated by what was implicitly alleged to be a 'new monarchy' – aptly symbolized by the ancient British name of Arthur given by Henry to his first-born son in 1486, by the imperial coin-image introduced possibly as early as 1487, and by the kneeling effigy of himself receiving the crown from God at Bosworth field which he willed to be placed over the most sacred shrine of English monarchy, St Edward's tomb in Westminster abbey.[12]

The view held at Henry's court that he had inaugurated a peaceful era after one of deeply entrenched division was to be powerfully developed in the early sixteenth century by Polydore Vergil in his *Anglica Historia*, and by Edward Hall's *The Vnion of the two noble and illustre famelies of Lancastre and Yorke*, published in 1548 by Richard Grafton. Vergil established the interpretation that the original cause of division was not *saevitia Anglorum*, but the usurpation of 1399. These views were to be propagated by the oft-printed chronicles of Grafton and Holinshed, and by Shakespeare's history plays, and were to be succinctly summed up by the phrase 'the Wars of the Roses', invented, apparently, by Sir Walter Scott.[13]

Recent historians have tended to play down the Tudor propositions that the wars were caused by the dynastic issue, and that they long engulfed society in chaos and misery. But they have mostly continued to see a value in looking at a scattering of conflicts over three decades as a whole, treating them as symptomatic of social, institutional and political tensions connected particularly with the role of the nobility. David Hume, in his *History of England*, had placed particular emphasis on the allegedly factious practices of the pre-Tudor nobility, and on how Henry VII's firm government induced cultural and social change:

There scarcely passed any session during this [Henry's] reign without some statute against engaging retainers, and giving them badges or liveries – a practice, by which they were in a manner enlisted under some great lord, and were kept in readiness to assist him in all wars, insurrections, riots, violences and even in bearing evidence for him in courts of justice. This disorder, which had prevailed during many reigns, when the law could give little protection to the subject, was then deeply rooted in England; and it required all the vigilance and rigor of Henry to extirpate it. . . . The nobility, instead of vying with each other in the number and boldness of their retainers, acquired by degrees a more civilised species of emulation, and endeavored to excel in the splendor and elegance of their equipage, houses, and tables: the common people, no longer maintained in vicious idleness by their superiors, were obliged to learn some calling or industry, and became useful both to themselves and to others.[14]

Hume's emphasis on the importance of aristocratic turbulence and its institutional forms was to be reinforced and refined by Charles Plummer's well-known critical edition (Oxford 1885) of Sir John Fortescue's brief treatise *The Governance of England*. Fortescue had been chancellor to Henry VI and his son Prince Edward in the 1460s: the *Governance* dates in its present form from soon after 1471, when Fortescue had perforce to accept Edward IV's allegiance. The work distils the mature reflections of a former chief justice of the King's Bench and royal councillor, about current problems of English monarchy which had absorbed his own career for at least a decade. He entitled his ninth chapter: 'Here he showith the perils that may come to the king by over mighty subjects':

> Whereof it hath come that often times, when a subject hath had also great livelihood of his prince, he hath anon aspired to the estate of his prince, which by such a man may soon be got. . . . For the people will go with him that best may sustain and reward them. . . . We have also seen late in our own realm, some of the king's subjects give him battle, by occasion that their livelihood and offices were the greatest of the land, and else they would not have done so.[15]

In his introductory discussion of this passage, Plummer put forward ideas about how changes in the system of military service in the fourteenth century increased the danger to the crown from the influence of 'over-mighty subjects': the reign of Edward III

> saw the beginning of that bastard feudalism, which, in place of the primitive relation of a lord to his tenants, surrounded the great man with a horde of retainers, who wore his livery and fought his battles, and were, in the most literal sense of the words, in the law courts and elsewhere, 'Addicti jurare in verba magistri;' while he in turn maintained their quarrels and shielded their crimes from punishment. This evil, as we shall see, reached its greatest height during the Lancastrian period.[16]

Plummer's casual phrase 'bastard feudalism' was to be given wider currency by the late K. B. McFarlane, who used it in his penetrating – and more sympathetic – explorations of later medieval patronage and clientage, especially in papers published in the 1940s, and in the Ford Lectures for 1953.[17] McFarlane bequeathed a new understanding of the social and political mechanics of later medieval aristocracy – in some ways a parallel achievement to Sir Lewis Namier's exposition of eighteenth-century 'connection'. In a similar vein, McFarlane regarded gentlefolk as generally motivated by self-interest rather than ideological conviction: the Wars of the Roses presented them with no 'cause worth dying for'; 'it is easy to see why opportunism rather than loyalty prevailed among those with most to lose, the heads of the great landed families'. He used the word 'opportunism' in a non-pejorative sense, taking a Whiggish view of noble patronage as social cement rather than (as Plummer) dissolvent. McFarlane denied that civil war was caused by the existence of armed bands of retainers or that it grew out of the local quarrels of magnates: the reason for central government's collapsing authority was the inanity of Henry VI.[18]

More recently, historians have illuminated facets of the politics of the nobility, and of the workings of 'bastard feudalism' in the period, confirming previous historians' insistence on their relevance to an understanding of the wars. Professor R. L. Storey has surveyed the widespread, increasing violence of 'faction' up to 1461, and, in a masterly biography, Professor C. Ross has shown how Edward IV gradually asserted his control over the disordered political scene.[19] Professor Ross has also written a succinct account of the Wars of the Roses.[20] The work of Storey and Dr R. A. Griffiths in particular has taught us much about the origins of the political instability of northern society, which was to help prolong the wars.[21] As yet less is known about political relationships in Henry VII's reign, though his methods of government have been studied exhaustively.

This book is intended to illuminate the Wars of the Roses through a study of the campaigns, military organization and methods, and social consequences. Indeed, the consequences were not as profound as those of the Hundred Years War in France, since commanders were especially concerned to keep campaigns brief and localized, and to minimize disruption of civilian life. But military activity does not have to be prolonged, wide-scale and devastating to produce significant social and political effects. As we are experiencing, late-twentieth-century society is vulnerable to mere threats from minute groups of terrorists. Normally, the main consequence of warfare for fifteenth-century society was the cost of sustaining soldiers, unwonted burdens on a largely subsistence economy. However few, however briefly engaged, the soldiers of the Wars of the Roses had to be armed, fed and billeted. Artillery, munitions, entrenching tools, transports and camp gear had to be assembled. The efforts required – even though no blows might be exchanged – had complex social effects, as did casualties, executions and forfeitures. An examination of such phenomena may help to explain the sixteenth-century conviction – transmuted by Tudor historians and poets into flights of classically inspired hyperbole – that recent ancestors had profoundly experienced the agonies of civil tumult.

Modern historians' concentration on socio-political aspects of the wars has led many to neglect their military context.²² Indeed, patchy evidence about the armies and campaigns has been a deterrent to study — and has led all too often to surmise in the following pages. Contemporary descriptions of engagements are often so vague that it is impossible to pinpoint details topographically with assurance, or even fix on their sites. Changing land-usage has often altered sites drastically. But one can walk round the centre of St Albans and trace the course of the 1455 *mêlée*. One certain, relatively unchanged battle-site, Bosworth, has recently been adorned with flag-poles and notices purporting to explain the course of the battle.

It has generally been too readily assumed that military methods in the Wars of the Roses were of little intrinsic significance. Supposedly they were insular and conservative — surprising suppositions, considering that before the wars the English had been so heavily involved in Continental warfare, and that during them there were notable Continental developments in the roles of infantry, cavalry and artillery. In the later stages of the wars foreign mercenaries were particularly prominent. Scientific study of warfare was encouraged at the highest levels of English society, and mercenary service by veterans of the wars was valued on the Continent. It is argued in this book that the wars helped to adapt historic English military methods to what was required of expeditionary forces crossing the Channel to the Continent in the new military age of the Italian wars.

In this study, the period of the Wars of the Roses has been taken as running from 1452 to 1497, not from 1455 to 1485. The 1452 campaign — which Professor Storey has described²³ — was the first large-scale one, with more magnates and soldiers involved than in 1455. It ended without the threatened battle, but its military and political lessons had some influence on subsequent campaigns. In a long-term perspective the battle of Bosworth in 1485 marks a decisive turning-point — the inauguration of the Tudor dynasty. But it did not, as Henry VII's propaganda suggested, inaugurate an era of peace. His seizure of the crown prolonged the rebelliousness which had reappeared in 1483. In 1486–7 his rule was dangerously beleaguered. Perkin Warbeck's attempted invasions in 1495, 1496 and 1497 petered out so quickly that they have not been seriously considered as a phase in the wars. But the forces he mustered on each occasion were not negligible — they were just mustered to little purpose. Henry would have faced a more formidable dynastic rebellion in the 1490s but for his success in penetrating his opponents' plans and arresting noble dissidents. 1497, not 1485, is the year in which the last dynastic rebellion occurred.

With one major exception, the literary sources used in this study were all written in the fifteenth century. Persuasive details given by Edward Hall and later Tudor writers have been ignored, because it is impossible to check on the sources of much of their information. There is a large amount of historical writing surviving from the later fifteenth century, much of it anonymous and primitively annalistic in form and content. Historiography was in a transitional phase. The tradition of monastic chronicle-writing was moribund: only two abbeys provide important sources for the wars. Abbot Whethamstede of St Albans (d. 1465) compiled a *Register* concerned mainly with the abbey's affairs, written up in its surviving form after his death. This contains a valuable, independent account of national politics up to 1461, with vivid details about the battles fought, so to speak, on the abbey's doorstep in 1455 and 1461.[24] At Crowland abbey (Lincs.) continuations of older chronicles produced in the house were made in the fifteenth century, which are prime sources for the wars. The 'first continuation', compiled by a former prior, narrated events until Warwick's triumph over Edward IV in 1469. The 'second continuator', who wrote in more polished vein some time after April 1486, started his account of events up to that year in October 1459: weight is added to it by information derived from an anonymous doctor of canon law who had been a councillor of Edward IV.[25]

The writing of Latin chronicles had become rare outside as well as inside monasteries. A particularly valuable non-monastic example, with many unique details, is that ending in 1462 and transcribed into his commonplace book before 1471 by John Benet, vicar of Harlington (Beds.). The single author of this account of events from 1440 onwards was probably a cleric living in London, perhaps Benet himself.[26] Another Latin writer who contributed unique details of early stages of the wars was an annalist writing in 1491, whose account of events from November 1459 to May 1463 contains a number of autobiographical entries. K. B. McFarlane disproved the accepted ascription of the chronicle of which this forms a section to William Worcester, a gentleman-bureaucrat of literary and antiquarian tastes whose Latin notebooks contain information about some episodes in the wars.[27] Humanist Latin historiography was slow to take root in England, and had few major practitioners. The founder of humanist historiography there (as practised in the vernacular as well as Latin) was Polydore Vergil of Urbino. When he arrived in England in 1502, he already had a distinguished scholarly reputation; and with some encouragement from Henry VII, Vergil undertook to write a history of England from Romano-British origins to the present day. He completed a draft up to September 1513, which he subsequently altered and added to: the first edition was published in Basel in 1534. Vergil set new standards of literary elegance and interpretative coherence for English historians. For events of the later fifteenth century he obtained information from those who had held high office in the period. This is reflected in the many unique details which he gives of rebellions and campaigns of the 1480s and '90s.[28]

The most powerful influence on the form of chronicle-writing in the fifteenth century was the spread of vernacular literacy among secular elites of gentlefolk and citizens. Many of their commonplace books have survived, into which they copied or had copied material relating to history and politics, such as royal genealogies, exhortatory and satirical verses, and chronicles of Anglo-British history going back to mythical times, notably the *Brut Chronicle*, so called after Brutus, the legendary Trojan founder of the ancient kingdom of Great Britain. Owners were eager to bring chronicles up to date, copying sets of borrowed annals, sometimes making personal insertions as they copied, or composing their own continuations. The Wars of the Roses in themselves probably helped to stimulate these literary activities. The largest corpus of burgeoning contemporary or near-contemporary annals, overshadowing all others in bulk and influence by the later fifteenth century, were the 'chronicles of London'. Dozens of manuscripts of these survive, some of them continuations of the *Brut* or older city chronicles, all differing in various degrees, but inter-related in complex patterns. They were written in the first instance for or by London citizens and residents: their preoccupations are reflected in the prominence allotted to city as well as national affairs, and to the record of commodity prices and matters of urban gossip.[29]

The London chronicles have drawbacks as sources for national politics. They are mostly anonymous compilations, a patchwork of annals, and their authors characteristically lacked literary skill or good sources of information about court politics and distant events. The annals are consequently often a hotch-potch of bald and inaccurate facts. But their great value is that they reflect contemporary rumour and prejudice – the marked pro-Yorkist bias of London annals dealing with the events of the 1450s and early '60s is a pointer to opinion in the city. An example is *An English Chronicle from 1377 to 1461* (a continuation of the *Brut*), the last eleven years of which, the work of a single author, are fullest, and distinguished by their Yorkist fervour.[30] Strong personal opinions about events in the early stages of the wars (notably about the second battle of St Albans in 1461) are found in the continuations of a city chronicle to 1470, in a commonplace book written in a fifteenth-century hand. There is tantalizing evidence that one of its continuators may have been William Gregory, a skinner who was mayor in 1451–2.[31] These are London chronicles with an exceptional amount of unique information for periods of the wars. More generally in this book recourse has been had to a London chronicle which embraces their whole span, and contains a great deal of information found in other London chronicles – British Museum, Cottonian MS Vitellius A XVI, which C. L. Kingsford edited in *Chronicles of London* (Oxford 1905). The core of this is a version of what he termed the 'Main City Chronicle, 1440–85'.

One of the few vernacular chronicles of the period whose authorship is definitely known is the short but valuable one which John Warkworth, master of Peterhouse, Cambridge, tacked on to a *Brut Chronicle* which he presented to the college in 1483.[32] Warkworth gave an account of national politics from Edward IV's accession in 1461 to the end of the last rebellion against him, the surrender of St Michael's Mount in 1474. Warkworth coolly appraised Edward's fumbling responses to the problems confronting his early rule, and provides one of the few accounts of the struggles of 1469–70. Knowledge of some campaigns in this period is provided by two early manuscript examples of a genre which was to be stimulated by the growth of vernacular literacy and printing – the propaganda pamphlet. The *Chronicle of the Rebellion in Lincolnshire, 1470*[33] is a brief account of Edward IV's campaign in the shire and its aftermath, which makes use of rebel confessions to prove Clarence's and Warwick's complicity. Another, more polished and informative official account is the *Historie of the Arrivall of King Edward IV, A.D. 1471*, written by 'a servant of the King's that presently saw in effect a great part of his exploits, and the residue knew by true relation of them that were present at every time'.[34]

These two works have affinities with documentary genres, now written mainly in the vernacular, numerous examples of which survive – public proclamations and political manifestos, semi-public letters of denunciation and summons addressed to individuals, and private newsletters. All these were heavily utilized by chroniclers. The Castilian Mosén Diego de Valera incorporated the substance of his letter to the Catholic kings about Richard III's fall and Henry VII's early months of rule in his *Crónica de los Reyes Católicos*.[35] Newsletters, and news items in letters, are to be found in the English family collections of vernacular correspondence, which become a substantial source in the second half of the fifteenth century. Our knowledge of politics and domestic conflict in the period would be a great deal poorer but for the survival of its most voluminous correspondence, that of the Norfolk family the Pastons.[36] The fact that their propertied fortunes were especially bound up with magnate politics made them great retailers of political gossip. Shafts of information about politics can also be found in the correspondence of two knightly families, the Yorkshire Plumptons, dependants of the Percies, and the Stonors of Stonor (Oxon).[37]

The frequent international repercussions and involvements of the Wars of the Roses led not only to the writing of informative diplomatic reports about them by foreigners, but to mentions of them in foreign chronicles – particularly in the compendious and sophisticated works produced for the edification of courtiers and councillors by French and Burgundian historians. Thomas Basin, bishop of Lisieux, was interested in recording information particularly about Anglo-French relations in the 1460s;[38] Philippe de Commynes, in his celebrated *Memoirs*, made some characteristically succinct judgments about English politics and warfare.[39] In view of the close English links with the Low Countries, and the marriage of Edward IV's sister Margaret to Charles the Bold, duke of Burgundy, in 1468, it is not surprising that the official historiographers of the ducal house of Burgundy provide considerable information about English affairs. Georges Chastellain (d. 1475) provides some about early stages of the wars; his official successor and the continuator of his chronicle, Jean de Molinet (d. 1507) was interested in the invasions of England from 1485 onwards.[40] Another servant of the ducal house, Jean de Waurin (d. *c.* 1474) produced a collection of sources of English history from the earliest times (for which he depended heavily on the *Brut*) to 1471. The section from 1444 onwards is more original: it contains the fullest account of the wars from 1459 to 1471. He used the official accounts of the rebellion of March 1470 and of Edward's campaigns in 1471 – but the sources of most of his unique details (such as those of the battle of Edgcote) are unknown. Like Froissart when writing about English affairs from abroad, he demonstrably relied on muddled hearsay on occasion, and gave garbled versions of English personal and place-names. Possibly this is why his accounts have sometimes been neglected – an undeserved fate for the commentator with the best appreciation of military matters to write about a broad sweep of the Wars of the Roses.[41]

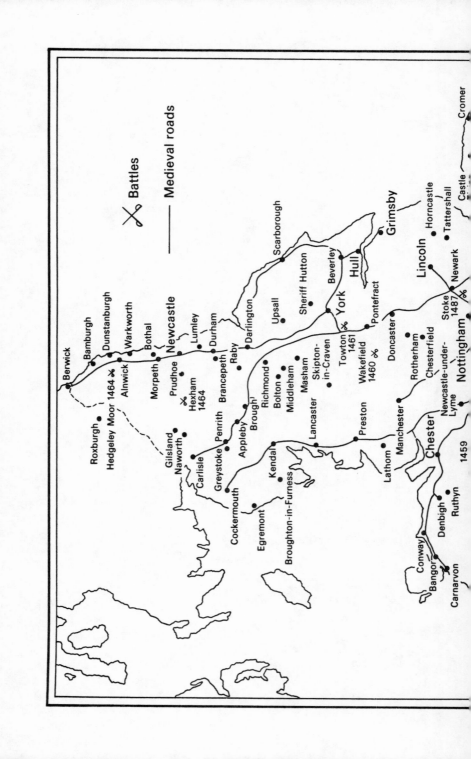

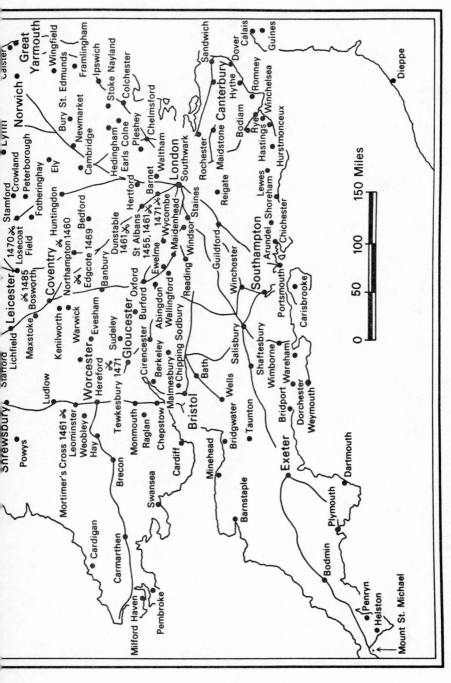

Map I   England and Wales during the Wars of the Roses

Part One

The Campaigns

Chapter 1

Yorkist Rebellions, 1452–60

Richard duke of York's elaborate and widespread propaganda campaign in the winter of 1451–2 gave the court ample warning of rebellion. In September 1451 he wrote to towns and individuals in Norfolk requesting support for his aims. In November, according to later indictments, his chamberlain Sir William Oldhall was inciting uprisings in eastern England.[1] Tense reactions at court are reflected in a letter which the duke wrote to Henry VI from his castle at Ludlow on 9 January 1452. Informed that, as a result of defamations, Henry was displeased with him, he had declared himself a true liegeman to Reginald Boulers, bishop of Hereford, and the earl of Shrewsbury. He had asked them to report to Henry his willingness to swear his loyalty on the Sacrament in the presence of two or three lords, if Henry cared to send them to Ludlow.[2]

The duke is unlikely to have received such deferential treatment. He was visited by the mere clerk of the council, who set out from Westminster on 1 February to summon him to a council at Coventry.[3] The mission proved vain. York was on the verge of rebellion. On 3 February he wrote a letter from Ludlow castle addressed to the bailiffs, burgesses and commons of Shrewsbury, blaming the duke of Somerset for the great losses in France, and for the king's failure to implement the articles which York had put before him in 1450, and accusing Somerset of continually labouring about the king for York's undoing. Consequently the latter had 'fully concluded to proceed in all haste against him [Somerset] with the help of my kinsmen and friends'. He requested the town of Shrewsbury to send him in support as many 'goodly and likely men as ye may'.[4]

The clerk of the council, who returned to Westminster on 12 February, doubtless confirmed rumours of York's warlike intentions. There were reports, too, of stirrings in the West Country, where the earl of Devon was preparing to join the duke in arms: on 14 February the duke of Buckingham and Lord Bonville were appointed chief commissioners to proceed against the rebels there.[5] Two days later the king rode northwards out of London, getting that day as far as Barnet, on his way to meet and consult with lords in arms, and perhaps to confront York, in case he advanced eastwards through the Midlands from Ludlow.[6] A peremptory royal mandate to Lord Cobham dated 17 February, upbraiding him for failure to attend the king like other lords who had been summoned, and enjoining immediate attendance, shows suspicion that he was involved in the rising.[7] The king headed for Northampton, where he stayed on 22–23 February, and 'took his counsel and sent for his lords'. He then turned back towards London, pausing at Dunstable, where he was well attended by magnates – the dukes of Exeter, Buckingham and Norfolk; the earls of Salisbury, Shrewsbury, Worcester and Wiltshire; Viscounts Beaumont and Lisle; Lords Clifford, Egremont, Moleyns, Stourton, Camoys and Beauchamp. By their advice he sent letters to the duke of York. These may have been carried by the envoys whom he dispatched to the duke – William Waynflete, bishop of Winchester, Viscount Bourchier and Lord Stourton. They relayed the royal prohibition of the rising: York tried to justify it and refused to obey. Henry also wrote, on 24 February, to the mayor, aldermen and commons of London, forbidding them to receive the duke.[8]

Henry's advance northwards and speedy concentration of formidable support posed a serious threat to the rising. Between 19 and 23 February there were Yorkist demonstrations in eastern England, but the assembly of the royal army may have deterred the demonstrators from moving westwards to join the duke.[9] York 'went another way' to avoid confrontation with the king, possibly through the southern Midlands, a convenient region in which to meet his southern allies, Devon and Cobham. The king's reversal of direction and message to the Londoners were probably responses to this Yorkist line of advance. The duke may have hoped to make Henry amenable by occupying the city. He and his allies sent a herald requesting the citizens to give them and their army passage. But the governors, obeying the royal command, refused and manned their defences. The Yorkist army abandoned the direct approaches to London, crossing the Thames into Surrey over Kingston bridge.[10]

York remained at Kingston for three days, perhaps waiting for reinforcements to come in, perhaps debating the next move, in view of the strength of royal support. But on 29 February, having traversed Surrey, the Yorkists arrived at Dartford in north-west Kent. The following day they were arrayed nearby at Crayford. Possibly they occupied ground between Crayford and the Darent estuary, with the Thames shore on their right flank, and on their left the river Cray, a tributary of the Darent crossed by Watling Street just south-east of Crayford church. York commanded the 'middleward', with Devon in command of a 'battle' 'by the South side' (bounded by the Cray?) and Cobham of one 'at the water side' (near the Thames shore?). There was a considerable array of ordnance – perhaps aligned in front of these positions in anticipation of a royal advance from the East along Watling Street.[11]

To counter York's move from Kingston to the vicinity of Dartford, the royal army had returned to London. Its 'foreward' had arrived there early in the morning of 27 February and passed over London Bridge, lodging in Southwark. The following morning it set out for Kent. That afternoon Henry VI reached London with the rest of his army, and lodged in Southwark at the bishop of Winchester's hostel by the church of St Mary Overy (now Southwark cathedral). Thence he dispatched bishops to negotiate with York. The latter 'said he would have the Duke of Somerset, or else he would die therefore'. His situation was not hopeless. Some chroniclers stress that he had a large, well-equipped army in a strong defensive encampment. Though the author of *An English Chronicle* said that his army was 'not strong enough for the king's party', the author of Arundel MS 19 said that allegedly he had as many soldiers as the king, and 'great stuff and ordnance'. Seven ships laden with 'stuff' kept open a line of riverine communication for the duke.[12]

On 1 March Henry moved from Southwark with his troops, to Blackheath, and over Shooter's Hill to Welling, where he lodged that day and the one following, about three miles from the Yorkist position. Bishop Waynflete of Winchester and the bishop of Ely, the earls of Salisbury and Warwick, Viscount Bourchier and Lord Sudeley rode to and fro from the king's camp as royal emissaries. Strenuous conciliatory efforts may have undermined the will of nobles on both sides to commence what promised to be bloody slaughter of their peers and kinsmen. The Yorkist lords' will to fight may have been sapped too by the amount and quality of noble support the king had rallied, and by the Kentishmen's failure to bring promised support. Henry, who hated the effusion of Christian blood, consented to receive York's petition. Terms were agreed on the afternoon of 2 March, presumably laying down conditions for York's reception, the disengagement of the armies and the right of Yorkist soldiers to unharmed egress. About noon the next day York, Devon and Cobham rode with forty horsemen into the royal army, which had withdrawn to Blackheath. The Yorkist lords knelt before the king, and the duke presented his articles of accusation against Somerset. To no avail: York was escorted to London, and before being allowed to return to Ludlow he was obliged to make public oath in St Paul's cathedral that he would never again instigate a rising.[13]

York's political humiliation stemmed from strategic failure. He had failed to co-ordinate the widespread stirrings which he had incited into a united movement. Constrained by the need to avoid outrageously rebellious behaviour, he did not move boldly against the king. The duke's unsure progress gave the royal commanders time to assess and respond to the challenge. The king's strategy may have benefited from the presence in his army of the most famous English soldier of the day, the venerable John Talbot, earl of Shrewsbury. The following year Talbot was to be killed at Castillon in Périgord, leading an Anglo-Gascon army as aggressively against the French as Henry's army had gone against York, and attempting an assault on a camp fortified with artillery like York's at Crayford.[14]

In his 1455 rising York avoided the mistakes of 1452. By basing it on the support of magnates coming from the remote north of England, instead of attempting to appeal widely to southern communities, he achieved a degree of surprise. By heading swiftly for the king's person, he kept the initiative. The campaign was one of the shortest in the Wars of the Roses. Henry, whose retinues were under Buckingham's command, was overwhelmed when defending the town of St Albans by York's forces and those of 'the captains of this field' under him, the earl of Salisbury and his eldest son, the earl of Warwick.[15] The king had set off from Westminster the previous day (21 May) on his way to Leicester. There he intended to hold a great council, which the insurgent lords feared might be turned to their disadvantage. About Christmas 1454 or New Year 1455, Henry VI had recovered from the mysterious illness which had incapacitated him mentally. The protectorship of the realm conferred on York to cope with the crisis had been terminated, and his deadly enemy Somerset had been released from prison and reinstated in favour at court. York and his Neville allies felt the situation to be intolerably threatening to their political interests.

When Henry set out from Westminster, he had fewer adult lay peers in his company than at Welling in 1452, and some of these may have come prepared to give counsel rather than military aid. Nevertheless, his tally of thirteen such peers was respectable, and there were well-founded hopes that he would soon be joined in arms by other lords and retinues, belatedly summoned to muster probably for his arrival at St Albans. In response to a royal mandate, the town of Coventry was preparing to send a contingent there, which was disbanded on news of the battle. The earls of Oxford and Shrewsbury, Lord Cromwell and Sir Thomas Stanley all arrived with contingents in the vicinity just too late to participate.[16]

The three Yorkist magnates probably had at most only four adult peers in their company, three of them minor barons.[17] But they had a larger army, perhaps outnumbering the king's, Mr Armstrong conjectures, by two or three thousand men. The date and place of their assembly is not known. A large number of the Yorkist troops were raised in the Marches towards Scotland. Warwick had 'the March men' fighting in his retinue, and the Northumbrian knight Robert Ogle led 600 'men of the Marches'.[18] Salisbury's castle at Middleham in Yorkshire, so often to be used as a rallying-point in the wars, is a likely place of assembly. The council knew of the rising by 18 May. On the 20th the Yorkists were as far south as Royston (Herts.) and on the 21st were at Ware. They may have been hoping to reach London before the king left, or were moving parallel to his intended route to Leicester because they were as yet hesitant about a direct confrontation. Moreover, York was particularly anxious to gain the duke of Norfolk's support, and felt perhaps that an easterly route would facilitate a juncture with his East Anglian contingents. In the event Norfolk brought a retinue into Hertfordshire, but remained militarily neutral.[19]

The king and his army spent the night of 21–22 May at Watford. Alerted about his advance there, the Yorkists had turned westwards from Ware in the direction of St Albans. When the king set out on his way there early on the morning of 22 May, news was brought indicating that the Yorkists were much nearer than expected. In a council of war, the duke of Buckingham argued in favour of pushing on to St Albans ($7\frac{1}{2}$ miles from Watford), confident that York would wait to negotiate.

This course was adopted, and Buckingham's assessment proved correct. The king's army moved unmolested into the town, which they 'strongly barred and arrayed for defence'.[20] The topographical spine of the town – which lacked stone fortifications – was formed by a south-west to north-east succession of streets running from the river Ver about 900 yards to St Peter's church. Holywell street, the road from Watford, climbs up from the river, with the abbey lands to the west of it, into the centre of the town, the market-place, which extends north-east as the broad St Peter's street. On the abbey and river sides, to the south-west, the ground slopes away steeply. But to the north-east the approaches are more level, especially to St Peter's street. Its wide northern end was particularly accessible: here 'at the barrier of the said town . . . which is high near the parish church [St Peter's]' York's emissary Mowbray Herald was challenged on one of his missions.[21] The comparative difficulty of assaulting the town up its western slopes – and the inherent danger of becoming involved in an assault on the abbey – probably determined the Yorkists' lines of attack from the east on the royal position centred on the market-place. The direction of their approach to the town inclined them the same way.

The Yorkist army arrived to the east, probably approaching from Hatfield, soon after the king was installed. They halted the length of a crossbow shot away, in Key Field, and barred exits from the town. The

Yorkist lords failed in their strenuous attempts to secure an undertaking from Buckingham that Somerset (in the royal army) should be imprisoned and tried: they were threatened with the penalties of treason. On the stroke of 10 o'clock, according to the *Dijon Relation*, battle commenced. York's main assault may have been around the barrier near St Peter's church. His attacks were frustrated: Lord Clifford 'kept strongly the barriers'.[22] Warwick attempted to break the deadlock by a diversionary attack to the south, through the back closes of Holywell street. He and his men

> ferociously broke in by the garden sides between the sign of the Key and the sign of the Chequer [inn signs] in Holywell Street; and anon as they were within the town, suddenly they blew up trumpets, and set a cry with a shout and a great voice. 'A Warwick! A Warwick! A Warwick!'[23]

Entering 'the other end of the town' (further south-west than expected?) Warwick's men disconcerted the defenders. When Ogle's Marchmen penetrated to the market-place, 'the alarm bell was rung, and every man went to harness, for at that time every man was out of their array, and they joined the battle anon; and it was done within di [a half] hour'.[24] The alarm bell may have been the early-fifteenth-century bell in the clock tower in the market-place, built between 1403 and 1412.[25]

The king's men had rallied desperately to defend Henry, who took his stand under his banner in St Peter's street. The Yorkists burst into the street in several places. Their opponents, hemmed in and densely packed, were unable to deploy effectively, and presented a good target for archers. They soon disintegrated into a rabble seeking mercy or attempting flight. Shamefully the royal banner was abandoned, propped against a house, and so was the king, his neck bleeding from an arrow wound, in a tanner's.[26] The author of *Benet's Chronicle* estimated that about 100 were killed in the battle.[27] Somerset, Northumberland and Clifford perished. Buckingham was among the prisoners, as was the king himself. He was escorted to the abbey, where the Yorkist lords treated him with due reverence. Next day they took him back to London.

The Yorkist victory was facilitated by royalist tactical miscalculations and failures. The crucial decision was the one pressed by Buckingham – to head for St Albans rather than make a stand on the way. He may have considered that, since the king's forces were probably outnumbered, it would be easier for them to hold out, well victualled and housed, in a town, until the anticipated reinforcements arrived. If this was his reasoning, he probably hoped that negotiations would meanwhile sap the Yorkist lords' determination to attack. Hence his willingness to hear their envoy, Mowbray Herald, and his insidiously tempting suggestion that they might retreat to Barnet or Hatfield for the night.[28]

Yet Buckingham's preference for a defence of St Albans had its disadvantages. When a king and his banner could be clearly viewed in the open field – as at Ludford in 1459 – his troops enjoyed a psychological advantage over rebels.[29] It is unlikely that the Yorkists attacking barriers and breaking down houses and pales at St Albans were daunted by a clear view of majesty. Moreover, an army in the field – particularly a small one, like the king's – could be more tightly controlled and mutually supportive than one strung out to defend a lengthy urban perimeter. The royal soldiers at St Albans had at most a few hours to familiarize themselves with the town and improvise defences. The failure to prevent or plug Warwick's breach in Holywell street, and the unpreparedness of many men to defend the market-place, imply serious defects in Buckingham's co-ordination of defences. Had he been able to prolong negotiations overnight, these might have been remedied. So might a possible fundamental tactical defect dictating the decision not to stand in the open: it is very likely that the royal army was short of archers.[30] But York did not oblige Buckingham by surrendering the initiative, as he had done in 1452. The Yorkist commanders daringly scrambled to the attack within hours of their arrival at St Albans: *their* gamble paid off.

No more fighting centring on the person of Henry VI occurred for four years. The Yorkists who had fought at St Albans were anxious to reaffirm their allegiance to the king and excuse themselves from blame for causing the disgraceful fight. A parliamentary Act of 1455 embodied a justification for their actions at St Albans and a pardon for nearly all the participants. In November York was appointed protector in parliament on conditions similar to those of 1454. But in February 1456 the king personally relieved York of the protectorate in parliament. The duke did not resort to extremes. His reluctance was shared by his opponents, headed at court by the queen, Margaret of Anjou.[31]

The circumstances which sparked off the Yorkist rising of 1459 had some resemblances to those of 1455. Several years of muted political tensions between the court and York and his allies erupted into violence after the king had held a great council at Coventry in the summer of 1459. York and his friends were conspicuous by their absence. At the queen's instigation, indictments were made against them.[32] According to the Act of Attainder passed on the leading rebels in the Coventry parliament the following November, the Yorkist lords planned to come in arms to Kenilworth, taking the king by surprise there.[33] If so, they probably had in mind their success of 1455. But Henry had advantages on this occasion. He was already centrally placed in the Midlands, whereas the Yorkist lords were widely scattered. York was in the Marches of Wales, probably at Ludlow; Salisbury was in Yorkshire at Middleham castle, and his son Warwick was across the Channel in his captaincy of Calais.[34] The king's councillors, with the lessons of 1452 and 1455 in mind, reacted promptly to the threat of a rising. They showed a disconcerting grasp of the strategic situation, giving priority to the need to move and recruit, and to isolate the northern Yorkists who had bruised the royal household so violently at St Albans.

Warwick, having to cross the Channel and traverse southern England to meet his allies, was a man in a hurry, with no time to attempt extensive Kentish recruitment. On 20 or 21 September he was admitted into London with a few hundred well-armed soldiers. He stayed in the city only for one night and next day rode out through Smithfield on his way to Warwick castle. Possibly that was the rendezvous for the Yorkist lords before their confrontation with the king at Kenilworth. In fact royal soldiers were active thereabouts. They were at Warwick before the earl's arrival, and he narrowly missed an encounter with Somerset at Coleshill. Warwick's small numbers, the lack of support from his allies, and the king's northward movement from Coventry determined his exit from the Midlands in another direction, towards the duke of York at Ludlow.[35]

Shortly before the earl of Salisbury set out from Middleham, the king, according to the Act of Attainder on the 1459 Parliament Roll, had taken the field with those lords about him, and advanced 'with great celerity' towards the earl's line of march. From Coventry Henry went to Nottingham, whence he summoned the Lancashire landowner Lord Stanley – and probably other northern lords – to bring military aid. The royal advance, according to the official version, caused Salisbury 'to divert from his first enterprise and purpose [i.e. to go to the king] and to take another way' to assemble with York and Warwick.[36]

Probably in order to block Salisbury, the king shifted his headquarters westwards, from Nottingham into Staffordshire. But Salisbury nearly got through unscathed to the duke of York at Ludlow. The king's main force was not responsible for his interception, but one raised mainly in the young prince of Wales's earldom of Chester, under commission from his father. In the prince's name the queen sent out from Chester urgent summonses for military support, to which there was a ready response from her 'gallants', the local knights and esquires among whom she had recently held open house, and to whom her son had given livery tokens depicting swans (a Lancastrian badge). Margaret and her son moved to Eccleshall castle (Staffs.), the residence of the bishop of Coventry and Lichfield, probably on their way to join the king.[37] But the prince's army apparently intercepted Salisbury without having linked up with the forces which the king was bringing. Moreover, it lacked an important component – the 2,000 Lancashiremen whom Lord Stanley had under arms. In answer to the prince's summons, Stanley sent only fair promises to Chester and Eccleshall, according to the charges brought soon afterwards against him in parliament. On the day on which the prince's forces fought Salisbury at Blore Heath (23 September), this circumstantial dossier alleged, Stanley lay idle with his men within six miles of the heath: in default of his aid, the king's people were 'distressed' there. Moreover, his brother William Stanley had sent reinforcements to the earl of Salisbury before the battle.[38]

There are no detailed accounts of Blore Heath.[39] Under the command of James Tuchet, Lord Audley (a prominent landowner in Staffordshire, Shropshire and Cheshire), the prince's army may have moved out from the neighbourhood of Eccleshall. They intercepted the northerners as they approached Market Drayton along the road from Newcastle-under-Lyme. Salisbury was forewarned of Audley's approach and tried in vain to negotiate an unmolested passage. Chroniclers had the impression that Salisbury was heavily outnumbered, though 'Gregory' was unique in thinking that he had only 500 men as against the prince's 5,000 – 'a great wonder that ever they might stand the great multitude not fearing'. He says that the battle lasted from one to five o'clock 'and the chase lasted unto seven at the bell in the morning. And men were maimed many one in the Queen's party.'[40] Perhaps borderers from the Anglo-Scottish Marches, as at St Albans, displayed their ferocious skills, this time against particularly green troops. The official account on the Parliament Roll does not minimize royal losses: Audley, and many Cheshire knights and esquires, were slain; others, including Lord Dudley, were captured.[41]

Salisbury spent the night a little further along the road to his objective, at Market Drayton. Morale was boosted by a congratulatory letter from Lord Stanley, promising future support, which the earl sent to Sir Thomas Harington. He showed it around, exclaiming, 'Sirs, be merry, for yet we have more friends.' But Harington was soon to be downcast. Next day he and Salisbury's younger sons Sir Thomas and Sir John Neville were captured in Cheshire, at Acton Bridge on the road between Nantwich and Tarporley. They may have been trying to get to Lancashire, seeking a haven for the brothers, who had been wounded in the fray.[42]

Their journey may have jeopardized their father's enterprise. For he lingered dangerously long at Drayton, perhaps in the hope of hearing news of his sons, or of distracting attention from their eccentric and hazardous movements. 'Gregory' believed that the earl narrowly escaped capture on the night after the battle:

But the Earl of Salisbury had been taken, save only a Friar Austin shot guns all that night in a park that was at the back side of the field [battlefield], and by this means the earl came to Duke of York. And in the morrow they found neither man nor child in that park but the friar, and he said that for fear he abode in that park all that night.[43]

Who was meant by 'they' in this passage? It is likely that they were part of the king's main force, belatedly arriving to reinforce the disarrayed Cheshiremen. That morning Salisbury was still at Drayton: a servant of Lord Stanley brought him a message there that his master had been summoned by the king, and that Stanley intended to ride to Henry with his 'fellowship', though he would continue to give the earl secret support. Stanley's abrupt change of conduct may have reflected the proximity of the king, and have snuffed out the embers of Salisbury's expectations of the previous night. The earl decamped from Drayton. It may have been a reflection of his haste that he left behind one of Lord Stanley's cooks, who had been wounded when fighting in William Stanley's company at Blore Heath. The cook was interrogated by gentlemen in the fellowship of one of the king's supporters, the earl of Shrewsbury, when they occupied Drayton.[44]

Salisbury's escape from the trap set for him was a measure of his desperate courage and that of his men. But fundamentally it resulted from failures to concentrate the much larger royal forces in time to stop him. The main army must have been near Salisbury's line of march, for, when the battle was fought, Henry was within ten miles of Blore Heath, and had on the day of the battle dubbed seven knights who fought there.[45] But the sources insist that the Cheshire army – handicapped by Stanley's absence – alone confronted Salisbury. Perhaps lack of co-ordination resulted from the separation of its command, nominally under the prince, from that of the main army. The Cheshiremen may have been eager to go it alone and their patroness, the queen, sympathetic in order to reflect honour on her son. Yet, even when the Cheshiremen had failed disastrously, the main command seems to have lost an opportunity to capture or rout Salisbury, resting with his battered force.

The sluggishness of Henry's command may have been increased by preoccupation with the need to co-ordinate the probably large number of noble retinues which he was soon to lead against the duke of York.[46] The duke of Somerset – possibly bringing a West Country contingent to join the king – was only at Coleshill in Warwickshire soon after 21 September, perhaps on the day of Blore Heath.[47] On 7 October the earl of Northumberland, his brother Thomas Percy, Lord Egremont, and Ralph Neville, earl of Westmorland, probably the leaders of the king's northern contingents, rode through Nottingham.[48]

The first known action of the united forces of Warwick, Salisbury and York was their move, probably from Ludlow, to the neighbourhood of Worcester. Their objective may have been to block a royal advance south from Drayton into the Midlands, which threatened to confine them to the Marches and cut them off from London and their English sympathizers. Probably on the road between Kidderminster and Worcester, the Yorkist army barred the way to the king's. Henry and his lords advanced to the attack with the royal banner displayed. York, not wishing to fight the king, retreated to Worcester.[49] This display of reluctance added credence to the indenture to which the three Yorkist leaders subscribed by oath after receiving the Sacrament in Worcester cathedral. In this they asserted their obedient respect to the royal 'estate and to the pre-eminence and prerogative thereof'. The dispatch of the prior of Worcester and other divines to present the indenture to the king seems to have had no effect on royal strategy. Henry advanced on Worcester: the duke retreated again, south to Tewkesbury.[50]

Henry, though he amply displayed his wonted mercy during and after the campaign, may have been in an uncharacteristically bellicose mood, moved by the slaughter of his faithful lieges, especially those dear to his wife and child, at Blore Heath. Whilst he paused at Worcester to take counsel and refresh his foot soldiers, he studied military problems, probably having in mind particularly those posed to his many hastily raised and ill-equipped levies by Salisbury's patently formidable company, and the professionals whom Warwick had brought from Calais. He considered accounts of past deeds in many annals, and was above all struck by the passage in the classic military textbook, Vegetius' *Epitoma Rei Militaris*, in which he affirmed that a small well-trained force usually defeated a large but inexperienced one, as the example of the ancient Romans' conquests of more numerous peoples showed.[51] The decision to send Richard Beauchamp, bishop of Salisbury, to the Yorkist lords with royal offers of pardons if they submitted was probably made at Worcester. This amnesty was publicly rejected on their behalf by Warwick. The king's army advanced on the Yorkist position at Tewkesbury. The Yorkists crossed the Severn and headed for Ludlow, with Henry in pursuit.[52]

The Yorkist retreat across the Severn was the turning-point of the campaign. York's decision to defend his Marcher lordships against plundering and confiscation involved the abandonment of immediate hopes to gain a wider spectrum of English support.[53] He and his colleagues may have hoped that the relative inaccessibility of Ludlow would shake off pursuit by a large army. But by 10 October the king was at Leominster. On that day the Yorkist leaders addressed a letter to him from Ludlow, protesting their loyalty and their intent to 'the prosperity and augmentation of your common weal of this realm', in accordance with the terms of the Worcester indenture and their subsequent letters to king and lords, and a message conveyed by Garter King of Arms. In effect, they served notice of their intention to defend themselves against royal attack.[54]

South of Ludlow, on the opposite side of the river Teme, near Ludford Bridge, the Yorkists were drawn up on 12 October. According to the official account, they 'fortified their chosen ground, their carts with Guns set before their Battles, made their Skirmishes, laid their Ambushes there, suddenly to have taken the advantage of your Host'. These traps, and the customary skill with which York had chosen his position, slowed royal progress. Because of the 'impediment of the ways and straitness [narrowness] and by let of the waters, it was nigh even' before the king was able to get his men into battle order and his tents pitched. He had it proclaimed within the enemy's earshot that whoever came over to him would be pardoned. The Yorkists fired their guns at his lines.[55]

Despite the strength of the Yorkist lords' encampment, that evening they considered their troops' morale to be critically low. An accumulation of factors contributed to this. It was probably clear that the king had a much larger army.[56] Salisbury and Warwick, dashing to link up with York, had not had time to recruit extensively in their 'countries', but the king's circuitous journey through the Midlands had given him the opportunity for widespread recruitment. The Yorkist lords probably had as scant support from their fellow peers as at St Albans: only two adult ones, both relatively insignificant, participated – Clinton and Grey of Powis. The king is likely to have been supported by an impressive number of peers and their 'fellowships'.[57] The Yorkist army had endured a prolonged retreat in face of the king's advances, involving at least one demoralizing failure to stand up to him in the field. Discontent may have been long simmering among Warwick's Calais soldiers at being brought into the field to oppose their royal master. Dissension in the ranks may have come to a head with the appearance of the 'army royal' in battle order at Ludford and the spread of rumours about the royal offer of pardons.

The Yorkist lords allegedly resorted that day to the desperate expedient of bringing persons before their soldiers who swore that Henry was dead. If so, this carried little conviction. Many deserted, to take advantage of the king's mercy – under cover, probably, of fading light. The key desertion, according to several chronicles, was that of Andrew Trollope, who led over a group of Calais soldiers.[58] The Yorkist leaders certainly left precipitately. According to the official version, about midnight they pretended that they were going to 'refresh' themselves across the river in Ludlow. Leaving their army arrayed with standards and banners flying, they fled from the town with a few companions. Desertion from the field when the banners were flying, as Dr Keen has shown, was regarded as particularly ignoble.[59] York made his way to Ireland, where he had been well liked as royal lieutenant, with his second son Edmund earl of Rutland. His eldest son, Edward earl of March, with Salisbury and Warwick, managed to reach Calais. But on the morning of 13 October, York's shamefully deserted army had to capitulate, and the king's men occupied Ludlow. Many of the leading Yorkists who were to purchase pardons were probably captured then. The king dismissed his arrays, by now weary and undisciplined, and returned to Worcester. The sudden end of the campaign may have come just in time to prevent his army from disintegrating, after the privations in which he had shared, eloquently outlined on the Parliament Roll:

> not sparing for any impediment or difficulty of way, nor of
> intemperance of weather, jeopardy of your most Royal person, and
> continuance of labours thirty days or thereabouts, not to rest any one
> day where Ye were another save only on the Sundays, and sometime
> as the case required lodged in bare field sometime two nights together
> with all your Host in the cold season of the year.[60]

The crown still had the problem of rooting out the fugitives from their havens overseas. Arguably the royal councillors underestimated the rebels' ability to maintain themselves there, and to organize an invasion. Such laxity is not the impression given in the poem *Knyghthode and Bataile*, a vernacular treatise on warfare based mainly on Vegetius' precepts. This was composed probably in the period between the Yorkist lords' flight to Calais and their return to England in June 1460. It was intended by the poet's patron, Viscount Beaumont, for Henry's edification.[61] The anonymous poet was above all concerned with the military and naval problems posed by the Yorkist occupation of overseas posts, drawing out lessons from recent as well as classical campaigns. He probably reflected military thinking current among magnates with influence in the royal council, and their wish to stiffen Henry's martial backbone.

His councillors were confronted with the difficulties of striking at the Yorkist bases in wintertime, probably with financial resources depleted by the costs of the recent campaign. They persisted doggedly with measures of defence and attack.[62] In November measures were being taken to fit out a force of 1,000 at Sandwich (Kent) to recover Calais, commanded by Somerset (the son of the duke killed at St Albans), who had officially superseded the attainted Warwick as its captain. But when the duke appeared before Calais, he was resisted by the garrison and deserted by some of his ships. With Trollope in his company, he was lucky to secure Guines castle.[63] Thence the pair of them harried the

Yorkists in Calais, a thorn in their side, posing a threat to the loyalty of the Calais garrison.[64] Meanwhile efforts had been made in England to reinforce Somerset and check Warwick's privateering navy. On 10 December orders were given for the muster near Sandwich of forces commanded by Lord Rivers and Sir Gervase Clifton. But soon after Christmas, John Dinham and a force sailing from Calais surprised the defenders of Sandwich in a pre-dawn attack, capturing Rivers and 300 of his men (15 January 1460).[65]

The failure of royal plans to recover Calais and the appearance of Yorkist forces on English and Welsh soil in the New Year may have led the council to give priority to naval action, in case of an invasion attempt in the spring. The author of *Knyghthode and Bataile* certainly envisaged the final defeat and submission of the attainted lords as taking place in a vigorously imagined naval battle.[66] On 1 February Sir Baldwin Fulford was empowered to keep the seas, and on 19 March the duke of Exeter, admiral of England, contracted to do so for three years. Their forces were ready by the third week in April. Preparations may have been spurred on by news presaging a Yorkist initiative: Warwick boldly sailed from Calais to Ireland, where by 16 March he was reunited with the duke of York.[67] In his absence Somerset attacked. But his loss of many men near Newnham Bridge altered the balance of forces in the March of Calais decisively in Yorkist favour.[68] However, around 25 May royal forces again took the initiative. Exeter embarked from Sandwich with fourteen ships and 1,500 men. Tension probably mounted along the south coast, especially in the Cinque Ports. It may have been about then that Rye corporation paid 6*d.* to John Pampulon for his trouble in sailing to Camber to inquire for news of Warwick from mariners coming from the west. Flosie, mariner of Rye, received 8*d.* for his expenses in going to Lydd to inquire what was the great fleet at sea. The duke of Exeter may have had good intelligence about Warwick: his timing was superb. About 1 June he sighted the earl's ships, returning from Ireland, off the Cornish coast. But the duke, despite superior force, showed no more eagerness to attack than the earl. One chronicler says that Exeter lacked confidence in his men's loyalty: he put in at Dartmouth and discharged them, short of victuals and pay. Perhaps Exeter would have been better advised to send reinforcements to the duke of Somerset during Warwick's absence – which had been causing tension at Calais. His fleet's collapse opened the Channel to Yorkist invasion, for subsequent royal naval activity was negligible, as a result, probably, of lack of funds.[69]

Somerset had not been completely neglected by the crown since the reverse at Newnham Bridge. On 23 May Osbert Mountfort, esquire, and John Baker were appointed to take reinforcements to him. Mountfort collected several hundred men at Sandwich, where they waited for a favourable wind, intending to escort Somerset back from France. He had presumably concluded that his presence in England was militarily more crucial. But Mountfort apparently failed to take adequate precautions against another cross-Channel attack on Sandwich. This is extraordinary, for he was a professional soldier – he had been marshal of Calais in 1452. One might have expected the recent capture of Rivers at Sandwich to have been much in the minds of its defenders. The author of *Knyghthode and Bataile* may have been alluding to it:

> For fault of watch, has worthy
> > not mischieved
> Now late, and all too soon?
> > Is this not proved?

Nevertheless, in June Lord Fauconberg (Salisbury's brother), Dinham and Sir John Wenlock sailed across and seized Sandwich (which had stone fortifications), capturing Mountfort. Dinham and Wenlock re-embarked, but Fauconberg garrisoned Sandwich. The Yorkists were once more embattled on English soil. This proved to be the spearhead of their invasion from Calais.[70]

Fauconberg's temerity signalled a striking revival of Yorkist opportunities. The Yorkist lords had taken unseasonable risks which had paid off handsomely. Royal councillors had certainly been tireless in devising counter-measures. But there had been a dismal series of royal failures, partly perhaps because no magnate was prepared to co-ordinate efforts in a recalcitrant region – and because some of those willing to captain wearisome and sometimes unglamorous enterprises showed incompetence. Buckingham, as constable of Dover castle and warden of the Cinque Ports, and a noble of some popular repute, would have been well placed to direct south-eastern efforts.[71]

As a consequence of royal failures and Yorkist improvisation, the Calais lords were able to maintain their outpost gallantly through the winter of 1459–60. But their future, and York's, remained dubious. They were cut off from their main regions of territorial influence, which the crown and its partisans gobbled up. Their fellow magnates remained ranged against them, though the sympathies of some may have been veering their way. No foreign power offered real help, though Warwick set store by the projects of the legate Francesco Coppini, bishop of Terni, who hoped by such partisan schemes to favour Milanese diplomatic interests rather than the reconciliatory papal ones he was supposed to forward.[72]

Yorkist political and military strategy was probably concerted during the Irish conference. It was decided to launch appeals championing popular grievances, more in the style of 1452 than of 1455 or 1459. According to Waurin, a decision was taken at a council of war in Ireland, and confirmed in Calais, to invade England, despite the strong feeling in Calais that Guines should be dealt with. York was to land in the north, the Calais lords in Kent.[73] They were doubtless aware of the grudging response on the south-east coast to measures against them. In Kent the habit of criticizing the court, which had erupted particularly in 1450, may have again intensified in the winter of 1459–60, because of the unseasonable attempts to raise soldiers, sailors and finance against Warwick, popular as a result of his naval attacks on aliens. Royal attempts to cut English communications with rebel Calais may have been particularly annoying in east Kent, for which it was in some respects a commercial and social centre.[74] According to 'Gregory', the Yorkist lords

> sent letters unto many places of England how they were advised to reform the hurts and mischiefs and griefs that reigned in this land; and that caused them much the more to be loved of the commons of Kent and of London; and by this means the commons of Kent sent them word to receive them and to go with them in that attempt that they would keep true promise and as for the more part of this land had pity that they were attaint and proclaimed traitors by the Parliament that was held at Coventry.[75]

In a series of articles addressed to the archbishop of Canterbury (Thomas Bourchier) and the 'Commons of England', York, March, Warwick and Salisbury said that they had sued to come into the king's presence, to declare to him a comprehensive list of ills afflicting the realm. But the earls of Shrewsbury and Wiltshire, and Lord Beaumont, 'our mortal and extreme enemies, now and of long time past having the guiding about' Henry, would not allow him to receive them, as he wished. These evil counsellors dreaded that oppressions would be laid to their charge. They had procured the condemnations in the Coventry parliament 'to the intent of our destruction and of our issue, and that they might have our livelihood and goods'. The Yorkist lords declared that they would offer again to come into the royal presence and declare these mischiefs 'in the name of the land', humbly suing remedy. They requested assistance and gave fulsome assurance of their faithful allegiance.[76]

This manifesto probably accompanied, or shortly preceded, their renewal of domestic conflict in June 1460. Near the end of the month March, Salisbury and Warwick, supported by their former prisoner, Audley, joined Fauconberg at Sandwich with their main force, estimated by one contemporary as 2,000 strong.[77] On 26 June, according to the chronicler John Stone, they approached Canterbury.

Next morning those appointed by the king to resist – Robert Horne, John Scot and John Fogge – met them at St Martin's church outside the walls, and negotiated the city's surrender. Despite their local renown, these Kentishmen can have had little hope of standing up to popularly supported lords of the king's blood, especially when two Kentish peers, Cobham and Abergavenny, were about to join the Yorkists, or perhaps had already done so.[78]

The Yorkist lords summoned help from the Cinque Ports. The mayor and bailiff of Rye, receiving a letter from March and Warwick summoning them to Canterbury next day, prudently dispatched Morris Gedard by boat to Winchelsea, to inquire whether the mayor and bailiff there intended to answer a similar summons.[79] The Yorkist lords, having paid their respects at the shrine of St Thomas of Canterbury, moved swiftly via Rochester and Dartford towards London, recruiting by the time they arrived on Blackheath what contemporaries considered to be a large army. Meanwhile the government of London, as in 1452, had taken measures of safeguard. But in the two days before the army reached the banks of the Thames (1 July), Common Council changed its mind and negotiated terms of admission with the lords. Next day the bishops of Ely and Exeter met the lords in Southwark and accompanied them across London Bridge. This was a crucial bloodless victory for the Yorkists. Had the mayor and commonalty accepted the counsel of those who urged them to lay guns at the bridge to keep the Yorkists out, a delay diminishing their chances of victory might have been imposed.[80]

The sudden capitulation of London was a blow to the king's party – and apparently an unexpected one.[81] There were a reasonable number of loyal peers in or near the city, though no leading lay magnate. The lieutenant of the Tower was the energetic veteran Lord Scales, eager to take command of the city and keep the rebels out. He was joined by Jean de Foix, earl of Kendal, and Lords Delaware, Lovell, Hungerford and Vescy.[82] One might have thought that their presence, the relative proximity of the king in the Midlands, and memories of the Kentishmen's conduct in 1450, would have kept the citizens in their resolve not to admit the Yorkist lords. But we know that they were divided in opinion.[83] One reason why the appeasers among them won the day may have been fear of the London commons. The latter 'would not have' Scales as captain of London.[84] Perhaps, as initially in 1450 and 1471, they were sympathetic to the Kentish rebels. Moreover, the city government may have been swayed by more weighty Yorkist sympathizers. Several peers in the vicinity were about to join the Yorkists in arms, or had already done so – the archbishop of Canterbury's brother Viscount Bourchier, Lords Abergavenny, Clinton, Say and Scrope. It was a fortunate conjunction for the Yorkists that the convocation of Canterbury was then meeting at St Paul's.[85] For even bishops opposed to them found it hard to stand out against the exhortations of the papal legate in their company. On 4 July, in full convocation at Paul's Cross, Coppini published the text of a lengthy letter to Henry VI echoing the Yorkist case, which was immediately dispatched to the king.[86] Whilst in London, March, Salisbury and Warwick swore an oath in St Paul's, in the presence of Archbishop Bourchier and two bishops, that they intended nothing contrary to the estate of King Henry.[87]

Henry had been in the Coventry region from the latter part of May, showing concern for defence measures. On 11 June a royal proclamation had been issued denying the Yorkist allegation that he had not freely consented to the attainders of York and his partisans enacted in the Coventry parliament of 1459, and bidding obedience to commissioners of array.[88] Henry may have stayed in the Midlands because his councillors considered, not unreasonably, that the main threat lay in a landing by York in Wales to raise support in his former Marcher lordships in order to strike at the court as he had attempted in 1452 and 1459. His supporters had been active in Wales as recently as the month of March.[89] Till the end of May it may have seemed less likely that the main threat would come through Kent from Calais, since Exeter had his powerful fleet based on Sandwich, and Warwick lingered in Ireland. The deterioration of Somerset's position, the collapse of Exeter's and Mountfort's commands, and the speed with which the Yorkists invaded Kent so soon after Warwick's return from Ireland may have taken the court by surprise.[90]

Probably in response to the invasion, the king shifted his base nearer London, from Coventry to Northampton.[91] But he made no attempt to recover the city or relieve the beleaguered Tower garrison.[92] The royal army covered the southern approaches to Northampton, on the banks of the Nene, across the river from the town, in an encampment positioned rather like York's at Ludford Bridge. The royal commanders may have wished to use the formidable arsenal accumulated at Kenilworth, difficult to transport far, and to wait for more distant regional contingents. In answer to summonses, Shrewsbury dispatched fifty-one men, and Beverley (Yorks) twenty.[93] Soon it was to be rumoured in London that the duke of York was about to invade. In the royal camp there may have been fears that, if the king moved further south, the duke might intercept or deter remoter supporters.[94]

The Calais lords did not waste time waiting for York. Their objective, once they had gained entry to London, was to reach the king before the bulk of his supporters could rally – as they had failed to do the previous year when he was in the Midlands. Their concern about being vulnerably bogged down before an impregnable royal redoubt may be reflected in the report that they feared that Henry and his army intended to withdraw to the Isle of Ely, 'where the king's counsel had proposed as was said to have left the king and for their strength and safeguard thereto have hidden'.[95] As early as 5 July, according to *Benet's Chronicle*, Fauconberg set out from London northwards with an advance-guard of 10,000.[96] Salisbury remained in London with 2,000 of the Yorkist army and the city forces, to safeguard London and besiege the Tower.[97] The main army, under March and Warwick, set out for St Albans, meeting reinforcements on the way, and spending the night there. They went on to pause two days at Dunstable, allowing contingents to assemble.[98] The first Yorkist soldiers arriving near the royal encampment at Northampton may have occupied Hunsbury Hill, to the south-west, whence they could keep it under observation.[99]

The sight may well have been a daunting one. The king, according to a pro-Yorkist London chronicler, had 'ordained a strong and mighty field beside a nunnery, having the river at his back'. His position was entrenched and provided clear fields of fire for his batteries. It was in low fields on the river bank, with Delapré abbey to the west, Sandyford mill to the east, the river Nene to the north, and open fields rising to the village of Hardingstone to the south.[100] Sticking to their manifesto and their oaths, the Yorkist lords attempted, as on previous occasions, to negotiate the peaceful presentation of their petitions to Henry. The fact that they were accompanied or joined by the papal legate, the archbishop of Canterbury and a bevy of mostly sympathetic bishops gave them a powerful mediating hand. But the envoys whom they sent, bishops and heralds, got nowhere. Buckingham in particular was credited by chroniclers with a brusquely dismissive attitude.[101] He was probably supported in this by his sons-in-law Shrewsbury and Beaumont, and by Lord Egremont.[102] They may have feared that the pious king would give in before formidable clerical pressure. On the 1459 campaign he had shown himself eager to pardon the rebels – and in the different circumstances of that campaign his mercifulness had been an effective weapon. Beaumont's concern about Henry's readiness to believe the honest intent of his adversaries is probably reflected in the recent warning to him in *Knyghthode and Bataile* against oaths sworn on the Sacrament 'thy true intent for to beguile'.[103]

Fears of Henry's pliability may have been a principal reason why Buckingham and his fellow magnates rejected the good reasons which they had to temporize. For the royal army was outnumbered: contingents were still on the way.[104] Besides Buckingham, his two kinsmen and Egremont, there was only one other lay peer in the king's company – Edmund Grey, lord of Ruthin. But the Yorkist leaders, for the first time, had a respectable company of lay as well as clerical peers with them – Viscount Bourchier, and Lords Abergavenny, Audley,

Fauconberg, Say, Scrope of Bolton, possibly Clinton, and perhaps even Stanley.[105]

But there were other likely reasons for the royalist readiness to give battle. Buckingham and his colleagues may have misjudged the strength of their encampment and the loyalty of the soldiers. They may have been impressed by the urgent need to relieve the beleaguered garrison in the Tower, and by the opportunity to defeat March and Warwick whilst they were separated from York and Salisbury. Despite the presence of eminent veterans in the Yorkist army, notably Bourchier and Fauconberg, the king's command may not have been over-impressed by its leadership. Warwick's performance at Ludford had been lamentable, and March was young and untried. Buckingham may have misread Warwick's frenetic attempts to put the Yorkist case to the king as a sign of weakness.

The battle was fought on 10 July 1460, less than three weeks after the main Yorkist landing in Kent.[106] According to Whethamstede, the Yorkist lords divided their army into three 'battles' (*turmae*), the first commanded by March, the second by Warwick and the third by Fauconberg. These, he says, did not attack in turn, but simultaneously, along different sections of the entrenchments. In order to overcome a difficult obstacle, the Yorkists took advantage of their superior numbers, making an enveloping assault.[107] The heavy rainfall put the royal artillery out of action, and also probably made the entrenchments sodden and slippery. Progress was made by the attackers when the soldiers of Lord Grey, commanding the 'vaward', helped them up, in accordance with his prior understanding with Warwick. This precipitated the collapse of the royal army. Within half an hour or so of 2 o'clock, when the assault commenced, the battle was over, a cheap victory for 'the true commoners of Kent', to whom it was attributed soon afterwards in some anonymous celebratory verses.[108] 'So few men slain in so great a fight', rejoiced the poet. The Yorkist casualties were negligible, but a number of royal soldiers perished in the pursuit, many of them drowning whilst trying to escape through the swollen river near Sandyford mill.[109] According to one London chronicler, Buckingham, Shrewsbury, Beaumont and Egremont were slain by the Kentishmen beside the king's tent; according to another, Buckingham was slain 'standing still at his [own] tent'.[110] The king was captured by an archer, one Henry Mountfort. Warwick, March and Fauconberg found Henry sitting in his tent. They showed him due obeisance. He was escorted first to Delapré abbey, then to Northampton. Within a few days the lords took him to London, where the Tower garrison soon capitulated.[111]

The battle of Northampton was a day's work in some ways reminiscent of that at St Albans five years before. The fact that Henry and his faithful nobles were trapped near the tents suggests that they did not anticipate that they and the main 'battle' needed to be ready to engage. The vanguard, as was to be so often the case in the Wars of the Roses, was to fight beforehand. The débâcle compounded military and political miscalculations. If the guns had cut Warwick's men up badly, Grey might not have given the order to help them. The reason why he was granted command of the vanguard is puzzling. He was less distinguished by rank and military experience than other peers present. Perhaps the honour was conferred on him for his prompt assistance to the king.[112] Since he had considerable landed power in neighbouring parts, he may have staked a claim to high command by bringing along many of his tenants. Even without Grey's treachery, it is likely that the Yorkists would have won at Northampton, through weight of numbers. But the battle would have been longer and bloodier: there would have been less chance for the Yorkists to emerge personally unscathed, with the king a prisoner and all the opposing nobles dead.

The aim of the lords who rose in arms in the period 1452–60 was simple and consistent. They wished to go to the king and get him to deal satisfactorily with grievances which they had against other nobles. They went in this politically explosive manner because they were convinced that it was the only way in which to make their influence felt in royal council and court. Their imperative need was to take the king by surprise – a difficult task, since they had to organize military contingents from their several 'countries'. Once the king had had time to summon the superior forces he could command, and put his opponents publicly in the posture of rebels, their determination and that of their men to confront the sovereign and other nobles in battle started to decline. York, forced on the defensive by royal armies in 1452 and 1459, resorted to an expedient popular in Continental warfare. He drew up his forces in a fortified camp, defended by entrenchments and batteries, and on rivers which provided or protected lines of communication. He doubtless hoped that royal commanders would be deterred from making potentially bloody assaults with hastily raised levies, and would therefore become more amenable to political compromises. In 1452, when he was entrenched at Crayford, the king was certainly prepared to negotiate a settlement. York may have believed, mistakenly, that he had won concessions. But at Ludford Bridge the royal army seems to have been more willing to assault field fortifications. They were never tested, as a result of the disintegration of Yorkist morale.

But the defensive encampment was not discredited, at least among royal councillors. Their concentration of artillery at Kenilworth castle suggests their belief that the king needed a defensive base, centrally placed, to guard against threats from different directions, and to which reinforcements could be summoned from different parts of the realm. The circumstances before the Yorkist invasion in 1460 particularly fitted in with this concept. It was applied at Northampton by Buckingham, Shrewsbury and Beaumont who, taught in the same school of warfare as York, resorted to his expedient of the armed encampment.[113] The utter débâcle which they suffered there, though stemming only in part from inherent military problems, may have finally discredited such defensive strategy in the eyes of younger nobles, such as Somerset, Exeter, Warwick and March, who were to play dominant roles in the next stages of the conflict.[114]

Chapter 2

The War of Succession, 1460–1

The consequences of the battle of Northampton differed greatly from those of the first battle of St Albans. The latter had so shocked contemporaries that it had ushered in a period of political compromise, leading eventually to the new court ascendancy against which York rebelled in 1459. But the compromise after Northampton rested on a novel, even more unstable basis – the recognition of Yorkist dynastic claims. York's acceptance as Henry's heir in parliament in October 1460 immediately provoked a struggle for the crown, a war of succession, producing widespread involvement and lasting bitterness as it developed into what some contemporaries regarded as a war of the north against the south.[1] Once the dynastic issue had been raised, with such dramatic and extreme consequences, it was hard to bottle up again, and, in various guises, it was to be a long-lasting problem in English politics and a principal cause of the recurrence of the wars.

The duke of York returned to England in September 1460. He was determined never again to be treated as a political outcast and branded as a traitor. The only way which he could fix on to prevent this was to put forward his own claim to the throne in parliament, despite adverse reactions, even among some of his closest allies. By the compromise Act of Settlement (10 October), Henry was to keep the throne for life, but York and his heirs were recognized as Henry's heirs. This cut out the claims of Henry's son, Edward prince of Wales. Such disinheritance was totally unacceptable to the boy and his mother, who after Northampton had fled with him from Eccleshall through Cheshire and taken refuge in a Welsh castle.[2] It was also unacceptable to a formidable body of magnates who had not experienced defeat at Northampton or been present in parliament to accept the settlement. The queen consulted Henry's half-brother, Jasper Tudor, earl of Pembroke. She summoned Somerset, Devon and Sir Alexander Hody to meet her speedily with armed companies, informing them that Exeter, with

Lords Roos, Clifford, Greystoke, Neville and Latimer, were to meet her at Hull. Similar summonses were sent to her chief officers. Somerset, who had surrendered Guines to his opponent Warwick, had returned to England about 21 September and taken up residence at Corfe castle (Dorset). He and Devon, with a strong force including many western knights and gentlemen, moved via Bath, Cirencester, Evesham and Coventry to York. The concentration in Yorkshire of an army from different regions (though mainly from the north) out of the campaigning season was a striking achievement, a measure of the fury caused by the Act of Settlement. According to the Londoner 'Gregory', it was achieved in such secrecy that the duke of York and his supporters were taken unawares.[3]

The Yorkist lords could not ignore such a challenge in their own 'country'. Early in December, York secured a loan of 500 marks from the Common Council of London towards the expenses of his intended campaign – though their grant was only half what he had requested, since he would not provide satisfactory securities.[4] The Londoners watched York riding off through Cheapside with a few hundred men, accompanied by Salisbury with at most a hundred. Recruiting on the way, they went northwards, passing through Nottingham, and in three or four days arrived at the duke's town of Wakefield, in or by which their forces encamped. They had already suffered a reverse. According to the *Annales*, their 'aforeriders' (*praeeuntes sui*) were killed by Somerset's men at Worksop (Notts.).[5] York and Salisbury seem to have underestimated Lancastrian determination to force the issue, and the strength the queen's captains had to do so. Lord Neville visited the duke of York, receiving his commission to array under pretence of being an ally, but joined the enemy with his recruits. Somerset also visited the duke and arranged a truce to last till after Epiphany.[6] Nevertheless, on 30 December the Lancastrians launched a full-scale attack at Wakefield. They fielded a respectable array of peers with their retinues – Exeter, Somerset, Devon, Northumberland, Clifford, FitzHugh, Greystoke, Neville and Roos. York and Salisbury had no adult peers in their company.[7] Waurin has a circumstantial but largely uncorroborated account of the ruses which the Lancastrians employed to undermine Yorkist defences. The day before the attack, they had insinuated 400 of their best men into the duke of York's garrison, welcomed by it as a reinforcement from Lancashire. At dawn more Lancastrians, under Trollope's command, appeared before the defences, claiming to be reinforcements for York, and flaunting Warwick's badge of the ragged staff. This lured the unsuspecting duke out to greet them. Somerset's men then attacked, aided by all the pretended reinforcements.[8] Writers in southern England lacked convincing details of the engagement. They were uncertain which side had numerical superiority.[9] The Milanese agent Antonio della Torre, in a letter of 9 January 1461, gave a version which had probably circulated in London. York and Salisbury, he said, were three times stronger than their adversaries, but gave them opportunity to attack through lack of discipline – they allowed a large part of their force to go pillaging and searching for victuals.[10] Whethamstede had heard that the northerners had attacked in bad faith, before the day agreed for battle, when they realized that the southerners were foraging without proper precautions.[11]

To southern writers the battle was a disaster – 'execrabile bellum' in the author of the *Annales'* phrase. Many Yorkists were killed. Among the dead in the field were York, Salisbury's son Sir Thomas Neville, Sir Thomas Harington, Sir Thomas Par, Sir Edward Bourchier, Sir James Pickering and Sir Henry Retford. In the pursuit Lord Clifford killed York's young son Rutland on Wakefield bridge. That night Salisbury was captured by a servant of Trollope and was executed next day at Pontefract.[12]

The Wakefield campaign reveals a new style of military leadership among the Yorkists' opponents – devious, inventive and quick to exploit opportunities. The complacency shown by York and Salisbury over Christmas may have stemmed partly from a failure to grasp that they were dealing with opponents no longer prepared to keep faith with them. But, even during periods of truce, lax discipline within a few miles of the enemy was militarily inexcusable. The Yorkists, unlike their opponents, do not seem to have reconnoitred well. Moreover, their strategy was fundamentally flawed. They lost, as the bishop of Terni wrote, because they made a 'rash advance'.[13] It was imprudent to advance into enemy territory and there remain passive. York might have been better advised to halt at Doncaster, or even at Nottingham, accumulating supplies from the south and tempting the northern army to take the offensive in less favourable circumstances. But he led his army to Wakefield, according to Whethamstede, in order to have better lodging.[14] A middle-aged man who had returned from exile to his greatest political triumph, he may not have relished this irritating, unseasonable campaigning, consoling himself with the prospect of celebrating the New Year peacefully in one of his own castles. His men could expect a better welcome in his lordship. He and Salisbury were doubtless anxious to rescue their Yorkshire tenants from the harassment which they had endured.[15] Such considerations may have inclined the Yorkist leaders to commit a cardinal military sin – the underestimation of their opponents. The Lancastrians had, indeed, recently lost some of their most experienced and forceful captains (Buckingham, Shrewsbury, Beaumont and Egremont); and two of their present commanders, Somerset and Exeter, had recently failed dismally.

The quality of the northern command was again demonstrated after Wakefield in their ability and determination to launch an invasion of the south in midwinter, culminating in a second victory only about seven weeks after the first. The queen, 'Gregory' exaggerated, 'came ever on from the journey of Wakefield till she came to St. Albans'. The northern army, said another London chronicler, 'came down suddenly to the town of Dunstable'.[16] The Yorkist leaders had set in motion widespread defence measures, and heightened tensions, by encouraging the belief that the queen's army of northerners was licensed to plunder the south.[17] On 5 January 1461 Warwick, Bourchier and Lords FitzWarin and Rugemont-Grey came before the London Common Council, and had a gratifying response to their request for a loan for the defence of the realm. Two thousand marks were at once granted by unanimous consent.[18] On 12 January a civic assembly at Norwich considered a royal demand for military aid dated 3 January, and decided to engage and finance a company of 120 men in response.[19] On 17 January the royal council ordered the burgesses of Stamford (Lincs.) to co-ordinate local defences.[20] On 23 January Clement Paston wrote from London: 'I have heard said the further Lords [the queen's supporters] will be here sooner than men wean, I have heard said, ere three weeks to an end.'[21] On 28 January the royal council drafted letters to county arrayers and to the urban officials of Bury St Edmunds and Ipswich (Suffolk), Salisbury (Wilts.) and Colchester (Essex) requesting them to hasten contingents: the council had sure knowledge that the 'misruled and outrageous people in the north parties' were coming.[22] On 5 February the royal council ordered Sir William and Thomas Bourchier and other arrayers to call together the Essex lieges and bring them to the king.[23] On 12 February a civic assembly at Lynn (Norfolk) ordained measures for the defence of the urban constabularies under the captain appointed, and for the keeping of night watches.[24] John Devyn, warden of the town of Henley (Oxon.), paid out of his own pocket the costs of having a watch kept in the guildhall and of having staples and rings made for the bars of the bridge over the Thames.[25]

The effects of the widespread measures stimulated by the king's council may have been to thwart the plans of the queen's sympathizers in the Midlands and south. This deprived the northern army of one vital source of support, just as the earl of March's rout of the army coming to its aid from Wales was to knock away another. Yorkist propaganda's success has concealed the fact that the queen had support in the Midlands and southern England. Amongst those who were attainted for fighting for Henry in March were twenty-four whose residence was given as being in those parts.[26] The council had certainly feared subversion in the regions under its control as well as their invasion. On 12 January the bailiffs and constables of Kingston-upon-Thames

(Surrey) were commissioned to arrest and imprison anyone uttering false news and carrying bills and letters to disturb the peace. On the 20th Richard Hotoft and the sheriff of Leicestershire were ordered to suppress dissentients who made unlawful gatherings or hindered those coming to defend the king. On 3 February Sir John Howard was appointed to head a similar commission in Suffolk.[27] On 28 January and 7 February measures were ordered to prevent the shipment of victuals to the rebels from Norfolk and Cambridgeshire respectively.[28] There may have been a Norfolk conspiracy to aid the northerners. On 7 February the council gave orders for the seizure and garrisoning of Rising castle.[29] The youngest John Paston's remarks in an undated letter probably have a bearing on this order: 'there is at the Castle of Rising, and in other two places, made great gathering of people, and hiring of harness, and it is well understood they be not to the King ward, but rather the contrary, and for to rob.'[30] Rising castle was the residence of one of the best-known partisans of the Lancastrian court in Norfolk, Thomas Daniel, esquire.[31] He had been associated with William de la Pole, duke of Suffolk's, government of Norfolk in 1447–8.[32] In 1449 he was squire for the king's body and in 1450 steward of the duchy of Lancaster beyond Trent.[33] In December 1451 he was closely associated with the duke of Somerset, father of the queen's leading partisan in 1461.[34] In a letter written by Friar Brackley to John Paston senior probably in October 1460 he is denounced as one of her partisans in Norfolk about whom Brackley wanted Paston to warn the earl of Warwick. If the friar was not exaggerating, there was dangerous anti-Yorkist activity in the shire. He names Bishop Lyhert of Norwich and the dowager duchess of Suffolk among the disaffected.[35] Daniel was to be attainted for fighting in the Lancastrian cause at Towton in March 1461, and in 1464 he was said to be in Cheshire, involved in the rising associated with Somerset's pro-Lancastrian treason.[36] It may be that before the queen's army came south Daniel was a leader of a Norfolk conspiracy to support it, whose success would have been a considerable aid.

That there was a sound basis for the fear of the queen's army felt in the south is shown by the pillage carried out at Beverley (Yorks.) by Lord Neville's soldiers on 12 January.[37] Plundering *en route*, the army advanced south via Grantham, Stamford, Peterborough, Huntingdon, Melbourn (Cambs.), and Royston, then turned west to Luton (Beds.) and on 16 February defeated the defenders of Dunstable.[38] On 12 February Henry VI and the duke of Norfolk had led one retinue out of London through Barnet, linking up at St Albans with one which Warwick had led out on the same day through Ware.[39] The earl's preliminary line of advance may have been a precaution in case the northerners failed to swing westwards to St Albans, as he had swung when advancing from Royston in 1455. The difference was that, unlike the king on that occasion, he now easily beat his opponents to St Albans. Nevertheless, as 'Gregory' makes clear, Warwick failed to realize how near the northerners were to St Albans on the 16th.[40] The Yorkist leaders thought that they had time to shift their main position: 'The lords in King Harry's party pitched a field and fortified it full strong, and like unwise men brake their array and took another.'[41] The new position was 1½ miles north-east of St Albans, on Nomansland Common, west of Sandridge.[42] Why was there a radical change of plan? The original Yorkist position may have centred on St Albans, in whose market-place Warwick had signally helped to hem in the king's army in 1455. Warwick now led a much larger army than the king had had then, with levies from Kent and neighbouring shires, London and East Anglia.[43] Since the leading magnates with him — the dukes of Norfolk and Suffolk, and the earl of Arundel — lacked his military experience and repute, they probably deferred to his judgment.[44] Warwick may have become convinced that the army needed to occupy a larger, flatter and more open ground in order to deploy properly. The new choice of field implies the expectation that the northern army would advance on St Albans down either the Luton or the Wheathampstead road, threatening the town from the north-east. Thus the move perhaps indicates indecisiveness and hidebound thinking on Warwick's part.

Opposed to him were Exeter, Somerset, Devon, Northumberland, Shrewsbury and Lords Clifford, FitzHugh, Grey of Codnor, Greystoke, Roos, Welles and Willoughby, most of them recently engaged at Wakefield.[45] The Lancastrian command, showing the flair which Waurin attributes to them at Wakefield, were able to achieve a degree of surprise by moving on the town of St Albans along the Dunstable road, from the north-west, so threatening the main Yorkist position from the rear, on 17 February. The fullest account of the battle is that by Abbot Whethamstede of St Albans, who had known the ground since childhood and was at the abbey during the fighting.[46] He says that the northerners got into St Albans, but were forced back to the western outskirts by the fire of a few Yorkist archers stationed at the Great Cross. The attackers managed to bypass this blockade of the centre of the town by getting up a lane which led to the northern end of St Peter's street, the street leading to the main Yorkist position. Before advancing on that, they had to overcome the stiff resistance of a company of commons who blocked their exit from the town. These delaying actions presumably alerted the Yorkist camp. The vanguard was got into the field to counter this unexpected attack from the south rather than the north. The defence was for a time well maintained, but suddenly collapsed. The Yorkist soldiers did not attempt to stave off their opponents in hopes of relief by reinforcements from their main 'battle'.

Instead they scattered in blind panic in all directions, pursued and slaughtered by northern horsemen, as the appalled bystander Whethamstede graphically recounted. Many were saved, he says, only by the fading light. The main Yorkist 'battle', guarding the king, melted away, leaving him in the company of a few apprehensive nobles. Soon he was to be reunited with his vengeful queen and triumphant little son.[47]

Scraps of information retailed by correspondents and chroniclers reflect contemporaries' awe, and in some cases fear, at the magnitude of the Yorkist disaster. Some attempted to explain it. The Londoner 'Gregory', possibly present among the city levies, railed at the scouts' incompetence, the commanders' untimely decision to shift camp, and the uselessness of the foreign gunners' paraphernalia.[48] Others blamed the defeat on the treachery of the captain of Kentishmen, Lovelace.[49] Two days after the battle an Italian correspondent relayed the generally accurate information which he had gleaned about it.[50] The battle had begun, he said, about one o'clock with a skirmish with the king's vanguard, and lasted until six. Despite the rout of the Yorkists and the loss of the king to their opponents, 'there is less harm done', he remarked mysteriously, because the Kentishmen, said to be commanded by the duke of Norfolk and the earl of Arundel, were not at full strength.[51] Prospero di Camulio wrote from Ghent on 9 March that many of the king's men at St Albans deserted for lack of victuals, and that Somerset attacked after midday with 30,000 horse. The duke wore down his opponents: Warwick decided to quit the field, by breaking through their lines (presumably, in order to get back to London). With 4,000 men he pushed into St Albans, but being heavily outnumbered withdrew to his camp. Hearing shouting thence to the queen's men, he feared treason and fled.[52] Warwick and most of his fellow nobles escaped. Lords Berners and Bonville, and Warwick's brother John Neville, were captured.[53]

According to 'Gregory', most of the northern army had proved useless: 'the substance that got that field were household men and feed men'.[54] The sources give the impression that the bulk of both armies was made up of hastily raised levies whom their commanders were unable to train, discipline or feed adequately. The disintegration of the northern army was well under way by the time it reached St Albans — success in the field, with the attendant orgy of slaughter and plundering, probably accelerated the process. The Yorkist levies, who had not come so far but may have been awed by rumours of their opponents' ferocity, disintegrated in the fight. Some, indeed, may have felt lukewarm about the Yorkist cause. One wonders how wholehearted the duke of Suffolk's retainers were, in the light of Brackley's doubts about the loyalty of the Suffolk political interest, and his opinion that it would be good for the young duke with his knights and esquires to use his spurs and prove in battle where his loyalty lay – though in fact he amply demonstrated himself a Yorkist in 1461.[55]

How did the Lancastrian commanders win with such a volatile army? They boldly exploited Warwick's strategic errors, concentrating their more reliable troops in a disciplined and well-led attacking group. Warwick and his colleagues proved unable to recoup initial mistakes by a similar concentration. Their spirited archers in the market-place at St Albans, the company defending the exit from St Peter's street, the good troops in the vanguard, and the foreign mercenaries, all seem to have fought without cover and reinforcement from their fellows. By getting the vanguard into line the Yorkist commanders reasserted some control, but after that their grip once again fatally slackened. In retrospect, it seems that Warwick was taking unnecessary risks by advancing to St Albans when he did, with the sort of forces he had. He might have won by sitting tight in London with a smaller and more reliable levy, and waiting for March's victorious army to arrive from the west before striking at exhausted and probably retreating northerners.[56] Such a course would have called for single-minded generalship which put strategic considerations before popularity. To some extent the Yorkists were victims of their own propaganda. Their emphasis on evil northern intents had helped to raise a large levy which it would have been difficult to maintain garrisoned in London. The fears there and in the neighbouring regions put pressure on Warwick to go out and repel the invaders long before they approached the city walls, thus enhancing his popular reputation. Ten years later, Warwick was to show that he had learned the wisdom of not always sallying forth to answer the call to battle, but instead braving reproaches passively behind city walls.[57]

'On an Ash Wednesday we lived in mykel dread', wrote a Yorkist versifier, recalling emotions felt the day after the second battle of St Albans.[58] Bishop Beauchamp sonorously recounted his experience of the 'general dread'.[59] The scattering Yorkist leaders were too demoralized to organize the defence of London. Mayor and aldermen kept the city under guard, and hastily opened negotiations for its surrender with the king and queen, who advanced to Barnet. They shared the citizens' anxiety about letting their undisciplined troops near London, and withdrew to Dunstable. Some of their men rode in to Westminster, but the prime royal concern seems not to have been to pluck the natural fruits of victory, by occupying the city. Rather, the Lancastrians were anxious to receive pickings in the shape of urban victuals. Whatever the reason for the Lancastrian command's priorities, their hesitation was fraught with danger when there was another Yorkist army – a victorious one – in the offing. The London commons were emboldened to prevent the dispatch of victuals by the city governors to the king and so hamper negotiations. Less than a fortnight after St Albans, March, accompanied by Warwick, who had met him in the Cotswolds, was welcomed into London at the head of his troops. If the Lancastrians had not already withdrawn northwards from Dunstable, March's arrival necessitated their retreat – a galling decision for mettlesome, victorious young nobles such as Somerset.[60]

Edward earl of March, York's eldest son, had celebrated Christmas at a friary in his father's town of Shrewsbury,[61] and it was probably there that he heard the terrible news of the deaths at Wakefield of his father, his brother Edmund, his cousin Thomas Neville and Neville's father Salisbury. March levied forces from various shires and was preparing to set forth against the northern army when he received news that the earls of Wiltshire and Pembroke had landed in Wales. Their intention, according to what Pembroke was to write on 25 February, had been to go to the king's support. March promptly reversed direction. He mustered his forces outside the town wall at Hereford, and at the beginning of February confronted the two Lancastrian earls at Mortimer's Cross on the river Lugg, about six miles north-west of Leominster. They were utterly defeated. Pembroke and Wiltshire managed to escape, but many of their captains were taken and executed. The engagement is one of the obscurest decisive battles of the Wars of the Roses. What is known about the leadership and composition of the armies suggests a Yorkist advantage.[62] March, though only eighteen, was militarily experienced. He had been present at St Albans in 1455 and Ludford Bridge in 1459, and had been a leader of the advance from Calais to Northampton in 1460. In his company at Mortimer's Cross were many from the Yorkist lordships in the Marches of Wales, probably keen not to see their estates overrun by their opponents and their local interests threatened, as were three leading supporters from the Anglo-Welsh border regions – Lord Audley, Sir Walter Devereux and Sir William Herbert. Other notable knights then with March were Lord Grey of Wilton, Lord FitzWalter and Sir William Hastings. But the Lancastrian force consisted chiefly of Welsh squires. Its leaders were militarily unimpressive. Pembroke had not yet distinguished himself, and Wiltshire's more prominent roles in 1455 and 1460 had provoked insinuations about his lack of martial attributes.[63]

March, as we have seen, speedily capitalized on his victory, averting the ruin staring his father's surviving allies in the face. The queen's cruel invasion, the horror at St Albans and the spiriting of the king northwards help to account for the readiness of many southerners to cast off their tenacious allegiance to the House of Lancaster and acquiesce in the acclamation by his soldiers of the little-known, youthful earl of March as Edward IV in London on 4 March. Despite the time of year, the insecure, fledgling king showed determination to proceed against his rival. There may have been fears of a renewed Lancastrian offensive. Henry's carver Sir Edmund Mountfort, Sir Harry Everingham and the prince of Wales's squire William Elton may have recently visited Coventry in the Lancastrian interest.[64] On the day after his acceptance of the crown, Edward wrote to the governors of Coventry exhorting them to keep the city safely against the rebels, and promising them relief if necessary.[65] On the same day the duke of Norfolk set off hastily into his 'country' to recruit.[66] On 7 March, Warwick left London with a large number of men to secure support in the Midlands; on the 11th the new king's footmen, mainly Welsh and Kentish, set out, and on the 13th Edward himself rode out through Bishopsgate.[67] He passed through St Albans, Barkway (16 March) and Cambridge (17th), where Sir John Howard met him with a contribution of £100 from the abbot and convent of Bury St Edmunds 'by way of love'. Contingents joined him *en route*.[68] He may have had a good deal of urban support. Coventry arrayed and financed a company of 100 men in response to his request of 12 March, and an anonymous poem on the battle of Towton may allude to the presence, besides, of contingents supplied by London, Canterbury, Bristol, Salisbury, Worcester, Gloucester, Leicester, Nottingham and Northampton.[69]

According to Waurin, reports reached Edward that Henry VI was based on Nottingham. Edward arrived there by 22 March, when it was reported that Somerset and Rivers were holding Ferrybridge on the river Aire. One might have expected the Lancastrians to try to hold the line of the Trent at either Nottingham or Newark, but perhaps they decided it was necessary to withdraw nearer York to 'refresh' their troops and link up with northern reinforcements. At a Yorkist council of war, the decision was made to advance to Ferrybridge.[70] Waurin, who gives unique details of the engagement, says that the Yorkist vanguard, commanded by the duke of Suffolk, fought the Lancastrians south of Ferrybridge – this may have been on 28 March.[71] The duke had halted within two miles of the enemy, but was drawn into battle in order to save his reconnoitring force, which had got too near the enemy. The vanguard threw the Lancastrians back to the southern end of the ferry bridge. Edward, informed of the encounter, came up with his main force. He said that the river passage must be gained and ordered an attack. The following month Bishop George Neville recalled what a stiff fight took place. The Lancastrians (presumably after withdrawing to the northern bank) sabotaged the ferry bridge. The Yorkists constructed a narrow raft to get their troops across, but their opponents seized it, and it was recovered only after bloody hand-to-hand fighting.[72] The Yorkist Lord FitzWalter was killed, and many of his men were killed and drowned; Warwick was injured in the leg.[73] The Yorkists got across the river, however, and encamped there amidst snow and hail.[74] A powerful Lancastrian force, with Somerset, Devon, Exeter and Lords Grey of Codnor, Willoughby and Roos present, had been worsted.[75]

The significance of the battle of Ferrybridge needs to be stressed. The Yorkists surmounted a highly defensible natural obstacle on the road to York. Their command demonstrated superior generalship – which Waurin attributed to Edward. The vanguard had been determinedly reinforced in order to gain a crucial advantage. But though the Lancastrian commanders on the spot showed equal determination, it seems that they were not reinforced by many of the nobles whose companies were in the field next day. An opportunity to tip the wavering balance in the fight at the ferry, and inflict a bloody check on Edward, seems to have been lost.

Next day (29 March) Edward's army was drawn up in battle array at Towton, near Sherburn-in-Elmet, about six miles north of Ferrybridge on the road to Tadcaster and York. Dr Richmond has listed eight peers in his company.[76] Opposing him in Henry's army were at least nineteen peers.[77] Contemporary correspondents and English chroniclers had little information about the tactics at Towton: they agreed in thinking that the armies were very large and that the death-toll was quite exceptionally large.[78] The governors of York recalled in 1485 that, whereas they had sent contingents of 400 to support the Lancastrians at the battles of Wakefield and St Albans, more than 1,000 men from the city went to 'the lamentable battle of Towton . . . of which many was slain and put in exile'.[79]

Waurin gives the one detailed account of the battle which, though largely uncorroborated, is followed here.[80] He says that Henry's vanguard, under Somerset, Exeter and Rivers, initiated the fight by attacking and putting to flight Edward's cavalry wing. They continued in hot pursuit, believing that Northumberland, in command of the main Lancastrian 'battle', had also joined the fray. But he was slow to engage. This gave Edward time to retrieve the situation, preparing and putting heart into his remaining troops. A tough struggle ensued, especially in Warwick's part of the line. Eventually the Lancastrians broke and fled. Many died on the road to York. At Tadcaster, according to George Neville, there were heavy drownings in the river Ouse, as the bridge had been broken down to stop the Yorkist advance.[81] The earl of Northumberland and Lords Clifford, Randolph Dacre, Neville and Welles were among the Lancastrian dead.[82]

Correspondents and chroniclers give a few scraps of information about the battle. According to Richard Beauchamp, the outcome remained doubtful all day. The author of *Hearne's Fragment* said that the battle was long, and that it snowed throughout. He believed that Norfolk's reinforcement of Edward during the fight with 'a band of good men' was important.[83] Though we cannot be certain why the Yorkists won, it may be that both sides had a problem in imposing command on exceptionally large forces – and that Edward achieved a unity of aim which eluded the huge number of peers fighting against him.

Next day Edward entered York, where he captured Devon and others, who had taken refuge in the old castle there but were apparently unable to withstand their opponents long enough to make terms. Devon and Wiltshire – a habitual fugitive whose luck had also run out – were executed.[84] Edward resumed the pursuit north of York, but returned there to celebrate Easter (5 April). Henry VI, Margaret of Anjou, the prince of Wales, Somerset and a few others had escaped to Newcastle, George Neville reported on 7 April. Exeter and Roos also got away. Edward raised new levies – a contingent went from Beverley – and after Easter passed through Durham to Newcastle, where he arrived on 1 May. He left next day, entrusting the custody of Newcastle to Fauconberg, and set out for Westminster and the coronation for which he had fought so tenaciously. Edward's striking victories had not brought him full control of the realm, however: he had failed to assert control of the Marches towards Scotland, probably because his troops and resources were exhausted.[85]

Why did the Yorkists win the war of succession in 1461 after the vicissitudes they had experienced? The forces which Edward confronted on the Yorkshire plains in March reflected, in their size and composition, the continuing strength of Lancastrian allegiances. At Towton Edward could muster probably fewer than half the peers that Henry could. Lancastrian commanders had recently inflicted shattering defeats on Edward's father and Neville kinsmen. The new Lancastrian leadership had displayed a more dynamic style of warfare than the static mode favoured by their predecessors at Northampton. Who was principally responsible for their ruses, surprise attacks and the daring winter march on London? Waurin rated highly the military partnership in 1459–61 of Somerset and his councillor, the veteran Trollope.[86] Waurin was not alone in singling out the fighting qualities of duke and esquire. Chastellain described Somerset as 'un des beaux jeusnes chevaliers qui fussent au royaume anglois'.[87] 'Gregory' was impressed by the duke's 'manly' assaults on Calais in 1459–60.[88] The author of the *Annales* remarked on his sterling support of Edward at the siege of Alnwick in January 1462 – and Edward's astonishingly favourable treatment of him showed how highly he valued his support.[89] Another English chronicler described Trollope as 'magno capitaneo et quasi ductore belli' at St Albans, and singled out his capture and wounding for comment.[90] 'Gregory' says that Trollope was wounded in the foot by a caltrop, and was the first of those knighted by the prince of Wales after the battle, to whom he declared, 'My lord, I have not deserved it for I slew but fifteen men, for I stood still in one place and they came unto me, but they bode still with me.'[91]

The dashing exploits of Somerset and Trollope may have masked and, indeed, exacerbated weaknesses and tensions in the Lancastrian command. 'Gregory's' testimony suggests that many of the northern levies had lost any military value by the time they reached St Albans. Waurin names southern lords as leading the attack at Towton, poorly supported by a force commanded by a northern one. Perhaps Somerset or a group of southern lords pressed bold courses on reluctant northerners who were dubious of the prolonged effectiveness of their forces.

The winter invasion of the south is the most striking strategic feature of the war of 1460–1. Persistence with it, after the suppression of southern and Welsh allies, was hazardous. Its failure exposed the queen's relative military weakness and created in the south a political climate for the acceptance of Edward's usurpation. He capitalized on this by mobilizing the superior resources of the richer parts of the realm in his control and striking swiftly at the Yorkshire heart of his opponents' resistance.

Thus the overthrow of the old Lancastrian leadership in 1460 had facilitated the emergence and dazzling successes of Somerset, a kind of Prince Rupert. But his efforts probably exhausted the resources of the Lancastrians' somewhat restricted provincial base of resistance. Moreover, the Lancastrian victories killed off or discredited the Yorkist leaders of 1455–60, facilitating the political and military emergence of Edward IV. His ability to organize armies and lead men to victory appeared conspicuously in 1461, strongly suggesting that he had considerable military talent, or recognized it in his counsellors, as Somerset did in Trollope.

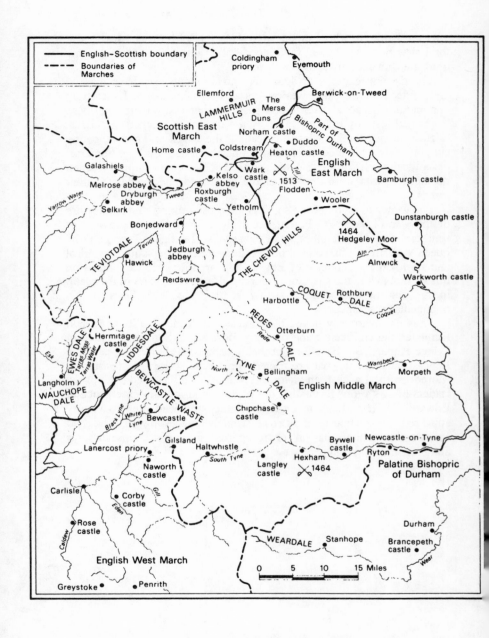

Map 2   The Anglo-Scottish Borders during the Wars of the Roses

Chapter 3

Lancastrian Risings and Invasions, 1461–4

It was more than two years after Towton before the Lancastrians were able to mount a sustained threat to Edward IV's rule – but it was not for want of trying. Many Englishmen continued to resent what they considered to be Edward's usurpation of the crown and his followers' usurpations of estates and offices. In the early 1460s there were frequent Lancastrian attempts to seize castles and towns, particularly on the fringes of the realm, which they hoped would be a prelude to rallying regional and foreign support. Fugitive Lancastrians vigorously intrigued and attacked. Henry himself appeared incongruously as a leader of Border raiding parties. But unlike the Yorkists, the Lancastrians did not succeed in mobilizing an effective domestic insurrection. This may have been partly because some of their leading magnates had died in the Towton campaign and others had been cut off from their areas of territorial influence. Moreover, the Lancastrian leadership apparently failed to copy the Yorkist device of stimulating domestic rebellion by playing on popular grievances. It was to be Warwick who revived this against Edward in 1469, and thenceforward the manifesto airing complaints and promising reform was to be a standard item in rebel baggage. Perhaps the Lancastrian leaders preferred to maintain an inflexibly legitimist stance, considering populist rhetoric, such as Warwick and his allies had directed against them, demeaning. Instead they set store by the need for foreign support – an emphasis most probably reflecting the convictions of Margaret of Anjou, shared at least to some extent by her principal councillors, such as Somerset, Hungerford and Whittingham. By involving foreign help in the wars on an unprecedented scale, Margaret handed the Yorkists effective propaganda material. Since the fourteenth century, the English had become accustomed to royal calls to prepare defences against the intended malice of foreign invaders. In 1485 Richard III was to proclaim that Henry Tudor plotted to allow foreigners to despoil crown and realm. Leaders of invading foreigners in 1487 and 1496 – Lincoln and Warbeck – showed awareness of the need to reassure subjects and protect them against their troops.

In the 1450s the Yorkist leaders had angled for foreign support, but it was Margaret who effectively 'internationalized' the domestic conflict.[1] The diplomatic precedents set by the Lancastrians in the 1460s after Towton were to be copied by those who wished to prolong dynastic strife for the rest of the century – for instance, there are many parallels between Lancastrian activity then and Yorkist attempts against Henry VII. Foreign rulers saw advantages to be gained in embarrassing English kings by aiding dynastic attempts. Plotters saw the foreign mercenaries and financial aid they could gain abroad as providing a more reliable backbone for domestic rebellion. Conversely, for English kings – for Edward IV in the 1460s and Henry VII in the 1480s and '90s – one key to dynastic peace came to be the establishment of good relations with neighbouring powers.

Frequent commissions of array in the spring and summer of 1461 testify to Edward IV's fears of insurrection and invasion. He had no certainty that Towton had halted the violent reversals of fortune of the last few years. The Lancastrian leaders showed no disposition to allow him peace.[2] His prolonged failure to consolidate his rule in the March of Calais must have seemed ominous, in view of the Calais garrisons' propensity to support rebellion as a means of getting wage arrears, and Charles VII of France's Lancastrian sympathies. In April 1461 a Lancastrian garrison in Hammes castle was besieged by Lord Duras, marshal of Calais, and Richard Whetehill, lieutenant of Guines. They raised the siege when Charles VII appeared with a force nearby. In July Duras, Whetehill and others were empowered to negotiate terms for the castle's surrender. But on 4 October it was reported that Sir Walter Blount, treasurer of Calais, was heavily involved in besieging it with a large force from the Calais garrison. Hammes was handed over by treaty by the end of the month – the defenders having first received £250 in Blount's name.[3]

But it was in the far north of England, in regions where many had allegiances to 'Lancastrian' families, and within reach of Scottish aid, that the first serious threats to Edward's rule developed in the summer of 1461. As early as 18 April Thomas Playter reported the story that the Lancastrians were hanging on to a Yorkshire castle and that its besiegers, Sir Robert Ogle and 'Conyrs' (Sir John Conyers?), had repulsed a relieving force led by Percy squires, inflicting heavy losses. The Percy force had been sent to 'bicker' with them, in order that King Henry 'might have been stolen away at a little postern on the back side. . . . Some say the Queen, Somerset and the Prince [of Wales] should be there.'[4] In fact Henry and 1,000 horsemen had entered

Scotland with safe-conducts by the first week in April. He, his wife, son, and principal lords, such as Somerset and Exeter, were honourably lodged there, and secured an offensive alliance with the regency government of the young James III, headed by his mother Mary of Guelders. In return, they ceded a great English prize to the Scottish crown – Berwick.[5] Probably in June 1461, Margaret, her son, Exeter, Lord Rugemont-Grey, Sir Humphrey Dacre, Sir Edmund Hampden, Sir Robert Whittingham, Sir Henry Bellingham and Sir Richard Tunstall crossed the Border with Scottish support, besieged Carlisle and burnt its suburbs.[6] On 3 June Edward IV wrote to Archbishop Booth of York ordering him to have proclamations made for his clergy to be ready to serve under Fauconberg and Warwick's brother Montague. On 18 June Coventry waged forty soldiers to serve under Warwick for twenty days.[7] Montague soon succeeded in worsting the besiegers of Carlisle and relieving the town.[8]

The Lancastrians promptly tried their luck on the eastern side of the Pennines, where they were probably well entrenched in Northumberland. Some of the Carlisle besiegers linked up with reinforcements, before advancing to threaten Durham, perhaps even hoping to move on York. On 26 June, 'Standards and Guidons' were raised at Ryton, and at Brancepeth, perilously close to Durham, by King Henry, Lords Roos and Rugemont-Grey, Dacre, Sir John Fortescue, Sir William Tailboys, Sir Edmund Mountfort, Thomas Neville, clerk, and Humphrey Neville, esquire, of Brancepeth. The attempt on Durham probably petered out because the bishop, Laurence Booth, held the bishopric's forces to Edward's allegiance – and because the Yorkist Nevilles were not far off.[9] On 28 August Giovanni Pietro Cagnolla reported from Bruges to the duke of Milan that Warwick had frustrated the Yorkshire Lancastrians' intention to rise.[10] Lancastrian strength in Northumberland faded. On 13 September Sir William Bowes assumed the keeping of the Percy castle at Alnwick for Edward IV, and before the end of the month Sir Ralph Percy (younger brother of the earl of Northumberland killed at Towton) had submitted to Edward and was holding the royal coastal castle at Dunstanburgh on his behalf.[11]

By July 1461 the balance in the north had swung in favour of the Yorkists. Both sides were now preoccupied with the fate of King Henry's supporters in Wales, where they held several castles. Edward planned an expedition to supplement the efforts of his local supporters. The Lancastrians essayed a powerful counter-move. An embassy, nominally headed by Hungerford but covertly including Somerset, was dispatched from Scotland to Charles VII. One of its aims was to procure from him 2,000 men to operate in Wales and a loan of 20,000 crowns. But the death of Charles on 22 July, before the embassy's arrival, and the succession of his son Louis, hitherto pro-Yorkist, fatally upset Lancastrian plans. The envoys lacked safe-conducts from the new king. A doleful letter from Hungerford and Whittingham, written at Dieppe on 30 August, and intercepted on its way to Margaret in Scotland, revealed that they were under arrest, and that Somerset was confined nearby at Arques.[12] Two letters written by Italian envoys towards the end of August show that men were breathing more easily at Edward's court, as the likelihood of French intervention dimmed. A recent Yorkist convert, Lord Rivers, crowed to Ludovico Dallugo that Henry's cause was 'lost irremediably'.[13]

Some urgency probably went out of the preparations for the intended royal expedition to Wales. Edward arrived at Hereford on 17 September, nine days after the date set for the muster of his army. He stayed at his castle of Ludlow from the 18th to the 26th, then abandoned the expedition. It must have been concluded that his lieutenants, notably Ferrers and Herbert, could deal with the Welsh Lancastrians. Commissioned to take Pembroke castle, they received it from Sir John Scudamore, who was granted a pardon by Herbert dated at Pembroke on 30 September.[14] On 4 October Henry Wyndesore reported from London that all the castles in North and South Wales were yielded into the king's hands, and that the duke of Exeter and Jasper Tudor, earl of Pembroke, had fled into the mountains.[15] On 16 October or earlier in the year they and Thomas Fitzherry, esquire, of Hereford were in the field at Tuthill near Caernarvon – perhaps in the hope of surprising the town and castle.[16] The Lancastrians hung on to Harlech castle till 1468, but lost Carreg Cennen castle in 1462. Herbert sent his brother Sir Richard to besiege it with Sir Roger Vaughan of Tretower. The garrison submitted, and 500 men were employed to demolish the castle, to prevent it from becoming a refuge for 'rebels and robbers'.[17]

Lancastrian plans in 1462 once again depended on substantial foreign as well as domestic support. They received a blow through the discovery of a conspiracy whose leadership was promisingly rooted in southern England. According to an official Yorkist account written in March 1462 by Antonio della Torre, Edward set out for Northumberland on 24 February to deal with the Scottish threat. Eleven days before his departure, a conspiracy headed by the Essex magnate the earl of Oxford was discovered. The plotters had intended to follow the king with his 1,000 horse northwards, leading retinues of 2,000 or more as if to support him, but in reality to attack. Meanwhile Somerset, then in Bruges, would sail to England, King Henry would cross the Border with the Scots, and Pembroke would come from Brittany.[18] Nevertheless, Somerset's safe voyage with Hungerford from Flanders to Scotland in March appeared to presage an invasion, and defence measures were put in hand.[19] In the north the Yorkists took successful preventive action against Scottish intervention. That month the earl of Douglas, long an exile at the English court, struck a blow at possible Lancastrian allies by raiding the Scottish West March.[20] In April Margaret, despairing of immediate Scottish support, left Kirkcudbright to sail to Brittany, with her husband's commission to treat with Louis XI. In May or June Warwick raided across the Border and captured a castle. At the end of June Mary of Guelders came to Carlisle and made a truce with him, to last till 24 August. There were impressions in England that this would lead to a more comprehensive and lasting settlement. It was rumoured that the Scots had agreed to hand over Henry and his adherents. In return, Warwick had leashed Douglas, who was ordered south, 'a sorrowful and a sore rebuked man'. The Yorkists were able to concentrate on reducing isolated northern strongholds: Dacre yielded his ancestral castle at Naworth to Montague, and on 30 or 31 July Tailboys surrendered Alnwick castle, which had been once more in Lancastrian hands. Sir Ralph Grey, who had commanded the siege with Lord Hastings, was made captain at Alnwick.[21]

The Lancastrian situation was not as hopeless as these diplomatic and military reverses seemed to imply. It was transformed by Margaret's successful diplomacy. In June she had reached agreement with Louis XI: the Lancastrians were to receive a subsidy from him and were authorized to recruit in France. With this aid they attempted to re-establish control in Northumberland in the autumn. Factors in the decision to strike there were probably the expectation of renewed help from the Scots and from Percy adherents, and appreciation that strong castles in the region could be held in defiance of a regime based in the remote south of England. Though the Lancastrians were to fail to extend their power significantly outside Northumberland, their incursions there from October 1462 to June 1464 placed a grave burden on Edward's resources. He had to continue exasperating his subjects by financial demands. Moreover, the Yorkist efforts to reconquer Northumberland led to his continued dependence on the Neville brothers, and their consequent aggrandizement. This contributed to the political strains which resulted in the decline and overthrow of his rule (1469–70) and the brief re-establishment of Henry VI.

The Lancastrian invasion of Northumberland in 1462 thus had a profoundly disquieting effect on Edward's and, indeed, his successors' rule, helping to revive and prolong traditions of dynastic revolt which persisted to the end of the century. Yet, arguably, the decision to strike in Northumberland was a mistake, for Scottish support had previously been wavering and of only limited military value. In 1496 Lord

Bothwell opined that a projected Scottish invasion of Northumberland was a hazardous enterprise, and that the army would agitate to return home after four or five days, being 'so weary for watching and for lack of victuals'.[22] As Perkin Warbeck found on this expedition, Scottish forces, plundering as usual, alienated any local inclination to support a dynastic claimant.[23] Perhaps the Lancastrians would have been better advised to delay their invasion until the spring of 1463, and then concentrate on reviving Welsh support. For the aggrandizement of Edward's lieutenants is likely to have caused as much resentment in Wales as in the north of England,[24] and landing in Wales had the advantage, as Henry Tudor showed in 1485, of providing speedy access to the English heartlands.

The queen embarked at Honfleur in Normandy and landed on the Northumbrian coast near Bamburgh on 25 October 1462. With her was a sizeable French force, at most about 2,000 strong, commanded by the distinguished soldier Pierre de Brézé, *grand sénéchal* of Normandy – according to the chronicler Warkworth 'the best warrior of all that time'. Henry VI, Somerset and some Scottish soldiers had been picked up in Scotland on the way.[25] The invaders speedily took the royal coastal castles at Bamburgh and Dunstanburgh, and the Percy castles at Alnwick and Warkworth, 'which they had victualled and stuffed both with Englishmen, Frenchmen and Scotsmen; by the which castles they had the most part of all Northumberland'.[26]

The Yorkist government reacted quickly: Edward had for some time been alert to the threat of a new Lancastrian invasion.[27] The king 'did make great guns and other great ordnance at London, and did do carry it into the north country'.[28] But the organization and movement of a royal expedition northwards took time. Meanwhile Warwick was commissioned to attack the Lancastrians.[29] Henry VI, his queen and Brézé did not feel strong enough to challenge the Yorkists in the field, and on 13 November they withdrew to seek reinforcements in Scotland, leaving garrisons in the castles which they had captured. The shipwreck of a large company of the queen's Frenchmen on the Northumbrian coast was a blow. The fact that two local gentlemen, the Bastard of Ogle and John Manners, esquire, attacked and overcame them on Holy Island shows that there were limitations to Lancastrian control even in the parts of Northumberland where they were strongest.[30]

Early in November Edward set out from London for the north.[31] He arrayed probably the largest number of peers to serve in a later medieval English army – there were thirty-nine adult ones on service, including recent Lancastrian activists and 'neutrals' who doubtless considered it politic to demonstrate their commitment to the new allegiance.[32] At Durham Edward was incapacitated by measles. He had to leave Warwick to conduct the sieges.[33] On 21 December garrison strengths within Alnwick and Bamburgh castles were said to be 300, in Dunstanburgh 120. Somerset, Pembroke, Roos and a deserter from Edward's allegiance, Sir Ralph Percy, were in Bamburgh, Sir Richard Tunstall and Sir Thomas Finderne in Dunstanburgh. Hungerford and Whittingham were at Alnwick, whose garrison was probably predominantly French.[34] John Paston the youngest, in the duke of Norfolk's military retinue at Newcastle, wrote on 11 December that Warwick was staying not far from Alnwick, at Warkworth castle, 'and he rideth daily to all these castles for to oversee the sieges'. The earl of Kent (Fauconberg) and Rivers's son Lord Scales were at the siege of Alnwick, the earl of Worcester and Sir Ralph Grey at Dunstanburgh, and Lords Montague and Ogle at Bamburgh.[35]

Bamburgh and Dunstanburgh were formally surrendered on 26 and 27 December respectively. Most of the gentlefolk received safe-conducts to withdraw from the realm, but Somerset and Percy paid allegiance to Edward, Percy receiving custody of the two castles.[36] Edward probably had pressing reasons for granting imprudently generous terms. He is likely to have been reluctant, as he was to be in 1464, to cause damage by bombardment to castles useful for the defence of the realm. The continued maintenance of his army was presenting problems. His forces at Alnwick were soon to show that 'they had lie there so long in the field, and were grieved with cold and rain, that they had no courage to fight'.[37] Above all, Edward believed that belated Scottish intervention to save the tottering Lancastrians was imminent. On 31 December, in a mandate under his signet seal dated at Durham and addressed to Archbishop Booth of York, he alleged that the Scots intended to enter the realm on 3 January to rescue 'our enemies of France closed within our castle of Alnwick' and to give him battle. The archbishop was to warn the clergy of the province to be with the king in defensible array on Newcastle moor on 4 January, to assist him in the battle which he anticipated the next day.[38] Edward's appraisal is likely to have been based on reports of the concentration of an army in the Borders by George Douglas, earl of Angus, warden of the Marches.[39] In response to appeals to relieve the hard-pressed and famished garrison in Alnwick, Angus selected his best troops for a foray across the Border. But he was to show no desire to stay for a confrontation with Edward. At about five o'clock on the morning of 6 January he and Brézé reached Alnwick with their forces. Its besiegers withdrew in some confusion, and part of the garrison sallied forth and disappeared with their rescuers. Angus, the Scottish chronicler Major boasted, set the Frenchmen free, and in sight of the mighty English army, carried them with him into Scotland; the English were paralysed by divided counsels as to whether or not they should attack Angus. The English chroniclers Warkworth and the author of the *Annales*, though under no illusions as to their countrymen's poor showing, professed themselves unimpressed by Angus's achievement. They thought that the invaders, fearing a trap, had missed an opportunity to defeat the disarrayed Yorkists. The upshot was in fact to the latter's gain: those remaining in the castle surrendered on terms.[40]

Angus's brief foray and the surrender of Alnwick virtually ended the winter campaign. Edward and his great army withdrew southwards, leaving Warwick to guard the frontier, which he did energetically. One English chronicler commented scornfully on the failure of 'practically the whole knighthood of England' to achieve anything memorable in their long stay, apart from the capture of three castles.[41] His attitude perhaps reflects Englishmen's expectations of brief campaigns and decisive battles in the dynastic conflicts, and their failure to appreciate the handicaps of winter campaigning in the region. Nevertheless, the Yorkist showing was not brilliant. Edward's enforced absence at Durham may have hampered firm directions. Warwick may have found it difficult to impose discipline on a great, motley assembly of fellow nobles, all doubtless as concerned with their precedence and the comforts of their winter quarters as with the business, novel to some, of prosecuting sieges. The Lancastrian leaders, on the other hand, had no cause to celebrate. They had failed to consolidate their hold in Northumberland. Scottish help had been disappointing. Their French force was depleted, and one of their principal supporters had deserted the cause.

Despite disillusion among the French soldiers, in 1463 the chivalrous Brézé displayed his habitual loyalty and tenacity in supporting Lancastrian efforts in Northumberland. There castellans on whom Edward had been constrained to rely, treacherously undermined the recent Yorkist success. In March 1463 Sir Ralph Percy, captain at Bamburgh and Dunstanburgh, delivered the castles to Henry. By May Alnwick castle was once again in Lancastrian hands, betrayed to Hungerford and the French by Sir Ralph Grey. Yorkist counter-measures were entrusted principally to the Nevilles.[42] They were soon faced with a more serious threat: on 11 July Warwick wrote as royal lieutenant from Middleham castle (Yorks.) to Archbishop Booth, saying that he knew for certain that the Scots and 'the king's traitors and rebels' had entered the realm 'with great puissance'. The earl wanted the clergy of the province to be assembled, defensibly arrayed, at Durham on 15 July.[43] Henry and Margaret, Mary of Guelders, the youthful James III, and Brézé laid siege to the bishop of Durham's exposed castle on the frontier at Norham – a move more calculated to suit Scottish than Lancastrian interests. After eighteen days of siege, Warwick and Montague relieved the castle with local forces and put the invaders to flight. Hotly pursued, in great disarray, Margaret fled to the

Northumbrian coast with Brézé and the French. It was the end of Franco-Scottish military co-operation in the Lancastrian interest in the Borders. Waurin, Basin and Chastellain all reflect French bitterness at the failure of the Scots to provide them with the anticipated support in the Border campaigns.[44]

Margaret, with the prince, Exeter, Brézé, Fortescue and other councillors sailed to Flanders. The conclusion of an Anglo-French truce in October 1463 dashed their hopes of aid against Edward. The truce made his threatened invasion of Scotland more dangerous: in December an Anglo-Scottish truce was concluded.[45] The renegade Somerset, Edward's travelling-companion and even, on occasion, bedfellow, may have ruefully reflected that autumn that the Lancastrian cause looked as if it might indeed be irretrievably lost, unless he helped to revive it. Since he was so unpopular with Yorkist partisans, some time after 25 July Edward sent him from court for his own protection to a royal castle, probably in Wales. The king showed his continued trust in Somerset by sending the duke's men to guard Newcastle. But before 20 December the duke, without royal licence, left North Wales for Newcastle, which he had plotted with his men to betray. On the way he was recognized and had to flee from his bed near Durham, in his shirt and barefoot. He reached the Lancastrian garrison at Bamburgh safely, but his supporters in Newcastle had to flee too. The king made the town secure for the winter by sending a force of his household men there and appointing Lord Scrope of Bolton captain of the town.[46]

There were other ramifications of Somerset's plot to be dealt with. On 1 March 1464 John Paston the youngest, in the duke of Norfolk's retinue at Holt castle (Cheshire), wrote about the duke's progress in suppressing and punishing Somerset's adherents in the region. Welsh gentlemen who had assisted his flight had to be dealt with. The commons of Lancashire and Cheshire had risen to the number of 10,000, 'but now they be down again'.[47]

Nevertheless, the Lancastrians were sufficiently well based in Northumberland to conduct offensives without foreign or other substantial help. They captured Langley and Bywell castles, and the town tower at Hexham, establishing a threatening presence in upper Tynedale. They even seized a Yorkshire castle, at Skipton in Craven.[48] On 1 April the irrepressible Humphrey Neville of Brancepeth, breaking the terms of his pardon, joined the Lancastrians at Bamburgh.[49] That month they attempted to disrupt the intended Anglo-Scottish negotiations. Somerset and Sir Ralph Percy placed Neville with eighty spears and bowmen in a wood near Newcastle to ambush Montague on his way to Norham to meet the Scottish envoys and escort them to York. He evaded the trap, but about nine miles from Alnwick, at Hedgeley Moor, was attacked by Somerset, Roos, Hungerford, Sir

Ralph Percy, Sir Richard Tunstall and Sir Thomas Finderne, leading 500 men-at-arms, on 25 April. The attack was repulsed and Percy was killed, a blow to Lancastrian loyalties in Northumberland.[50] Montague carried on to Norham and brought in the Scots, returning to Newcastle. Despite the reverse, the Lancastrian leadership, including Henry, held on in Tynedale. Presumably they hoped to score a success before Edward could bring up overwhelming southern reinforcements. But Montague caught them unprepared: on 15 May, with Lords Greystoke and Willoughby, and, according to the *Annales*, 4,000 men against not more than 500 Lancastrians, he attacked by Hexham. The common soldiers deserted the Lancastrian lords, who were captured thereabouts or hunted down in the next few days. Henry VI made a lucky escape from Bywell castle, leaving behind his helmet with its crown, and his sword. Montague was able to publicize the downfall of the Lancastrian leadership in a series of executions, at Hexham, Newcastle, Middleham and York. Somerset, Roos, Hungerford and Finderne were among the victims.[51]

As a result of Hexham there was a general crumbling of the Lancastrian cause in Northumberland. Commanders of castles abandoned them or negotiated terms.[52] After the battle some fugitives took refuge in Bamburgh castle.[53] Diehard gentlefolk from Northumberland and Westmorland may have congregated there from the end of May.[54] Warwick arrived before Alnwick castle on 23 June and received its surrender, as he did that of Dunstanburgh castle, where he lodged the next day. On 25 June he and his brother Montague (newly created earl of Northumberland) laid siege to Bamburgh castle, whose hard-core garrison was led by Sir Ralph Grey and Neville of Brancepeth. Chester and Warwick Heralds were sent to offer pardons to all the besieged except these two. Grey's reply was defiant, but he was told by a herald, 'My Lords ensurith you, upon their honour, to sustain siege before you these seven years, or else to win you.' Grey had changed his coat too many times. The king, it was intimated, was particularly anxious that the castle should not be damaged by artillery — every shot fired would cost a defender's head. Nevertheless, the besiegers had to bombard: Warwick 'ordained all the King's great guns that were charged at once to shoot'. *Newe-Castel*, the king's great gun, and *London*, 'The second gun of iron', knocked stones off the castle walls into the sea. *Dysyon* (i.e. *Dijon*), a brass gun, often loosed shot through Grey's chamber. He was concussed by a fall of masonry and given up for dead. The bombardment assisted an assault on the castle, but Neville managed to bargain for his life and the lives of the other defenders, except for Grey, who was to pay the penalty for his tergiversations.[55]

From Margaret of Anjou's landing in Northumberland in October

1462 till the surrender of Bamburgh in June 1464, Lancastrian resources were concentrated on controlling this peripheral part of the realm. The attempt was intensely troublesome and repeatedly alarming to Edward IV. Lancastrian threats contributed to his failure to consolidate his rule until after 1471. But at no time were the Lancastrians able to tighten their hold in the Marches sufficiently for the invasion of the realm. They never secured the requisite base – a major town. The attempts to take Carlisle in 1461 and Newcastle in 1464 were failures. The numerous, well-maintained Northumbrian castles provided a means of maintaining their interest there, but local factors made it necessary for them to devote their energies just to hanging on to the castles. Supplies were difficult to come by; local nobles and commons were by no means unanimously pro-Lancastrian, and were liable to flinch from a cause supported by Scottish arms. Apart from Perkin Warbeck in 1496, no claimant to the throne after the 1460s was to make his principal effort in the Marches towards Scotland. The invaders of 1469–71, 1485 and 1487 preferred other entry points, and pushed as fast as they could towards the central parts of the realm, sometimes with foreign support less impressive than that at Margaret's disposal in 1462. Lancastrian strategy took a disastrous turn in the 1460s. The choice of and persistence with the Northumbrian option cost the lives of some of the best of Henry's knights and disillusioned many English and foreign supporters. Nevertheless, it must be remembered that concurrent attempts were made to develop an alternative strategy.

Chapter 4

Local Revolts and Nobles' Struggles to Control the Crown, 1469–71

From 1464 onwards the few remaining prominent Lancastrians were unable to pose a major threat to Edward IV, who was militarily and diplomatically successful. Henry VI was captured, hiding in Lancashire, in 1465 and imprisoned in the Tower. Margaret of Anjou and her son Prince Edward maintained a threadbare court in Lorraine. Their former patron Louis XI had his hands full with the revolts headed by Charles the Bold of Burgundy, and Margaret's doughty champion Brézé died in them, at the battle of Montlhéry in 1465.[1] Somerset's heir, his brother Edmund Beaufort, became absorbed in fighting for Charles, not Henry.[2] Only in Wales did continued Lancastrian activity necessitate royal counter-measures. The bailiffs of Shrewsbury accounted in the year 1466–7 for the financing of soldiers raised on royal command to accompany John Tiptoft, earl of Worcester, to Denbigh and Harlech castles. Men were sent from the town to ascertain the truth of rumours that the Lancastrian Sir Richard Tunstall was at Wrexham with a force, and whether he and other men of Harlech 'intended any evil to this town or not'.[3] In September 1467 the Milanese agent Panicharolla reported from Paris: 'the Welshmen have taken up arms against King Edward and proclaim King Henry, whose next brother [Jasper Tudor], late resident here, is going over there, and the late queen is sending him some of her followers to make their party take the field if possible'. Jasper was provided with enough aid by Louis XI to equip a tiny force of three ships and fifty soldiers. His landing in Wales was reported by Panicharolla on 2 July 1468, and on the next day Lords Herbert and Ferrers were commissioned to array men in the Marches of Wales and adjacent shires for service against him. Jasper Tudor raised enough support to occupy Denbigh, but was defeated by Herbert and his brother Sir Richard. Harlech castle at last capitulated the following month.[4]

The crown was alarmed by the possibility that prominent

Englishmen were involved in this resurgence of Lancastrian activity. Heads of noble families which had lost estates or influence as a result of past rebellion were especially suspect. Among those arrested in the autumn of 1468 were Henry Courtenay, brother and heir of the earl of Devon attainted in 1461, Thomas Hungerford, whose father was also attainted then, and John de Vere, earl of Oxford, whose father and elder brother had been executed in 1462. Oxford was soon released, but in January 1469 Courtenay and Hungerford were convicted of plotting with Margaret of Anjou and executed.[5]

But in 1469–70 it was northern discontent with aspects of Yorkist rule, discontent encouraged by leading Yorkist nobles, which posed dire threats to Edward's rule. The Lancastrian exiles were not to be involved until the summer of 1470 – and then not of their own volition. The first major stirrings were in the spring of 1469. There were popular assemblies centred on Yorkshire, about which the sources are confusing and unenlightening. One aim of the rebels in the East Riding, captained by 'Robin of Holderness', had possible Lancastrian, and certainly anti-Neville, overtones. They wanted the restoration to the earldom of Northumberland of Henry Percy, whose father had forfeited it in 1461. The present earl, Warwick's brother John Neville, took the lead in suppressing these stirs.[6] But about 28 May there started another Yorkshire outbreak, whose leaders had completely different sympathies. Captained by 'Robin of Redesdale', they complained, according to the first Crowland continuator, that they were grievously oppressed by taxes and annual tributes instigated by the favourites of the king and his queen Elizabeth Wydeville. This rising was in fact firmly controlled by Yorkshire gentlefolk acting in the interests of a Neville coterie – Warwick, his brother George archbishop of York, and the king's brother George duke of Clarence, allied to destroy the influence of rivals at court. 'Robin of Redesdale' was probably Sir John Conyers of Hornby (Yorks.), related to the Nevilles by marriage. In his company were the sons of Lords Latimer, FitzHugh and Dudley, also Neville kinsfolk. The royal response to the rising was sluggish. Edward may at first have regarded it as another of the tiresome Yorkshire discontents whose impact had been mainly local. In the first week of June he set out on a tour of East Anglia. The first day on which there is evidence that he was preparing to act against the risers in person is 18 June. On 5 July he addressed a signet letter from Stamford (Lincs.) to the mayor of Coventry, expressing his determination to go into northern parts to suppress the riots, and asking him to send hastily 100 archers in assistance. Five days later he wrote even more urgently from Newark asking for whatever support Coventry could send. When at Newark, he found himself outnumbered by the northern rebels by three to one. He retreated to Nottingham and remained there, presumably unwilling to give the appearance of flight, and hopeful that he would be reinforced in response to the privy seal letters he had sent into the north, Wales and the West Country.[7]

The northerners, remonstrating against royal favourites, were as anxious as Edward's father had been to avoid the appearance of attacking the king. They bypassed Nottingham, moving southwards into the Midlands, doubtless with the intention of linking up with their Neville mentors as soon as possible. Warwick re-enacted his 1460 role as a 'Calais lord'. On 4 July he, his brother-in-law Oxford, and Clarence crossed to his captaincy of Calais. There his daughter Isabel married the duke. On 12 July Clarence, Archbishop Neville and Warwick set their signets and sign manuals to a letter addressed to a 'right trusty and beloved' correspondent. In it they declared that subjects had delivered to them bills containing articles about the 'deceivable rule and guiding of certain seditious persons' – Lord Rivers and his wife the duchess of Bedford (the queen's parents), William Herbert, recently created earl of Pembroke, Humphrey Stafford, recently created earl of Devon, Lord Scales (Anthony Wydeville, the queen's brother), Lord Audley, Sir John Wydeville and his brothers, Sir John Fogge and their supporters. The three said that they intended with other lords to show these articles to the king, and asked for military support to accompany them. They would be at Canterbury on 15 July. In fact they crossed the Channel the day after, to be greeted by a large number of Kentishmen at Canterbury. On 18 July they left the city for London, whose governors allowed them to pass through on their way to join the northerners.[8]

But before the conjunction could be made, the issue was settled in battle. The northerners intercepted a Welsh force commanded by Pembroke, hurrying to reinforce the king, on the 'plain of Edgcote' near Banbury (Oxon.) and decisively defeated it on 26 July. Contemporary accounts of the battle are meagre, apart from Waurin's, whose circumstantial details lack independent confirmation – and who is contradicted by English sources on an important point. Waurin says that the armies converged on a river crossing (presumably on the Cherwell) and encamped at some distance on either side for the night. Next morning both armies advanced to secure the crossing. Pembroke, not realizing how near the enemy was, went on ahead of the infantry with his horsemen, who had to defend themselves against heavy attack. They held the passage, however. The bruised northerners drew off, inclining to wait for Warwick to reinforce them. But two insistent knights got them into line for another assault to secure the crossing. Sir William Par ('Appare') and Sir Geoffrey Gate ('Guat') may have arrived with some reinforcements, part of the vanward of the magnates' army. Waurin says that Pembroke, though now reinforced, was outnumbered, and that the Welshmen were overwhelmed when Devon and his men withdrew from the fight on hearing that Clarence was coming to aid the northerners. However, Warkworth and the author of *Hearne's Fragment* state that Devon and his company had parted company with Pembroke before the battle. The latter author thought that the northerners owed their victory to the 15,000 household men and soldiers from Calais under Clapham whom Warwick sent ahead as a reinforcement from London. Contemporaries regarded the death-toll as high on both sides, but disastrous for the Welsh. Pembroke and his brother Sir Richard Herbert were captured, and executed the following day on Warwick's arbitrary orders. The earl was able to dismiss his Kentish supporters. Too late, on 29 July Edward at last left Nottingham, moving southwards. At Olney (Beds.) he heard about the battle. Deserted by his men, he had to submit to Archbishop Neville. Probably early in August, Earl Rivers and his son Sir John Wydeville were captured and executed.[9]

Warwick's ambitious strategy in 1469, involving the conjunction of forces from the south-east and north, echoed that in which he had been disastrously involved ten years before. But in 1469 he laid the ground well, working up prior support in Yorkshire and Kent, and was sufficiently well informed and organized after reaching London to react speedily to the needs of his northern allies when things did not go according to plan. Edward, however, seems to have been more than usually misled by the fog of war. He failed to exploit interior lines in the Midlands, unlike the royal commanders in 1459. Unlike Henry then, he remained for too long at Nottingham, perhaps hanging on for reinforcements, perhaps uncharacteristically relying on a subordinate commander, Pembroke — who had a good military reputation. Had Edward made a dash to place himself at the head of the Welsh and western men, he would have had a good chance of defeating the northerners at Edgcote, before they were able to link up with Warwick, and consequently might have enforced the latter's submission or flight. For the royal army, though outnumbered at Edgcote, was an excellent one. Its weakness lay in the enmity of its commanders, two parvenu earls. The royal presence would have damped that down, and disheartened the northerners. Basically Edward lost because he failed to achieve a sufficient concentration of forces, whereas his enemies did so.

The civil war of 1469 demonstrated to Lancastrian sympathizers the enmities splitting the Yorkist establishment and the slender hold which Edward and some of his magnates had over local loyalties. Northern Lancastrians attempted to exploit Edward's humiliating tutelage under Warwick's control. Humphrey Neville of Brancepeth had escaped from the rout of Hexham in 1464 and since lived in hiding around Derwentwater. He and his brother Charles now raised revolt in the

Borders. Warwick found that his imprisonment of the king was so unpopular that he could not raise sufficient arrays until Edward was released and appeared at liberty in York. Humphrey Neville was captured by Warwick in Holderness: he and his brother Charles were executed at York on 29 September in the king's presence.[10]

Clarence and Warwick thus soon found that the 1469 rebellion had brought them few political gains. So they planned a repeat performance for 1470, possibly with the more extreme aim of deposing Edward. They covertly encouraged rebellion in the north, planning to join up with the rebels – this time with forces brought from nearer at hand – and trap the unwary king. But Edward had learnt a bitter lesson. Though again operating in a haze of misapprehension, he grappled with the local rebels as quickly as possible. They were unable to withstand the king. Their leaders lacked the calibre of the previous year's, and this time Clarence and Warwick were not in time to give help. Once Edward had won in battle, he began to bring up support, and the frantic efforts of the two lords were unable to stop theirs from petering out.

At the start, besides hoping for support in Yorkshire once again, they tried to exploit tensions among Lincolnshire gentlefolk. Richard Lord Welles and Willoughby, his son Sir Robert Welles, his brother-in-law Sir Thomas de la Launde, and Sir Thomas Dymoke resented the aggrandizement of a knight of the king's body, Thomas Burgh of Gainsborough. He was driven out of the shire and his house was sacked. The Welles interest's fears of royal disfavour for local stirs inclined them to accept the patronage of Clarence and Warwick: some even succumbed to their incitement to rebel.[11] On Sunday 4 March 1470 Sir Robert Welles, 'great captain of the commons of Lincolnshire', had proclamations made in churches, in the name of the king, Clarence, Warwick and himself, ordering the people to meet him armed on Ranby Hawe (seven miles north of Horncastle) in order to resist the king, who was coming, so he said, to destroy the commons of the shire. But fears of royal displeasure had driven other members of the Welles interest to adopt what turned out to be a disastrously contradictory policy. When Sir Robert was having his proclamations made, his father and Dymoke were in London, in answer to royal summonses – and they and, indeed, Sir Robert received pardons for previous disturbances. Sir Robert, according to his confession, relied on Clarence's promises to go to London, excuse Lord Welles to the king, and delay the latter's counter-measures. The duke in fact arrived at court on 4 March, the day of Sir Robert's proclamations, but he does not seem to have effectively delayed Edward's expedition or cleared Lord Welles. The king set out northwards from London on 6 March, the day of the intended assembly at Ranby, and on the following morning, at Waltham (Herts.) received news of the Lincolnshire proclamations. He promptly summoned Welles and Dymoke from London. Clarence's dissimulation left Edward disinclined to believe that his brother and Warwick were mixed up in the business. From Royston (Herts.), where he arrived on 8 March, he dispatched the commissions of array made out to them at Waltham.[12]

Edward reached Huntingdon on 9 March, and his ancestral castle of Fotheringhay (Northants.) on the 11th. There it was reported that the rebels were south of Grantham, less than forty miles away. But they were veering south-west, out of his path, towards Leicester, in response to Warwick's promise to meet them there on Monday 12 March with 20,000 men. According to the Lincolnshire captains' later confessions, the plan was for the rebels at Leicester to allow the king to pass northwards, then cut off his retreat, surrounding him with their northern allies – such as, presumably, the Yorkshire dissidents. This alleged intention seems to have relied heavily on Edward displaying uncharacteristic foolhardiness. In fact he undermined enemy strategy, unknowingly, by a neat piece of psychological warfare. On the 11th Sir Robert received a letter from his father, in the king's army, making plain that Edward would have him executed unless Sir Robert submitted. Sir Robert made a fateful decision. Calculating that the king would get from Fotheringhay as far as Stamford on 12 March and spend the night there, he decided to turn away from Leicester, attack the king's army as it settled into Stamford, and rescue his father.[13]

However favourably this sudden decision displayed Sir Robert's filial and chivalrous instincts, by rushing at Edward single-handed he was providing the king with an opportunity to nip rebellion in the bud. He was negating the strategy agreed with his sluggish magnate allies, whose fair promises had not relieved his father's plight. Early on the morning of 12 March the royal army took the road from Fotheringhay. When it reached Stamford the same day, the rebels were still five miles to the west of the town, at Empingham. Edward pushed his 'foreward' on towards them. A message to him from Clarence and Warwick saying that they would be at Leicester that night and promising help did not delay him. Edward's generalship is seen at its best in his determination to force the issue that day, after a hard march. His soldiers were probably impressed by the ruthless execution of Lord Welles and Dymoke, in accordance with his nobles' wishes, before engagement. Sir Robert Welles, shocked by what he regarded as royal perfidy, refused an offer of grace. But his rustics, daunted by the sight of Edward's great host, soon broke and scattered in what contemporaries referred to contemptuously as Losecoat Field – so unmemorable, if decisive, a fight that no surviving chronicle records details.[14]

One of the fruits of victory was firm evidence of Clarence's and Warwick's complicity. On the battlefield the corpse of one of

Clarence's servants was found to be carrying in a casket 'many marvellous bills, containing matter of the great sedition'. In the pursuit Sir Thomas de la Launde was captured; Sir Robert Welles and Richard Waryn were among the rebel captains brought to the king when he had moved on to halt at Grantham (14–15 March). These three publicly confessed in the royal presence that Clarence and Warwick had promised them assistance, and they confirmed this at their executions. The magnates' repeatedly asserted purpose, Welles alleged, was to make Clarence king.[15]

After his victory, Clarence and Warwick were disinclined to attack the king. On 13 March Edward dispatched a squire of the body, John Donne, from Stamford with letters to them at Coventry, commanding them to dismiss the bulk of their troops and attend on him with select retinues. But they dissimulated, hoping to stir rebellion anew, north of the Trent. They sent messages charging Yorkshiremen to make proclamations ordering military assistance to them on pain of death. From Coventry they went with their whole fellowship through Burton-on-Trent and Derby, arriving at Chesterfield on 18 March.

Moving on a parallel course, an increasingly recalcitrant Edward set out northwards from Grantham: he had information that there were rebellious moves in Yorkshire, in the honour of Richmond. He arrived at Newark on 16 March; there signet letters were drafted to the two magnates, summoning them to the royal presence to answer the charges against them. *En route* from Newark to Doncaster, Edward received a message from them promising to meet him at Retford. This they failed to do. After his arrival at Doncaster (18 March), their envoys came requesting sureties if they were to come to Edward's presence, which he brusquely refused. The execution of Sir Robert Welles and another Lincolnshire captain there on the 19th showed his confidence and determination. He had beaten his indecisive opponents, who were advancing less directly, in the race for Yorkshire. Appreciating their dilemma, he determined to bring matters to a head. On 20 March 'at nine of the bell, the King took the field, and mustered his people; and it was said that were never seen in England so many goodly men, and so well arrayed in a field'. Abandoning the route north, the royal army turned aside to advance on the lords at Chesterfield. Edward spent the night at Rotherham, since the lords' aforeriders had been there to requisition lodgings. Their appearance may have been a feint, or part of a move to trap the king in conjunction with the Yorkshire rebels, whose leaders were to confess that they were to have 'drawn to' Rotherham, encountered the king there and attacked his host. But at Rotherham Edward had firm news that the lords had given him the slip. They retreated westwards towards Manchester, hoping that Lord Stanley would reinforce them with his Lancashiremen before they joined up with their Yorkshire allies. But it may be that a crisis in the lords' camp necessitated a drastic change of plan. Waurin picked up a story that at some point Warwick was prepared to fight the king, but that the night before, one of his 'great captains', son of the renowned 'Thalbot', deserted with his company of about 3,000 to the king's side so suddenly that Warwick and his army had to make a disorderly flight. 'Thalbot' may have been either John Talbot, earl of Shrewsbury, or his brother Sir Gilbert, grandsons of the great fighting earl who died in 1453.[16]

Acting on the counsel of his lords, Edward broke off the pursuit, deciding to go to York before venturing into Lancashire. Pausing for a night at Pontefract castle, he entered York on 22 March. He wished to 'refresh' his army and secure the submission of Yorkshiremen who remembered well the rout of his army the previous year. Lord Scrope's efforts to raise Richmondshire, in the North Riding of Yorkshire, had been deterred by news of Edward's victory near Stamford and of his commissions of array directed to the Border shires and the earl of Northumberland. At York he received the submissions of Scrope, Sir John Conyers, 'young Hilyard of Holderness' and others who liberally confessed that they had been incited to revolt by Clarence and Warwick. Edward had now decided to treat the pair as incorrigible traitors. In a proclamation dated York, 24 March, he accused them of collusion in the Lincolnshire rising and of subsequent rebellious defiance. He charged them to appear before him on 28 March at the latest, or else be branded as rebels and traitors. They were both denounced as such in commissions of array dated 26 March.[17]

About 27 March Edward set out from York in pursuit. The rebel magnates' plans for resistance in the north collapsed. Finding no support in Lancashire, they retreated south-west all the way to Exeter. Edward, advancing through Nottingham, Coventry and Wells, arrived there on 14 April to find that they had taken ship with their wives and a small fellowship. Heading for Calais, they put in at Southampton, hoping to seize Warwick's great ship the *Trinite*, docked there. But Anthony Wydeville, Earl Rivers, and Lord Howard staved them off. The Calais garrison, despite the sympathy of Warwick's deputy there, Lord Wenlock, made clear that it would oppose the landing. The earl and Clarence had to take refuge in Normandy, putting in at Honfleur about 1 May.[18]

Why were the risings of March 1470 so unsuccessful, despite Edward's dangerous slowness in realizing who the instigators were? Their defeat was due in large measure to Edward's energy and speed of action. He was determined not to be overtaken by events, as he had been in 1469. He matched the ruthlessness his opponents had displayed then by his executions before Losecoat Field, at Grantham and Doncaster, tempered by a politic willingness to grant pardons to the volatile Yorkshiremen. But Clarence and Warwick again relied too readily on raising rebellion by proxy: Welles and his army lacked the ability which their Yorkshire allies of 1469 had exhibited. The sudden, solitary collapse which the Lincolnshiremen brought upon themselves caught the two magnates and their sympathizers in the north on the wrong foot. They were never able to get back into their stride for a challenge to the victorious Edward. Welles's confession strongly suggests that Clarence had a large share of responsibility for inciting the rising prematurely.

The failure of Clarence and Warwick enabled Louis XI of France to give an extraordinary twist to dynastic allegiances by reconciling them to Margaret of Anjou and the prince of Wales. They reverted to the allegiance of Henry VI (still a prisoner in the Tower), and Warwick betrothed his daughter Anne to the prince.[19]

Warwick once more planned an invasion of England – bewilderingly, in the Lancastrian interest with French royal backing. On 2 June commissions of array were appointed for defence against Clarence and Warwick in southern and western shires.[20] On 28 July Sforza de' Bettini, Milanese envoy at the French court, reported from Angers that in two days Warwick would leave for his fleet to undertake the enterprise of England. Just over a week later he reported that the earl had departed for Normandy, and that news of his sailing was expected at any moment.[21] On 5 August Sir John Paston reported from London that 'it is said Courtenays [the Lancastrian family which had held the earldom of Devon] be landed in Devonshire, and there rule' and that Clarence and Warwick 'will essay to land in England every day, as folks fear'.[22] But Warwick was unable to invade. Delays were imposed by organizational problems and a blockade instigated by Charles the Bold of Burgundy, whose alliance with Edward IV was the motive for Louis XI's support of Warwick's extraordinary enterprise.[23]

In anticipation of the earl's arrival, his English adherents rose in arms. In the north, Neville supporters – probably smarting at their recent humiliation and angry at Henry Percy's restoration to the earldom of Northumberland in place of John Neville in March – were dry tinder. In Yorkshire they rose in July under Henry Lord FitzHugh, Warwick's brother-in-law. On 5 August Sir John Paston commented on the inability of Percy to suppress the northern rebels: 'and so the King hath sent for his feedmen to come to him, for he will go to put them down'. On 8 August Coventry dispatched forty soldiers to the king at Nottingham. By mid-August Edward was once again in arms in Yorkshire, advancing from York to Ripon. Deterred by Warwick's failure to appear, and by news of Edward's approach, FitzHugh fled to Scotland.[24]

At last, on 9 September, Clarence and Warwick were able to embark from Normandy, after the Burgundian fleet had been dispersed in bad weather. On 13 September their English and French ships put into West Country ports. In the company were the earl of Oxford, Jasper Tudor, and Warwick's cousin Thomas Neville, Bastard of Fauconberg (the son of Lord Fauconberg). Edward was still at York. His delay there has been considered ill-adjudged; but he may have been concerned about a recurrence of northern rebellion, and he was well placed for a swift advance southwards towards Nottingham and Leicester, to rally retainers and secure London, as he was to do in 1471.[25]

In fact the start of the invasion was inauspicious. It was late in the campaigning season. Due possibly to prevailing winds, Clarence and Warwick had landed in a remote part of the realm, where they had little influence, far away from their Kentish adherents, who were to rampage in Southwark in a manner little calculated to win over London citizens.[26] The invaders advanced into the Midlands, presumably in order to cut Edward off in the north and to recruit in Warwick's shires. By the time they reached Coventry, according to the city's official account, they were 30,000 strong.[27] Edward was moving southwards, perhaps intending, as in 1469 and 1471, to make Nottingham his base for rallying supporters. But, whilst his numbers were still insignificant, he was undone by an outstanding act of treachery. He was roused from his bed by the serjeant of the minstrels, Alexander Carlisle, who came in great haste with the news that his enemies were poised to capture him. Warwick's brother John Neville, Marquess Montague, aggrieved at being recently deprived of the earldom of Northumberland in favour of the Percy, was advancing with 6,000 men arrayed under commission from Edward – against him. The king, with less than 2,000 under arms in his company, could not make a stand. With his young brother Richard duke of Gloucester, Earl Rivers, and Lords Hastings, Howard and Say he fled to Lynn (Norfolk). On 2 October they embarked, seeking refuge in Charles the Bold's county of Holland.[28]

On 5 October Archbishop Neville entered London with a strong force and took over the Tower from the garrison which the perplexed civic authorities had placed in it. Next day Clarence and Warwick appeared in the city. With the archbishop, the earl of Shrewsbury and Lord Stanley, they escorted Henry VI from the Tower to the bishop's palace by St Paul's, and made him take the crown once more.[29]

About five months later, on 11 March 1471, Edward sailed from Flushing to challenge Henry's title, with a force not exceeding 2,000, subsidized by Charles of Burgundy.[30] Next day his ships hove to off Cromer (Norfolk). Sir Robert Chamberlain and Sir Gilbert Debenham landed to reconnoitre. But it was clear that the Lancastrians had a tight grip on East Anglia. One of Oxford's brothers, Thomas de Vere, with the Norfolk levies, appeared too strong.[31] Prevailing winds probably forced Edward to adopt the disagreeable alternative of sailing away from the routes to London and his Midland and southern sympathizers, towards the northern parts whose lukewarm loyalty to his person had undermined his rule since 1469. The weather was so bad that the ships ran for the Humber estuary. Edward landed on the tip of Holderness at Ravenspur on 14 March. Gloucester landed four miles away, and Rivers fourteen away at Paull – he nearly sailed into Hull. By the next day Edward had assembled his force. A council of war was held, and the decision was made to march boldly on York. Local levies to the number of 6,000–7,000 milled menacingly, but luckily for Edward no local noble appeared to give them leadership. He descended to the abject but effective expedient of meeting one of their leaders, to whom he exhibited a letter from Henry Percy, earl of Northumberland, and explained that he had come only to claim his patrimony of the duchy of York. This blatant deception continued to bemuse the more gullible Yorkshiremen. The Holderness levies let Edward pass and, though Hull would not receive him, Beverley did. York, too, where he arrived on 18 March, presented a grudging official face. He was permitted to enter with a few companions. The north was mainly stony ground, however, and Edward moved quickly southwards, reaching Tadcaster the next day, and on 20 March skirted round the hostile but indecisive Montague, whose force was based on Pontefract castle, to pick up some recruits in the Yorkist lordship of Sandal and Wakefield. From Wakefield he moved via Doncaster to Nottingham. There, poised on the borders of southern England, he first issued royally styled proclamations, and received his first significant reinforcements.[32]

Yorkist 'scourers' based on Nottingham reported that a large Lancastrian force – 4,000 strong – had occupied Newark, north-east of Nottingham. This was commanded by the duke of Exeter, Oxford and Lord Bardolf. It comprised levies from East Anglia, Cambridgeshire, Huntingdonshire and Lincolnshire. On 19 March (the day Edward had left York), Oxford had written to his supporters from Bury St Edmunds (Suffolk), asking them to bring contingents to the Norfolk array at Lynn on the 22nd. Thence they would set out for Newark, to combat the invaders in the north – an intention fulfilled with admirable speed.[33]

Edward reacted to their presence at Newark by setting out to attack. Within three miles of the town, he found that they had abandoned it. The Lancastrians had decamped at two o'clock in the morning, precipitating large-scale desertions. Why did their leadership show signs of panic? The author of the *Arrivall* says that they thought the reconnaissance of Edward's aforeriders foreshadowed his arrival, and that they would not be able to withstand him. Warwick, writing on 25 March, emphasized the insignificance of the force with which Edward had landed, and the fewness of his recruits. But the Lancastrian command at Newark may have worried that their levies would be no match for Edward's foreign mercenaries – and perhaps they were rattled by Montague's failure to oppose him or reinforce them. The Yorkist scouts' appearance from higher up the Trent may have intensified their alarm, for it suggested that Edward had outflanked them and might cut their communications with Warwick in the Midlands. Welles's defeat in 1469 was a warning to them – and earlier to Montague – not to face Edward before linking up with Clarence and Warwick. Edward may by then have had a high reputation as a field commander, and this could have been a significant factor in his opponents' calculations. According to Basin, the Lancastrians in the West Country were soon to be reluctant to face him in battle because of his great reputation – this was after his victory at Barnet.[34]

Edward returned to his base at Nottingham. The curious Lancastrian behaviour at Newark may have convinced him of the necessity of getting to grips with Warwick in the Midlands before the latter could concentrate the forces of his hesitant regional allies. He advanced on Leicester. Warwick apparently did not oppose him, but withdrew his substantial forces behind the town walls of Coventry, one of the finest urban defence systems in the realm. On 29 March, only ten days after leaving Tadcaster, and with a greatly increased force – albeit one probably inferior to Warwick's – Edward encamped outside Coventry. For four days he tried to persuade Warwick to come out and fight. But the earl stuck to his policy of waiting for his allies to come up, even when Edward tried to tempt or shame him out by withdrawing to the earl's castle and town of Warwick. Unlike Malory's King Mark, Warwick was not to be shamed into emerging from behind his walls. Up to a point, the earl's policy worked: Edward failed to intercept completely reinforcements which reached him, commanded by Exeter, Montague and Oxford.[35] But as so often in the campaigns of 1469–71, success or failure was swayed by defections. Warwick was probably waiting above all for Clarence before attacking Edward. The duke, who moved south-westwards from Bristol to Wells soon after Edward's landing, recruited over 4,000 men and turned back towards the Midlands, reaching Burford (Oxon.) by 2 April.[36] But Edward suborned him, as he probably suborned other magnates. Probably on 3 April he and Gloucester met their errant brother for a formal reconciliation. They all moved with their men to Warwick. They tried to tempt the earl of Warwick with offers. But even he lacked the nerve to turn traitor again, nor would he and the Lancastrian lords who had joined him come out of Coventry. Despite the blow of Clarence's abysmal defection, he had hopes of reinforcement.[37]

Heartened by Clarence's support, Edward and his council took the bold decision to turn their backs on Coventry and attempt the seizure of London. On 5 April they withdrew south-eastwards, reaching Daventry the next day, and passing through Northampton and Dunstable to arrive at St Albans on the 10th. Warwick set off urgently in pursuit. He wrote to his brother Archbishop Neville in London, urging him to hold the city until his imminent arrival. Neville called together his supporters – not exceeding 7,000 – and paraded Henry VI round the city in an attempt to raise recruits. But the appearance of the saintly king and the worldly ecclesiastic failed to stir military ardour. In fact the Lancastrian lords who could have organized resistance – Somerset, his brother John Beaufort, and Devon – had recently left London for the West Country, to prepare for the arrival from France of Margaret of Anjou and Prince Edward.[38]

The city governors, with their militia in harness, and in receipt of contrary exhortations from Edward and Warwick, were in a fearful dilemma. One king was in their midst, another practically at their gates. Two opposed armies were on the horizon; they risked the penalties of treason and an assault on the city by defying either. In the event they decided not to oppose Edward: it may have been some consolation that his army was well disciplined, and not composed of northerners. On the night of 11 April his supporters opened a way into the city by gaining control of the Tower. Edward entered London next morning. The city governors had got their harnessed men out of the way by telling them to go home to dinner.[39]

Warwick, who had advanced from Coventry via Northampton, may have pinned his hopes on a swift attack on Edward whilst he and his forces were busy celebrating Easter and settling down in London. But Edward, however conventionally pious, was not the man to be distracted by religious observance, unlike King Henry, once more in his hands. He set out with his army from London two days after entering it, on 13 April, the eve of Easter Sunday. In his company, besides his brothers, were Henry Bourchier, earl of Essex, his brother Lord Berners and his son Lord Cromwell, and Lords Hastings and Say – some of whom had swelled Edward's ranks in London. In the afternoon Edward's aforeriders flushed Warwick's from Hornsey Park back towards Barnet, whence the earl's men were driven too. The main body of the Yorkist army came up against the Lancastrians lining a hedge half a mile or so out of Barnet. Despite the fading light, Edward had pushed his men on to camp ready for a dawn attack – in fact, they were closer to the earl than Edward at first realized. Edward's insistence on getting his men into position that night had significant consequences. Warwick failed to realize how close the royal encampment was, and his night bombardment overshot it. But Edward had failed to align his troops precisely opposite Warwick's: on the eastern flank his men overlapped the earl's, and vice versa on the west. When battle commenced early the following morning, the need for swift action may have prevented commanders from altering their alignment, and weather conditions in any case may have prevented them from fully appreciating the situation.[40]

In Warwick's company were Exeter, Montague, Beaumont and Oxford. The sources agree that they outnumbered Edward's army. Zannoto Spinula reported from Bruges on 26 April that Edward had about 7,000 men on entering London, and that Warwick's force was then about 10,000 strong. The author of the *Arrivall* (intent on glorifying Edward) put his forces at Barnet at not more than 9,000 against 30,000. Warkworth says that the day after entering London Edward's strength had risen to 7,000, and that on the eve of Barnet, according to Edward's information, Warwick had about 20,000. The conviction that his opponent had a considerable numerical superiority may have made Edward anxious to take him by surprise at Barnet: he may have recalled how successfully Somerset had hustled the earl at St Albans in 1461, and that the latter had been unable then to assert control over his large army.[41]

On Easter morning (14 April), despite heavy mist, Edward launched his attack between four and five o'clock. The effects of surprise may to some extent have been nullified by those of non-alignment. Though the right (eastern) wing of Edward's 'battle' wheeled in effectively against Warwick's left flank, Edward's left wing was routed by Warwick's overlapping western one, commanded by Oxford. But these reverses did not spread panic down either line because mist concealed what was happening. Fighting was intense in the centre. Edward's right wing, after their preliminary success, joined the fight here. On the western flank, Oxford's victory was so complete that he had difficulty in extricating his men from Barnet to regroup for an attack on Edward. In the mist Warwick's men mistook the livery of Oxford's returning company for Edward's, and attacked them. This brought to the surface the Lancastrian fears that Warwick might do a deal with Edward, which must have simmered since Clarence's desertion. Oxford and his men cried 'Treason! treason!' and, 800 strong, they fled. This apparently was decisive: after at least three hours' fighting, Lancastrian resistance broke. Montague and Warwick were killed; Exeter lay, seriously wounded, abandoned among the dead. Casualties were heavy on both sides. Sir John Paston, writing on 18 April, listed among the slain the king's supporters Cromwell and Say, Berners's son Sir Humphrey Bourchier 'and other people of both parties to the number of more than 1,000'. The author of the *Arrivall* noted that Edward's household had sustained heavy casualties. It was probably a chastened royal army which returned to London that day. Edward's determination to press home a dawn attack in the particular circumstances had created a tricky tactical situation for both sides. But in the fight Warwick does not seem to have maintained as firm control over an army which, despite its fighting qualities, was flawed by suspicions.[42]

The same evening (14 April), Margaret of Anjou and her son landed at Weymouth, with 'knights, squires, and other men of the King of France'. They moved inland to Cerne abbey, where they were met by the duke of Somerset and John Courtenay, earl of Devon. On receiving news of Edward's victory at Barnet, it was decided not to challenge him directly, but pass as quickly as possible through western England, via Bristol, Gloucester and Chester, to recruit skilled Lancashire archers – and link up with Jasper Tudor, earl of Pembroke, who had gone to rally Welsh support. Arrayers were sent to raise contingents in Somerset, Dorset and parts of Wiltshire. Queen, prince and lords first went westwards to Exeter: their appearance helped to attract the 'whole might' of Devon and Cornwall. To disguise their intention to head north-west, the Lancastrian commanders dispatched aforeriders on routes implying an eastward advance.[43]

Edward moved from London to Windsor, the assembly-point for his army, on 19 April.[44] He needed to know as soon as possible which way the Lancastrians would jump, in order to intercept them before they could roll up more support. Intelligence sources soon convinced him that their main force, advancing through Taunton, Glastonbury and Wells, was indeed heading for the Welsh Marches. His objective was to prevent them crossing the Severn, at either Gloucester, Tewkesbury or, further north, at Worcester.[45]

The race was on for the bridges. On 24 April Edward set out from Windsor with his army, arriving at Abingdon on the 27th, Cirencester on the 29th. At Cirencester he had sure information that the Lancastrian army would be at Bath the next morning (as indeed they were) and that on 1 May they would come up against his position. So on the night of 29th–30th, he insisted that his army should lodge, not in the comfort of Cirencester, but three miles away, ready for battle. The next morning, having no news of the Lancastrians' advance, Edward turned southwards towards Bath to seek them out. At Malmesbury he learnt that they had given him the slip, avoiding battle by taking the road from Bath to Bristol, which they triumphantly entered.[46]

From Coventry on 12 May Edward was to write accusing the men of Bristol of having recently broken their allegiance, naming certain persons who had 'largely offended' against him – Nicholas Hervy (the city recorder slain at Tewkesbury), John Schepherd the elder, Robert Straunge, John Cogan, mercer, William Spencer, William Hynde, John

Sutton, goldsmith and John Body, 'staynour'.[47] The Lancastrians, refreshed and reinforced in the city, 'took new courage' to challenge Edward. On 2 May their aforeriders advanced nine miles east of Bristol to Chipping Sodbury, and Sodbury Hill was chosen to make a stand. Edward hastened to meet the challenge: advance elements of both armies skirmished at Sodbury. But when in the afternoon he reached the vicinity of Sodbury Hill, he found no sign of his opponents. He dispatched his scourers, but they could get no certain information. With his army exposed on 'a great and a fair large plain, called a wold', and believing the enemy to be near, he decided to encamp rather than advance without sure intelligence. The king and the main body of the army lodged at Sodbury Hill, the 'vaward' beyond it, in a valley between the hill and the town.[48]

Where was the Lancastrian army? The main force, before reaching Sodbury, had wheeled left, towards the Vale of Berkeley. Most unusually for an army of the period, it kept going all night, heading for Gloucester. Had the thrust towards Sodbury been a feint? The author of the *Arrivall* thought not. The night march bespeaks a desperate change of plan, likely to add to the weariness and demoralization of troops repeatedly marched away from the enemy. Perhaps the Lancastrian commanders' plans to fight at Sodbury were countermanded because the encounter there with Edward's harbingers convinced them that he would forestall their intention to prepare a strong defensive position.[49]

Soon after three o'clock on the morning of 3 May, Edward received news of the Lancastrian line of march. Clearly his opponents might cross the Severn at Gloucester or Tewkesbury. At about ten o'clock they arrived before Gloucester. The captain of the castle, Sir Richard Beauchamp, reassured by Edward's promise of relief, refused demands for entry. The Lancastrians had to go on towards Tewkesbury. They arrived there about four o'clock in the afternoon:

> By which time they had so travailled their host that night and day that
> they were right weary for travelling; for by that time they had
> travelled 36 long miles, in a foul country, all in lanes and stony ways,
> betwixt woods, without any good refreshing.

There, too weary to press on, they determined to spend the night and 'take a field'.

Meanwhile Edward had set out from Sodbury Hill early on 3 May with his army in battle array. The description of his march that day in the *Arrivall* is so vivid that it probably reflects the personal experience of a participant. His army covered over thirty miles 'through the champain country, called Cotswold' to Cheltenham. They shadowed the Lancastrians moving on Tewkesbury – whose pause at Gloucester had probably enabled the king to make up lost ground: 'all that day was evermore the King's host within five or six miles of his enemies; he in the plain country and they amongst woods; having always good espialls upon them'. But the Yorkists suffered from lack of victuals. They were parched in the warm sunlight, and had small refreshment at a brook which 'was so soon troubled with the carriages that had passed it'. At Cheltenham, having sure intelligence that his enemies had just halted five miles away at Tewkesbury, Edward was able to rest and feed his troops, before pushing on to encamp about dusk within three miles of the enemy position.[50]

Next day (Saturday 4 May) the Yorkists advanced to the attack. The Lancastrians held a strong defensive position on a hill not far from Tewkesbury abbey, approaches to which were hindered by dykes, enclosures and woods – 'it was right hard to approach them near' according to the *Arrivall*. But, once bombardment commenced, the defenders did not all remain in position. The foreward, commanded by Somerset, launched an attack which soon ran into difficulties; its retreat produced a swift crumbling of the Lancastrian defences. The prince of Wales, Devon, Wenlock and John Beaufort were killed in the rout. Many leading Lancastrians took refuge in the abbey and fell into Edward's hands. At Tewkesbury he executed many implacable opponents, including Somerset.[51]

Lancastrian tactics at Tewkesbury are hard to account for. Perhaps Somerset was a chivalrous hothead, frustrated by the failures to challenge Edward in recent days, and burning to emulate the deeds of his elder brother and of Charles the Bold, in whose army he had served. Perhaps the Lancastrian command decided that a desperate throw with their best troops was needed, rather like what Oxford may have tried at the start of the battle of Bosworth, and Richard III in its later stages. The Lancastrians had been beaten strategically in a nerve-racking advance through the West Country, and they may have rightly suspected that the bulk of their tired and perhaps demoralized levies had no stomach for a long defence.

The decisive move in the western campaign had been Edward's arrival at Cirencester. This had threatened Lancastrian strategy. But, going on from Bath, then from Bristol, the Lancastrians had shown considerable skill in shaking off Edward's threat. Their command may, indeed, have been divided at Bristol as to whether to go out and confront Edward or to run for the Severn bridges, for there seems to have been a drastic change of plan during the advance on Sodbury. The decision taken then turned out badly, for Edward could not be shaken off and was able to bring his men into battle less weary than their opponents.

Despite the death of the prince of Wales and the capture of Margaret of Anjou, Edward's labours were, he anticipated, not yet over. Rebels were stirring in Wales and the north. The day after the battle, Clarence wrote to Henry Vernon saying that Edward intended to go to the north in haste to establish peaceful government, and requesting Vernon to join him (Clarence) with an arrayed company at Coventry on 12 May. The king's need for fresh troops is reflected in his dispatch of signet letters requesting Vernon's aid on two successive days, from Tewkesbury on 7 May and Worcester on the 8th. In the second, Edward expatiated on the 'murmurs and commotions' being made by the commons in various parts of the realm. Clarence, again summoning Vernon, from Coventry on 10 May, elaborated on the destruction threatening the land. By 14 May, however, it was clear to Edward that there would be no large-scale northern rebellion: those in the field had submitted to the earl of Northumberland.[52]

But Edward received news of a dangerous rising in the south-east which he had been too busy to safeguard against. On 12 May a force commanded by the Bastard of Fauconberg, hoping to rescue Henry VI, appeared before London. Fauconberg, commander of his kinsman Warwick's ships in the Channel, had landed in Kent and raised the commons. Backbone was added to his army by the 300 soldiers under Sir George Broke sent from the Calais garrison by Sir Walter Wrottesley and Sir Geoffrey Gate. Edward, setting out from Coventry, reached London with 30,000 horsemen on 21 May, after the rebels' retreat. Many of them went home, but the Bastard with a nucleus of soldiers went via Rochester to Sandwich, which he garrisoned strongly, according to the *Arrivall*. The Bastard's attempt to rescue Henry seems to have been his death-warrant: on the night Edward entered London, Henry perished in the Tower.[53]

On 22 May Edward's forward set out from London into Kent under Gloucester's command; Edward soon followed with the rest of his army. He arrived at Canterbury on the 26th, making, according to the chronicler Stone, an impressive display of strength. His army was said to be 40,000 strong, and he was well supported by peers – the dukes of Clarence, Gloucester, Norfolk and Suffolk; the earls of Arundel, Wiltshire and Kyme; Lords Scales, Talbot, Grey of Ruthin, Hastings and Mountjoy. The Bastard of Fauconberg had probably not seriously intended to defy such an array at Sandwich, but to negotiate favourable terms of surrender. On 27 May Gloucester received his submission and took possession of his ships at Sandwich, and the Bastard received the promised pardon on 10 June. Edward was now well placed to regain control of Calais, whose soldiers also wished to bargain for its surrender. In July the new lieutenant of Calais, Lord Hastings, and Lord Howard crossed the Channel with a large force. Gate and his fellow captains submitted and gained pardons.[54]

After his arrival at Canterbury Edward was never again to campaign on English soil. Embers of rebellion flickered dimly, despite Louis XI's desultory attempts to breathe life into them. Sforza de' Bettini reported to the duke of Milan on 16 July 1471 that Louis, desirous of encouraging continued disturbance in England, had ordered financial assistance to Jasper Tudor who, with Scottish help, was holding 'a good number of towns' in Wales. On 27 August William Herbert, earl of Pembroke, and Lord Ferrers were commissioned to array in South Wales and adjacent shires and Marches against Jasper, and on 11 September the earl of Shrewsbury was commissioned to array in Shropshire, Staffordshire and the northern Marches to resist the rebels in North Wales and the Marches. Jasper soon had to give up, taking ship for France with his young nephew Henry, the future Henry VII. In 1473 Oxford, who had escaped abroad after Barnet, attempted with assistance from Louis to invade southern England, unsuccessfully. It is difficult to judge in whose dynastic interest Jasper Tudor and Oxford were operating, after the deaths of Henry VI, his son and Beaufort kinsmen. Contemporary sources are not explicit, and later writers were uninterested in these failures. It is hard to avoid the conclusion that Jasper's stir was the first attempt to put Henry Tudor on the throne – since there was no other Lancastrian heir available. The seriousness with which his claim was taken in Yorkist circles in 1483 may have been because it had become familiar to them in 1471.[55]

How good a general was Edward? Commynes certainly thought it was remarkable that he had fought in so many battles and never been on the losing side. The reasons for his failure in June 1469 are mysterious, but clearly he made a feeble and ineffective military showing. The Lincolnshiremen over whom he triumphed in March 1470 may not have been of high calibre, and his other opponents then were badly organized. Nevertheless, Edward's strategy in that campaign was impeccable: his army was well organized, and his speedy movements hampered co-ordinated resistance. The loss of his crown in September was simply due to betrayal – as in the previous March, and probably early in 1469, his military dispositions were influenced by faulty political assessments.

Edward's greatest test as a general was his invasion in 1471: he landed, like so many others in the period, as an adventurer, with a miniature army – though with considerable expectations of gaining support. The fullest source for the invasion is, unfortunately, completely biased in his favour: the *Arrivall* was written as a semi-official account of it. But other sources do not contradict its impression. There seems little doubt that Edward's forces were led in 1471 with speed, tenacity and, on occasion, great boldness in face of numerical superiority. Despite the considerable changes of size and composition in the Yorkist army during a campaign which ranged over most of the length and breadth of England, it remained well organized, efficient. Edward repeatedly took the initiative, against the threats from levies in Yorkshire and at Newark, against Warwick at Coventry and his allies in Leicester, against London, against Warwick advancing on London. Then there was Edward's brilliant disruption of the western Lancastrians' tricky and tenaciously executed strategy, a feat particularly admired by the second continuator of the *Crowland Chronicle*. After all this, Edward immediately prepared to mount expeditions, first against his northern opponents, then against his south-eastern ones. It cannot be proved that Edward was the military genius responsible for these achievements. At the very least the campaign of 1471 demonstrates that he had a flair for picking expert war counsellors, and for recognizing – and putting into execution – exceptionally good advice. Yorkist military efforts in 1471 showed a high degree of concentration. This was successful against the odds because Edward's opponents failed to concentrate their efforts against him. They had good commanders and good troops, but no captain-general with the authority to impose unity. Yet Warwick's passivity at Coventry may have had more justification than his tardiness in supporting allies in the previous two years. He probably appreciated that he would find Edward a tough opponent to take on single-handed, and that he needed time to get his Lancastrian allies to co-operate with him in the field. At Barnet he came near to destroying Edward. But the decision of the Lancastrian lords in the west after Barnet not to challenge Edward directly is less defensible than Warwick's passivity at Coventry. In the days after the battle Edward was vulnerable: his smallish army had been badly mauled and he had not had time to recruit widely. Lancastrian forces were astir at Calais and in the Channel. The Lancastrian cause died, and so did Henry, because the western lords lacked the offensive spirit to march on London to his rescue – as the young Edward had marched to save a faltering cause in 1461.

Chapter 5

The Later Risings, 1483–97

More is known, mainly from Polydore Vergil's account, of the complex plotting leading up to the rising in October 1483 against the new king, Richard III, than about the seemingly desultory fighting.[1] The second continuator of the *Crowland Chronicle* says that there was discontent in southern shires over the imprisonment of Edward IV's sons – and, presumably, over the dramatic deposition of Edward V and Richard's seizing of the crown. Nobles angered by these events fomented and attempted to exploit dissident feeling. According to Vergil, there was devised in London a 'ladies' plot' between Edward IV's widow, Elizabeth Wydeville, whose family had, as in 1469, been violently ejected from influence at court, and Margaret Beaufort, Lord Stanley's wife. Margaret was the daughter of John Beaufort, duke of Somerset (d. 1444), and the widow of Henry VI's half-brother Edmund Tudor, earl of Richmond (d. 1456). The ladies' objective was to displace Richard on the throne by Margaret's son Henry Tudor, who was to swear to marry one of Edward IV's daughters. He had fled abroad as a boy after the Lancastrian débâcle in 1471 and had lived ever since in the duke of Brittany's protective custody.[2]

Margaret Beaufort appointed as her 'chief dealer' in the conspiracy Reginald Bray, who speedily received oaths of adherence from gentlefolk, including Giles Daubeney, Richard Guildford, Thomas Romney and John Cheyney. The dowager queen drew in her kinsfolk and their adherents, notably her son Thomas Grey, marquess of Dorset, who, like his mother, had sought refuge from Richard in sanctuary. Other distinguished plotters were Peter Courtenay, bishop of Exeter, and his cousin Edward Courtenay, heir to the earldom of Devon.[3] Dissidence among Yorkist nobles, as in 1469–70, aroused the expectations of those sympathetic to 'the old cause'.

In its early stages the plot was given a new impetus and focus through the curious treason of the 'kingmaker' who had aided Richard's elevation to the throne – Henry Stafford, duke of Buckingham, who had been lavishly rewarded by his master.[4] Buckingham confided in John Morton, bishop of Ely, a former Yorkist councillor – and, before then, staunch attendant of Henry VI – whose arrest had been ordered by Richard when he was protector of the realm, and who was in the duke's custody at Brecon castle. Morton put the dissident duke in touch with Bray, the agent of Margaret Beaufort – who was Buckingham's aunt. Plans were laid for Buckingham to raise revolt in South Wales, at Brecon. In Brittany, Henry Tudor was visited by a succession of envoys who urged him to stake his claim. His mother's agent Hugh Conway brought money and the advice that he should land in Wales – advice echoed by Guildford's agent Thomas Romney. Buckingham accepted Morton's counsel to send a message to Henry, urging him to hasten over in order to marry Edward IV's daughter Elizabeth, and with her take the throne. Henry conferred with the duke of Brittany, whose strained relations with Richard inclined him to encourage Henry's attempt and offer substantial support.[5]

A revolt in Wales intended to link up with an invasion force from Brittany, and with widely scattered risings in southern England, was crucially dependent on good timing. Buckingham needed to rally his Welsh tenants and cross the Severn speedily in order to link up with his allies in England before the king could concentrate an army. But surprise was lost because the plot proved leaky: royal spies ferreted out information about it, and the king was able to plan his strategy. He entrusted the safeguard of London to the duke of Norfolk, who on 10 October summoned John Paston's aid for its defence against the Kentishmen who he said were 'up [in arms] in the weald'.[6] Richard concentrated his own and his other supporters' energies on the defeat of Buckingham. In the principality and Marches of Wales the king's men were warned to be prepared to occupy the duke's properties as soon as he made his move. His envious neighbours Roger Vaughan of Tretower and the latter's brothers and kinsmen needed little incitement to keep a watch on the duke's lordship of Brecknock. The Worcestershire landowner Humphrey Stafford raised a force to guard the passes and river crossings into England. On 11 October Viscount Lovell, in the king's company at Lincoln, wrote to the Oxfordshire landowner Sir William Stonor, relaying the command to Stonor to bring his company to the royal presence at Leicester on 20 October.[7] Next day Richard wrote confidently in his own hand to the chancellor Bishop Russell about the measures against Buckingham: 'We assure you there was never false traitor better purveyed for as this bearer Gloucester [a herald] shall show you.'[8] A royal signet letter dated Lincoln, 13 October, informed the corporation of Southampton of Buckingham's treasonable intentions and ordered the dispatch of an urban contingent, to report to the king at Coventry on 22 October.[9] Richard 'by word of mouth' issued a general commission of array to Lovell to raise forces against the duke, dated at Leicester on 23 October.[10]

Richard's foreknowledge of the rebels' plans gave him the luxury – unusual for a king defending his crown in this period – of being able to time counter-measures confidently. The plotters may have unwittingly given him time to prepare, and have let the campaigning season go by, because they were anxiously awaiting the arrival on British soil of Henry, an unsullied leader, better able to win men's hearts than the dubious Buckingham.[11] But royal preparations may have at last forced their hands. According to the 1484 Acts of Attainder passed against about 100 participants in the revolt, on 18 October there were risings at Brecon, Maidstone (Kent), Newbury (Berks.), Salisbury (Wilts.) and Exeter (Devon).[12]

Richard moved south-west from Leicester through the Midlands to isolate and confront Buckingham. The duke was unable to put up any opposition. He was effectively hemmed in by neighbouring Ricardians. His sullen Welsh soldiery deserted. At Weobley (Herefs.) he seems to have tried in vain to rally the local gentlefolk. Whilst he was there, the Vaughans sacked his castle at Brecon. From Weobley Buckingham vanished into hiding: betrayed, he was executed at Salisbury, during the king's stay there, on 2 November.[13] Richard soon afterwards reached Bridport (Dorset), and it was probably on this occasion that a prominent burgess of the town, Richard Orchard, provided 'the Kings Wyne' for which he was paid 13s. 4d. by the borough cofferer.[14] Richard's aims were to secure the coast and advance on the rebels in Exeter, who were headed by the marquess of Dorset and the Courtenays. Meanwhile the Kentish and other south-eastern rebels, prominent among whom was Sir Richard Guildford, seem to have been deterred from attacking London by the duke of Norfolk's defence. They may have concentrated at Guildford (Surrey), hopefully awaiting the arrival of Welsh, western or Breton allies.[15]

But the rebel leaders in Exeter were not prepared to trust to its sound defences till Henry arrived. They were intent on escaping from Richard. He occupied the city without difficulty, and there executed the captured Sir Thomas St Leger and Thomas Romney.[16] Henry, whose army of 5,000 Bretons in fifteen ships had been scattered in a storm, hove to off the West Country coast just too late. He prudently refrained from landing and sailed to Normandy.[17] The south-eastern rebels dispersed.

Edward Plumpton's letter of 18 October records how Lancashiremen had been troubled 'marvellously, that they know not what to do', as rumours had spread of Buckingham's strength, and messengers came daily from him and the king. They had particular reason for equivocation. The local magnate, Lord Stanley, an experienced 'trimmer', was Margaret Beaufort's husband. His son Lord Strange was about to set out from their place at Lathom with 10,000 men 'whither men cannot say'.[18] Such equivocations early in the campaign may have been resolved by Richard's success in catching Buckingham and his allies wrong-footed, and in pressing home his advantage. Other nobles besides Norfolk and Lovell had rallied to the king's support. By commission dated Bridport, 5 November, William Herbert, now earl of Huntingdon, was ordered to array in Wales to resist the rebels. Norfolk's son the earl of Surrey and Lord Cobham were commissioned (Exeter, 8 November) to besiege Bodiam castle (Sussex), and Lords Scrope of Bolton and Zouche to array against and punish rebels in western counties (Exeter, 13 November).[19] Among peers rewarded in 1484 for good service against the rebels were Viscount Lisle and Lords Cobham, Grey of Codnor, and Neville.[20] Richard's success against Buckingham seems to have disheartened the remaining rebels – though it might be viewed as a blessing in disguise for Henry's cause. They lacked the temerity displayed by West Country Lancastrians after Barnet in 1471, abandoning the game even though a powerful foreign force was hastening to their support. Had they known Henry's resolute character better, they might have shown more courage.

Despite Richard's brilliant victory, the revolt had ominous implications for his rule. Henry had been seriously promoted as a candidate for the throne: the tensions aroused by Richard's usurpation had revived dynastic conflict, quiescent since 1471. The flight abroad of distinguished dissidents and rebels gave continued credit to Henry's claim. Among his adherents were the queen dowager's brother Sir Edward Wydeville and her son Dorset, and Bishops Morton and Courtenay.[21] For the first time since 1470, a king was menaced by a formidable body of gentlefolk in exile. The large number of attainders enacted in 1484 partly reflect Richard's failure to reconcile opponents, though he did not give up hope of doing so.[22]

Henry's invasion in August 1485 was not unexpected. In a proclamation issued on 7 December 1484 and re-issued on 23 June 1485, Richard had particularized Henry's alleged machinations, and warned subjects to be prepared to resist in case he landed, and to array when commanded.[23] Henry cast off in the Seine estuary on 1 August. According to the newsletter written on 1 March 1486 to the Catholic kings of Spain by their retired councillor Mosén Diego de Valera, Charles VIII of France provided him with 2,000 soldiers paid up for four months, a loan of 50,000 crowns and a fleet for transport. In size, provision of finance, and calibre of leadership Henry's expedition compares favourably with foreign-backed invasions in 1462, 1470 and 1471.[24]

He landed on 7 August in Milford Haven (Pembrokeshire).[25] His sally at a remote part of west Wales rather than the heartlands of southern England was probably influenced by his own and Oxford's failures on the latter's shores, and by Jasper Tudor's successes since the 1460s in gaining support in his former earldom of Pembroke and elsewhere in Wales. Lovell's naval and defence measures centring on Southampton may also have been a determining factor.[26] Thus Henry eschewed the invasion strategy in vogue from 1469 to 1483, and adopted the Welsh option often considered by Lancastrians in the 1460s, and urged on him in 1483.

Henry's Welsh strategy paid off. Officials, gentlefolk and townsmen, when they did not actually welcome him, were slow to oppose his initially vulnerable and nervous force. Henry, his captain-general Oxford, and the captain of his French troops, Philibert de Chandée, were probably agreed on the desirability of getting through Wales quickly, not least in order to draw out Henry's sympathizers in England who had encouraged his enterprise.[27] He wrote to his mother, his stepfather Lord Stanley, the latter's brother Sir William Stanley (chamberlain of North Wales), Lord Talbot and other English lords that he was determined to cross the Severn and march through Shropshire towards London. He requested that they meet him in arms. With impressive speed he acted on his word. Evading potential opponents and exploiting their hesitations, he moved so rapidly up to and along the coast of Cardigan Bay, and inland through what the Crowland continuator described as 'rugged and indirect tracts', that he was before the gates of Shrewsbury on 15 August. *En route* he had attracted some recruits, notably, at Newton, Rhys ap Thomas, whose opposition he had feared, and who was won over, according to Polydore Vergil, by the promise of the 'perpetual lieutenantship of Wales'.[28] But perhaps memories of how their hopes of crushing 'the Saxons' in 1469 had been disappointed, deterred many Welshmen from joining this undoubtedly British prince. Thomas Mytton, one of the bailiffs of well-fortified Shrewsbury, put up what turned out to be only a token resistance.[29] Soon after Henry had left the town, when he was encamped at Newport, the earl of Shrewsbury's uncle Sir Gilbert Talbot joined him with over 500 men. Henry may have been moving north-eastwards towards Stafford because of news that Lord Stanley had advanced from Lancashire to hold the town with nearly 5,000 men. But when he heard of Henry's approach, Stanley abandoned Stafford and went south-eastwards as far as Atherstone (Warwicks.), presumably on the line of Henry's anticipated advance towards London. Sir William Stanley, who appears to have been operating with a retinue independently of his brother (as he had at Blore Heath in 1459), visited Henry at Stafford, but did not join him or send troops. There was a more urgent reason than usual for Stanleyan equivocation. Lord Stanley's son Lord Strange, who had plotted with Sir William to aid Henry, was in the king's hands. Henry thus found himself in the middle of England without the overt support of the nobles on whom he had particularly relied to augment his invasion force.

Richard had been in the north since May. He was at Nottingham when he received news of Henry's landing on 11 August.[30] Vergil says that he was relying particularly on Walter Herbert and Rhys ap Thomas, 'who ruled Wales with equal authority', to dispose of Henry's force. Perhaps he was remembering how Buckingham's rising had been hampered by Welsh opposition, and how Jasper Tudor's numerous attempts to raise revolt in Wales had never had more than local success. Nevertheless, he prudently summoned the military aid of Henry Percy, earl of Northumberland, and other nobles. Sir Robert Brackenbury, lieutenant of the Tower, was ordered to bring up a southern force. But Richard experienced some shocks. Lord Stanley, on the excuse of illness, evaded obedience to his summons. The thwarting of Strange's flight from court induced his confession of treason plotted with his uncle and Sir John Savage. The news of Henry's capture of Shrewsbury reached Richard on 15 August: he was enraged by it and the broken promises which had facilitated it.[31] He determined to go against Henry as quickly as possible. His decisiveness in 1483 showed that he had digested the lesson of the 1469–71 campaigns that chief rebels must be encountered before they could bring up support. Royal 'scurriers' reported Henry's encampment at Lichfield, threatening Richard's southern communications.

On 19 August the king moved from Nottingham southwards to Leicester. Next day the rebel army took a converging course from Lichfield to Tamworth. On the way Henry lost touch with his army. That night, with only twenty soldiers, he 'stayed by the way, uncertain what was best as to deliberate what he might do'. Vergil's elliptical words perhaps hint at contemplated flight – desertion by commanders was not uncommon in the Wars of the Roses. No wonder there was uneasiness in Henry's army. His appearance at Tamworth 'in the grey of morning' may have prevented its disintegration in the nick of time. It speaks volumes for his pertinacity.

On 21 August the large, augmented royal army set out westwards from Leicester, towards the line of Watling Street running south-east of Tamworth through Atherstone. Leading royal supporters were Norfolk and his son Surrey, Northumberland, Lovell and Lords Ferrers and Zouche.[32] On the night of the 21st, royal and rebel armies – and the ambivalent Stanley forces – were encamped at most a few hours' march from each other. Next morning Richard's army manned the eastern crest of Ambien Hill, less than two miles south of Market Bosworth, and the tip of higher ground running near Sutton Cheney.[33] Henry's army probably bivouacked between Atherstone and Ambien Hill (under six miles distant as the crow flies). His men foraged at Atherstone and places about three miles and less from it – at Witherley, Mancetter, Fenny Drayton and Atterton to the south and east.[34]

According to Vergil, Richard's army was more than twice as large as Henry's army of 5,000, well supplied with cavalry as well as infantry, and well equipped with artillery.[35] But Henry had some advantages. Nervousness about treason in the royal camp on the eve of battle is strongly attested: it may have affected Richard's tactical judgment the next day. Well-paid foreign mercenaries, such as Henry deployed, had often fought more tenaciously than native conscripts.[36] Henry had some artillery, though probably of light calibre.[37] He had experienced captains in Jasper Tudor and Oxford, and a galaxy of competent knights, including Edward Wydeville, John Cheyney, John Savage, Robert Willoughby, Richard Edgcombe, Edward Poynings, Giles Daubeney and Richard Guildford.[38] Above all, in conference with the Stanley brothers at Atherstone on 21 August, according to Vergil, Henry gained what he considered a firm commitment of Stanleyan aid in the imminent battle.

Early on the morning of 22 August, Henry's army deployed for battle. To his consternation, Lord Stanley sent an evasive reply to his request to set his soldiers in array, instead approaching the field 'as in the mid way betwixt the two battles' (Vergil). Thus far committed, Henry had to go on. He sent his vanguard forward, captained by Oxford, with archers in the front line, and himself followed with a meagre main 'battle' – a troop of cavalry and a few footmen. Confronting them was the king's much larger vanguard, comprising horse and foot, with archers to the fore, according to Vergil, 'like a most strong trench and bulwark'. Norfolk and Brackenbury were in command.[39] Richard followed with the main 'battle', a 'choice force of soldiers'. According to Vergil, the rebel army's line of approach took advantage of a marsh between the armies, skirting to the left of it, and getting the rising sun behind them. This is puzzling. The east is not the direction from which one would have expected Henry's army to assault the king's force, and nothing in the sources suggests that it did. If the marsh mentioned by Vergil was the one at the bottom of the long southern slopes of Ambien Hill, it may be that Oxford advanced there, on the enemy's southern flank below the marsh, then turned back to approach the enemy's front from the south-east. This unconventional manoeuvring might have been aimed at disconcerting the royal forces and getting closer to them with the marsh's protection. Scraps of evidence give some support to Vergil's statement, and hint at the reasons for his manoeuvre. According to the poem *The Rose of*

England, the 'blue boar' (Oxford) who commanded Henry's van,

> the right hand of them [the king's troops] he took
> the sun and wind of them to get.[40]

In so doing he would have applied precepts laid down by the classical military writer Vegetius, who stressed the advantages to be gained from overlapping the enemy's flank, and from having the sun and wind behind one.[41] Such may have seemed crucial advantages in neutralizing royal firepower and increasing the effectiveness of Henry's archers. According to Molinet, Richard had his guns fired at the rebels: then Henry's Frenchmen, gauging the king's position by the firing, counselled that, to escape bombardment, the assault should be made on the flank (*costé*) of the king's 'battle', not on its front – and as a result of this course, the royal vanguard was eventually defeated.[42]

Vergil says that as soon as the king saw that the rebels had passed the marsh, he commanded his men to charge them. Oxford's expert direction and the good discipline of his troops enabled them to withstand and confuse the royal vanguard. Whilst the two vans were engaged, Richard received reports that Henry was 'afar off' with a small force, which he confirmed by personal observation. It may be that, in the movements before the battle, a wide gap had opened up between Henry's van and main 'battle'. But the separation may have been deliberate. Perhaps it had been decided that Oxford and some of his best troops should test the uncertain will of the royal army whilst Henry held off, so that, in the event of disaster, Henry could escape the fate of the prince of Wales at Tewkesbury in 1471. He and Oxford were to follow similar tactics at Stoke in 1487, and near Blackheath in 1497 Henry apparently remained stationary with the main 'battle' again, whilst the vanguard under Daubeney engaged the western rebels.[43]

The crisis of the battle resulted from Richard's reaction to the gap between Henry's vanguard and unimpressive main 'battle'. The king may have discerned in this an opportunity to curtail Henry's challenge abruptly – and one which might speedily evaporate, since Oxford's defeat would leave the retreating Henry a chance to fight another day. Vergil says of the king: 'all inflamed with ire, he struck his horse with the spurs, and runneth out of th'one side without the vanwards against him'. In face of the violence of Richard's attack, Henry's retinue faltered and his life was in danger. He was rescued by the intervention of the hitherto neutral Sir William Stanley with 3,000 men. The king's supporters broke under this pressure – and the earl of Northumberland failed to come to his rescue, possibly because he had an understanding with Henry.[44] Richard rejected a captain's expert advice to flee: 'Salaçar, please God that I do not take one step backwards, for I want to die like a king or win victory in this battle.' Donning the royal crown, he encouraged his remaining supporters to fight to the death.[45] Molinet says that, after fighting valiantly, crown on head, Richard, finding himself utterly abandoned, in the end tried to escape. But his horse leapt into marshy ground. Whilst the king floundered, a Welshman killed him with a halberd's blow.[46] According to Henry's proclamation after the battle, Richard was killed at a place called 'Sandeford', which Gairdner plausibly identified as a ford across a brook, nearby where there is now a road between Shenton and Sutton Cheney.[47] This low-lying, damp spot, seen on a wet August day, conjures up a vision of Molinet's marsh.[48]

Once the king's death was known, his remaining soldiers fled or surrendered. Oxford had already independently routed the royal van.[49] According to Vergil, about 1,000 were killed, scarcely 100 of them on Henry's side.[50] Among the slain were Norfolk, Ferrers and Brackenbury. Lovell and Salaçar made good their escape. Surrey was captured on the field, injured.[51]

Richard's defeat can be attributed to treacheries in the field. The day after the battle, the council of the city of York debated reports that Richard III 'through great treason of the Duke of Norfolk [sic] and many other that turned against him . . . was piteously slain and murdered'.[52] But were Northumberland's and Lord Stanley's failure to support the king, and Sir William Stanley's intervention against him, inevitable? The earl and the Stanleys played a waiting game – had tactical developments been different, perhaps they would have felt obliged to support Richard. When his impressive vanguard was skilfully pinned down by Oxford, the orthodox move for him would have been to reinforce it with his main 'battle'. But Richard – presumably, with his picked household cavalry – moved boldly out of his lines. His erratic boldness perhaps confirmed the lukewarm in their desire not to hazard themselves, and gave the dissident hopes of picking him off. It is remarkable that two widely separated sources, the Crowland continuator and Vergil, emphasized Richard's disturbed spirits on the morning of the battle. Perhaps the treasons already manifest, and his fears that others might occur, clouded his tactical judgment, so that he angrily cast away his crown and his life, and the fortunes and lives of loyal followers.

Yet the course of the battle might not have gone so badly for Richard but for Oxford's initial success in confronting his vanguard. Though Ambien Hill is a good place for an overnight encampment, it is flawed as a defensive position. The marshy ground to the south provides cover for attackers as well as defenders, and the frontal western slopes can be rushed. Richard had been schooled in his brother's campaigns – and may have learnt his preference for the offensive. Perhaps he never intended to fight at Ambien Hill, but to advance thence on Henry's camp. Henry's captains, some of whom were familiar with the methods of the Yorkist princes, may have decided that their only hope of victory lay in seizing the initiative and forestalling an attack from the much larger royal army, whose size would make it slower to get under way. The Crowland chronicler mentions incidents in Richard's camp which might imply that his troops had to array in haste in face of an unexpected emergency. At daybreak there were no chaplains present to perform divine service for the king, and there was no breakfast prepared for him. Yet it is unthinkable that he should have been in the field without chaplains or cooks. A likely explanation is that they were still asleep, and Richard had to arm and array hastily. Then, says the Crowland continuator, as the rebels advanced, Richard ordered the traitor Strange to be executed instantly. But his servants delayed carrying out the order. Richard's failure to make an example of Strange is in glaring contrast to Edward's execution of Lord Welles before his troops engaged the Lincolnshiremen in 1470, and bespeaks too a Richard thrown off balance by an unexpected attack. He may have underestimated the offensive spirit of his opponents, some of whom had not shown any in 1483.

On the morrow of Bosworth, Henry doubtless realized that his victory, despite its magnitude, gave no prospect of stable rule. Though he had declared his intention of marrying Edward's eldest daughter, Yorkist claimants were likely to be countenanced by some of that majority of subjects who had shown no interest in his claim to the throne. The triumph of the candidate supported by Lancastrian, Wydeville and Buckingham partisans automatically threatened the interests of those favoured by Richard, including leading families such as the de la Poles, Howards and Scropes. Richard's overthrow unbalanced the precarious stability of northern society. He had gained popularity in the north by reconciling and favouring the interests of gentlefolk and townsmen. As Edward's lieutenant, and as lord protector and king, he had used his control of former estates of Warwick the Kingmaker as a means of attaching loyalties and asserting authority. Neville adherents there, and in Warwickshire, Worcestershire and other Midland and southern shires, had no initial expectation of a ladder to royal redress and patronage under the rule of a Tudor with whom they had no 'natural' ties. They were attracted by the claim to the throne of an impeccably Neville and Yorkist candidate, Clarence's fifteen-year-old son, Edward earl of Warwick – heir, since the death of his aunt, Richard's wife Anne Neville, in 1484, to the whole of the Kingmaker's inheritance.[53] Thus Henry's conquest of England had a disruptive effect, producing, like Edward's in 1461, dynastic strife fuelled by the disarray of lords' interests, particularly in the north.

But swift action by Henry after Bosworth was to hobble dynastic opposition. Before he left Leicester for London, he dispatched Sir Robert Willoughby to Sheriff Hutton castle (Yorks.) to secure Warwick's person and bring him south, to be kept in custody in the Tower.[54] But according to the Castilian correspondent, Valera, Henry, after he was installed in London, ordered the arrest of 'lord Tamorlant', who, he had been informed, really intended Clarence's son to be king, and to marry one of his daughters. 'Tamorlant' was released only after Clarence's son had been received into royal custody, and after two 'counts' who were his kinsmen had sworn homage and perpetual fealty to Henry. Valera's informants may have been referring to the earl of Northumberland. It is plausible that he was tempted by the prospect of Warwick as a pliant young son-in-law on the throne, confirming and enhancing a Percy hegemony in the north which Richard had limited, and which there was no certainty that Henry would promote. The earl was certainly imprisoned by Henry: Giovanni de' Giglis reported on 6 December that he had been released 'sub cautione' of the lords and commons in parliament.[55]

One reason for Henry's imprisonment of Northumberland may have been his fear that the earl would be unable or unwilling to control hostile northern reactions to Richard's overthrow. On 15 October Henry wrote to Lords Stanley and Strange and Sir Edward Stanley, sheriff of Lancashire, ordering them to have the county's levies ready to move under their leadership, since the Scots intended to besiege Berwick and plunder the Marches, trusting to the favour of local dissidents.[56] In a letter to Henry Vernon requesting his armed attendance, dated two days later, Henry stated that rebels allied with the Scots were making insurrections in the northern parts – rebels who, in a spirit reminiscent of 1469, took captains with pseudonyms associated with popular protest – 'Robyn of Riddesdale, Jack St[raw], Thomolyn at Lath and Maister Mendall'.[57] But the alarms quickly subsided. In a proclamation of 20 October, Henry allowed the preparations for arrays to be suspended, since the rebels, understanding that he had made 'politic and mighty purveyance for the recounter and subduing of their said malice and rebellion', had dispersed.[58] Nevertheless, it was realized at court that this was unlikely to be the end of the affair. A correspondent, Betanson, wrote from London on 13 December that there were expectations there of rebellion 'and no man can say of whom; but they deem of Northernmen and Welshmen. And much speech is in the King's house and of his householdmen.'[59] It may have been as a bold device to quieten the north that Northumberland had recently been released, and in January 1486 received northern commissions.[60] Moreover, according to Betanson's letter of 15 February, 'the King proposeth northward hastily after the Parliament, and it is said he purposes to do execution quickly there on such as have offended against him' accompanied 'as it is said, with ten hundred men in harness and with him more than five or six score lords and knights'.[61] Betanson was writing to a Yorkshire landowner: if such rumours gained currency in the shire, it is not surprising that (as in Lincolnshire in 1470) men were prepared to resist the king, and dissident nobles quick to exploit their fears. About 11 April, when Henry had progressed as far as Lincoln, it was reported to him that notable fugitives from Bosworth, Viscount Lovell and Humphrey Stafford, had abandoned sanctuary at Colchester.[62] When he arrived in Ricardian York, there was news that Lovell had assembled a large force a little beyond the Neville castle of Middleham, attracting support within its lordship and that of Richmond, and intending to march on York. Stafford, it was reported, had raised revolt in Worcestershire. According to the testimony of some of his indicted sympathizers, he had spread the false news that the king had pardoned his attainder, and that he was a true liegeman. He may have been trying the old trick of arraying under the pretence of supporting the king against rebellion – whereas in fact he intended to go to Lovell's aid. But many of his supporters wanted to promote the earl of Warwick's claim to the throne, including, possibly, some of the townsfolk of Warwick who received general pardons in 1486–7 – Oliver Alwode, clerk; Robert Beverley, chaplain; William Wellys, mercer alias vintner; John Smyth, barber alias vintner; Robert Barlowe and Ralph Betery, yeomen.[63] Henry, at York, and militarily unprepared, was, according to Vergil, 'struck by great fear'. Nevertheless, he scotched these over-hasty risings by wresting the initiative. He dispatched his poorly armed retinue, 3,000 strong, against the northern rebels' encampment. The Yorkshiremen accepted the terms offered to them; Lovell fled. Alarmed by news of this débâcle, and despite his success in gaining entry to Worcester, Stafford also deserted his men, entering sanctuary at Culham (Berks.) on 11 May.[64]

Pardons enrolled in 1486 reflect Henry's anxiety to reconcile dissidents. On 6 August Sir William Tyler and others were empowered to receive into the king's grace and to grant pardons of life and lands to all rebels in Yorkshire, especially in the lordships of Middleham and Richmond.[65] Pardons granted to north-westerners show how Henry's rule stimulated continued discontent among gentlefolk there, upsetting Ricardian loyalties and the relative influence of rival affinities. Writs to the sheriffs of Northumberland, Cumberland and Yorkshire dated 16 July alleged that Sir Thomas Broughton, Sir John Hudleston, William a Thorneburghe, William Ambrose and others 'for their great rebellions and grievous offences lately by them done . . . keep them in huddle and secret places and over that have disobeyed divers and many his [the king's] letters and Privy Seals'. They were charged to appear before the king within forty days or be reputed traitors.[66] This threat elicited some response. General pardons dated 17 August were granted to them and to Richard Middleton, Geoffrey Fraunke and Henry Hudleston, esquires, and George Middleton, gentleman.[67] By commission dated the following day Sir Richard Tunstall, one of Henry's most trusted retainers, and Sir Thomas Wortley were empowered to take oaths of allegiance and sureties from this group, with the addition of Sir James and Sir Robert Harington and Sir Robert Middleton, who had all been attainted in the 1485 parliament.[68] Sir Thomas Broughton was lord of Broughton-in-Furness (Lancs.).[69] Sir John Hudleston of Millom (Cumberland) was a kinsman and long-time associate of Sir James Harington. Another of his old allies was Sir Thomas Pilkington of Pilkington (Lancs.), attainted in 1485 and fully pardoned on 14 August 1486.[70]

The reason for the reluctance of Harington and his friends to swear allegiance to Henry may have been that they feared he would favour north-western landowners whose interests were inimical to theirs. One of these may have been Tunstall – royal councillor and knight of the body in 1487. As Henry VI's chamberlain, he had faithfully helped to hide the fugitive king in Lancashire and Westmorland after the battle of Hexham (1464). Sir James Harington had played a leading part in Henry VI's capture in 1465, and was rewarded by a royal grant of Tunstall's forfeited Lancashire lordship of Thurland.[71] Harington also had a long-standing, bitter dispute with the Stanleys. He was the younger son of Sir Thomas Harington of Hornby castle (Lancs.), who was killed fighting in the Yorkist interest at Wakefield in 1460. His eldest son, John, was mortally wounded there, leaving two infant daughters, Ann and Elizabeth, as co-heirs to the Harington estates. In 1468 they were in the custody of their uncle Sir James and of Sir John Hudleston. In an undated petition to the king the girls complained that Sir James had 'kept them as prisoners contrary to their will, in divers places by long space, intending the utter destruction and disinheritance of the said complainants'. In 1468 Sir James was occupying Hornby castle and other estates of the inheritance, including Brierley (Yorks.) and a group of properties granted him by Archbishop Neville, Hudleston and others of his father's feoffees in 1463.[72]

But a powerful kinsman of the Haringtons, Lord Stanley, emerged as the girls' self-interested protector. His influence may have procured the commissions appointed in 1468 to inquire into the heirs and inheritance of Sir Thomas and John Harington. The verdict of the inquests, that the girls were the co-heirs, and that Sir James had held the manors and lands since their father's death without title or right, was accepted by the chancellor on petition, and he committed the culprit and Hudleston to the Fleet prison. On 6 December the pair appeared in chancery to present a bond guaranteeing the submission of their disputes with Stanley, especially concerning the wardship and marriage of the girls, to arbitrators headed by the earl of Warwick. Ann and Elizabeth were in fact delivered from Sir James's to Stanley's keeping. Stanley married the former to his younger son Edward, and the latter to his nephew John Stanley.[73]

Sir James clung tenaciously to the family estates, however. On 5 March 1471, a few days before Edward IV's invasion, the government of Henry VI and Warwick ordered provision of a carriage to convey the cannon *Mile Ende* from Bristol to Hornby castle, to assist in Stanley's siege of it, doubtless against Harington's supporters.[74] Not surprisingly, Harington was one of the first to bring a company in support of Edward, to Nottingham, according to the *Arrivall*. But Warkworth says that Stanley's brother Sir William joined Edward with a company there – a characteristic piece of Stanleyan reinsurance.[75] In June 1473 a commission headed by Gloucester, and including Hudleston, Sir John Pilkington, and Thomas Pilkington, esquire, was ordered to take all the properties of the late Sir Thomas and John Harington into the king's hands, displacing the possessors, Sir James Harington and his brother Sir Robert. Seemingly Edward was not prepared to back Sir James fully at the Stanleys' expense. But in Edward's later years Sir James was holding on to Farleton and Brierley (Yorks.), and in 1476 his offences against the crown, and debts to it, were pardoned. The 1483 revolt against Richard III, involving Stanley's wife, may have raised the expectation among Sir James and his friends that their interest might be revived at Stanley expense: conversely, they may have considered that Henry Tudor stood for unalterable Stanley hegemony. Sir James, Sir Robert and Pilkington fought for Richard at Bosworth, and afterwards Henry granted Sir James's forfeited estates to Stanley's son Edward.[76]

These complications hampered Henry's attempts to win north-western allegiances. In 1487 Sir Thomas Broughton, Thomas Harington, Broughton's brother John, James Harington, Edward Frank and Richard Middleton joined in an invasion aimed at overthrowing Henry's rule.[77]

This invasion, escalating from an implausible posture originating among relatively humble folk, demonstrated Henry's continued dynastic weakness, despite his marriage to Elizabeth of York and the birth of their hopefully named son Arthur. A 'lowborn' priest studying at Oxford, William or Richard Symonds, trained the 'ignoble' Lambert Simnel, son of an artisan – perhaps an organmaker or a joiner – to impersonate a Yorkist prince. Symonds cannily conveyed his protégé to Ireland, where pro-Yorkist nobles and townsmen readily accepted him as the earl of Warwick and the rightful king. They sought the support of

Edward IV's sister Margaret (widow of Charles the Bold of Burgundy), and of dissidents in England, notably Lovell, who crossed to Flanders to encourage the co-operation of the dowager duchess. The wide network of plotting alerted king and council that a rising was afoot, but royal offers of pardon did not deter Sir Thomas Broughton from crossing to Flanders. More ominously, Suffolk's eldest son, John de la Pole, earl of Lincoln — the Yorkist kings' nephew — took the same route. On 3 April the earl of Northumberland wrote from his house at Leconfield (Yorks.) to the mayor of York that the previous day he had received the king's letters informing him of Lincoln's departure. According to Vergil, the latter aimed at the crown for himself.[78]

At first Henry feared that Lincoln would invade East Anglia, his ancestral 'country'. In the week commencing 12 March the king rode into Essex, and thence to Bury St Edmunds. On Maundy Thursday (12 April) he was at Norwich with Bishop Fox of Exeter, the earls of Oxford and Derby, Lord FitzWalter, Sir Robert Willoughby 'and in Substance all the Nobles of that Parties'. News arrived daily of invasion preparations on the coasts of Zealand and Flanders, but, like all recent kings threatened with invasion, Henry decided that it was more prudent to take up a central position in the realm, where recruits could reach him more easily from all directions, and whence he could reach the vulnerable north as well as the south-east. On 16 April he went to Walsingham, 'where he prayed devoutly before the image of the Blessed Virgin Mary . . . that he might be preserved from the wiles of his enemies'. He moved via Cambridge to Huntingdon, where on 20 April he wrote to the city council of York, warning them to safeguard the city against any rebel assault. Passing through Northampton, he arrived at Coventry on the 22nd. There his servants and subjects rode in to give support, and on 28 and 30 April he wrote letters to the city council of York about the measures concerted for that city's defence. He ordered the constable of Scarborough castle, William Tunstall, to deliver to the citizens twelve serpentines. On 1 May John Vavasour, recorder of York, reported from Coventry that a royal servant had ridden with 'writing and money' to Sir Richard Tunstall and leading Yorkshire knights, for their assistance in the defence of York in case of need. 'The King', Vavasour told his fellow citizens, 'is greatly accompanied and hath yet no certain knowledge when his enemies will take their shipping.'[79]

Three days later, however, Henry wrote to the York council saying he had sure knowledge that the rebels had left Flanders and departed westwards: consequently, he and his council thought that 'ye shall not need to have any strength or company of men of war for this season' under arms. He licensed the 'Nobles of the South Parties', expensively maintaining their retinues at Coventry, to return to their 'Countries' and make preparations for a summons. But some would not leave, sending 'Part of their People into their Countries for their Relief' till required. Henry retired to Kenilworth castle, writing from there to the mayor and aldermen of York on 8 May, commending their provision of victuals and other 'stuff' for the 'men of worship and their retinues' whom he had commanded to defend the city, and reassuring them that these would be ordered to return if danger threatened again; 'also our cousin the Earl of Northumberland intendith hastily to be in the country nigh unto you'. On the 13th, Henry wrote to the earl of Oxford, telling him that the rebels had landed in Ireland eight days previously, and requesting him to come and give advice and counsel on measures to subdue them.[80] A noble – possibly Oxford – wrote to the Norfolk landowner Sir Edmund Bedingfield about this time, saying that he had shown the king Bedingfield's letter about the execution of a commission of array. Henry, grateful for 'the right good minds and disposition of you and of other gentlemen there towards his Grace', would not as yet put them to 'any further labour or charge', as the rebels were in Ireland:

> nevertheless his Grace will that the country be ready at all times to do his Highness service upon reasonable warning; for so much as the King's Grace intendeth to make provision to send an army into Ireland in haste, not knowing as yet whether that ye, and other about you shall be desired to bear any charge thereto or no.[81]

On 24 May, in Dublin, Simnel was crowned as 'Edward VI' before a motley group, notable among whom was the leading Irish magnate Gerald FitzGerald, earl of Kildare. The most formidable rebel support was a force of German and Swiss mercenaries, 1,500 and 2,000 strong, supplied from the Low Countries by Duchess Margaret. They were commanded by the highly reputed Swiss colonel (and former Augsburg shoemaker) Martin Schwarz. The rebels moved on to the offensive with disconcerting speed, and soon shattered any illusions Henry may have had that he could tie them down in Ireland. The English dissidents, foreign mercenaries and a large Irish force commanded by Thomas Geraldine sailed to Lancashire, landing on 4 June at Piel castle on the Isle of Foudray, belonging to Furness abbey. This invasion point, on the tip of the Furness peninsula, was probably recommended by Broughton. Christopher Urswick, whom Henry had dispatched to Lancashire to ascertain which ports were capable of berthing the rebels' ships, brought him news of the invasion. Immediately the king summoned his council to concert military measures. Already he may have had seven secular peers or heirs presumptive to peerages in his company – the earls of Oxford and Shrewsbury, Viscount Lisle, and

Lords Grey of Ruthin, Hastings, Ferrers of Chartley, and Grey of Powis.[82]

There are four especially valuable accounts of the 1487 campaign. An anonymous account probably written by a soldier in Henry's army is graphically informative about its progress up to the battle of Stoke; but the author was largely ignorant of what went on elsewhere. The York civic archives contain an account of the campaign which is uniquely informative about events in the city and its environs. Two historians, Vergil and Molinet, were less well informed about particulars, but put the whole campaign into a general political context. Vergil was concerned to minimize the support which the invaders received in England; Molinet, sympathetic to the Yorkist cause, stressed the augmentation of their numbers in an allegedly favourable north.[83] Indeed, they aimed particularly to stir Yorkist and Neville sentiment there. James Taite alleged on 31 May before the mayor and leading officials of York that on 25 March he had fallen in with travellers who had a white horse which he recognized as the earl of Lincoln's 'hobby', stabled with Taite when the earl had been with the king in York the previous year. These travelling London merchants' servants reportedly had a bold line in subversive conversation, for example:

> John of Lincoln shall give them all a breakfast that oweth him no love nor favour . . . thou shall hear tell that right good gentlemen shall take my Lords part. Can ye oght me how far I have to Sir Thomas Mallevery place for we must have him writing or else send it to him?

When the merchants arrived in York, said the aspiring spy Taite, 'a servant of theirs showed me that they should meet the Prior of Tynmouth at the sign of the boar' – an appropriately named hostelry![84] At least two Yorkshiremen were attainted for their part in the rebellion – Robert Percy of Knaresborough, and William Kay of Halifax, gentleman. A week after the battle of Stoke, the earl of Northumberland wrote from Richmond to Sir Robert Plumpton with some urgency, saying that 'for [his] own discharge and mine' he should arrest 'divers gentlemen and other commoners' within the keepership of Knaresborough who had assisted the rebels in battle or otherwise, especially John Pullen and Richard Knaresborough.[85]

The most distinguished northern adherents were John Lord Scrope of Bolton and his younger kinsman Thomas Lord Scrope of Masham. They had Neville links – Scrope of Bolton had attempted to rally support in Yorkshire for the Kingmaker against Edward IV in March 1470, and Scrope of Masham was married to the Kingmaker's niece.[86] Nevertheless, the support the rebels gained in the north seems disappointing. In Yorkshire there may have been doubts as to who this

'Edward VI' was, as Henry's men had taken the real earl of Warwick from Sheriff Hutton in 1485. Henry's vigorous showing at York and Lovell's poor one at Middleham in 1486, may have been a deterrent to rebellion, as may the outlandishly foreign complexion of much of the present Yorkist army: the city of York no more wanted to admit Lincoln's German mercenaries in 1487 than it had Edward's in 1471.[87]

Taite had pertinently asked the agitator whom he had met in March whether Lincoln stood 'in condition' with the earl of Northumberland, and received the telling answer that 'as therefor we set little by him'. The preparedness of Northumberland and leading Yorkshire landowners stiffened the defensive backbone of the citizens of York and lessened the rebels' chances of capturing the city. Henry had worked strenuously to safeguard it. On 6 June Northumberland wrote from Leconfield to the York council, giving news of the rebels' landing and affirming his intention to resist: he would be in York for the purpose on the 10th. On the 8th he was still at Leconfield, promising the York citizens that he would be at Pocklington the following evening: '[I] shall not rest there but be with you the same night . . . and upon Sunday next coming [10 June] I will not fail to be with you at the farrest, and tofore if ye think it requisite.' But the earl was sluggish compared to the rebels, who speedily made the arduous crossing of the Pennines, descending through Wensleydale. On 8 June 'Edward VI' wrote a signet letter from Masham to the city of York, testing the water by requesting admission. In fact, like Edward IV in 1471, the rebels put a swift southward drive above securing the city's allegiance. The city chamberlains, returning from a meeting with Lincoln and Lovell the following day, reported that they were bypassing the city through Boroughbridge. Later that day, the pro-Tudor Lord Clifford was admitted through Micklegate Bar with 400 foot and horse; the following day (10 June), Northumberland, doubtless galvanized by the enemy's proximity, arrived at noon 'with many knights and lords of this country'.[88]

Clifford was chivalrously determined to take a crack at the disappearing enemy on his own. The prudent citizens laconically recorded the disastrous outcome. On the afternoon of Northumberland's arrival in York, Clifford sallied out, encamping that night at Tadcaster. In fact he had got too close to the rebels lying on Bramham Moor, and that night they attacked and scattered his panicked force. Clifford fled back to York, his baggage abandoned and captured. Two days later he set off again, with Northumberland and the Tudor Yorkshire forces (estimated by the city at 6,000), intent on linking up with the king. Once more Northumberland and Clifford were the victims of poor intelligence − there were other Yorkist forces hovering in the vicinity. The two Lord Scropes rode up to Bootham

Bar, 'there cried King Edward', and assaulted the gates, but the commons acting as watchmen put up a good defence and beat the rebels off. Northumberland, still within six miles of the city, returned with Clifford and garrisoned York for over a week, leaving on 14 June – not to link up with Henry in Nottinghamshire, but to go northwards, presumably to mop up Scrope's following.[89]

Thus Henry's commanders north of the Trent, though hanging on to York, had signally failed to hold the invasion forces there, and were deterred by relatively insignificant forces from adding to the king's main strength. If an uncorroborated episode related by Molinet is true, Tudor ineffectiveness in stopping the rebels was even more striking. Molinet says that Sir Edward Wydeville, with an advance force of 6,000 from the royal army, penetrated into Yorkshire as far as Doncaster, to reconnoitre the rebels' position. But their strength forced Wydeville to retreat for three days through Sherwood Forest to Nottingham, to link up with the king's main force.[90] Perhaps Lincoln and Lovell concluded that poorly co-ordinated enemy forces were reacting similarly to the opponents of Edward's bold advance through south Yorkshire and Nottinghamshire in 1471.

Henry, at Kenilworth when the invasion took place, had his main forces assembled and moving northwards within a week – as fast as might be expected, but too late to halt the rebels north of Trent.[91] According to the anonymous memorialist, he passed through Coventry and Leicester, enforcing strict discipline at Leicester and Loughborough, where he arrived on 11 June.[92] The following day, the army advanced north to encamp for the night 'under a Wood called Bonley [Bouley?] Rice'. This may have been the encampment near Nottingham described by Vergil as 'the wood which is called Banrys in the vernacular'. Possibly Henry's bivouac was at Bunny (Notts.), where 'Boneyris' is recorded in 1330 ('Bonnyrise' in 1572, 'Bonney Reyce' in 1582).[93] On 13 June, in fine weather, the army set out again, but may have lost its way, failing to reach Nottingham, perhaps the day's objective. The foreward and the main 'battle' spent the night in hastily selected quarters, the former below a hill, the latter in a village (where the king lodged in a gentleman's house) and adjacent beanfield. The village may have been Ruddington, three miles south of Nottingham.

Next day (the feast of Corpus Christi), after Henry had heard Mass in the parish church, and trumpets had sounded to horse, he seems to have puzzled some of his soldiers by leaving the army, riding 'backwards'. But this turned out to be (consciously or not) a neat morale-booster, for he returned with Lord Strange, who was accompanied by 'a great Host'. Nevertheless, there was some nervousness in camp that evening; many fled after a disturbance. Next day Henry had sure intelligence about the enemy's movements: they were just north of the Trent, passing away from him through Southwell towards Newark. So as not to be outflanked, on the 15th Henry moved, south of the river, on a parallel course, halting for the night at Ratcliffe. The nervousness in the army showed itself in the same way as the previous night. On the morning of 16 June, Henry, as before Bosworth, got his men on the road very early in the morning: guides from Ratcliffe led Oxford's foreward and the main 'battle' to arrive before nine o'clock at Stoke, not far out of Newark, where, now on Henry's side of the river, the rebels had encamped.

Lincoln responded vigorously to the king's challenge, leading his troops into attack. His force, which was to be officially estimated at 8,000, was heavily outnumbered: the observer in Henry's army thought that the 'great Host' which Lord Strange had brought to Henry's support was 'enough to have beaten all the king's enemies, only of Lord Derby's and his own folk'. The royal council of war at the start of the expedition had set up a powerful foreward under Oxford's command: with him were the earl of Shrewsbury, Viscount Lisle, Lords Grey of Ruthin, Hastings, and Ferrers of Chartley. There were appointed as foreriders, and as the 'right hand' of the foreward, Lord Powis, Sir Edward Wydeville, Sir Charles Somerset, and Sir Richard Haute, 'with many other Gallants of the King's House'; Sir Richard Pole was on the left hand. Some changes in the foreward command may have taken place by the time Stoke was fought: the York civic account mentions the presence there of the latecomer Lord Strange, and Molinet says that the right wing was commanded by Wydeville, the left by Sir John Savage.[94]

Despite the creditable array of magnates to support the king, he may not have been fully confident of noble support, especially in the light of his predecessor's experience at Bosworth. Before the invasion Henry had had the marquess of Dorset arrested by the earl of Oxford, as the marquess was coming to meet him at Bury St Edmunds; he had dispatched the duke of Suffolk, Lincoln's father, honourably to Windsor.[95] Henry's observation of the high morale of Lincoln's men in battle at Stoke convinced him, rightly in Vergil's opinion, that they were relying on secret allies. But the 'naked' Irish were ill equipped for English warfare: the rebels were unable to resist the powerful royal foreward which, alone committed to the fray, at length broke resistance in a vigorous charge. Lincoln, Geraldine, Schwarz and possibly Lovell were killed in the intense fighting. Simnel and his priestly mentor were captured. According to an Irish source, the *Book of Howth*, more than 4,000 Irish were slain. On the day of the battle, Henry wrote from Newark that it had been won 'without death of any noble or gentleman on our part'. Two days later, he dismissed thence all but 3,000 to

4,000 of his soldiers, according to Vergil, going to Lincoln, where several captives were executed, and then south to Kenilworth castle before a progress to York 'in order to reform the territory bordering on Scotland, in which his enemies had shortly before raised an army against him'. Henry arrived at York on 30 July with an army of 10,000 'with his banner displayed' and stayed a week, during which judgments for treason were pronounced and an execution was carried out.[96] Then 'with many lords and nobles' he set out for Durham and Newcastle, returning through Boroughbridge and Pontefract – he was at Pontefract on 25 August.[97]

Henry won a victory for which he had worked hard against a dangerous enemy. Like Richard in 1485, he had had ample warning of the danger of invasion, and gathered, at the same base, an army superior in numbers. But, again like Richard, he was unable to prevent the enemy from penetrating to the Midlands from the fringes of the realm, or to rely fully on the loyalty of his noble supporters. There were many to his rear, in the south, who did not rate his chances high, or who were eager for a Yorkist restoration. According to Molinet, on the day on which Henry's vanguard abandoned Nottingham, lord 'de Veals' (Welles?), who was bringing up a retinue of 10,000 to the king's support, turned in flight and retreated through London. The Yorkists in sanctuary there, thinking that Henry had been defeated, sallied out to rob his servants and well-wishers, and cry for Warwick as king.[98] A London chronicler tells a similar story:

> And yet was that time false Englishmen that were between the field
> and the king's true people that were coming towards him, which
> untrue persons said that the king was fled and the field lost; whereby
> the king was put from much of his aid.[99]

The rumour-laden atmosphere in London, and the danger it presented to Henry, is reflected in the story told by Thomas Howard, earl of Surrey, that the lieutenant of the Tower, where Surrey had been imprisoned since Bosworth, offered to release him.[100] Perhaps, if the real Warwick was also in the Tower, the lieutenant had it in mind that Surrey could have him proclaimed king. Surrey shrewdly stayed put. He may not have relished setting up as a rival kingmaker to his fellow East Anglian, Lincoln, or promoting Lincoln's kingmaking.[101]

How did Henry survive the crisis, amidst widespread lack of confidence in the outcome and treacherous meditations? Perhaps some nobles sympathetic to the Neville–Yorkist cause hesitated to support the invasion because they feared that it boded ill for the genuine Warwick. The frequently ambivalent Stanleys had in 1487 a strong stake in upholding Henry's rule, for it had aggrandized them – and the invasion was in part a protest against their gains. Despite Henry's suspicions of treason, he apparently kept calm at Stoke – unlike Richard at Bosworth – and, as was his wont, tried to remain detached and immune from the fighting. He had good reason for confidence in experienced commanders who had fought together for him in 1485.

The lack of a convincing, free Yorkist candidate for the throne, the formidable repute of Henry's commanders, and the tendency of his principal opponents to die in battle, may after 1487 have acted as deterrents to the continuing impulses to plot dynastic risings. In 1489 and 1491–2 there were popular rebellions in regions which had not been securely in Henry's allegiance since his accession. But they failed notably to develop into more general dynastic stirs. According to Vergil, in 1489 northerners refused to contribute to the subsidy for the Breton war, 'either because they found it too onerous or because they were instigated and urged not to pay it by certain individuals who secretly hated Henry'. When the earl of Northumberland reported to him that it was impossible to make them pay, the king ordered the earl to force those who refused.[102] On 24 April Northumberland wrote to Sir William Plumpton, summoning him on the king's behalf to come with an armed company, together with the earl's nephew Sir William Gascoigne, to attend the earl at Thirsk by the evening of 27 April.[103] The next day Northumberland met the commons at Cocklodge, his house nearby in his lordship of Topcliffe. There the commons slew him. Vergil's succinct explanation of their action was that when they heard the intransigent royal reply about the payment of subsidy, they 'assaulted the earl as though he were the author of their wrongs'. This rings true. Northerners looked to their magnates to represent and protect their interests at a southern court which, except under Richard III, they were inclined to regard as unsympathetic and alien.[104]

Contemporaries regarded the failure of the earl's retinue to protect him as the most shocking aspect of the affair. Dr Hicks has adduced reasons why his followers may have been lukewarm in their loyalty. Former retainers of Gloucester whom he had recruited may have had a cooling effect.[105] Their passivity probably stiffened the resolve of the more intransigent risers to prolong and indeed widen the scope of their protest. Writing from Hedingham (Essex) probably just before 12 May, William Paston relayed reports current in the south that the risers were still around the place where the earl was killed 'and not with no great number, they say not past with 5 or 600'. But they had made proclamations to meet others of their affinity, probably on 7 May. Paston had got hold of a copy of their proclamation: every 'lord, knight, esquire, gentleman and yeoman' in the north parts was to appear in defensible array, either on Allerton Moor (near Pontefract) 'in the east part' or on Gatherley Moor, in Richmondshire, 'in the west part'. No overt treason was suggested: they were 'to gainstand such persons as is aboutward for to destroy our sovereign Lord the King and the Commons of England, for such unlawful points at St. Thomas of Canterbury died for'.[106] But the rebels seem to have attracted insignificant 'gentle' support. Sixty-two out of sixty-six Yorkshiremen indicted for participating were yeomen, husbandmen, artisans and tradesmen. More noteworthy were Eli Casse and Thomas Bullock, two of the four governors of Beverley; Thomas Wrangwish, alderman of York; and Sir John Egremont, a former servant of Richard III who had enjoyed some favour from Henry.[107] According to the earl of Surrey, they captured York, 'won with assault by force' – this was before 17 May, when Egremont summoned the mayor to All Hallows church there, 'showing unto him and his brethren that there might be prepared shortly pretty men with horses to attend and go with certain fellowship of his into Richmondshire'. The mayor complied, for Egremont 'had rule and his people here'.[108]

Soon after Northumberland's death Henry VII had determined to lead a large army into the north. On 6 May the earl of Oxford requested Sir John Paston to meet him with a retinue armed for the king's service at Cambridge on 12 May.[109] Henry set out northwards with his army from Hertford castle. He appointed as 'chief Captain' of the vanguard the earl of Surrey, recently released from the Tower. Among those appointed under Surrey were familiar figures from Henry's campaigns: the earl of Shrewsbury, Lord Hastings (the son of William Hastings), Sir William Stanley, Sir Rhys ap Thomas, Sir Thomas Bourchier, Sir John Savage and Sir John Rysely. Vergil says that on the king's approach to York the rebels dispersed: according to a London chronicle, before Henry arrived, Surrey had 'distressed' the rebels and captured their captain John a Chamber, who with some of his supporters was hanged at York. Egremont showed Yorkist colours by fleeing to the court of Duchess Margaret.[110] Surrey's funeral inscription says that

> for the singular trust, that the King had to the said Earl, and the activity that he saw in him, he left him in the North, and made him his Lieutenant-general from Trent Northward, and Warden of the East and Middle Marches of England against Scotland, and Justice of the Forests from Trent Northwards.

At last Henry had found a magnate able and dedicated enough to rule the north in his interest, whose Ricardian background perhaps made him acceptable there. In the second year of his lieutenancy, however, Surrey had to face an insurrection in 'the West part of the Country', but defeated the rebels at Ackworth near Pontefract. He captured and executed their captains, but sued the king for pardons for the rest, a successful intermediacy (unlike Northumberland's in 1489) which 'won . . . the favour of the Country'.[111]

Surrey's ability to rule the north, and the measures which Henry took to strengthen his position in Ireland, deprived Yorkist plotters in the 1490s of promising bases of support.[112] But tensions between Henry and his former patron Charles VIII of France, James IV, who succeeded as king of Scots in 1488, and the rulers of the Low Countries, gave Yorkists continued hopes of foreign help. Perkin Warbeck, claiming to be a Yorkist prince, landed in Ireland at Cork in November 1491. Henry dealt effectively with the threat that Warbeck's claim might be exploited by Irish lords, as Simnel's had been, by dispatching a force the following month under the lieutenant's deputy James Ormond and Captain Thomas Garth. Warbeck found what appeared a more promising field of support in France: in March 1492 he was received as a prince by Charles VIII. A consequence of Henry's invasion of France the following October was to scotch these hopes. For a condition of the Anglo-French peace of Etaples in November was the banishment of Warbeck from France. But he soon received encouragement from Duchess Margaret and the principal rulers of the Low Countries – her son-in-law Archduke Maximilian, king of the Romans, and his son Philip.[113] A letter from Henry to Sir Gilbert Talbot (20 July 1493), requesting that Talbot have a military company in readiness, reflects his fears that the duchess would soon once again launch a mercenary force in favour of a Yorkist impostor.[114] Warbeck's plotting in 1493–4 had some distinguished connections in England, but his hopes of gaining support there were badly dented by the information about it elicited through the activities of Henry's spies in the Low Countries. In January and February 1495 there were treason trials. Among those convicted were the Norfolk landowner Lord FitzWalter, Sir Simon Mountfort of Coleshill (Warwicks.), William Worsley, dean of St Paul's, William Richford, provincial of the Dominicans in England, and Thomas Powys, prior of their house at Langley, Herts. Most spectacularly of all, a man to whom Henry was heavily indebted for his crown – his chamberlain, Sir William Stanley – confessed to having been in contact with Warbeck in 1493. He was executed.[115]

Disappointed by the arrest of plotters in England, Warbeck nevertheless persisted in attempting invasion. In Flanders, with the aid of Duchess Margaret and Maximilian, he collected ships, troops, victuals and artillery, sailing with what Vergil termed the 'human dregs' of neighbouring regions, including English exiles (his denigration is characteristically sweeping). According to Molinet, Warbeck had in his company Roderick de Lalain and other experienced soldiers. Lalain was an ornament of chivalry, who was to excel in Scottish jousts. One of

Warbeck's two Spanish captains, Don Fulano de Guevara, was referred to by de Puebla, the Spanish envoy in England, in a letter to the Catholic kings, in terms which implied their familiarity with his family. One of his English captains, Mountfort, was the son of the recently executed Warwickshire landowner. Warbeck's expedition was comparable in size as well as calibre with other invasion forces during the Wars of the Roses – he probably had at least 1,300 men. He planned to raise the Kentishmen. According to what his captured English captains were to tell Robert Albon of Yarmouth, the intention was to seize 'a town of strength', with Sandwich in mind – Warwick the Kingmaker's and the Bastard of Fauconberg's old base. With over fourteen sails, Warbeck hove to in the Downs off Camber sands near Deal. Calm weather facilitated operations. On 3 July a landing party reconnoitred, to see if Kentishmen would give support. Though tempted, the locals decided to dissimulate with the invaders until levies could assemble to oppose them. Warbeck prudently remained on shipboard with a majority of his troops, but landed reinforcements who fanned out to raise standards over three neighbouring villages. They were attacked – and probably taken badly by surprise – by the mayor of Sandwich and a scratch force of commons. Kentish archery took its toll. The invaders were driven back to their ships. It was a disaster: besides about 150 killed, there were many captives, including a clutch of captains.[116]

Very soon afterwards Warbeck's fleet slipped away from its anchorage. There was speculation as to his intentions. One captured captain, Belt, told Albon 'they will have Yarmouth or they shall die for it'. Another report received by Yarmouth corporation was that 'they be forth out of Camber westwards'. De Puebla reported from London on 19 July that the fleet was believed to have gone to Ireland or Scotland.[117] But Warbeck returned to Flanders, according to Vergil. At Duchess Margaret's court it was planned that he should attempt an invasion of the west of England, first having raised Irish support, or, if this did not work out, that he should sail to Scotland and attempt to exploit the bad relations between James IV and Henry VII.[118] Warbeck appeared in the summer off the earl of Desmond's territory of Munster, the region where he had been welcomed in 1491. From 23 July to 3 August he and Desmond besieged the vigorously defended port of Waterford. It was relieved by Henry's lieutenant, Sir Edward Poynings, with a force from Dublin. As in 1491, Warbeck found the Tudor interest too strong in Ireland to use it as a base for the invasion of England. He moved on to Scotland: in November or December he was received as a prince by James IV.[119]

Henry VII seems to have particularly appreciated the value of spying as a means of disrupting plots – a lesson probably imprinted during his youthful exile. He had penetrated the plotting centring on Warbeck in 1493–4; prior to James IV's invasion of September 1496 in support of Warbeck, he knew what was afoot at the Scottish court. His informant was Lord Bothwell, who emphasized in his letters the unpopularity of James's intention to go to war with England. He recounted his own attempts to temper the king's determination to promote the claim of the 'fenyt boy'. Nervousness among English Border gentlefolk is reflected in his report that on 28 August Warbeck had a visitor from Carlisle. 'I was informit secretely yat yis man sould have commyn fra Randell of Dacre, broder to ye lord Dacre, and fra the Sceltonis for mekyll [Michael?] Scelton yat is her had ye convoyanc[e] of him.'[120] On 8 September Bothwell wrote that five days previously Warbeck had agreed conditions with the king and council for royal intervention in support of his claim. Warbeck was to hand over Berwick, and pay 50,000 marks towards James's military costs. It was planned that the Scottish army and Warbeck's international company, 1,400 strong, should rendezvous at Ellem kirk on 15 September, and cross the Border two days later, despite the opposition of nearly all the barons and people both 'for ye danger that thereof might follow, and for the inconvenience of the season'. Bothwell believed that James was ill prepared for war, and predicted that within four or five days of invading, his men would be 'so weary for watching and for lack of victuals' that they would oblige James to go home. He advised Henry on how to entrap the Scottish army. Besides describing Warbeck's Scottish support unflatteringly, Bothwell insinuated that some of his leading followers were less than devoted to his cause. He represented Warbeck's principal councillor, Sir George Neville, as an unprincipled adventurer. His captain of 1495, Roderick de Lalain, who arrived from Flanders with two little ships and sixty 'Almains' (Germans), emphasized that he had come to serve James, snubbing Warbeck in the royal presence. Perhaps Lalain had been disgusted by Warbeck's failure to attempt the rescue of his captains near Deal.[121]

The invasion got under way not long after Bothwell predicted that it would. On 13 September carters received their wages. The artillery was assembled near the coast east of Edinburgh, at Restalrig: on 14 September the priests of the collegiate church at Restalrig received payment to say Masses for the king before Our Lady and St Triduana, and that day royal forces probably reached Haddington. The army set out to cross the Lammermuirs, probably going up from Garvald by Whiteadder Water, and down from Ellem to Langton. The treasurer made payments on 16 September 'For walking of the guns that night at Johnscleugh' (in Whiteadder valley), and on the 17th for their being 'walked' at Langton. On the 19th, payments were made to 'Henric, gunnar, at Ellem' and to 'the man and the wif of the hous quhar the

King Iugyit at Ellem'. Some difficulty was encountered in getting heavy equipment across the Tweed. The treasurer records under 21 September payment to 'The cobill men of Tweid, that helpit the artailȝerj oure the watir'; the next payment is 'to the men that brocht the clos cart furth of the watir, quhen scho stude in the watir all nycht'. R. L. Mackie thought that the invaders crossed near Coldstream: that is where Warbeck received a large sum at the king's command on the 21st. The army probably crossed and bivouacked south of the confluence of the Tweed with the Till, so that the cumbersome equipment was protected from the English garrisons at Norham and Berwick by this tributary. James appears to have confined his operations to the Till valley. Presumably Twizel bridge, a key feature, was quickly seized and guarded: peels on the north bank at Twizel, Tillmouth and as far east as Duddo were sacked, probably in part to prevent them from being used as forward English bases. The centrepiece of James's campaign turned out to be a test of his siege equipment, a brief and unsuccessful siege of Heaton castle on the south bank of the Till. This was conducted with some urgency, probably because James feared an attempt at relief. On 24 September, drinksilver was paid to masons 'to mine all night at the house of Hetoune', and on the 25th payment was made to workmen to work in the mine that night.[122] According to a London chronicler, James withdrew into Scotland in some disorder, on receiving news that Lord Neville with 4,000 men and other companies of marchmen were approaching. The Londoner crowed that the Scots had only 'Entered four miles within this land, and burnt houses and cast down two small Towers or peels, making great boast and brag'.[123] Heaton is, indeed, less than four miles from the frontier. Vergil, untainted by London chauvinism, painted a bleaker picture of the effects of invasion. James 'penetrated a considerable distance into the country and . . . widely devastated the countryside of Northumberland'; terrified by the Scots' pillage and slaughter, the gentlefolk took refuge in their castles. When his men were sated with booty, and the gentlefolk's resistance stiffened, James retreated. Vergil's account makes plain that Henry's fears that northern nobles would embrace the Yorkist cause proved groundless. The brusque reply which James made to Warbeck's complaint about Scottish ravaging may have stemmed from disillusion with a similar overestimation.[124]

In his limited strategic commitment, as well as his failure to curb pillaging, James had displayed a disinclination to do much to help the Yorkist cause militarily. His achievement in 1496, in terms of his own as well as Yorkist interests, was unremarkable. But he had shown realism. He got away with more than Bothwell thought he would deserve, and rattled the English. The greatest feat was getting the artillery all the way from Edinburgh, across the Lammermuirs and the

Tweed, and back again – an experiment probably not previously tried by a Scottish king on the same scale, which could have easily ended in disaster, and which provided useful operational lessons. To achieve this, there had been hired in Edinburgh 143 carters with 196 horses, to carry guns, covered carts, gunstones, pavilions and other gear, and 76 men with spades, shovels, and pick mattocks to pass with the artillery and draw the guns 'in peththis and myris'.[125]

Why, then, after parting the mountains, did James merely manoeuvre and mine mouselike for a few days in the Till valley? He may have felt that he had insufficient time and resources for deeper penetration, for the reasons outlined by Bothwell. The carters hired on 13 September had received wages from the treasurer for only fourteen days 'fra this day furth'.[126] The hope of Yorkist rebellion provided another reason for sitting down near the frontier. So did a military constraint currently imposed on Scottish royal expeditions by frontier conditions. The prized artillery train, cumbersome to move in an emergency, had to be put at risk across the Tweed – and even on the Scottish bank there was no formidable fortress to protect it from pursuit. Possession of Berwick, taken by the English in 1482, was the best strategic remedy. But Berwick was difficult to besiege, being well fortified, strongly held, and easy to reinforce by land and sea.

The 1496 invasion appears to have been a trial run for James's later forays, in which he again threatened the English higher up the Tweed, hoping, perhaps, to lure and disarray their field forces, then rush the defences of isolated Berwick. In 1497 he besieged Norham castle and attempted to get the earl of Surrey to fight. On his last campaign, in 1513, James again advanced along Whiteadder Water and through Ellem to attack castles in the Till valley, and to meet his death at Flodden.[127]

The 1496 invasion demonstrated what the Lancastrians had discovered in 1462–3: that Scottish intervention in the dynastic quarrel was likely to be of little military value. Moreover, it revealed that the north, in the energetic and tactful care of Surrey, was a barren field for Yorkist rebellion. Warbeck's preoccupation with Scotland and Ireland, and his failure to rebuild a network of supporters in England after the arrests of 1494, led to his inability to exploit fully a dangerous rebellion against Henry in the summer of 1497, a rebellion which was an indirect consequence of his invasion of Northumberland. Rising in protest against taxation for the war with Scotland, the commons of Cornwall were a principal constituent of a West Country army which advanced, recruiting support, through Wells, Salisbury and Winchester and across Surrey, to Henry's mortification encamping intact on Blackheath, the *champ de Mars* of Kentish rebels. They intended to punish the councillors whom they held responsible for taxation, especially

Archbishop Morton of Canterbury and Sir Reginald Bray. But the mayor and aldermen of London took firm defence measures and kept in daily communication with the king and the chancellor, Morton. George Grey, earl of Kent, Lords Abergavenny and Cobham, and Kentish gentlefolk guarded against a rising in their shire. Henry left London with his army to confront the western men. His captains, the earls of Essex and Suffolk, Sir Rhys ap Thomas and Lord Daubeney, surrounded and overcame them with comparative ease at Blackheath on 17 June.[128]

The 1497 rebellion was the first major one since 1460 in which the dynastic issue was not raised. Contemporaries surely expected it to be. It is inexplicable that a peer, Lord Audley, took the captaincy of the rebels at Wells unless he thought he was the first swallow in a Yorkist summer. According to a somewhat suspect allegation made in 1506, Abergavenny, when with soldiers at Ewelme near Wallingford (Berks.) to oppose the rebels' advance, urged the later Yorkist claimant the earl of Suffolk to join them. A letter to the earl when he was a Yorkist pretender (1505?) shows that his circle then affected to believe that Warbeck had indeed been the duke of York. Perhaps in 1497 Suffolk was hesitant about asserting his own claim because he was not sure whether Warbeck was an impostor. On the other hand, if 'York' had appeared at the head of the westerners, Suffolk might have been inclined to join them.[129]

Three days after the battle, on 20 June, the sheriffs of Cornwall, Devon, Somerset, Dorset, Gloucestershire, Wiltshire, Hampshire and Surrey were ordered to have it proclaimed that pardons would be granted on submission to the king's mercy of all offenders in the insurrection subdued at 'the Blackheath beside Greenwich'. But some rebels probably remained recalcitrant, fearful of harsh punishments. On 28 June the earl of Devon was appointed to head a large commission to inquire into all insurrections in those counties and elsewhere, and to punish or pardon the delinquents. On 5 July Sir John Digby and Sir Robert Clifford were appointed to execute respectively the offices of constable and marshal with respect to the rebels who had levied war.[130]

Warbeck was slow to take advantage of the smoulderings of rebellion. Rejected by James IV, he left Scotland on 6 July, and appeared at Cork on the 26th, but was unable to raise support there. On 7 September he landed on the far tip of Cornwall, at Whitesand Bay near Land's End.[131] By 12 September Henry VII, at Woodstock (Oxon.), had heard that Warbeck was on his way from Ireland to Cornwall with two small ships and a Breton pinnace. The king wrote to Sir Gilbert Talbot that he had sent Lord Daubeney westwards to array against Warbeck, and Lord Willoughby of Broke with a fleet to cut off his retreat. He assured Talbot that, if necessary, he would go without delay to subdue Perkin.[132] Reports from Milanese and Venetian agents in London gave particulars of Warbeck's landing, his favourable reception by the Cornishmen, and the impressive royal counter-measures. The agents were confident of Henry's victory. Raimondo de Soncino, writing on 16 September, said that Warbeck had landed with eighty 'savage' Irishmen, and that Henry had dispatched against him the earl of Devon and the lord chamberlain (Daubeney). Next day Andrea Trevisan wrote that Warbeck had raised 6,000–8,000 insurgents and marched sixty miles inland. Among royal measures he mentions the dispatch of the chamberlain and the earl of Kent with 12,000 men.[133]

Warbeck secured St Michael's Mount and, passing through Penryn, displayed remarkable energy by arriving before and assaulting Exeter on 17 September. His attempts to rush the defences on that day and the one following failed against a hastily organized but energetic defence by the earl of Devon, leading gentlefolk of Devon and Cornwall, and the citizens. Why did Warbeck attempt to seize Exeter? Henry VII was to note with satisfaction that, on the 18th, Warbeck had not one gentleman with him. He can hardly have hoped that, once he had occupied the city, the local pro-Lancastrian and pro-Courtenay gentry would flock in. Perhaps both he and the Cornishmen believed that possession of the city would be a counter with which to bargain for pardons and favour from Henry.[134]

On 18 September the earl of Devon wrote to Henry that the rebels had withdrawn from Exeter to Collumpton, and that many had deserted. According to what was reported to the mayor and aldermen of London, Warbeck withdrew to Taunton on hearing of the approach of the king's forces.[135] Like the Lancastrians in the West Country in 1471, Warbeck was anxious to avoid confrontation with a royal army. On 20 September Henry sent news of Perkin's invasion and assaults on Exeter to Oliver King, bishop of Bath and Wells. If, he said, Perkin and his company 'come forward' (eastwards?), they would find 'before' them Daubeney, Willoughby of Broke, Seymour, Sir John Cheyney and the noblemen of South Wales, Gloucestershire, Wiltshire, Hampshire, Somerset and Dorset, and 'at their back' the garrison of Exeter. Henry with his 'host royal' would be not far off for the conclusion. Vergil confirms this strategy of encirclement. Henry dispatched light cavalry, then moved with his main force towards Taunton. He was joined by the duke of Buckingham and an impressive force of western knights. Characteristically, Henry sent on ahead with the main body of his army Daubeney, Broke and Rhys ap Thomas, following himself to trap Warbeck.[136]

At Taunton Warbeck soon concluded that the game was nearly up. He had already shown himself adept at escaping from the Kentishmen and the men of Waterford. With John Heron, Edward Skelion, Nicholas Ostelay and a small company, he rode off from his men at Taunton by night. They were to escape south-eastwards, where, probably, the ways were less infested with Henry's cavalry and the ports less closely guarded than in the West Country. Warbeck nearly reached the Hampshire coast, but had to take refuge in sanctuary at Beaulieu abbey. By 12 October the king was able to inform the mayor and aldermen of London that Warbeck had voluntarily surrendered.[137] According to Vergil, almost all of his deserted followers at Taunton had received pardons on submission. Henry had entered Exeter and sent his cavalry to secure St Michael's Mount.[138]

Thus was extinguished what was arguably the last flare-up of the Wars of the Roses. In the 1490s, the far-flung demonstrations that the persistent and impressively patronized 'duke of York' was an inept plotter and military leader, and his unmasking in 1497 as an impostor, may have discredited Yorkist rebellion as a respectable and legitimate course in noble eyes. Dynastic rebellion had always been hazardous, and the efficiency of Henry's intelligence sources and military system and the competence of his captains worsened the odds. Moreover, gentlefolk may have looked more doubtfully at concepts of rebellion when in 1489 and 1497 they were so boldly appropriated by peasants and artisans – who in the second 1497 revolt had the temerity to take over the dynastic issue and proclaim 'Richard IV'. From the 1450s onwards the rule of kings, their councillors and courtiers was repeatedly and often successfully challenged – by risings of discontented magnates, dynastic plotting and popular demonstrations of discontent. These sorts of movement interacted to give each other more strength and impetus. By 1497 they were manifestly no longer doing so. Such kinds of rebellion all revived in the sixteenth century, with novel features, sometimes in a heady and potent mix. Even the old Yorkist claims were to be canvassed. But this was part of a different drama.[139]

Part Two

Military Organization and Society

Chapter 6

Military Convention and Recruitment

In the fourteenth century, English kings' involvement of subjects' resources and fortunes in the pursuit of royal claims in Scotland and France had led to a renewed emphasis on their personal duty to lead armies, displaying the strength of their resolve to defend subjects against the oft-proclaimed malice of foreigners, and to secure a just peace. Edward I, Edward II and Edward III went abroad at the head of armies. Richard II and Henry IV both led invasions of Scotland, and had their intentions of invading France affirmed on occasion in parliament.

When faced with domestic uprisings, too, kings had powerful incentives to appear armed in the field. Their presence was likely to spur recruitment of levies and infuse them with zeal. According to an official account, the gentlefolk in Henry VI's army in 1459 were stimulated to make great efforts by his exhortation

> made by your own mouth, in so witty, so knightly, so manly, in so comfortable wise, with so Princely apport and assured manner, of which the Lords and the people took such joy and comfort, that all their desire was only to haste to fulfil your courageous Knightly desire.[1]

It may have been with Henry's behaviour then in mind that the author of *Knyghthode and Bataile* wrote

> Therefore our eye is to the king's sign,
>   We hear his voice, as trump and clarion,
> His eyes are obeyed, we incline
>   At once unto him, his legion
> We are . . .[2]

The king's demeanour could have a vital effect on morale. At St Albans in 1461 the Yorkist lords in Henry VI's company despaired and fled from the field when it was clear that he would not attempt to rally his men, since his sympathies lay with their opponents: 'nec spiritum esse, nec animum, immo, nec vultum nec alloquium, ad consolandum sive animandum populum suum'.[3]

Another incentive for the king to ride against rebels was to emphasize the dubiousness of their undertakings. Aquinas had written that the first condition for a just war was 'the authority of a ruler by whose order war is declared, for no private individual may declare war, since he may seek justice at the hands of a superior'.[4] Canonists insisted on the restriction of the right to wage public war to superior authority: 'Every hostile act except immediate self-defence required superior authority.'[5] A state of public war was declared by the unfurling of the prince's banner: subjects who then rode in warlike array in the realm, displaying unauthorized banners, courted the penalties of treason.[6] To do so in the king's presence demanded cool nerve.

York and his noble allies, to counter the unfavourable impressions which they made by raising warlike banners in Henry's vicinity in 1452, 1455, 1459 and 1460, implicitly defended themselves against charges of waging unlawful public war, and flaunting the king's declarations of it. For in their proclamations they asserted that they were in fact petitioning their royal superior, their unconventional manner of proceeding necessitated by scandalous circumstances. They were bearing arms merely in self-defence against the malign intent of the traitors around the king. Rather than risk the accident of an assault on the king's person, at St Albans in 1455 they strenuously tried to negotiate a settlement, protesting that they were loyal subjects whose aim was to procure the condemnation and punishment of traitors. York urged his men to attack only after Henry threatened them with the penalties of treason, refusing to accept the duke's explanation of 'the intent that we be come hither and assembled for and gathered at this time'. York argued that they were cornered men with no alternative to self-defence, for, if they were taken, Henry would 'give us a shameful death losing our livelihood and goods and our heirs shamed for ever'.[7] Immediately after the battle, and in the following months, the Yorkist lords tried to eradicate the treasonable impression which they had made by resorting to arms against a king whose banner was displayed. They escorted him back to London with royal honours, reaffirmed their oaths of fealty at a solemn crown-wearing ceremony, and secured pardons which were ratified in parliament. These pardons put the blame for the battle on the deceased duke of Somerset and two relatively obscure royal bureaucrats, Thomas Thorpe and William Joseph. The pardons cited in some detail the Yorkist lords' attempts to negotiate and the frustration of these efforts by their enemies in the royal entourage.[8]

Chroniclers' accounts of the Ludford Bridge campaign of 1459 and the battle of Northampton reflect the Yorkist lords' attempts to publicize the fact that their primary intention was to negotiate rather than to fight.[9] A conversation between two Nottingham men, probably referring to news of the Yorkist retreat in face of the royal army in October 1459, emphasized the risers' political disadvantage. According to Thomas Bolton:

Robert Shirwood, baker, said that if the Lords [i.e. Henry's supporters] would have put the King's banner from them, the Earl of Salisbury would have fought with them and proved on them that he had been true lord, as he heard it reported. And I answered again, that it were no wisdom to put ye King's banner away, if they might have it with them.[10]

At Ludlow the Yorkist lords made a virtue of necessity by claiming:

hereto we have forborne and avoided all things that might serve to the effusion of Christian blood, of the dread that we have of God and of your royal majesty, and have also eschewed to approach . . . [Henry] of the humble obedience and reverence whereon we have and during our life will have the same.[11]

But according to the crown, once Henry had approached them, they did not hesitate to attack him: they 'falsely and traitorously reared war against You [Henry], and then and there shot their said Guns, and shot as well at your most Royal person, as at your lords and people with You then and there being'.[12] The raising of the dynastic issue in 1460 provided a different justification for much of the subsequent campaigning. Resort to public warfare was authorized by rival sovereigns: the waging of battle was an appeal to God's judgment on their royal claims. Pro-Neville, ostensibly non-dynastic rebels in 1469–70 publicly alleged supplicatory or defensive motives for their appearance in arms, but after Wakefield there were no more elaborate attempts by risers to negotiate over grievances before attacking. The sort of negotiations which took place in the later stages of the wars (e.g. in March 1470 and in 1486) were concerned with offers of pardon to rebels and terms of submission.[13]

The dynastic basis of confrontation gave an added incentive to kings and claimants to appear regally in arms, prepared to put themselves to divine judgment. In his proclamation against the Lancastrians who invaded the West Country in 1471, Edward IV emphasized his recent military success. His right to the throne had been made manifest 'by Victory given unto us by our Lord Almighty God in divers Battles against our Great Adversary Harry and his adherents'.[14] To stress his regality, Richard III – like Henry V at Agincourt – appeared crowned at Bosworth. Henry VII's reception of the crown, allegedly found discarded, on the field, and the degradation and exposure of Richard's corpse, were ritual occurrences, unmistakable signs of the divine will.[15] Henry VII was always prepared to ride in person against rebels, including comparatively insignificant ones, like those in Yorkshire in 1489 and in the West Country in 1497. But, perhaps with Richard's fate in mind, he always held back whilst the foreward went on ahead to probe the opposition.[16]

By the mid-fifteenth century, kings of England had for long habitually commissioned lieutenants to exercise royal rights in the waging of war, in the areas of their particular commands. Jurisdiction as lieutenants was conferred on commanders of expeditions abroad, on wardens of the Marches towards Scotland, and on the captain of Calais for its march, within their spheres of operation. The lieutenancies in the north conferred by Edward IV on Lord Fauconberg in 1461 and Warwick in 1462 were probably similar in terms, with powers to raise and discipline soldiers, lead them on expeditions and make local truces.[17] In March 1471, on Edward's invasion, Warwick apparently exercised general military command by virtue of a royal commission: he styled himself 'Lieutenant to the king our sovereign lord Henry VI'.[18] Those who patently lacked such justification for raising war in a land at peace sometimes invoked, besides the right of self-defence, the ideal of championship of those being oppressed: allusions were sometimes made to Robin Hood.[19] In 1471 the Bastard of Fauconberg, anxious perhaps not to be caught out in a deception by the governors of London, or not to give offence to eminent Lancastrians, carefully refrained from claiming to act as Henry VI's lieutenant. He styled himself clumsily 'Captain and leader of our liege lord King Henry's people in Kent'.[20]

Before moving on St Albans in 1455, Henry VI appointed the duke of Buckingham as constable and lieutenant to command the army. The appointment may have been considered especially appropriate because the duke held the office of constable of the realm, by hereditary right.[21] The constable and marshal of the realm were the king's chief customary lieutenants, exercising military justice as well as command.[22] In 1464 some of the Lancastrians captured around Hexham, and Sir Ralph Grey, were convicted of treason in the court of the constable, the earl of Worcester.[23] In 1495 Sir John Digby, the king's marshal, was commissioned to cite before himself and pronounce sentence on the rebels and aliens from Warbeck's invading force captured at Deal, and in 1497 he and Sir Robert Clifford were ordered to execute the office of constable and marshal with respect to the West Country rebels.[24] The constable and marshal of the realm, and the *ad hoc* constables and marshals appointed for particular campaigns, were responsible for trying offences against the code of discipline issued by the king or his lieutenant – the ordinances of war.[25] The importance of discipline was appreciated in English military circles. The author of *Knyghthode and Bataile* emphasized it,[26] and so did the anonymous author of the account of the Stoke campaign. At the start of this campaign Henry 'ordained by his proclamations, for good rule of his host'. At Leicester, by the archbishop of Canterbury's command, the royal proclamations were put in execution: 'And in especial voiding Common Women, and Vagabonds, for there were imprisoned great number of both. Wherefore there was more Rest in the King's Host, and the better Rule.' At Loughborough 'the Stocks and Prisons were reasonably filled with Harlots and Vagabonds. And after that were but few in the Host, unto the Time the field was done.' In 1489 Henry VII wrote to the earl of Oxford that the English army in Brittany 'blessed be God, hath among themself kept such love and accord that no manner of fray or debate hath been between them since the time of their departing out of this our Realm'.[27] In ordering the proclamation of disciplinary ordinances in 1487, Henry was probably following a standard practice in the Wars of the Roses. The key role of the marshal is reflected in his injunction that every man should endeavour to bring makers of quarrels and affrays into 'the marshal's ward to be punished according to their deserts'.[28] The task of disciplining the often hastily assembled, motley armies of the wars was probably eased by the royal presence – except perhaps in the case of the notoriously merciful Henry VI. Abbot Whethamstede recounted how, after the second battle of St Albans, he prevailed on Henry to issue a proclamation against plundering – which, the abbot said, was disobeyed. Malory's ideal king had no such problem.[29]

The roles of kings and magnates in decision-making about strategy and tactics in the wars are difficult to discern. Chroniclers tended to attribute initiatives uncritically to leading protagonists. Waurin's accounts of Somerset's consultations with Trollope, 'ung tres soubtil homme de guerre', are an unusual acknowledgment of an expert subordinate's influential counsel.[30] The commander, the author of *Knyghthode and Bataile* opined, must rely for counsel on 'olde and exercised sapience'.[31] Most chroniclers failed to stress the importance of councils of war – they were ill placed to find out what went on in these highly confidential and unrecorded sessions. The anonymous writer about the Stoke campaign knew something about the 'ordering of his Host' settled by the council which Henry VII summoned for the purpose. There are mentions of councils held in armies faced with a tricky set of circumstances – in Henry VI's on the road from Watford to St Albans in 1455, in Edward IV's after the landing in Holderness in 1471. Later that year the nobles in Margaret of Anjou's army 'deliberated in council how they might contrive most speedily to pass along the west coast'.[32] Waurin is almost the only writer who shows considerable appreciation of the vital significance of councils of war.[33]

I have argued above that, as kings, Edward IV and Richard III took a leading role in strategic and tactical decision-making, whereas Henry VII, lacking comparable field experience on his accession, tended to be a figurehead, relying heavily on the expertise of his skilled commanders.[34] There was one king to whom contemporaries did not usually attribute an active role in command – Henry VI. As we have seen, he delegated it in 1455, and may have done so in 1459 and 1460. Buckingham's refusal to allow Yorkist envoys to have direct dealings with the king at Northampton may have rested on his possession of a lieutenancy again.[35] But Henry's detachment from command, at least in the early campaigns, must not be exaggerated, though his interest may have been characteristically bookish. There is some evidence that he bestirred himself particularly in 1459 and 1460. As we have seen, his strenuous part in the 1459 campaign was officially emphasized, and Whethamstede pictures him on it pondering Vegetian doctrine. The author of *Knyghthode and Bataile* bestowed on Henry the title 'Tryumphatour' afterwards. The author, in order to provide counsel for Henry's war against the fugitive, attainted Yorkists, with Viscount Beaumont's encouragement presented the king with his updated translation of the classical writer Vegetius into English ballad form. Beaumont may have hoped to keep alive Henry's military interest by a work written, congenially, by a cleric professedly ignorant of warfare, and keen on religious symbolism.[36]

The traditional English preference was that noblemen should command armies and their constituent 'battles'.[37] The majority of English lieutenants in France during the Hundred Years War were of royal or noble birth, and captains of English-held coastal fortresses there were usually from either baronial or knightly families.[38] Peers expected to receive commands which they considered commensurate with their rank and honour. Lord Stanley allegedly requested Margaret of Anjou and the prince of Wales in 1459 'forasmuch as he understood, that he was had in jealousy, that he might have the vaward against the earl of Salisbury, and his fellowship'. When the prince, whose council considered that Stanley's force was too small to challenge Salisbury, ordered him to join up with the rest of the army, he disobeyed. In 1487, before Henry's army set forth to fight the rebels, 'the Earl of Oxford desired and besought the King to have the Conduct of the Forward, which the King granted, and accompanied him with many great courageous and lusty knights'.[39]

In a society which inculcated the divine sanction behind hierarchical proprieties, peers, especially those of royal blood and highest rank, were, next to kings, best fitted to secure obedience. The aristocratic Malory would probably have found commoners as well as gentlefolk who agreed that association with noble knights was most desirable and beneficial. His Sir Pryamus declared: 'I had liever have been torn with four wild horses than any yeoman had such a loose won of me, other else any page other pricker should win of me the prize in this field gotten.' Pryamus placed reliance in knights: 'harlots and henchmen will help us but a little, for they will hide them in haste for all their high words'.[40] Nobles were most likely to have funds or credit available to lay out on arms, armour, supplies and wages, and to have the patronage and prestige necessary to recruit large and skilled retinues. The political circumstances of the Wars of the Roses enhanced traditional needs for noble command: authoritative example and persuasion were needed to stir or restrain men in the potentially anarchical conditions of civil war. York in 1455 and Montague in 1470 were probably not alone in having to commit their personal prestige by cajoling their soldiers.[41] In the disturbed situation in London after the surrender of the Tower in 1460, Warwick's intervention was needed to restore order. He 'rode to the Tower, and there he made a proclamation, and all about the city, charging that no manner of person should not slay, nor steal, nor murder, on pain of death'.[42]

But there were precedents from the Hundred Years War for the elevation in command and rank of gentlefolk of lower status (esquires and gentlemen) and of men of non-gentle status. In 1460 John Harowe, mercer of London, was a commander of Yorkist companies (probably ones raised by the city) both there and at Wakefield.[43] The ten Lancastrian captains captured at Mortimer's Cross and executed at Hereford in 1461 were esquires. They included, besides a knight's son and the exalted Owen Tudor, father of the earls of Richmond and Pembroke, an estate steward, an esquire with an income of five marks *per annum*, and a lawyer.[44] Sir Edmund Fish, one of the Lancastrian leaders executed after the battle of Hexham in 1464, was a former tailor (*scissor*) of York.[45] The 'chief captain of the army' of southern rebels in 1483, Edward Peningham, like some of the other rebels, does not seem to have been a knight – perhaps he was selected for his military experience.[46]

Methods of recruitment and the nature of the forces recruited probably encouraged the appointment of captains with professional skills or influence over their non-noble neighbours, but of lesser or no gentility. Urban corporations, concerned that their well-equipped and -financed contingents should honour the town's name, were anxious to appoint captains for competence and trustworthiness, rather than because of their great name. William Tybeaudis, appointed as captain of Coventry's company to support the king, by the mayor and council in May 1455, was not accorded any title of rank in the city's records.[47] William Rokewode, who, the mayor of Norwich declared in January 1461, as a result of 'great labour and supplication' had consented to be captain of the city's company going to the king, was a local esquire.[48] In the early 1460s a Nottingham company intending to join Edward IV at York was captained by the city sheriff, Walter Hilton.[49] However, sophisticated burgesses are likely to have been especially concerned to avoid laughably incompetent captaincy by any of their number. The London author of *Gregory's Chronicle* parades his military expertise and mercilessly denigrates the noble Yorkist commanders at St Albans in 1461, but he also pours contempt on the butcher of Dunstable who had been beaten out of town by the northerners, and as a result of whose 'simple guiding' the contingent of which he was 'chiefest captain' was routed.[50]

The involvement of the commons threw up such rustic captains. According to Warkworth, after Edward landed at Ravenspur in 1471 there was a rising against him of 'all the country of Holderness', captained by a local parson, John Westerdale. The author of the *Arrivall* says that the leaders of the assembly, which was 6,000–7,000 strong, were a vicar and a gentleman called 'Martyn of the See'. Their indecisiveness illustrated the need for the superimposition of noble command on the captains of rural arrays, impressively organized as they often may have been.[51] Prejudice in favour of noble commanders was not just a noble prejudice. Vergil says that the West Country rebels of 1497 were at first captained by 'two men out of the dregs of the population, to wit Thomas Flammock, a lawyer, and Michael Joseph, a blacksmith'. The rebels, though not likely to have put the point with Vergil's elitist waspishness, would have agreed with him, for, when Lord Audley joined them, they acclaimed him as a leader.[52] In default of such leadership, Jack Cade, leading the rebels of 1450, bestowed on himself the aristocratic name of John Mortimer, dressed in the guise of a knight and kept table like one, with a gentleman to carve his meat.[53] Nevertheless, it is likely that noble commanders of armies were often highly dependent on rustic captains of low rank, as well as on captains of mercenaries and urban companies with little or no nobility. The constables of townships played a key role in recruiting and arraying contingents; they may often have been given command roles after contingents had joined up. Rustics were most likely to obey their richer neighbours, men possessed of or aspiring to gentility who knew them and spoke the same dialect. When Audley was in command of the rebels in 1497, he would have remained highly dependent on the mediation of rural captains such as Flammock and Joseph, for most of his men are unlikely to have spoken English, and he is unlikely to have spoken Cornish.

There is a little information about a few men of relatively low status who rose to high military influence through their expertise. One such was the esquire Lovelace. By February 1461 he 'had the reputation of being the most expert in warfare in England': according to Waurin, Warwick had made him captain of Kent and steward of his household, and given him command of the foreward in his campaigns.[54] He took the Yorkist guns and supplies through London northwards in October 1460 and was captured at Wakefield. But by the time the queen's northern army had reached St Albans, he was acting as captain of the Kentishmen in the Yorkist forward. He betrayed the Yorkists there by withdrawing the Kentishmen. A London chronicler had heard that this was because Lovelace had saved his life after Wakefield by taking an oath never to fight against the northerners. Waurin says that he confessed to Edward IV that he had been bought by the queen, who had promised to have him created earl of Kent with a suitable endowment.[55]

Another soldier who rose to high command in the wars was Andrew Trollope, who considered his advancement to knighthood after the second battle of St Albans to be a reward for valour, not a right of birth.[56] Master porter of Calais, he crossed with Warwick from Calais in 1459, and his desertion to the king, and persuasion of Calais soldiers to desert, was an important element in the royal success at Ludford Bridge.[57] According to Waurin, Warwick, having 'greater faith in him than any other', had put Trollope in command of the foreward, but he was suborned by a secret message from the duke of Somerset. Thereafter Waurin represents him as the duke's principal military counsellor, advising him over the defence of Guines and negotiations with Warwick for its surrender, and over his assembly of forces to support the queen, suggesting and helping to execute the plan which brought victory at Wakefield.[58]

For over a century before the outbreak of the Wars of the Roses, the crown's need to mount campaigns and maintain garrisons in the wars with the French, Scots and other foreigners had led to the development of well-tried methods of military recruitment and of the organization of companies. A principal method, the raising of companies by contracted captains, was used mainly in a modified form in the domestic conflicts, and continued to flourish in its normal form as a means of raising forces for service abroad into the sixteenth century. The crown negotiated with its lieutenants and captains to settle their individual terms of service and those of the retinue which they would be responsible for raising, leading, and paying the king's wages. The terms were embodied in indentures interchangeably sealed by the contracting parties. They contained variations on standard, largely traditional conditions – stipulations as to the nature and duration of the captain's and his men's service, as to their rates of pay, and obligations and entitlements regarding war profits and losses. The retinue captain, after his company had been mustered to the satisfaction of the king's or his lieutenant's officials, received a wages advance. He had responsibility for the pay and conduct of his retinue.[59]

In order to recruit the retinue which he had contracted to provide, the retinue captain made a series of indentures with knights and men-at-arms, very similar in form to those which he had made with the crown, stipulating their terms of service and those of the men-at-arms and archers which they often undertook to contribute to the retinue.[60] The captain is likely to have sought to find such subcontractors among kinsmen, servants, tenants and neighbours, and among soldiers with whom he had become acquainted on previous campaigns. Since peers and knights were often eager to contract with the crown as leaders of military retinues, they had an incentive to take permanent contingency measures, so that they would be well placed to respond to a call to arms. This was probably one of the main purposes which led magnates to contract for the service of retainers for life. Indentures were made between the parties stipulating that a knight or esquire was to do service to the lord in peace and war when required: the conditions on which he was to serve in war, such as reception of the king's wages, are often laid down in quite specific detail, reflecting terms usually found in the purely military, and temporary, war contracts. The life retainer, his indenture stated, was to receive a generally substantial annuity, in the form of fee or rent. Such retainers, who were frequently officers in the lord's household or in his estate administration, were presumably expected to provide key segments of his military retinues. Thus a characteristic organizational device of the Hundred Years War stimulated magnates' development of the means of constituting military companies.[61]

In the period of the Wars of the Roses there are numerous examples of customary indentures for paid military service made between the crown and its lieutenants and captains. For instance, there are the indentures contracted by Edward IV with the earl of Northumberland for the keeping of the East and Middle Marches in July 1470, and with Lord Howard as lieutenant and captain of the king's forces for the invasion of Scotland in 1481.[62] But the crown did not normally make this sort of contract with English subjects intending to serve in the wars. An exception is the contract made by Sir Baldwin Fulford in February 1460. He undertook to serve Henry VI at sea with 1,000 men, receiving royal wages for himself and his men for three months. The object of the expedition was to destroy Warwick's naval power based on Calais.[63] The contract reflected conventional aspects of the proposed service, more characteristic of foreign than domestic war. Fulford was undertaking a voluntary command, with a strong profit motive, which would take him to sea and perhaps overseas. He had several weeks in which to prepare and receive finance for his expedition.

In many of the campaigns in the Wars of the Roses, the swift defensive measures required by the crown precluded the negotiation and fulfilment of such elaborate terms of service, which the frequently sudden and unexpected turn of events might render unrealistic. Moreover, when there was rebellion the king was not going into the market-place to negotiate for his nobles' voluntary proffers for a command. He was peremptorily and desperately demanding, on pain of allegiance, whatever support subjects could muster in the time available – an obligation especially pressing on peers, members of the royal household, and other livery-holders of the crown. Even when there was time to commission a commander – in the case of domestic sieges – he was not contracted as for service against foreign enemies, though provision to cover expenses was probably made for him.[64]

Wages were indeed the fuel of warfare: compelled for service or not, men hoped to receive wages from one source or another. The Yorkist leaders of 1459, according to the Act of Attainder passed against them, rebelled at Ludford 'with other Knights and people, such as they had blinded and assembled by wages, promises, and other exquisite means'.[65] The capture of William Tailboys near Newcastle in 1464 with the Lancastrian war-chest of 3,000 marks was a crushing blow to the cause. Henry VI 'had ordained harness and ordnance enough, but the men would not go one foot with him till they had money. And they waited daily and hourly for money that this Tailboys should have sent unto them or brought it.' Instead, the money went to the men of the opposing commander, Montague: it 'was a very wholesome salve' for their wearisome labours.[66] The 1483 revolt may have attracted support because Margaret Beaufort's agent Reginald Bray 'had made up no small sum of money to pay soldiers' wages withall'.[67] But when kings peremptorily summoned nobles to bring retinues for service in the wars, they had no formal obligation to provide the latter with wages for their men, and often no means of doing so. Nevertheless, it was unrealistic to expect individuals to provide expensive service, digging deep into their pockets for their companies' wage bills, without inducement. During the crisis of Edward V's reign, on 11 June 1483, Richard of Gloucester wrote to Lord Neville, asking for his support with a military retinue: 'And, my lord, do me now service, as ye have always before done, and I trust now so to remember you as shall be the making of you and yours.'[68] More tartly than usual, this distilled what is likely to have been an essential spirit in the generation of military support in the wars. Henry VII, thanking Sir Robert Plumpton in 1491 for his part in suppressing Yorkshire commotions, needed only to hint at royal practice: 'we . . . shall not forget the disposition you have been of in that behalf, etc.'.[69] Writing 'in haste' from Knaresborough on 17

September 1497 to his cousin Sir William Calverley, Sir Harry Wentworth relayed news of Warbeck's landing and urged his cousin to prepare a company for the king's service 'for the which I doubt not but his highness shall give you thanks according'.[70]

There are numerous examples of royal cash remunerations for past military service in the wars. Sir John Clay received his costs after serving Edward in the north in the campaign of 1462–3.[71] Edward, after his victories in 1471, ordered payment of '£100 by way of reward' to Lord Grey of Codnor, for the costs which he had incurred in 'attending in his own person upon us in this our great journey as in bringing unto us a great number of men defensibly arrayed at his cost and charge'.[72]

Rewards sometimes took the form of life-grants of offices, annuities and estates, and of perpetual grants of property. The long-term return on some of these rewards represented a potentially large profit on the individual's military investment. A factor determining participation must have been the noble's ability and preparedness to lay out a large sum in the hope of winning a lasting income. The esquire Lovelace dreamt of getting the earldom of Kent – but Lord Fauconberg actually did so.[73] The inducement of large-scale profit was as important in getting men to fight in the Wars of the Roses as in the Hundred Years War, though the mechanics of compensation and reward were markedly dissimilar. Indeed, pressure for compensation and reward, particularly on kings who in the early stages of the wars were short of ready cash, led to the employment of a means of gratification which was a key factor in perpetuating rebellion. The trend was initiated by Henry VI's government after the 1459 forfeitures. Nobles who had given unpaid service against the rebels were rewarded with grants of their lands; lesser men received appurtenant fees and offices.[74] These grants – and the similar ones made by Edward IV after his attainders of 1461 – created a new dimension to the wars: they became recurrent flare-ups between claimants to inheritances as well as to the crown. The earl of Pembroke and Lord Roos, who surrendered at Bamburgh in 1462, did not enter into Edward's allegiance, since they were unable to receive back their lands – presumably because he had granted them to his supporters.[75] Richard III's supporters eagerly occupied Buckingham's lands when he rebelled in 1483, for the king had already promised them ducal wealth.[76] The exiled Henry Tudor's pledge to marry Edward IV's daughter may have been seen as some sort of guarantee that his accession would not lead to an upheaval of the existing landed settlement. Indeed, in his first parliament there was bitter but unavailing opposition to his determination to date the start of the reign from the day before Bosworth, threatening with the penalties of treason any who had taken arms against him. But Henry soon showed his sensitivity to the need to preserve landed stability, in his attempts to reconcile past and potential opponents, and provision of guarantees against forfeiture for all those who supported the crown against rebellion.[77]

We have seen that the nature of the domestic conflicts precluded resort to customary forms of military contract between crown and gentlefolk. The raising of many noble retinues probably stemmed from verbal, sometimes secret, agreements between kings and their noble allies, perhaps sworn on the Sacrament. But agreements for foreign help doubtless continued to be embodied in written contracts. Treaties were made with foreign princes, such as the rulers of France, Scotland and Brittany, which contained promises of aid. The making of written contracts and the provision of wage advances are likely to have been standard practices in gaining the services of reputable foreign mercenary captains and their companies.[78] The text of a distinctly idiosyncratic agreement for foreign noble help survives. On 22 November 1462, at Edinburgh, Henry VI and George Douglas, earl of Angus, sealed an indenture by which Angus was retained to pass with the king into England against the rebels. Within a month of recovering his realm, Henry promised to grant Angus a duchy with lands to the value of 2,000 marks in the north of England. He would be free to hold it in time of war between England and Scotland, and, when fighting in support of the king of Scots, to send up to twenty Scotsmen to govern his lands in England, where they would be treated as if they were Englishmen.[79] The indenture reveals well the kind of ambition which may have animated English as well as foreign nobles' participation. But it is a mad agreement. The implementation of the grant under a restored Henry would have been likely to provoke new domestic conflicts, with greater Scottish involvement.

To resist rebellion, as we have seen, kings perforce relied heavily on the support of influential individuals whom they trusted to bring retinues. Among those whom they turned to were the men whose services in peace they had retained, especially the leading denizens and officers of their households. Under the pressure of domestic conflict, royal military needs became a factor in their retaining policies, and the satisfaction of these needs a more pressing obligation of royal retainers. In 1459 the queen was attempting to rally provincial support; she 'allied unto her all the knights and squires of Cheshire' and had her little son distribute a 'livery of Swans' among them. Some of the recipients were probably among 'the Queen's gallants' who were soon to suffer heavy losses at Blore Heath.[80] At the second battle of St Albans, according to 'Gregory', 'The substance that got that field were household men and feed men.'[81] After Edward's accession, some former members of the Lancastrian household showed tenacious dynastic loyalty, doubtless inspired partly by the conviction that only the reinstatement of King Henry could lead to the recovery of their lost offices and annuities. In 1462 his former steward of the household Sir Thomas Tuddenham, intensely unpopular in some Norfolk circles, was executed for his part in Oxford's conspiracy.[82] A number of former household servants were captured in and after the battle of Hexham in 1464 and executed.[83] A tenacious loyalist was Robert Whittingham, esquire, receiver-general to the prince of Wales in 1456.[84] He was with Somerset at Guines in 1459–60, was knighted by the prince after the second battle of St Albans, in 1461, and later in the year was plotting in France in the Lancastrian interest, for which he died fighting at Tewkesbury in 1471.[85] Richard Tunstall of Thurland (Lancs.) was luckier. In 1452 he was appointed for life as one of Henry's four esquires of the body; in 1457 he was the king's knight and carver, and in 1459–60 his chamberlain.[86] He was with the Lancastrian invaders in Northumberland in November 1462, and took part in the epic defence of Harlech castle.[87] Pardoned by Edward IV in 1468, during Henry's Readeption he was again high in Lancastrian favour: in October 1470, when royal chamberlain, he received a grant made verbally by Henry. The restored Edward immediately pardoned him and made him a king's knight, and he was to serve Richard III and Henry VII as knight of the body.[88]

Edward IV and his immediate successors placed particular reliance on the ability of their retainers to give military as well as political support.[89] In a commission of array by signet letter sent to Coventry corporation (9 February 1470), Edward commanded military service in person or by substitute from all those holding offices of his or the queen's gift with wages of 3*d.* or more a day.[90] On 5 August following, Sir John Paston wrote that the king had 'sent for his feedmen to come to him' to put down the northern rebels.[91] Advancing south from Yorkshire in 1471, Edward rallied his household men. At Barnet many of his 'menial servants' were slain.[92] In 1473 he relied heavily on John Fortescue, esquire of the body, and other household men to oppose the earl of Oxford in the West Country.[93] At Bosworth loyal retainers probably charged with Richard and defended him against odds: Valera says that 'the majority of those who loyally served the king were killed'.[94] Henry VII, according to Vergil, instituted a bodyguard of about 200 retainers, who were among those dispatched from York against rebels in 1486.[95] According to Trevisan's memorialist (1498):

> the present King Henry has appointed certain military services, to be performed by some of his own dependants and familiars [*suoi domestici, e famigliari*], who he knows can be trusted on any urgent occasion; and can be kept on a much smaller number of fees [than *milites* can].[96]

In the 1495 parliament it was enacted that all those in receipt of royal 'grants and gifts of offices fees and annuities', having the obligation to give military attendance in person on the king, were to forfeit their grants if they defaulted, unless licenced not to attend, or sick.[97] In 1504 this Act was extended to include all those holding grants of property from the crown, with the proviso that all those in these categories giving attendance 'shall have the King's wages from the time of coming from his House toward the King when they come to the King, and from the King home again at the time of their departing . . . and whilst they be with the King's Grace to have also the King's wages'.[98]

After the battle of Tewkesbury, when Edward was at Coventry preparing for a new campaign (May 1471), he 'forgot not to send from thence his messengers, with writings, all about the countries near adjoining, to such in especial as he trusted best that they would do him service'.[99] Some examples of royal summonses to individuals – not all royal retainers – survive. They seem to reflect a trend towards more insistent, and more elaborately specific requests, and a tendency for kings to make prior agreement with individuals about the nature of the support which they would provide in emergencies. On 13 March 1461, by signet letter dated at York, Henry VI wrote to Sir William Plumpton outlining the 'earl of March's' misdeeds: 'we therefore pray and also straitly charge you that anon upon sight hereof' you come as soon as possible 'with all such people as ye may make defensibly arrayed' to Henry 'as ye love the surety of our person, the weal of yourself, and of all our true and faithful subjects'.[100] Thomas Stonor received a signet letter from Edward IV dated at Coventry, 3 April 1470, informing him of the flight of Clarence and Warwick westwards, and of the royal intent to pursue them and suppress their traitorous purpose: 'Wherefore we will and strictly charge you that immediately after the sight of these our letters ye array you, with such a fellowship on horseback in defensible array as ye goodly can make, to come unto us wheresoever ye shall understand that we then shall be.'[101] Edward's signet letter to William Swan, gentleman, dated at York 7 September following, charged him to array with a fellowship 'upon the faith and liegance that ye bear unto us'. Since the strategic circumstances differed from those of the previous April, Edward did not specify that Swan's company must be horsed, and, in anticipation of a landing in Kent or nearby by Clarence and Warwick, commanded him to be ready to act on several alternatives, in accordance with the information he might receive about rebel movements.[102] In contrast to these summonses, Edward's signet letter to Henry Vernon, esquire (Tewkesbury, 7 May 1471), specified the size of Vernon's company; he was charged 'as our trust is in you' to bring twenty men, defensibly arrayed, to meet the king for his entry into Coventry. But more urgent circumstances made the king less specific and more peremptory. Edward's letter to Vernon from Worcester the following day desired and charged him to bring 'such fellowship defensibly arrayed as ye goodly can make' immediately to meet the king – to resist the rebellious commons – on his allegiance 'and forfeiture of all that ye may forfeit'.[103] Richard III's signet letter dated Beskwood Lodge, 11 August 1485, willing and strictly charging Vernon, squire for his body, to attend the king with a company to resist the malice of Henry Tudor, is also insistent on the penalty of forfeiture. Vernon is to attend 'without failing, all manner excuses set apart'. The king in fact had made prior agreement with Vernon as to the numbers and equipment of the company that he should bring at need: he was to come 'with such number as ye have promised unto us sufficiently horsed and harnessed'. Richard's desire to have his followers' strength prepared is reflected in a list in the duke of Norfolk's papers, dated 26 February 1484, giving some particulars of the 1,000 men 'that my Lord hath granted to the King'. Men were listed under the duke's lordships 'to be ready at all times at my Lord's pleasure': individuals who had promised to come, with or without men, were listed, some with the proviso 'at my Lords cost'.[104]

Though, in a military summons to Vernon, Henry VII did not allude to any prior agreement about the nature of the fellowship that Vernon was willed and desired to bring, his letter to Sir Robert Plumpton dated Sheen, 28 May 1491, shows that he, too, was concerned to have companies organized by trusted gentlemen ready for use in emergencies:

> We therefore, intending to provide for the time to come, desire you that forthwith and by as wise wages as ye can, ye put yourself in a surety of your menial servants and tenants, and to know assuredly how many of them will take your part in serving us according to your and their duties foresaid. When ye have demeaned the matter in this wise, which we would that you did as above with all diligence, then we pray you to certify our cousin, the Earl of Surrey, of the number of such assured men, etc.[105]

In a letter to Sir Gilbert Talbot (July 1493), he willed him to have a company in readiness to resist the malice of Margaret of Burgundy. Henry was highly specific about the composition of Talbot's company. It was to be horsed, eighty strong, 'whereof we desire you to make as many spears, with their custrells [attendants], and demi-lances, well horsed as ye can furnish, and the remainder to be archers and bills, ye be thoroughly appointed and ready to come upon a day's warning for to do us service of war in this case'. The king laid down the rates of pay which Talbot was to receive for different categories of soldier.[106] Thus Richard III and Henry VII appear to have made greater efforts than their predecessors to constitute a select force in readiness to oppose rebellion or invasion, consisting of private companies commanded by trusted gentlefolk, about whose terms of service and composition there was a degree of prior agreement.

In 1497 Henry expected Talbot to bring to his aid promptly a company of 120 men. The need of gentlefolk, especially magnates, to widen potential military as well as political support because of the wars may have encouraged the habit of breaking the 1399 statute enacting that no one 'shall use or give any livery or sign of company'. In 1468 it was enacted that all statutes and ordinances hitherto made against the giving or receiving of liveries and badges should be kept. Great numbers of people were said to be daily breaking them. The grant of liveries or badges was prohibited: no one was to retain another except his menial servant or a lawyer by any writing, oath or promise.[107]

But a body of evidence indicates that one leading participant in the wars, Edward's chamberlain Lord Hastings, retained by indenture for services for life in peace and war, partly as a means of forming companies to participate in the wars. There survive sixty-nine indentures which he entered into in the period 1461–83 with sixty-seven out of the total of two peers and eighty-eight knights, esquires and gentlemen whom he is known to have retained. According to Professor Dunham's analysis of these contracts, the retainer commonly agreed to ride and go with Hastings, to aid and succour him, and to take his part and quarrel against all others, his liege lord the king excepted. The retainer was to come, upon reasonable warning, with as many men defensibly arrayed as he could assemble, or as accorded with his rank. In forty-two contracts, the obligation to attend Hastings was restricted to English soil – a restriction indicating their relevance to the Wars of the Roses. In all but a few cases, Hastings was required to pay the costs and expenses of the retainer and his company for their service.[108]

Other peers and gentlefolk may not have reacted to contemporary· domestic political and military stresses with such a widespread making of life-contracts. Some apparently preferred to make relatively few contracts and to grant fees on a less permanent basis.[109] The nature of Hastings's indentures may reflect exceptional features in his political and military career. Something of a parvenu, he came to exercise great influence in some Midland shires, and needed to build up networks of connection: by far the greatest number of his known retainers, thirty-two out of ninety, were from Derbyshire, though his principal family estates were in Leicestershire. Identifying his political fortunes closely with Edward's, he habitually fought for him, and consequently required ready military support, for which he was well placed to guarantee remuneration.[110]

There are some surviving letters from magnates summoning

individuals to bring military support in the wars. Presumably the recipients had made verbal or written promises to provide such support, or it was hoped that they would do so because of their tenure of offices, fees and land grants. The responses to the letters provide some indications as to whether expectations were fulfilled. Henry Vernon, esquire, an officer of the duke of Clarence, received the first of a series of summonses from his master, by signet letter dated Bristol, 15 March 1471. He was to 'see that as well all your tenants and servants as ours in those parts be ready upon an hour's warning to wait upon us in def[ensible] array whensoever we send for you and them'. The following day, from Wells, the duke reiterated this request, emphasizing the importance of the preparations in the light of rumours of Edward IV's imminent invasion, and on 23 March, when sure news of it had arrived, he desired and prayed Vernon to join him immediately with as large a defensibly arrayed company as possible, on the king's service, and that ye fail not hereof as our special trust is in you'.[111] But two days later Warwick dispatched a letter to Vernon with news of Edward's landing, willing him to join him with a company at Coventry 'as my vray singular trust is in you and as I mowe do thing to your weal or worship hereafter'. The earl tellingly added the autograph postscript: 'Henry I pray you fail not now as ever I may do for you.' However, Vernon must have failed either Warwick or Clarence — possibly both of them. Though he sent information to the duke about Edward's movements, Clarence had to send further requests to him for military service in similar urgent terms from Malmesbury on 30 March and Burford on 2 April. Vernon did not take part in the battle of Tewkesbury: Edward IV's signet letters to him (7–8 March) reinforced one from Clarence desiring him to join king and duke with soldiers for the latter's retinue on the northern expedition projected after the battle. Writing on 6 May from Tewkesbury, with Edward's weight behind him, Clarence had adopted a more peremptory tone with Vernon: 'we desire and for your weal advise you, and also in my said lord's [the king's] name charge you, to dispose you to come and attend upon us'. But, summoning him again four days later, Clarence accepted the reasons reported to him for Vernon's failure to attend, and assured him of ducal favour on compliance:

> letting you weet that it hath been reported to us that ye have heretofor put you in devoir to have come to us if ye had mought, wherof we thank you, the matters and causes of the let and impediment of your coming now ceased, blessed be God. . . . [The summons follows.] And ye shall find us your good lord, and thereof ye shall not need to doubt in any wise.[112]

The group of summonses received by Vernon provide a unique

insight into the pressures for military support on one influential esquire, and the difficulties experienced by lords in mobilizing a retainer or well-wisher in a doubtful politico-military situation. Not all other surviving summonses by magnates were complied with. On 11 October 1483 Viscount Lovell wrote to his 'cousin' Sir William Stonor about the arrangement approved by the king that their companies should go together, Stonor's men in Lovell's livery. Lovell held out in return promise of his future goodwill – but Stonor joined the rebels.[113] The day before Lovell addressed his summons to Stonor, the duke of Norfolk wrote to a well-to-do East Anglian neighbour, his 'welbeloved friend' John Paston, requesting his help to defend London with a company of 'six tall fellows in harness', promising 'ye shall not lose your labour, that knoweth God'.[114] In 1485 he prayed Paston to meet him at Bury, in order to join the king,

and that ye bring with you such company of tall men as ye may goodly make at my cost and charge . . . and I pray you ordain them jackets of my livery, and I shall content you at your meeting with me. Your lover, J. Norffolk.[115]

Since Paston was appointed sheriff of Norfolk and Suffolk soon after Bosworth, it is unlikely that he complied.[116]

It seems, then, that it was not uncommon for lords (like kings) to be disappointed in domestic emergencies by the gentlefolk they had trusted and favoured. Kings could, indeed, call on a firmer obligation to allegiance – but there is no evidence that they resorted to forfeiture as a penalty for its non-fulfilment. Both kings and nobles punished failure by loss of office, fees, goodwill. Because Sir William Skipwith did not comply with York's summons to join his army in 1455, the duke revoked his offices and annuities. But in 1459, after York's forfeiture, they were restored to Skipwith by the crown.[117] This illustrates limitations on the crown's and nobles' ability to punish the unwilling. They were reliant on gentlefolk to extend their local political influence: if they withheld gracious lordship, there was likely to be someone else eager to step in with it. Clarence in 1471 was being realistic when he accepted Vernon's excuses with a good grace, despite the fact that Vernon was failing him at a crucial stage of his career. For king and lords, the key to gaining the military support of substantial followers was the offer of inducements rather than the threat of disfavour.

There was one other principal means of raising forces in the later Middle Ages, besides the recruitment of companies by individuals. Commissions of array were used more especially to provide for the defence of the realm, as well as for expeditions abroad. This system had its roots in Anglo-Saxon obligations owed by men of shire and borough to give armed support to the king and his officers. In the thirteenth century, able-bodied men between the ages of sixteen and sixty were sworn to allegiance, grouped under the constables of cities and boroughs, hundreds and vills, and were obliged to have adequate arms. They were summoned and mustered to serve under the sheriff or regional constable, and followed his orders to hunt down criminals or rebels, or guard the coasts against invasion. The Statute of Winchester (1285), which laid down the types of arms which possessors of chattels or rents of various worth were to have in readiness for service, remained the basic legislation on military obligation until the sixteenth century.[118]

The systematic use of commissions of array to assemble selected communal recruits for expeditions out of the realm, as well as to supply the backbone of local defences, was developed by Edward I for his Welsh and Scottish wars, and exploited by Edward II and Edward III for their commitments abroad. Under Edward III, arrayers were appointed to raise a company for a French campaign within a single shire or borough. The shire arrayers were usually gentlefolk – particularly knights – with some military experience. The number of men whom they were asked to raise varied according to the size of the county.[119] The sort of instructions which they received were to choose, test and array, ensuring that recruits were suitably clothed, equipped and mounted,[120] and had received pay. Thus communities were expected to supply some finance and, in some circumstances, equipment and weapons.[121] Sheriffs, bailiffs and other officers as well as the faithful men of the communities were bidden by writ to assist the arrayers. Constables of townships probably had some responsibility for securing recruits, ensuring that they were adequately set up, and levying aid from their neighbours. The constables may have also made preliminary groupings of the men into scores and hundreds (*vintaines* and *centaines*) for inspection by the arrayers.

The political weakness of the crown after Edward III's accession in 1327, and his increasing dependence, for waging the French wars which commenced in 1337, on political and financial support from parliament, induced royal concessions in answer to the communities' protests at harsh exploitation by the crown of this system of military obligation. A statute of 1327 conceded that levies were to arm at their own expense only in the manner laid down by the Statute of Winchester, and were not obliged to provide the elaborate and expensive arms which Edward II had on occasion specified. The ancient obligation of men to provide unpaid service was not to be stretched: they were not to have to go out of their counties at their own costs except in the case of the sudden coming of foreign enemies into the realm. From 1343 men could gain exemptions from service by payment of fines. In 1344 it was enacted that those chosen to go on the king's service outside England were to receive his wages from the day on which they left the county in which they were chosen until the day they re-entered it. But for service out of the country in other parts of the realm, the community remained obliged to provide wages. In 1402, at the request of the commons, the statutes of 1327 and 1344 were re-enacted, as was one of 1352 which curbed royal demands on individuals to pay soldiers' costs.

Therefore the kings of the later fifteenth century could turn for defence against rebels to a traditional, well-tried, universally accepted and understood system of raising troops from communities in general. Many commissions to counter internal rebellion and invasion during the Wars of the Roses were of the customary kind, letters patent addressed to a group of influential, reliable military gentlefolk in a shire, or to the ruling elite in a city or borough. Such were the commissions issued in December 1459, intended to prepare forces to resist invasions by the attainted Yorkist lords.[122] But domestic emergencies often led to less conventional, less cumbersome authorization and greater reliance on influential individuals to control arrays. According to William Paston, it was being said that Henry VI, on his way to London in January 1460, 'reareth the people as he come'.[123] In 1471 the Lancastrian forces in the West Country raised men as they moved, presumably by virtue of the prince of Wales's commission of lieutenancy.[124] Kings sent privy seal or signet letters requesting cities and boroughs to dispatch companies, such as those sent by Edward IV to the mayor of Coventry under his signet in July 1469.[125] They turned too to trusted noble friends. In February 1460, to guard against Yorkist invasion, Henry VI's half-brother the earl of Pembroke was empowered to call up all Welsh lieges.[126] In Jamuary 1461, when preparations were being made to resist the queen's advance on London, Sir John Wenlock had his commission to suppress her sympathizers strengthened by the power to call together the lieges of Hertfordshire and five other shires north of the city.[127] The following month, the earl of March was empowered to call together, to resist the rebels, the lieges of Bristol, Staffordshire, Shropshire, Herefordshire, Gloucestershire, Worcestershire, Somerset and Dorset.[128] Two letters in the Paston correspondence show magnates acting under a commission of array addressed to them. In March 1471, the earl of Oxford, citing his commission for Norfolk to resist Edward, wrote to five individuals commanding them to come 'with as many men as ye may goodly make'.[129] In October 1485 the duke of Suffolk wrote to John Paston as sheriff of Norfolk and Suffolk, reciting the ducal commission to array received from Henry VII, and ordering Paston to have proclamations made 'in all possible haste' warning 'all manner men able to do the King service, as well knights, esquires, and gentlemen, as townships and hundreds, as well within franchise and liberties as without' to be prepared to attend on king and duke when required. The promptness with which commissions were expected to be fulfilled is reflected in Suffolk's stipulation that the arrayed men were to be ready at all times upon an hour's warning, and his information to Paston that his letter was dispatched 'this same day we received the King's commission at four after noon'.[130]

The need to rely on individual nobles to enforce commissions posed dangers. They might use the arrayed men against instead of in support of the author of the commission. In 1460 Lord Neville raised men under a commission from the duke of York and subsequently joined with them in the attack on him.[131] Even when a lord could not exhibit a commission, there was a danger that he might hoodwink men into believing that he was ordering them to serve at the king's command. Warwick's letter of 28 June 1469 to his 'servants and wellwillers within the city of Coventry' disingenuously asserted that he wished them to array to accompany him in answer to the king's summons for attendance against the northern rebels – when in fact the latter were acting *for* Warwick. Edward was to realize that deceits were being practised against him, for in a signet letter commanding a Coventry array dated 10 July he ordered that

> in no wise ye make any rising or assemblies with any person
> whatsoever he be, nor suffer any of our subjects within our City of
> Coventry to do upon the said pain, without that we under our privy
> seal or signet or sign manual command you to do.[132]

In 1470 Clarence and Warwick perverted the purposes of the commissions which they had received from Edward. According to his proclamation of 24 March,

> his said Highness authorised them by his commission under his great
> seal to assemble his subjects in certain shires, and them to have
> brought to his said Highness. . . . [they] under colour thereof, falsely
> and traitorously provoked and stirred, as well by their writings as
> otherwise, Sir Robert Welles . . . to continue the said insurrections
> and rebellions, and to levy war against him, as they, by the same, so
> did with banners displayed.[133]

Fear of their misuse of the commissions of array which he had issued was probably the spur to his proclamations of 13 March commanding

> that none of his subjects presume, nor take upon him, to rise, nor
> make any assembly or gathering, by reason of any of the said
> commissions or writings, nor by moving, stirring, writing, or
> commandment made, or hereafter to be made, by any person or
> persons of what estate, degree, or condition soever he be of, lest that

it be by the King's commission, Privy Seal, or writing under his signet, of new to be made after this the 13 day of March.[134]

Nevertheless, later in the year Marquess Montague destroyed Edward's rule by misusing his commission of array.[135]

Such notorious treacheries may have made some men wary. In 1487 Sir Edmund Bedingfield had difficulty in persuading Norfolk gentlemen to assist him in executing a commission of array received by the earl of Oxford, until he could authenticate it:

it was thought I ought not to obey no copy of the commission, without I had the same under wax, wherein hath been great arguement, which I understood by report a fortnight past, and that caused me to send unto my lord [Oxford] to have the very commission, which he sent me.[136]

Commissions of array indicate the powers granted to arrayers, and provide some information about the recruitment and nature of the forces raised, and their intended spheres of operations. The arrayers in Westmorland in June 1463 were authorized to summon all lieges, who were to array according to their degree. The arrayers were to hold a muster and ensure that the men were continually prepared to serve. On receiving a royal summons, they were to lead the shire levy to the king or others, and were to exercise powers of command over it on the journey. All sheriffs, mayors, bailiffs, constables and other officers within and without liberties (areas of private jurisdiction) were to assist the arrayers in their tasks.[137] In May 1464 sheriffs of sixteen counties were instructed to have proclamations made ordering every man between the ages of sixteen and sixty to prepare to attend Edward IV at a day's notice 'well and defensibly arrayed'.[138] The commission for Cornwall to guard against invasion threats (July 1468) specified that 'hobelars' (light horsemen) and archers were to be arrayed, and that arrayers were to divide them into companies of a thousand, subdivided into hundreds and twenties.[139] Since the direction of threats was often uncertain in the wars, arrayers had on occasion to prepare the levies for a variety of contingencies. A commission for South Wales and its Marches to guard against the return of Edward IV (January 1471) specified that the levy was to repel invasions of particular regions, suppress rebels there or go to the king or his deputies.[140]

Writs to the sheriffs of Kent and Sussex, the mayor of Canterbury, and the constable of Dover and warden of the Cinque Ports, dated August 1492, commanded:

all and every his subjects inhabited within this his shire of Kent, having harness of his own and being of ability in his person to serve his highness if need be, that they and every one of them prepare themself to be ready in their said harness, upon an hour warning, to serve our said sovereign lord at his wages.

Constables of hundreds were to make search for all inhabitants 'of ability and harnessed to serve' and to certify the king of their names and apparel without delay.[141] The workings of the array system are more fully revealed in a writ under Henry VII's sign manual to the chancellor, dated November 1509, which was intended as a basis for writs ordering the shires communities to overhaul the system. Those able in person and goods to serve the king were to prepare 'horse and harness competent, and weapons convenient' for themselves and, if their 'degree, power and substance' warranted it, for two or three more. Those wealthy enough to serve, but unable to do so because of sickness or old age, were to provide, equipped, one, two or more soldiers. Sheriffs, bailiffs and constables of cities, towns and boroughs, and constables of hundreds, were to warn every city, town, borough, village and hamlet within their offices to prepare one or more able men harnessed and weaponed. All the prospective soldiers were to remain during the following months ready to appear and muster before the commissioners of array whom the king would commission, at the time and place appointed by them.[142]

Features of this system as it worked in the Wars of the Roses may be reflected in a hostile account of the Bastard of Fauconberg's levy in Kent in 1471, raised by authority allegedly received from the earl of Warwick, Henry VI's lieutenant:

> Other of Kentish people that would right fain have sitten still at home, and not to have run into the danger of such rebellion . . . for fear of death, and other great menaces, and threatenings, were compelled, some to go with the bastard, in their persons; such specially, as were able in their persons if they had array, and might not wage to such as would go, they were compelled, by like force, to lend them their array, and harness; and such as were unharnessed, aged, and unable, and of honour, they were compelled to send men waged, or to give money wherewith to wage men to go to the said bastard's company.[143]

It may be that other arrays during the wars were as unwelcome as this, involving what was perceived as compulsion and extortion. Proclamations ordering an array in May 1464 enjoined obedience 'under the Pain that shall fall thereupon'.[144] A hostile writer alleged that Warwick, as Henry VI's lieutenant in 1471, 'whereas he could not arraise the people with goodwill, he straitly charged them to come forth upon pain of death'.[145] The comprehensive powers to array throughout the realm granted to the prince of Wales in March 1471 threatened the disobedient with the penalties of treason.[146] Richard III is said by a hostile writer to have dispatched letters in 1485 threatening those who failed to respond to his summonses with forfeiture and death.[147]

The provision of wages for the levy must have been one of the most widespread and resented burdens of the arraying system. The account of the Bastard's recruitment in the *Arrivall* implies that he expected the Kentishmen arrayed to have their wages provided by themselves or their neighbours. Chamberlains' accounts in urban records often state sums provided for the wages of companies raised: urban sources sometimes record in detail the raising of taxes for military wages in the wars and how they were allotted.[148] A letter written by John Paston in 1461 gives information about the 'waging' of Norfolk levies summoned to resist the northerners:

> most people out of this country have taken wages . . . the towns and the country that have waged them shall think they be discharged . . . . And yet it will be thought right strange of them that have waged people to wage any more, for every town hath waged and sent forth, and are ready to send forth, as many as they did when the King [Henry VI] sent for them before the field at Ludlow [in 1459].[149]

The chronicler Warkworth, discussing the reasons for Edward's loss of the crown in 1470, lists among the common people's discontents the fact that throughout his reign they had 'at yet at every battle to come far out their countries at their own cost'.[150]

Knowledge of the array system is handicapped by a dearth of information about its local organization. There survives a partially defective roll of a muster held at Bridport (Dorset) on 4 September 1457 before the town's two bailiffs and two constables. This may have had some connection with a commission issued on 16 December following, according to which arrayers delivered indentures into the Exchequer, certifying how many archers shires and ten cities were to supply. The respective totals were 10,993 (254 for Dorset) and 1,602.[151] The Bridport Muster Roll lists over 180 individuals with the 'harness' which they presented for inspection, and a note of the additional equipment which some were ordered to produce, often within a fortnight, under pain of fine. No harness is listed after at least sixty names — perhaps because these were absentees or for some reason incapable of complying. Just under two-thirds out of about 100 of those who presented arms had either a bow and sheaf of arrows (or half a sheaf or a specified number of arrows). Seventy or so were equipped with parts or the whole of what seems to have been the standard full complement for an arrayed man-at-arms — a sallet (helmet), jack (reinforced tunic, not unlike a modern flak jacket), sword (the commonest weapon at the muster after bow and arrow), buckler and dagger. Ten had the full equipment; about a dozen lacked buckler and dagger. A few duplicated one or more items: one man had three sallets. With seeming arbitrariness – but presumably in accordance with assessments of property and wealth – some who lacked items of the standard harness were ordered to provide one or more of them, such as a sallet and jack, or a dagger; bucklers, less in evidence, were not *de rigueur*. Some who paraded sallets nevertheless had to provide an additional one.

A sprinkling of other sorts of weapons were produced, often supplementing bows, swords and daggers – there were poleaxes, glaives, spears, axes, custills (two-edged daggers), bills, staves and a hanger (short sword). One man, in addition to a bow, twelve arrows and a sword, had a gun, but despite this unique weapon he had to double his bundle of arrows. There were also odd items of armour, some possibly cannibalized from gentlefolk's superior armours – habergeons (jackets of mail or scale armour), pairs of gauntlets and brigandines (body armour of metal on material), leg harness and a kettle hat. At least two arrayed men brought a pavis – a large shield, probably of a sort fixed on the ground in front of an archer. The bailiffs' and constables' consciousness that more pavises were needed is reflected in their orders to individuals to provide them, in two cases with a lead mallet, presumably intended to hammer pavises into place, or protective stakes set up in front of archers.

The Bridport Muster Roll gives the impression that the leaders of the community were determined that well-equipped archers should be provided. There was a good stock of harness among the inhabitants: some, indeed, were excellently equipped, such as the man who had two sallets, two jacks, three bows and sheaves, two poleaxes, two glaives and two daggers. As a compact, relatively wealthy community uncomfortably close to the Channel coast, Bridport was armed to the teeth.

A few documents concerned with arrays survive from the archives of noble families. A valuable survival is a muster certificate of the later fifteenth century compiled for Sir William Stonor on the information of the constables of the half hundred of Ewelme (Oxon.), 'of men that make harness and be able to do the king service and not able to make harness'. The constables of seventeen vills named more than eighty men, a few of whom were said to be not able for service. All except two of the constables categorized their men as being with or without harness. Over forty had harness. John Pallyng of Ewelme may have inherited his from someone of different build, for he was 'not able to wear it'. Constables often noted whether their men were archers – as many of them were – or whether they fought with what were the other characteristic weapons in this region: bill or staff. Some were noted down as good archers or able with bill or staff. One Brightwell man was armed with an axe. Sir William Stonor thus had precise information about the military strength of the half hundred. The compilation of such certificates was probably unexceptional. Other sorts of array records are to be found copied into a book which contains household accounts of John de Vere, earl of Oxford. There is the commission to the earl to array in Essex, Norfolk, Suffolk, Cambridgeshire and Huntingdonshire for Henry VII's northern expedition after the battle of Stoke, dated Lincoln, 21 June 1487. There follow Oxford's instructions to the arrayers, telling them to inform all knights, esquires, gentlemen and constables of townships about the king's victory, the royal intention to lead 'a mighty power' into the north, and the royal command that individual gentlefolk and townships 'after their degree and substance' should assist the king by personal service or by the provision of men or money. The commissioners were to examine what services had been done in the recent campaign and what would be in the coming one 'and there of make a remembrance, to the intent that the King . . . may give every of his subjects thank after his demerit': those who had aided the Stoke campaign were excused further obligation. The commissioners were also to command constables to ascertain whether men were adequately arrayed, and to certify defaults.[152]

The book also contains notes of the numbers of soldiers that individual gentlemen had undertaken to 'find and purvey' to 'await upon my Lord into the North Country' and of those whom other gentlemen had undertaken to bring at the costs of the king and earl. Also listed were those who 'found men with my Lord in the other voyage' (i.e. the Stoke campaign) at their own cost, and those who paid 'to wage men with' on the same expedition. The latter included Lord Willoughby (£12 for six men) and the towns of Bury St Edmunds, Walden and Ipswich (respectively, £10 for five men, £12 for six, £15 for blank). There follows a list of 'such receipts as I have received of certain hundreds and townships' for the wages of those attending Oxford northwards, waged from 18 July for a month. Some sums were sent to the receiver by a whole hundred, some by an individual township, and in some cases he noted that a constable had given him the money – though a knight, Thomas Grey, did so for three townships.

Some precise information about the organization of arrays is to be found in urban archives. The administrative mechanisms of leading cities were well fitted to raise, equip and provide pay for contingents. In May 1455 the mayor of Coventry received a royal signet letter addressed to him and the sheriffs, summoning them to come armed with a retinue. He convened the council; he and his brethren decided that 100 'of good-men defensibly with bows and arrows, Jakked and saletted, arrayed', should be provided hastily for the king. A captain was appointed, and 38s. 6d. was spent on a new ribanded and tasselled standard for the company, a gaudy multi-coloured garment for its captain, and 'bends' of green and red cloth to be worn by the soldiers. As the company never went to war, these accoutrements were committed to the city wardens' keeping.[153] In a Norwich assembly of 12 January 1461, a royal commission dated 3 January ordering the mayor to summon military aid from the city for Henry VI was read out. It was decided that the aldermen and past and present sheriffs should find forty soldiers and the commonalty eighty: costs were to be assessed by wards and parishes at the mayor's discretion. On 26 January he reported that the captaincy of the company had been filled and that the soldiers were pledged to serve for six weeks at the city's wages. The costs of the captain's outlay were to be borne by the city treasury and sums paid by the cathedral prior and various ecclesiastical bodies.[154] The Nottingham chamberlains' accounts for 1463–4 list expenses of 56s. 3d. for the cost of making jackets for the soldiers riding to the king at York. Payments were made for red cloth for the soldiers' jackets and fine red cloth for their captain's, the sheriff, for white fustian to make letters, and for the cutting out and threading on of the letters.[155]

Unfortunately we lack descriptions or illustrations of the appearance of arrays in the Wars of the Roses. Clearly some of the urban levies were, in their way, as brave a sight as the knights whose deeds and accoutrements were of more interest to courtly chroniclers and illuminators. Perhaps the nearest we can get to a description of levies is Dominic Mancini's one of the soldiers whom he observed in London in 1483, summoned there by the dukes of Gloucester and Buckingham. Among those he saw may have been the northerners (who included a company raised by the city of York) and Welshmen prominent among the dukes' supporters:

> There is hardly any without a helmet, and none without bows and arrows: their bows and arrows are thicker and longer than those used by other nations, just as their bodies are stronger than other peoples', for they seem to have hands and arms of iron. The range of their bows is no less than that of our arbalests; there hangs by the side of each a sword no less long than ours, but heavy and thick as well. The sword is always accompanied by an iron shield. . . . They do not wear any metal armour on their breast or any other part of the body, except for the better sort who have breastplates and suits of armour. Indeed the common soldiery have more comfortable tunics that reach down below the loins and are stuffed with tow or some other soft material [i.e. jacks]. They say that the softer the tunics the better do they withstand the blows of arrows and swords, and besides that in summer they are lighter and in winter more serviceable than iron.[156]

Bishop Latimer, in a sermon preached before Edward VI, gave a vivid glimpse of how as a boy he had helped to equip his father, Hugh, setting out to serve Henry VII against the Cornish rebels in 1497:

> My father was a yeoman, and had no lands of his own, only he had a farm of three or four pounds by year at the uttermost, and thereupon he tilled as much as kept half a dozen men. He had walk for a hundred sheep; and my mother milked thirty kine. He was able, and did find the king a harness, with himself and his horse, while he came to the place that he should receive the king's wages. I can remember that I buckled his harness when he went unto Blackheath Field.[157]

His father, a well-to-do tenant at Thurcaston (Leics.), possessing his own harness and mount, was doubtless better equipped than the generality of levies.

How efficiently were commissions of array fulfilled? Many contingents were doubtless tardy, inexperienced, ill equipped, unruly. There were the green Cheshiremen slaughtered at Blore Heath, the inadequately armed ('naked') men in the royal army which advanced to Ludlow, the 'new men of war' routed by the northern army at Dunstable in 1461, and the king's people who, at St Albans the next day, 'would not be guided nor governed by their captains'.[158] Whether the arrays were adequate, and whether they came at all, was highly dependent on the zeal and ability of the arrayers, and on the co-operativeness of local communities. Dire threats in proclamations from kings desperate for support are more likely to have repelled than attracted their services. On occasion arrayers were confronted by a stubborn refusal to budge. At Newark in 1469 Edward IV had to give up his intention of confronting the northern rebels, 'finding that the common people came into him more slowly than he had anticipated'.[159] Later in the year Warwick was unable to get an adequate response to proclamations ordering the lieges to rise against the northern rebels, because the king was his prisoner.[160]

But it is likely that arrays often provided sturdy, reliable companies, especially in the years 1459–64 and 1469–71, when frequent summonses tested arraying organization. The formidable military reputation of northerners may have been based partly on their more habitual arraying, to combat Scottish raids. Cities and boroughs, needing defence against sack, and the goodwill of crown and nobles to maintain their privileges and interests, had incentives to keep their arraying capacity in good order. In February 1460 the mayor of Coventry was concerned because no action had been taken on a royal commission received over a fortnight before ordering a muster in preparation against any invasion attempt by the exiled Yorkists. By the advice of the city council, the mayor waited on the duke of

Buckingham, then lodging in Coventry at 'the Angell', to have the duke's advice 'of his demean in the said commission because his receipt was so late, if any peril or hurt might grow unto the city for the late certificate thereof'.[161] Cities' good repute as paymasters and providers of equipment doubtless enabled them to attract able services.[162] It was probably a point of pride and prestige that civic companies should behave creditably: as we have seen, they were sometimes decked out with a banner and smart new uniforms. Shires and their constituent hundreds, like cities and towns, probably vied to make good array for war, as they did for peace. William Paston reported to his brother in 1489:

> Sir, my lord [the earl of Oxford] hath sent on to the most part of the gentlemen of Essex to wait upon him at Chelmsford, where as he intendeth to meet with the King, and that they be well appointed, that the Lancashire men may see that there be gentlemen of as great substance that they be able to buy all Lancashire. Men think that ye among you will do the same. Your country [Norfolk] is greatly boasted of, and also the inhabitors of the same.[163]

Had Sir William Stonor arrayed a scarecrow levy from the half hundred of Ewelme — like the Essex levy in 1471 and the Cornish levy in 1497 which were sneered at as ragtag and bobtail by London chroniclers — he might have earned ridicule, and certainly no royal thanks.

Edward IV may have had some impressive arrayed levies as well as lords' companies when he mustered his army at Grantham in March 1470. According to a correspondent of John Paston, 'it was said that were never seen in England so many goodly men, and so well arrayed in a field. And my Lord [the duke of Norfolk] was worshipfully accompanied, no lord there so well; wherefore the King gave my Lord a great thank.'[164] But even poor contingents had their uses. Their inadequate equipment or inexperience might be compensated for by the quality of nobles' retinues and by a weight of artillery. Massed behind ditches and hedges, relatively 'naked' men, armed with bows, bills, staves, axes, could fill in or extend a defensive position. Their manpower was required to assist carts, particularly those loaded with guns and shot, through foul ways, and to set up artillery positions and encampments. In 1486, when threatened with rebellion in Yorkshire, Henry VII summoned Lincolnshire levies to come unarmed, wishing, says the Crowland continuator, 'to appear rather to pacify than exasperate the people who were opposed to him'.[165] Perhaps he — and other commanders in the wars — had another motive for arraying: to prevent the enemy from recruiting.[166]

A crucial organizational point was the timing of the summons of arrayed men. This is reflected in the emphasis in commissions that arrayers should select their contingents in readiness to array at short notice. John Paston's comments on the Norfolk levy in January 1461 illustrate the importance of timing. He thought that the council's and the commission of array's procrastinations were in danger of causing the disintegration of the levy. Most of the arrayed men believed that their services were needed in London. They had therefore drawn their wages, 'but they have no captain, nor ruler assigned by the commissioners to wait upon, and so they straggle about by themselves, and by likeliness are not like to come at London half of them'. Orders had come from London that people should not come till sent for, but they were unlikely to get more men than the mere 400 or so who had reportedly passed Thetford without the issue of new commissions. Since the communities considered themselves discharged of all expenses, they would think it 'right strange' if they had to pay for new levies.[167]

The exceptional circumstances of January 1461, when the invasion by the northern army was feared, may account for the urgency with which Norfolk constables and bailiffs had organized levies, and the latter's unwonted zeal to commence their service and even depart from the county. But the basic problem on this occasion was a normal one: communities were prepared to 'wage' soldiers for only a few weeks' service. Some of the frequent military débâcles of the Wars of the Roses may have been basically caused by mistimings of summonses. Kings and captains had an incentive to delay them dangerously – the need to husband the short period of waged service available. Paston's letter suggests that Warwick may have been deprived of support at St Albans because arrays had been summoned too early. Henry VI in June 1460, Edward IV in July 1469 and September 1470, Richard III in 1485, and Henry VII in 1486 may have jeopardized their cause by leaving summonses late.

The prolongation of levies' service beyond the period for which they had been paid was also risky, unless the commander could provide wages – and even then, some levies may have murmured against the extension of their term. 'Gregory' thought it worthy of remark that in February 1461, March, when he met Warwick at Burford (Oxon.), was 'sorry that he was so poor, for he had no money, but the substance of his men came at their own cost'.[168] The disintegration of the northern army in the same month may have been because the wages which their communities had provided had run out – they may have been in arms for several months.[169] John Paston wrote to his elder brother John from Newcastle on 11 December 1462

In case we abide here, I pray you purvey that I may have here more money by Christmas Eve at the farthest, for I may get leave for to send none of my waged men home again; no man can get no leave for to go home but if they steal away, and if they might be known, they should be sharply punished.

This prolongation of service, and probable delays in receiving extra wages, help to account for the dismal performance of Edward's army at Alnwick the following month.[170] In his reconquest of the realm in 1471 (14 March to 26 April), faced with a sequence of threats, he raised a succession of levies round a stable nucleus of nobles' and royal retainers' companies. After the hard-fought battle of Barnet, he 'sent to all parts to get him fresh men' to meet the Lancastrian threat in the west.[171] These levies, after their victory at Tewkesbury, were presumably dismissed, for to oppose the rebels in the north he promptly 'prepared a new army'.[172] Until the fresh levies arrived, Edward was so low in manpower that he 'by possibility could not by power have resisted the Bastard' (of Fauconberg). But he 'made out commissions to many shires of England; which in a ten days there came to him, where he was, to the number of 30,000'.[173] Edward's need to rotate arrays, and the intermediate periods of vulnerability which he endured, reveal defects in the array system. Yet in 1471 he got speedy and weighty support from arrays arriving from different parts of the realm – as, indeed, did his opponents. The system, put to the test in preceding years, seems to have been working well – though not necessarily to the advantage of the throne's occupant.

Why did rulers continue to rely on methods of recruitment which produced variable levels of support for limited periods, and which might be turned against them? One reason was that these obligations were accepted as customary by communities. Rulers and their opponents struggling to win military and political support in emergencies could not risk alienation by making demands for unfamiliar services. The crown could not afford to maintain large standing forces as an alternative to arrays: it had a struggle to pay the wages of its frontier garrisons. The largest concentration of frontier troops, in the March of Calais, tended to grow mutinous when pay was in arrears – hardly an encouragement to kings to increase standing forces.

Nevertheless, some royal councillors may have toyed with the idea of establishing a standing army, as the French crown had done in the 1440s. In their 1460 manifesto the Yorkist lords alleged:

> now begin a new charge of imposition and tallages upon the said people which never afore was seen; that is to say, every township to find men for the king's guard, taking example thereof of our enemies and adversaries of France: which imposition and tallage if it be continued to their heirs and successors, will be the heaviest charge and worst example that ever grew in England.[174]

Sir John Fortescue, in *The Governance of England*, completed in the 1470s, argued that it would not be to the king's advantage if the commons were rendered poor, as some advocated, on the grounds that then, like the French commons, they would not be equipped to rebel. Fortescue's rejection of the idea was based partly on the argument that it would destroy the arraying system:

> Forsooth these folk consider little the good of the realm of England, whereof the might standith most upon archers, which be no rich men. And if they were made more poor than they be, they should not have wherewith to buy them bows, arrows, jacks, or any other armour of defence, whereby they might be able to resist our enemies, when them list to come upon us. . . . Item, if poor men may not lightly rise . . . how then, if a mighty man made a rising should he be repressed, when all the commons be so poor, that after such opinion they may not fight, and by that reason not help the king with fighting ? And why maketh the king the commons every year to be mustered ; since it were good they had none harness nor were able to fight ? O, how unwise is the opinion of these men.[175]

This is powerful testimony, from a leading participant in the Wars of the Roses, to the efficacy of the array system in the period. Indeed, that ancient system was to continue as the bedrock of Tudor and early Stuart military organization.[176] The fact that it had been found politically preferable and reasonably adequate in the Wars of the Roses had important long-term political consequences. Henry VIII and his successors, with their urgent new military requirements, found it simpler to adapt this existing system, revitalized by the wars and in full working order – a system which in the fourteenth century had had constitutional safeguards built into it to restrain its operations from oppressiveness.

As a complement to arrays and the hiring of foreign mercenaries, under Henry VIII the crown continued to rely for service abroad and during domestic disquiets on the recruitment and captaincy by nobles of military companies composed particularly of men customarily in some way in their 'lordship'. The survival of this complementary system owed something to its vigorous use in the Wars of the Roses. To cope with the problems of inducement in civil conflict, 'neo-feudal' ties had been emphasized. Grantors of offices and fees tried to extract support from retainers by promises to pay military wages and give rewards; indentures were drawn up with the object of guaranteeing military support. Random surviving evidence suggests that Richard III, Henry VII and some of their adherents were particularly concerned to secure the promise of service by specified companies beforehand.

The operations of 'neo-feudalism' in the Wars of the Roses have often been viewed as the characteristic expression of noble power threatening royal rule. But arguably 'neo-feudalism' in the long run strengthened rather than weakened the crown. For as a means of raising military support in domestic conflict, retaining had deficiencies which kings were best qualified to overcome. The fact that summonses to arms were on the whole occasional hardened the inclination of office-holders and fee'd men to regard such 'neo-feudal' military obligations as options attached to more basic administrative or political services. The crown was best placed to enforce the association of military demands with patronage, because it could invoke superior obligations of allegiance, and threaten the withdrawal of its exceptional stock of favour. From the 1470s onwards, the increase of royal resources enabled kings to offer more dazzling inducements. Moreover, in the legislation against livery and maintenance, they had a weapon with which to deter potentially hostile magnates from competing with their bounty. The relative infrequency of revolts after 1471 – except during the periods of unusual political tension triggered off by the usurpations of 1483 and 1485 – and the failure of all except one of these revolts, probably stem partly from the crown's successful manipulation of 'neo-feudalism'.

Chapter 7

Supply, Billets and Ordnance

The English, wrote the Milanese Raimondo de Soncino in 1497, 'require every comfort even in the ardour of war'. His words were echoed in the report written for the Venetian envoy Andrea Trevisan in 1498: 'I have it on the best information, that when war is raging most furiously, they will seek for good eating, and all their other comforts, without thinking of what harm might befall them.'[1] One of Malory's knights warned against such temptation: 'They will put forth beasts to bait you out of number.'[2]

There were well-tried methods of providing victuals for English armies and navies in the fifteenth century. The rights of purveyance customarily exercised by royal household officers were extended to licensed victuallers, sheriffs and other local officers, and to the soldiers themselves. These rights, and the limitations on them, were defined by Sir John Fortescue:

> the king, by his purveyors, may take for his own use necessaries for his household, at a reasonable price, to be assessed at the discretion of the constables of the place, whether the owners will or not: but the king is obliged by the laws to make present payment, or at a day to be fixed by the great officers of the king's household. The king cannot despoil the subject, without making ample satisfaction for the same.[3]

An example from the Wars of the Roses of a customary military licence to purvey is the commission granted to two officers in March 1460 to purchase provisions with funds in the duke of Exeter's hands for the fleet under his command, intended to flush out the Yorkists abroad.[4]

The author of *Knyghthode and Bataile* (c. 1460) emphasized the importance that commanders should attach to ensuring that there were sufficient victuals for their men on the march, and in camp or castle. They should show foresight, denying stocks to the enemy:

Have purveyance of forage and victual
For man and horse; for iron smiteth not
So sore as hunger doth if food fail.[5]

Malory appreciated the importance of stockpiling and foraging. One of his armies 'had great plenty of victual by Merlin's provisions'. Arthur declared, 'My folk is waxen feeble for wanting of victual', and dispatched knights to forage in forests where he was convinced his enemies had beasts.[6]

In the Wars of the Roses, prior provision of stocks was peculiarly difficult, for often commanders had not had either the time or the finance to accumulate them and the transports necessary to convey them. Urban and county communities do not seem to have customarily provided much in the way of victuals for the companies which they dispatched. Beverley's contingents for the Lancastrian armies in 1460–1 received wine for a send-off.[7] The forty soldiers which Coventry sent to Edward at Nottingham in August 1470 had been given by the city 16d. 'ad bibendum', a gallon of wine and six pennyworth of ale.[8] Footmen were expected to carry their rations: the author of *Knyghthode and Bataile* advised that they should be regularly sent on practice route marches in full harness, 'Vitaile eke born withal'.[9] Their dependence on daily foraging is suggested by 'Gregory's' remark that 'spearmen they be good to ride before the footmen and eat and drink up their victual'.[10] In 1471 Edward's soldiers were unable to forage in the Cotswolds 'in all the way, horse-meat, nor mans meat'. It was a tribute to his care for the commissariat, especially as his expedition had been hurriedly launched, that at Cheltenham he 'a little comforted himself, and his people, with such meat and drink as he had done to be carried with him, for the victualling of his host'.[11]

The armies' dependence on foraging emphasized the danger that they might oppress the civilian population and alienate support. Henry VII's army foraged in Atherstone and neighbouring villages in 1485 without payment.[12] He had with him many French troops whom he may have found difficulty in restraining from their extortionate customs. Sir John Fortescue, in exile in France in the 1460s, had graphically denounced these to the young, warlike prince of Wales (with whom French troops landed in England in 1471) as oppressive and impoverishing:

> the soldiers, though quartered in the same village a month or two, yet they neither did nor would pay any thing for themselves or horses; and, what is still worse, the inhabitants of the villages and towns where they came were forced to provide for them *gratis*, wines, flesh, and whatever else they had occasion for; and if they did not like what

they found, the inhabitants were obliged to supply them with better from neighbouring villages: upon any non-compliance, the soldiers treated them at such a barbarous rate, that they were quickly necessitated to gratify them. When provisions, fuel and horse meat fell short in one village, they marched away full speed to the next; wasting it in like manner. They usurp and claim the same privilege and custom not to pay a penny for necessaries ... such as shoes, stockings and other wearing apparel.[13]

Henry VII, despite his Breton sojourn, soon showed an appreciation of contrary English practice, and determination to guarantee more certain payment – and perhaps surer provision of victuals – than he had been able to do in 1485. He compensated property-owners who had suffered losses by his army's encampment before the battle of Bosworth.[14] On 5 June 1487, at the start of his campaign against the Simnel rebels, he had it proclaimed:

and for that his highness nor his said company in no wise should be destitute or wanting of victuals for man or horse: He strictly chargeth and commandeth every victualer, and all other his subjects dwelling in every town or place where his said highness and his said company shall come, to provide and make ready plenty of bread and ale, and of other victuals, as well for horse as for man, at reasonable price in ready money therefor to them: And every of them truly to be contented and paid.[15]

In the ordinances of war which he issued for the campaign at about this time, he insisted that no one 'take nor presume to take any manner of victual, horse meat, or man's meat, without paying therefor the reasonable price thereof assigned by the clerk of the market or other the king's officer therefore ordained, upon pain of death'.[16] His opponents, with foreign mercenaries in their army, feared that they would meet with opposition from those who believed their men would not follow such English conventions. On 8 June 'Edward VI' wrote to the civic governors of York: 'it will like you that we may have Relief and ease of lodging and victuals within our city there and so to depart and truly pay for that We shall take'. The York civic councillors were anxious to respond to Henry's determination to deal fairly: in anticipation of his arrival with an army the following month, they ordained that proclamation was to be made in the city that the common victuallers were to have adequate supplies for the army during his proposed sojourns. The council was concerned to prevent exploitation by the sale of unwholesome or dear food. A price limit of 10*d.* per gallon was fixed for red and white wine, and for claret.[17]

In the often large-scale, prolonged and unseasonable campaigning of the early 1460s it had been particularly important for commanders to ensure availability of stocks. Richard of York's troops at Wakefield in December 1460 were imperilled 'vagantibus per patriam pro victualibus quaerendis'.[18] The poor discipline and plundering habits of the queen's army on its advance southwards in February 1461 may have been intensified by seasonal shortages. The soldiers 'compelled, despoiled, robbed and destroyed all manner of cattle, victuals and riches'. After victory at St Albans their commanders were anxious to obtain 'both bread and victual' from London. But Henry VI, his wife, son and lords had to be content with relief from the city of York 'in victuals and other goods to the uttermost of their powers'.[19]

Possibly the Lancastrian army got into such dire straits because of the disruption of its victualling arrangements in fertile eastern regions before it crossed south of the Trent. On 28 January 1461 a Norfolk squire had been commissioned by the Yorkist government to inquire from what part of the country wheat and victuals were being shipped to the rebels, and to arrest the ships and men involved. Just under a fortnight later a commission was appointed to inquire where in Cambridgeshire wheat, malt and victuals were being shipped for transport to the rebels.[20] The rebels' base at Hull (whose corporation provided fodder for the queen's men) may have been the port to which shipments were being sent. But Yorkist control of Lynn, at the head of an extensive river network, must have hampered any efforts to victual the Lancastrian army from the south.[21]

The Yorkist army which was attacked by the northern men at St Albans may, like theirs, have had an inadequate commissariat. Prospero di Camulio reported that many of the Yorkist soldiers deserted for lack of victuals.[22] Next month Edward, organizing the large army he intended to take north from London, probably made strenuous efforts to overcome the difficult supply situation. Waurin remarks on the great number of waggons with victuals and ordnance parked in the fields outside the city.[23] Towns may have been scoured for contributions: the accounts of the jurats of Lydd record payment 'for vitelle sent to London, to the journey of York, £3. 11s. 9d.'[24]

In the struggle to control Northumberland and neighbouring parts which intensified with Margaret of Anjou's landing in November 1462, shortage of victuals in these relatively barren regions was a key factor: a memory of shortages 'in the extreme pressure of his wars in the parts of the North' was preserved by Henry VI's hagiographer, John Blacman:

it is told by some who came from that region, that when there was for a time a scarcity of bread among his [Henry's] fellow-soldiers and troops, out of a small quantity of wheat, bread was so multiplied by his merits and prayers that a sufficiency and even a superfluity was forthcoming for all of his who sought and asked for it, whereas the rest that were opposed to him had to suffer from lack of meat.

The speed with which castles changed hands in the northern Marches was probably due in part to inadequate stocking. The Lancastrians achieved some success because it took time for the Yorkists to organize the provision of supplies from further south on the scale necessary if they were to deploy their numerical superiority. Newcastle was probably the main Yorkist base to which shipments were sent. In a letter of 11 December 1462, John Paston referred to Yorkist victualling arrangements. From his base at Warkworth the earl of Warwick was supervising the sieges of Alnwick, Dunstanburgh and Bamburgh castles, 'and if they want victuals, or any other thing, he is ready to purvey it for them to his power'. Edward, at Durham, had commanded the duke of Norfolk to convey victuals and ordnance from Newcastle to the earl at Warkworth; the duke sent East Anglian knights and esquires to escort the convoy – 'and so we were with my Lord of Warwick with the ordnance and victuals yesterday'.[25] In the years 1461–3 Hull was obliged to provision Edward's forces in the north with corn and beer, without payment.[26]

Thus availability of victuals was crucial in determining the location, duration and outcome of campaigns. In relatively prosperous and accessible eastern parts of England, it was important to keep control of ports and coastal shipping. Domination of these regions depended on possession of towns on or near intersecting north-south and east-west routes, such as Newcastle, York, Pontefract, Doncaster, Newark, Nottingham, Stamford, Leicester, Coventry, Northampton – and, above all, London, the key not only to the Thames valley and estuary, but, with Canterbury and the Cinque Ports, to Kent and the main routes to northern France. In the west of England, the towns of the Severn valley and the cities of Exeter and Bristol were the keys which Welsh and western armies sought to turn, to give them access to the wealth of the Midlands and the eastern plains. Strategic dominance over the realm – including control of its major supply sources – depended on securing the route from London to York. This was demonstrated in the campaign of March–April 1470. Edward's victory near Stamford sealed his control of London, East Anglia and the eastern Midlands. Clarence and Warwick conceded this by withdrawing northwards from Coventry. They hoped to establish an alternative base in Yorkshire. But Edward, operating along the eastern plains, moved north too fast for them, forcing them westwards towards barren Lancashire. He broke off the pursuit,

as it was thought by his highness, his lords, and other noble[men there bei]ng with him that he might not conveniently p[roceed] with so [great an] host, for that the said duke and earl, with their fellowship [had consum]ed the [vitaile] afore him, and the country afore himself wo[s] not able to sustain so great an host as the king's highness had with him without a new refreshing.[27]

The rebels may have shaken off Edward by denying him supplies, but they had handed to him their principal northern source. He advanced to York 'fully determined there to have refreshed and vitailed his said host', which he did, before forcing the rebels to flee south-west.[28]

Principal towns were important strategic objectives for a number of reasons: one form of 'refreshment' which they provided was billets. In May 1471 Edward refreshed his army in Coventry for three days, not long after his victory at Tewkesbury; Warwick had recently billeted there for much longer.[29] In 1469 variance over lodging in a town (possibly Banbury) had, according to Warkworth, led to the split in the king's army.[30] The author of *Knyghthode and Bataile* described the task of assigning billets, performed by the harbinger ('herbagere'):

> A Mesurer, that is our Herbagere,
> For paviloun and tent assigneth he
> The ground, and saith 'Be ye there, be ye here!'
> Each hostel eek, in castle and city,
> Assigneth he, each after his degree.[31]

The author of the *Arrivall* mentions the arrival of five or six of Edward's harbingers in Sodbury in advance of his army in 1471, intending to 'purvey' his lodgings, and their 'distress' by the enemy's harbingers.[32] Henry VII's 1487 ordinances of war outlined the powers of the king's harbinger:

> Also that no manner of person or persons, whatsoever they be, take upon them to lodge themself nor take no manner of lodging nor harborage but such as shall be assigned unto him or them by the King's harbinger, nor dislodge no man, nor change no lodging after that to be assigned, without advice and assent of the said harbinger, upon pain of imprisonment and to be punished at the will of our said sovereign lord.

The anonymous author of the account of Henry's campaign thought that the 'Marshals and Harbingers of his Host' let him down one day on the march northwards: they

> did not so well their diligence that Way; for when the King removed, there was no proper Ground appointed where the King's Host should lodge that Night then following. . . . And the King and his Host wandered here and there a great Space of Time, and so came to

a fair long Hill, where the King set his Folks in Array of Battle.[33]

'In England', Fortescue wrote, 'no one takes up his abode in another man's house, without leave of the owner first had: unless it be in public inns.'[34] Malory describes how Sir Marhaute and a damsel

> came into a deep forest, and by fortune they were benighted and rode long in a deep way, and at the last they came unto a curtilage and there they asked harborage ['herborow']. But the man of the curtilage would not lodge them for no treaty that they could treat.

They accepted his refusal.[35] Kings and commanders probably considered it important that their harbingers controlled billeting in order to minimize the abuses of a compulsory enforcement which clearly went against the grain for Englishmen. They also wanted to minimize quarrels such as that which allegedly disrupted the royal army in 1469, and ensure particularly that every man was lodged 'after his degree'. For reasons of prestige as well as comfort kings and peers were anxious to secure the best billets on campaign, soft beds in castles, and religious or town houses. But necessity often forced them to lodge in their tents in fields, as Henry VI frequently did in 1459.[36] Elaborate camping gear was probably carted round for their convenience. But it is unlikely that the common soldier had much shelter, if he was forbidden to enter within town walls, or when the available dwellings in a village were occupied by the entourages of king or peers. Commanders were often keen to station their men in the open, to maintain good battle order as well as to avoid inconvenience to civilians. At Ludlow in 1459 and Northampton in 1460 armies encamped across the river from the town. In 1461 the Yorkist lords moved the bulk of their army to a heath near St Albans, possibly out of the town itself. In 1471, when engagements were thought to be imminent, Edward would not allow his men to billet in townships. Coming to Barnet, and understanding Warwick was encamped nearby, he 'would [not] suffer one man to abide in the same town, but had them all to the field with him, and drew towards his enemies, without the town'. At Cirencester he expected to encounter the Lancastrians the following morning, 'For which cause, and for that he would see and set his people in array, he drove all the people out of the town, and lodged him, and all his host, that night in the field, three miles out of the town.' At Sodbury, when uncertain of the enemy's whereabouts, he pitched camp outside the town.[37] In 1487 Henry VII kept his jittery army out of Nottingham.[38]

In domestic strife royal and noble commanders did not expect to have to provide the bulk of their soldiers with arms, armour, victuals, camping equipment, horses or transport. Officers inspected these commodities, and regulated their use and those of available billets. But there was one highly specialized branch of armaments which commanders were eager to make full provision for – ordnance. John Lord Howard's household accounts for April 1481 show him having serpentines cast – doubtless for use in the Scottish war.[39] The crown's long tradition of maintaining ordnance equipped it especially well to make such provision. By the mid-fifteenth century there was a permanent royal officer for ordnance commissioned primarily to supervise the receipt, upkeep and issue of the firearms and ammunition stocked in the Tower of London.[40]

The shock of York's rebellions in 1452 and 1455, as well as of the débâcles in France in 1449–51 and 1453, may have galvanized the Lancastrian council into improving its ordnance as well as its fortifications.[41] The warrant appointing John Judde, merchant of London, as master of the king's ordnance (21 December 1456) admitted that 'we [Henry VI] be not yet sufficiently furnished of guns, gunpowder and other habilments of war'. Judde contracted to 'do make and ordain' sixty field guns (serpentines) and twenty tons of saltpetre and sulphur for gunpowder.[42] He certainly fulfilled part of this contract, for on 19 May 1457 he was assigned at the Exchequer £133. 8s. 5½d. as payment for twenty-six new serpentines with their apparatus for the field, quantities of sulphur, gunpowder and saltpetre, a culverin and a mortar, and the cost of carriage and two carts to go from London to Kenilworth castle.[43] Judde was energetic in royal service till his death in 1460.[44] In the autumn of 1459, as master of the king's ordnance, he was commissioned to assist in fitting out ships for Somerset's expedition to Calais, to seize armaments which had belonged to York, Warwick and Salisbury, and to ensure that the royal ordnance scattered about in castles and walled towns throughout the realm was ready for use.[45]

The Lancastrian armaments programme of the mid-1450s probably stimulated the use of firearms in the wars, providing a substantial part of the stock of heavier ones deployed. Frequent domestic use of firearms may in turn have helped to stimulate the expansion of the royal ordnance department's activities and personnel. In the later fifteenth century there is more evidence for control of the purchase and manufacture of firearms and ammunition by the master of the ordnance, the king's smith, or a specially commissioned royal squire. They controlled workmen not only in the Tower but in various parts of the realm.[46] The function of the Tower arsenal as a munitions factory as well as a storehouse is seen in Richard III's appointment in 1484 of Patrick de la Motte as 'chief cannoneer' or master founder, surveyor and maker of all the king's cannon there and elsewhere, at a daily wage of 18d. Under his command were the 'gunnoures' Theobald Ferrount, Gland Pyroo and William Nele, who were paid 6d. a day for making cannon in the Tower and elsewhere.[47] The importance of the ordnance office is reflected in Henry VII's appointment of a more socially exalted master than hitherto – Sir Richard Guildford, a substantial landowner and early Tudor supporter experienced in warfare. In September 1485 he was granted for life the offices of master of ordnance and of the king's armour; according to his patent of March 1486, he was to receive wages of 2s. a day, and have a clerk, a yeoman and twelve gunners receiving royal wages from him as master of the ordnance.[48]

Thus the manifold use of artillery in the Wars of the Roses – and, doubtless, the royal invasions of France in 1475 and 1492, as well as other expeditions abroad – probably stimulated the expansion of the royal ordnance department. By the end of the wars, in size, activity and prestige it had attained a level which made it capable of worthily supporting the crown's ventures into sixteenth-century European warfare. Henry VII had good reason for pride in his ordnance, when he took Philip I of Castile to London from Barking abbey, probably up the Thames, in 1506: 'and so the Tower, and gun shot'. The Tower had been celebrated as an arsenal a few years before, by a Scottish poet – possibly William Dunbar: 'by Julyus Cesar thy Tour founded of old may be the hous of Mars victoryall, whose artillary with tonge may not be told'. In the year when Henry was showing off his guns there, Guildford, his old master of the ordnance, *en route* to Jerusalem, inspected with an expert eye the 'wondre and straunge ordynaunce' in the Arsenal at Venice. The English knight abroad on pilgrimage now had another interest besides the traditional pious and chivalrous ones.[49]

Chapter 8

Methods of Warfare

English fighting methods in the mid-fifteenth century, like English military organization, were heavily influenced by the experiences of the Hundred Years War. In the fourteenth century one classic form of attack perfected on expeditions in France and Scotland was *la chevauchée* — the 'ride' through hostile terrain by swiftly moving, unencumbered columns of mounted men-at-arms and archers. Such expeditions varied greatly in size, from armies of several hundreds or thousands down to raiding parties from garrisons of a few score. Besides specific strategic objectives, *chevauchées* had the general ones of undermining the enemy's resources and morale by destroying crops, beasts, buildings and chattels, and of enjoying the pickings of war — victuals, booty, prisoners. Unhampered by the drag of siege equipment or a long tail of non-combatants, the force on *chevauchée* cut a swathe through the fields, less concerned than more elaborately constituted armies about scarcity of victuals or the proximity *en route* of menacing enemy forces and garrisons.[1]

But when, during the Hundred Years War, the conquest of territory by the siege of towns was the principal strategic objective, expeditionary forces were in major respects differently constituted and equipped. Then they included siege engineers, miners, carpenters, smiths, carters and a swarm of servants to maintain an appropriate life-style for lords, who presided in the luxurious tents which are often such a prominent feature in contemporary manuscript illustrations of sieges. There were columns of waggons to bring up siege equipment, prefabricated residences and their furnishings, and to shuttle to victualling bases for supplies of foodstuffs. The army which Henry V led from Harfleur to Calais in 1415 — and with which he won at Agincourt — was fit for a *chevauchée*; that with which he landed in Normandy in 1417 was an army of conquest.

Both sorts of armies were commonly grouped for movement and for engagements into formations known as 'battles', often into the specific triple division of vanguard (also called 'foreward', *avauntguard*), main 'battle', and rearguard.[2] In the field the archers were concentrated in the front or on the wings of the vanguard. The longbowman, protected by the sharp-headed stake he planted before him, loosed off from his bow — six feet of yew, maple or oak — volleys which were highly effective at up to 165 yards' range.[3] The devastating effect of English and Welsh longbowmen's rapid and accurate fire was repeatedly demonstrated during the Hundred Years War — notably against the Scots at Halidon Hill (1333), and against the French at Crécy (1346), Poitiers (1356) and Agincourt (1415). The English military leadership's appreciation of the value of archers is reflected in contracts made by the crown with retinue leaders for military service abroad in the later fourteenth and early fifteenth centuries: these frequently show a ratio of three archers to one man-at-arms.[4] In the fifteenth century the French and Burgundians persistently copied the English use of longbowmen. Philippe de Commynes asserted that 'in my opinion archers are the most necessary thing in the world for an army; but they should be counted in thousands, for in small numbers they are worthless'.[5]

Edward III at Crécy and his son the Black Prince at Poitiers both commanded heavily outnumbered armies. Consequently they dismounted their forces, enabling knights and men-at-arms to seek defensive cover in woods and behind hedges, ditches and archers' stakes. The English commanders' good fortune on these occasions confirmed the advantages of using their usually mounted troops as blocs of infantry, co-operating closely with groups of archers, who enfiladed attacking cavalry and infantry.[6] In 1363 these infantry tactics were successfully introduced to Italian warfare by the White Company, partly English in composition. In Italy dismounted men-at-arms developed offensive tactics, advancing shoulder-to-shoulder, gripping in pairs a heavy cavalry lance.[7] Commynes's accounts of French and Burgundian armies in action in the 1460s and '70s, and his appreciative remarks about the excellence of English infantry, also reflect the deep impression which the English development of infantry tactics made on Continental warfare. In 1465, he says, 'it was . . . the most honourable practice amongst the Burgundians that they should dismount with the archers, and always a great number of gentlemen did so in order that the common soldiers might be reassured and fight better. They had learnt this method from the English.'[8]

The most striking technical innovation in warfare during the Hundred Years War was the development of artillery. Surviving fortifications in England dating from the second half of the fourteenth century onwards are commonly provided with gunports.[9] By the accession of Henry VI the defences of Calais were studded with them, and the artillery its captain had at his disposal included sixty iron guns to shoot stones, forty-nine brass guns, and nineteen iron and four brass guns designed to shoot lead pellets. During the reign additional works were carried out at Calais castle to accommodate the heaviest guns. In 1438–9 an opening was made in the east curtain wall for the insertion of a timber 'loop' through which the 'great bombards' were to shoot. By the mid-1450s two of the earthen bulwarks for artillery, projecting from the enceinte, had in recent years been rebuilt in more permanent materials, one in stone and mortar, the other in brick.[10]

From the 1370s onwards heavy guns had been inflicting significant damage on stone fortifications. Their effectiveness is referred to in the earliest English version of Vegetius, made in 1408 for Lord Berkeley, besieging Aberystwyth castle: 'Also great guns that shoot nowadays stones of so great weight that no wall may withstand them as have been well showed both in the north country and also in the wars of Wales.'[11] The guns of heaviest calibre were known as bombards. At Edinburgh castle can be seen one of the largest bombards ever made – *Mons Meg*, constructed at Mons in 1449 by order of Duke Philip of Burgundy, and sent in 1457 as a gift to James II of Scotland. It weighs about 8½ tons, has a calibre of nine inches, and it cast iron shot of 1125 lb, stone shot of 549 lb. By the 1450s there was such a variety of firearms that the author of *Knyghthode and Bataile* could not be bothered to enumerate them all: 'bombards . . . / And gun and serpentine . . . / Fowler, covey, crappaude and culverin / And other sorts more than eight or nine'.[12]

Heavier pieces were even more difficult to deploy effectively in the field than in sieges. They and their ponderous ammunition presented transport problems, their rate of fire was slow, and they lacked manoeuvrability. The use of more convenient, cheaper portable firearms spread more extensively in the early fifteenth century. By the 1430s there is growing evidence for the presence of companies of hand-gun men in Italian field armies.[13] In the mid-fifteenth century a Norfolk lady was well acquainted with the use of hand-guns: Margaret Paston wrote telling her husband how the company holding Gresham manor-house against him had made five holes for their shot with hand-guns 'scarce knee high' from the floor.[14] By then artillery was becoming more adaptable and efficient. The modern fixed-wheeled gun-carriage appeared, and the development of the trunnion facilitated speedier elevation and depression of the barrel.[15] In the 1440s the brothers Jean and Gaspard Bureau had begun their improvement of French royal artillery. Its deployment was probably a factor in the swift English surrender of towns and fortresses during Charles VII's conquest of Normandy (1449–50). According to the contemporary historian

Thomas Basin, the French besieging force at Castillon in Périgord (1453) had entrenched its artillery round its encampment. They had 'dug a deep ditch and added a wall of earth and even great tree trunks around it, placing on this elevation a very large number of machines of war named serpentines and culverins'. The assault on the camp by the relieving Anglo-Gascon force under the earl of Shrewsbury was broken up by their bombardment.[16] In the Wars of the Roses, by 1462 field artillery was clearly distinguished from siege artillery.[17]

In the phase of the wars up to 1460, most noble commanders had learnt the business of war in the Anglo-French conflict. Their knowledge may have sometimes turned out to be dated, inappropriate or rusty. Richard of York (d. 1460) had been Henry VI's lieutenant in France in 1436–7 and 1440–7, his rival Somerset (d. 1455) in 1447–50. Buckingham (d. 1460) had contracted to take a retinue to France as long before as 1421. He had been appointed constable of France in 1430 and granted the *comté* of Perche in 1431. But Lord Bonville (d. 1461) had probably taken part in Henry V's Norman conquests in 1418.[18] Lord Hungerford (d. 1464) had been captured in France in 1453.[19] Lord Scales (d. 1460) had had a distinguished career of service in France, stretching back to 1421. He was, a London chronicler wrote, 'well approved in the wars of Normandy and France'.[20] Another well-reputed noble veteran was Warwick the Kingmaker's diminutive uncle William Neville, 'little' Lord Fauconberg (d. 1463). He had accompanied York to France in 1436, and was captured there in 1449.[21] The youthful Warwick and March probably relied heavily on Fauconberg's expertise, and his part in the Wars of the Roses must have enhanced his military reputation. He performed a crucial task for Warwick in 1459 by maintaining control of his captaincy of Calais whilst the earl took to arms in England. In June 1460 the Yorkist lords dispatched him from Calais to Sandwich in command of the advance-guard of their invasion. The following month he set out from London towards Northampton with the vanguard of the Yorkist army, and he was to be a commander in the Towton campaign in 1461. After the king's withdrawal from the north he was given responsibilities to safeguard it, and on 1 November he was created earl of Kent. In July 1462 he was appointed admiral of England, and in September he raided Le Conquêt near Brest.[22] No other veteran of the Anglo-French wars won such distinction in the Wars of the Roses. Indeed, the reverses then endured by some veterans suggest difficulties in adjusting to the different conditions of civil war. Younger men, less blinkered by experience of command in other circumstances, proved more adaptable – notably Warwick, Henry duke of Somerset, and March.[23]

The major handicap of the civil-war commander was that many of his troops were likely to be less reliable than those usually recruited for campaigns in the Hundred Years War. A captain who had contracted with the crown to lead a military retinue to France often had weeks in which to select and subcontract with experienced soldiers, to inspect their weapons and general fitness, and to 'shake down' with them as a company on the bivouac at the port of embarkation, on the voyage, and on preliminary manoeuvres in France. In the Wars of the Roses, the captain often had to rely on men who were hastily recruited, inexperienced and inadequately equipped, and whom it was essential to deploy speedily. Nobles were consequently eager to secure the services of veterans, just as Sir John Fastolf (d. 1459) had been, when he recruited 'the old soldiers of Normandy' at Southwark in 1450 to guard his house against Jack Cade's rebels.[24] Fastolf was a distinguished veteran, whose secretary William Worcester collected materials for his biography.[25] Worcester's interest in veterans of the French wars led him to list those who fought at Mortimer's Cross in 1461. On Queen Margaret's side, he says, there were the brothers Sir John and Sir William Scudamore, 'in arms in France'. Six of the earl of March's esquires were either 'of war', 'a man of war' or 'a man of the war of France' — notably Philip Vaughan, 'captain of Hay, a man of the war of France, the most noble esquire of lances among all the rest'.[26] Chroniclers' accounts of the 1459–60 campaigns imply that the professional soldiers and veterans of the Calais garrisons exercised an important influence on their outcome. The desertion of Warwick's Calais contingent in 1459 was a prime blow to the Yorkists.[27] The captain responsible, Andrew Trollope, who was to play a notable military role in the next two years, had distinguished himself as a 'lance' in the Anglo-French conflict.[28]

Inexperience in warfare seems to have been recognized as a characteristic of English captains and men-at-arms in many campaigns in the Wars of the Roses. The author of *Knyghthode and Bataile* (c. 1460) wrote for the novice in command an elementary and comprehensive textbook, turning Vegetius' precepts into homely, and distinctly creaking, English verse. He was encouraged to do so by the veteran Beaumont.[29] In the epilogue to his translation of Christine de Pisan's compilation *Le Livre des Faits d'Armes et de Chevalerie*, William Caxton said that Henry VII willed him in Westminster palace on 23 January 1489

> to translate this said book and reduce it in to our English and natural tongue and to put it in enprint to the end that every gentlemen born to arms and all manner men of war captains, soldiers, victuallers and all other should have knowledge how they ought to behave them in the feats of war and of battles.

The veteran earl of Oxford, attending the king, handed Caxton a copy of Christine's book.[30]

The need to season raw levies with veterans strengthened the natural inclination of protagonists to stick to traditional formations and well-tried tactics. But the fact that captains and soldiers often lacked the capability of performing as well as the English were accustomed to do in France, and that opposing veterans had often been trained in the same school, stimulated some tactical diversification. Commanders relied on entrenching, brought up artillery and hand-gunners, and cherished cavalry. Experiment, indeed, had its pitfalls. 'Gregory' scornfully related how Warwick's foreign gunners at St Albans in 1461 failed to make an impression with their outlandish contrivances. All depended on the good old skills of the native infantryman:

> And as the substance of men of worship that will not gloss nor curry favour for no partiality, they could not understand that all this ordnance did any good or harm but if it were among us in our part with King Harry. Therefore it is much left, and men take them to mallets of lead, bows, swords, glaives, and axes.[31]

'Gregory's' scornful contrasts reflect a notable feature of the wars: their particular conditions stimulated attempts to combine innovations with traditional methods.

One tactical feature which outlasted the wars, and is sometimes referred to in accounts of them, is the threefold division of armies for movement or action, a traditional — one might almost say, natural — means of making a host more manageable. Henry VI's army advanced into Kent in 1452 in three divisions, and in 1482 Edward's ally the duke of Albany was said to have invaded Scotland 'in three battles'.[32] Henry VII's army at Calais in 1492, and Henry VIII's there in 1513, were organized in three wards. Henry VII's vanguard, commanded by Oxford, went by a separate route for its advance from base, and his son's three 'wards' all did in 1513. They were self-sufficient fighting forces of all arms, as were probably Henry VII's 'wards' in 1492.[33] In the Wars of the Roses, the need to recruit on the way and to link up with allies coming from different regions had sometimes reinforced logistic and strategic reasons for splitting armies into independent columns. On three occasions in 1460–1 Yorkist armies left London in two or more columns, often on different roads and days, with a rendezvous. On the first occasion, the Northampton campaign of 1460, the army was to go through a series of regroupings.[34] Bishop Neville wrote that Edward IV departed from London in March 1461 'having a week previously dispatched my said brother [Warwick] to muster forces': all the retinues linked up in Yorkshire.[35] However, in 1485, Richard III ordered his whole army into a tight defensive formation for the advance from Nottingham to Leicester, probably to guard against further desertions as well as attack: 'he commanded the army to march forward in square battle [*quadrato agmine*] that way by the which they understood their enemies would come . . . all impediments being gathered into the midst of the army'.[36]

The day before the battle of Tewkesbury in 1471, Edward, anticipating an engagement, 'divided his whole host in three battles'.[37] In 1487 Henry VII, when approaching the earl of Lincoln's camp at Stoke, 'formed his whole force into three columns'.[38] But commanders did not always adhere to the threefold battle order. At Stoke, Lincoln tried to co-ordinate and give greater weight to his ill-matched and outnumbered forces by concentrating them in one 'battle'.[39] Circumstances may have sometimes made the threefold order somewhat academic. The author of *Knyghthode and Bataile* — perhaps with the royal army of 1459 in mind — had warned about how slow and cumbersome 'Too great an host' was: it was preferable to take a smaller one 'of proved and achieved sapience . . . a learned host'.[40] The need for a reliable, speedy striking force led to a frequent division between the main 'battle' and a powerful vanguard, operating independently from it on the march and in the field. According to Waurin, the Yorkist vanguard set off from London to Northampton ahead of the main army in 1460: the following year, the Yorkist vanguard was engaged at St Albans and Ferrybridge before the main army arrived.[41] In 1470 Edward sent his vanguard ahead from Stamford against the Lincolnshire rebels, and in 1471 ahead from London against the Kentishmen.[42] At Bosworth, according to Vergil, Richard arrayed a formidable vanguard, 'stretching it forth of a wonderful length . . . that to the beholders afar off it gave a terror for the multitude'.[43] Both he and Henry committed their vanguards first (the latter's commanded by Oxford) and waited to see how they would fare before joining in with their main 'battles'. The deployment of a powerful advanced striking force moving ahead of the main force and engaging separately in the field became standard practice under Henry VII, perhaps as a result of Oxford's influence in particular. In 1486, when the king was taken unawares by rebellion whilst at York, 'since it was essential to act quickly . . . he dispatched against the enemy his whole retinue, including his bodyguard . . . even although they were ill-equipped'. This force advanced against Lovell at Middleham: Henry meanwhile assembled levies.[44] At Stoke 'the first line of the king's army . . . was alone committed to the fray and sustained the struggle'.[45] In 1489 Henry dispatched his 'foreward' under Surrey's command ahead of himself against the Yorkshire rebels.[46] When confronting the Cornishmen near Blackheath in 1497 he again dispatched the vanguard to envelop them, whilst remaining unengaged with the main 'battle'.[47]

The same year, to suppress Warbeck's revolt in the West Country, he sent the vanguard on ahead under Lord Daubeney's command.[48] Chroniclers had long recognized that a great deal hinged on the conduct of the vanguard in battle, where it was often first in line and heavily engaged. Some of them alleged that the Lancastrian defeat at Northampton and the Yorkist defeats at Ludford Bridge and St Albans stemmed from the treachery of vanguard commanders. The blame for the Lancastrian defeat at Tewkesbury was put on the indifferent command and consequent rout of its vanguard.[49] The Yorkist kings recognized the need to build up and deploy vanguards. The sources give the impression that under Henry VII they were elite bodies of veterans and professionals. The names of some of their commanders recur. Sir John Savage commanded the left wing of Henry's vanguard at Bosworth and, according to Molinet, at Stoke, and he was one of the commanders in the vanguard in 1489.[50] Probably he was a crack cavalryman.

As had become customary in English armies in the Hundred Years War, commanders concentrated archers in the vanguard for a preliminary 'shoot-out'. At Barnet they occupied the centre of Warwick's line, and at Bosworth were in front of Henry's vanguard – their importance in both cases recognized by the captaincy of a magnate.[51] But since England and Wales were nurseries of skilled archers, commanders are likely to have found it more difficult to establish tactical edge with the longbow in the Wars of the Roses than had often been the case abroad, unless they had a special recruiting advantage. There are hints that in a few fights one side enjoyed a telling preponderance of bowmen. At St Albans in 1455 Henry VI had to fight before many local levies could join him: he and his household suffered particularly from arrow wounds.[52] The failure of '7,000 of archers of the west country' to support the Welsh at Edgcote in 1469 was probably an important factor in their defeat.[53] At Tewkesbury Edward's bowmen may have gained an ascendancy over their West Country colleagues, who had not been joined by the Lancashire archers whom their commanders wished to recruit. His vanguard 'so sore oppressed' their opponents 'with shot of arrow, that they gave them right-a-sharp shower'. This barrage, combined with gunshot, the author of the *Arrivall* surmised, may have provoked the Lancastrian vanguard's fatal advance.[54] But at Bosworth, Vergil relates, there was an inconclusive, if fierce, preliminary archery duel between the vanguards.[55] This may have been because the rebels' oblique angle of approach brought them within close range of royal shot for a relatively brief period before battle was joined.[56] One battle in which English archers probably displayed their ancient mastery of the field was Stoke. Lincoln's oddly constituted German-Irish army, unlike French or Burgundian ones of the period, was not well supplied with archers, and was not sufficiently armoured: consequently their 'battle' 'could not withstand the fire of the archers of England'.[57]

Since commanders could not usually assume, as the English had often done abroad, that they would have supremacy in archery, they had an incentive to use, as a supplement in the field, artillery and hand-guns, and, when on the defensive, to reduce the effectiveness of the enemy's firepower by making field fortifications. A weight of noisily impressive guns and protective entrenchments might also reassure and steady raw recruits. These expedients are found in Continental warfare of the period: as we have seen, entrenched artillery contributed to the English defeat at Castillon in 1453.[58] Concerning Italian warfare in the fifteenth century, Dr Mallett has argued that it was the development of field fortifications which hastened the transfer of cannon from ramparts and siege emplacements to the battlefield.[59] Commynes's account of the manoeuvres of Louis XI and his princely opponents on the Seine in 1465 provides graphic illustrations of the combined use of artillery and entrenchments.[60] He also provides examples of the Burgundian use in this campaign of another fifteenth-century development – the *champ de guerre*. This comprised the formation round an army of a defensive enclosure made up of waggons and wooden barriers, which could strengthen slow-moving, encumbered forces and bivouacs against surprise attack.[61] The count of Charolais's army in 1465 had 'such a number of waggons that his alone could enclose the greater part of his host'.[62] After the battle of Montlhéry, the Burgundians used their waggons as a laager, and subsequently, when Charolais's army was encamped between Charenton and Conflans, along the Seine, the count 'enclosed a great stretch of country with his baggage train and artillery, putting all his army inside the enclosure'. When once more expecting battle, this allied army took up a position surrounded by its waggons, except for some cavalry.[63]

The chroniclers of the Wars of the Roses generally lacked Commynes's keen tactical eye. Their evidence of employment of entrenchments, laagers, and firearms is casual and patchy. As early as 1452, the duke of York resorted to characteristic Continental field fortifications. Near Dartford, in expectation of the advance of Henry's army, he 'marvellously fortified his ground with pits, paveys and Guns'.[64] The circumstances at St Albans in 1455 did not allow more than makeshift defensive measures by the royal army: it is not known whether they had guns, though their opponents did.[65] The only evidence for the presence of guns at Blore Heath in 1459 is 'Gregory's' tale of the versatile friar who facilitated Salisbury's escape by shooting guns off all night after the battle.[66] However, soon afterwards, at Ludford Bridge, York once more occupied an impressive field fortification: he 'let make a great deep ditch and fortified it with guns, carts, and stakes', and fired his guns at the royal army.[67] The Lancastrian command in 1460 shared the duke's enthusiasm for entrenchment, and to pander to it the author of *Knyghthode and Bataile* relayed reams of classical technical advice.[68] At Northampton the king held 'a strong and mighty field ... armed and arrayed with guns'. There were 'great ditches which they had dug around the field to the river banks, which enclosed the whole army'. Whethamstede attributed the intransigence of the king's lords partly to confidence in their artillery and entrenchments.[69] But 'the ordnance of the king's guns availed not, for that day was so great rain, that the guns lay deep in the water, and so were quenched and might not be shot'.[70] Apparently the royal high command – like the Yorkist command at St Albans the following year – had not fully grasped the limitations to the reliance which could be placed on artillery in the field. Perhaps the recent death of the master of the king's ordnance, John Judde, had removed an expert whose advice might have been heeded by the lords.[71] In December 1460 the Yorkist lords transported guns northwards from London – they now had possession of the royal arsenal. At Wakefield the duke of York probably once again created a strong defensive position with entrenchments and guns, but, since his soldiers were surprised while out of their lines, these would have been of no avail.[72]

In subsequent campaigns, chroniclers hardly mention field fortifications, and often say little or nothing about the presence of guns. One reason may be that these ceased to be novelties, as domestic conflict became frequent. But possibly recourse to elaborate field fortifications, the panacea of commanders in the fights of 1452–60, declined, since guns became better adapted to field use, and entrenchment was associated with too static a strategic approach. Commanders often placed priority on mobility, with the objectives of seizing towns, spreading recruiting nets, and above all intercepting the enemy chiefs before they could get their campaign rolling. In those circumstances commanders may have been in too much of a hurry to take any except the lightest field pieces and hand-guns. Guns were not a necessity. In November 1462, to counter the Lancastrian invasion, Edward rushed up to Durham with his men, leaving the artillery to follow when it could.[73]

The most detailed account of gunners in action in the Wars of the Roses is one which highlights their limitations – 'Gregory's' incredulously mocking account of the débâcle suffered at St Albans in 1461 by Warwick's foreign company of 'goners and borgeners' [Burgundians?]. This illustrates commanders' interest in bringing in foreign specialists, the cumbersome construction of some early field pieces, and the difficulties of co-ordinating action by specialists with that of the rank and file. This company's guns, unlike the single-barrel pieces more familiar in England, were 'ribaudekins' – multiple-barrels designed to fire simultaneously lead pellets, iron-headed arrows and 'wild fire'. They were aimed through the shutters of pavises, part of the gunners' elaborate defences. At St Albans the gunners were probably attacked before they could erect their booby-traps satisfactorily. Levelling their guns hastily, they injured themselves: 'in time of need they could not shoot not one of these, but the fire turned back upon them that would shoot these three things'.[74]

There is, surprisingly, no record of the presence of artillery at the battle of Towton in 1461, nor in the preliminary engagement at Ferrybridge, though Waurin says that Edward had set out from London with plenty of artillery, and one might have expected it to be useful in helping to force the Aire crossing.[75] But perhaps the foul weather – probably much worse than at Northampton in the summer of 1460 – again dampened the charges. Moreover, the destruction of the ferry may have made it impossible to get heavy artillery across in time for the fight at Towton. Later in the year Edward was having artillery prepared for his projected Welsh expedition, and in 1462 his army in Northumberland was reinforced with it. In September 1461 Philip Herveys, master of the king's ordnance, started out for Hereford with ordnance for the royal expedition.[76] On 11 December 1462 John Paston wrote from Newcastle that the royal commanders in Northumberland had been sent thence enough ordnance 'both for the sieges and for the field, in case that there be any field taken'.[77] In the 1460s artillery was certainly used against Lancastrian fortresses there and in Wales, but it is not evident that guns were used in the relatively small-scale engagements with Lancastrian risers and their foreign supporters – or at Edgcote in 1469.[78] In 1470, at Losecoat Field, Edward 'loosed his guns of his ordnance' on the Lincolnshire rebels.[79] When he invaded the realm in 1471, on landing in Holderness he had in his company 'three hundred of Flemings with hand-guns' – a quarter of his force, according to Warkworth.[80] At Barnet, according to the author of the *Arrivall*, he was outgunned by Warwick – probably because the earl had equipped his army from the royal ordnance. But, as at St Albans ten years before, Warwick does not seem to have benefited from his superior firepower. His night bombardment overshot Edward's army. The king kept most of his guns silent in case their fire enabled the earl's gunners to correct their range. The heavy mist the next morning may have prevented the earl from exploiting his artillery advantage, if he had enough ammunition left to do so.[81] Warwick's guns, undoubtedly among the spoils of Edward's victory, gave him an advantage over the Lancastrian army forming in the West Country. He was certainly concerned to equip his army with ordnance for the new campaign, and the *Arrivall*'s account of the battle of Tewkesbury implies that he outgunned his opponents.[82] Very little is known about the role of artillery in the later campaigns of the wars. It is unlikely that Henry Tudor, speeding through the Midlands in 1485 from a remote part of Wales, transported any but light guns to Bosworth. Richard III, long anticipating his invasion, had had an opportunity to prepare superior ordnance, but the haste with which he moved from Nottingham may have necessitated a reduction of his superiority. Molinet's account of the battle suggests that the royal artillery was superior, nevertheless. Henry's foreign specialists recognized his disadvantage and deployed his troops so as to benefit from defects in the siting of the king's guns.[83]

By then the use of a variety of guns had become a commonplace of warfare in England, no longer a wryly regarded wonder. Viscount Lisle had written to his enemy Lord Berkeley in 1470: 'I marvel ye come not forth with all your Carts of guns, bows, with other ordnance, that ye set forward to come to my manor of Wotton to beat it down upon my head: I let you wit, ye shall not need to come so nie.'[84] In 1475, on his expedition to France, Edward IV had an artillery train which impressed contemporaries, and which was clearly intended to provide for field actions as well as sieges. He had at least thirteen pieces of heavy artillery, including bombards, five 'fowlers' (long-range field guns), a 'curtowe' (short-range field gun) and three 'potguns' (mortars).[85] This splendid train – and the expansion of the royal ordnance department which was responsible for it – bear witness to how the Wars of the Roses had enabled new generations of English captains to keep abreast of military technology, which was developing relatively quickly in the period.[86]

Nevertheless, it is difficult to ascertain how generally and judge how effectively artillery was used in the Wars of the Roses. Chroniclers' references to the presence of guns suggest that they considered them to have been an important factor on occasion. Their presence may have been particularly useful in steadying hastily organized men. The manufacture of artillery and its ammunition was, in fifteenth-century terms, a complex and consequently expensive technology. Kings and nobles would not have paid out for field guns and the costs of transporting them, nor handicapped their progress by taking them sometimes long distances, if they had not considered it worthwhile. But since armies were frequently assembled in haste and on the move to deal with swiftly developing crises, the time factor probably made it difficult to assemble a formidable ordnance train such as Edward accumulated for his French invasion in 1475. In 1460 Henry VI's forces had lost the strategic initiative by tying themselves to their Midlands arsenal: the subsequent technical failure showed that reliance on entrenched artillery was a gamble. But Edward – perhaps inheriting an enthusiasm which his father had gained in the French wars – seems to have been particularly adept in the deployment of field artillery. However, in circumstances when it proved difficult for a force to bring a weight of supporting artillery into the field, commanders in the wars seem to have been prepared to go ahead regardless. Like the tank in twentieth-century warfare, artillery had become a symbol of military virility and prestige. A great bombard was a present fit for a prince to give a king. The 'long fowler' and the 'bumbardelle' which Edward took to France in 1475 were both named the *Edward*.[87] Yet leaders of risings and invasions in the fifteenth century were no more deterred than leaders of 'liberation movements' are today by a dearth of such prestige weapons.

The general vagueness of chroniclers about the use of artillery in the wars is symptomatic of their tendency to neglect tactical detail. Waurin, 'Gregory' and the author of the *Arrivall* are the main ones who write as if they had personal experience of soldiering. Most chroniclers inclined to regard the issue of battle as being settled, if not by treachery, then by flights of arrows followed by 'hand-strokes'. Because infantry fighting was a characteristic skill of the English, the chroniclers are rarely explicit as to whether soldiers had mounts, or whether engagements were entirely fought on foot. The tactical circumstances of some engagements imply that to all intents and purposes they were. At St Albans in 1455, Warwick's men must have been on foot when they penetrated the royal defences, bursting through pales, houses and street barricades.[88] The bulk of the Yorkists at Crayford in 1452 and Ludford Bridge in 1459, and of the royal army at Northampton in 1460, are likely to have been dismounted behind their entrenchments: the assault on them at Northampton must have been on foot. Vergil says that on the king's side there 'many of the horsemen had put their horses from them, and, as their manner [i.e. the English manner] is, fought on foot'.[89] According to *Benet's Chronicle*, in 1461 Edward fought on foot at Ferrybridge, and was unable to pursue the Lancastrians, who commandeered many of the Yorkist horses – presumably being held by pages whilst their owners, like the king, fought dismounted. The next day at Towton, according to Waurin, Edward dismounted at a crucial stage of the battle to encourage his men, saying that he intended to live or die with them that day.[90] Ten years later, at Barnet, Warwick was on foot when he decided to flee: he 'leapt on horse-back'.[91] Commynes, like Vergil, is more explicit about English practice. Edward IV, he says, won nine important battles 'all of which were fought on foot'.[92] Dominic Mancini described the practice of horsed English soldiers in 1483:

Not that they are accustomed to fight from horseback, but because they use horses to carry them to the scene of the engagement, so as to arrive fresher and not tired by the fatigue of the journey: therefore they will ride any sort of horse, even pack-horses. On reaching the field of battle the horses are abandoned, they all fight together under the same conditions so that no one should retain any hope of fleeing.[93]

Most arrayed men were trained only to fight on foot: they did not possess horses suitable for cavalry engagements. Moreover, they were probably anxious to dismount in the field, so as not to risk the loss of their horses, with no certainty of compensation. John Welles, esquire, was fortunate to receive 3s. 4d. as compensation authorized by the governors of Beverley for the loss of his horse at Northampton in 1460. The cryptic entry in their accounts seems to imply that Welles, a soldier in the royal army, had had his horse tethered in a wood during the engagement, but that a fugitive from the rout tried to swim the beast across the Nene, and it drowned in the mill race.[94]

Mancini, describing the troops which Richard III and Buckingham brought to London in 1483, says that 'there were horsemen among them'. There was an important difference between characteristic infantry forces in English armies abroad and those in the Wars of the Roses. Whereas the former had mounts, the bulk of the latter probably did not. When the crown contracted with a captain to bring a retinue of men-at-arms for service on expedition in France or Scotland, it could insist that they should be horsed for mobility. But in the often hasty, desperate conditions of civil war, commanders were anxious to increase manpower above all. The author of *Knyghthode and Bataile* frequently alludes to 'horsemen' and 'footmen', and is concerned about their mutually supportive roles on the march.[95] The distinction is probably not derived simply from his classical source, but based as well on the constituents of the royal army in 1459. Its 'naked men' are unlikely to have been horsed.[96] According to *Bale's Chronicle*, the Yorkist army which reached London in July 1460 had 500 horsemen and 'a host of footmen of commons of Kent, Sussex and Surrey numbered at 60,000'.[97] Advancing on Northampton, its leaders waited for two days at Dunstable for all the contingents to assemble, 'for those on foot could not go as fast as those on horse', especially since bad weather had rendered the ways foul.[98] John Harowe, a London mercer, was described as *dux peditum* ('captain of foot'?) in the Yorkist army at Wakefield.[99] Ruminating on the Lancastrian victory at St Albans in 1461, 'Gregory' expressed the footman's animus against mounted troops: 'As for spearmen they be good to ride before the footmen and eat and drink up their victual, and many more such pretty things they do, hold me excused though I say the best, for in the footmen is all the trust.'[100] Next month, when Edward was preparing to combat the Lancastrians in the north, his 'foot people' set out from London a few days ahead of him.[101] One of those who fought against him at Towton was Sir Thomas Hammys, 'captain of all the footmen'.[102] At Losecoat Field in 1470 Robert Waryn was 'captain of the footmen' in the Lincolnshire army. After the royal victory there, Clarence and Warwick promised to come to Edward from Coventry, leaving their footmen behind. Their excuse for taking a route away from the king was that they were going to contact a force of their footmen.[103] In 1471 Coventry sent twenty 'footmen' and twenty 'horsemen' to Barnet field, presumably to support Warwick.[104] The Lancastrians had to make a stand at Tewkesbury because only their horsemen could go on, in the general state of exhaustion, and 'the greater part of their host were footmen'. Edward achieved a notable feat by forcing on through the Cotswolds, his parched, hungry army, 'whereof were more than 3,000 footmen'.[105] Few of Warbeck's supporters in the West Country in 1497 are likely to have had mounts. Those who were at Bodmin when he was proclaimed Richard IV were 'men of Rascal and most part naked men'. The larger force which he and sixty horsemen abandoned at Taunton were 'poor and naked'.[106]

The fact that armies were partly or in substance composed of marching rather than mounted infantry probably had important tactical consequences. It may have stimulated the formation of specialized mounted vanguards to spearhead attacks. It may have encouraged the carriage of armaments which could not have kept up so easily with mounted troops – artillery, cannon balls and, besides, entrenching tools. But such slower forces were vulnerable to surprise attacks, all the more so as mounted contingents tended to move separately. There was an enhanced need for troops of light horse – 'scourers' (also termed 'aforeriders' or 'prickers') to protect the flanks of footmen and waggons, and maintain contact between columns, as well as watching enemy movements and reconnoitring objectives. Incidentally, aforeriders might cut fine figures: they were able to secure plum billets, and to avoid tramping along muddied lanes, well equipped to make a quick exit from a tight corner, and doubtless expert at scanning the horizon and detecting the whereabouts of a camouflaged pig, chicken or barrel of ale.

The author of *Knyghthode and Bataile* recognized the need for horsemen to provide good intelligence and protection for marching infantry. 'Escouring is to have of every coast', he wrote; the best horsemen, light-harnessed, were to shepherd the footmen.[107] The need for good intelligence was emphasized by some notable failures early in the wars. In May 1455, when Henry VI's retinue was leaving Watford for St Albans, the assembly-point for the royal army, his commanders were startled to discover that York had forestalled them, being near enough to offer battle, or occupy St Albans before them.[108] In 1459 the opponents Warwick and Somerset both passed through Coleshill (Warwicks.) without realizing their proximity.[109] Salisbury's peril at Blore Heath sprang from his failure to realize that superior forces were enveloping him.[110] Yorkist intelligence continued to be abysmal. After their scourers' defeat at Worksop (Notts.) in December 1460, York and Salisbury consistently failed to appreciate their opponents' dispositions in Yorkshire.[111] At St Albans the following February, Warwick's scourers failed him more seriously than at Coleshill. His army was attacked whilst moving to a new position, 'and then', declares the trenchant 'Gregory', 'all thing was to seek and out of order, for their prickers came not home to bring no tiding how nigh that the Queen was, save one, come and said that she was nine miles off'.[112] Waurin's account suggests that in the following months Edward was served better by his *avant coureurs* in the north.[113]

The militarily minded author of the *Arrivall*, in his account of the 1471 campaign, gives the best insights into scouting activities. By then there was probably more light horse available skilled in the techniques of observation and liaison. After his cautious advance from Holderness, Edward 'being at Nottingham, and or he came there, sent the scourers all about the countries adjoining, to aspie and search if any gatherings were in any place against him'. Those who reconnoitred the Lancastrian force at Newark in fact precipitated its withdrawal in the belief that they foreshadowed the imminent arrival of Edward's army.[114] The day before the battle of Barnet, Edward's 'afore-riders' secured an advantage by beating Warwick's out of the village.[115] When the king's army was soon afterwards pursuing the western Lancastrians through the Cotswolds, he always had 'good espialls' on them. The 'certain knowledge' that he had at Cheltenham of their halt at Tewkesbury enabled him to rest his weary army.[116] It seems that Edward appreciated the need for good intelligence, perhaps as a result of his seniors' failures to get it in 1459–61. It was certainly to be crucial to the opponents in the 1485 campaign. In his operations in Wales, Henry Tudor, unsure at each stage of his reception, was highly dependent on his scourers' reports; Richard's were eventually able to pick up his line of march in the Midlands. Henry's aforeriders in 1487, who also apparently formed 'the Wing of the Right Hand of the Forward', were from the pick of his household knights.[117]

Besides detecting and shadowing enemy movements, masking their own forces and securing advance positions, 'scourers' and aforeriders were by 1471 being used for a variety of tasks. In that year, to deceive Edward into believing that they intended to advance on London rather than northwards, the Lancastrians dispatched aforeriders on sweeps from Exeter to Shaftesbury and Salisbury, and from Wells to Yeovil and Bruton. They were to 'call and array the people to make towards them', and to spread false information that the army would advance on Reading, and, through Oxfordshire and Berkshire, on London.[118] In 1487 a weaker side was again resorting to deception measures. Whilst Henry VII confronted the earl of Lincoln's army at Stoke, the latter's scouts may have been spreading hostile rumours on approach routes to the royal army.[119] Vergil hints at another task of scourers, in forces which commanders often with good reason suspected of a lack of enthusiasm for fighting. He claims that many in the royal army would have deserted at the start of the battle of Bosworth 'if for king Richard's scurryers, scouring to and fro, they might so have done'.[120]

There is little evidence of light horse protecting companies of foot and waggon trains on the march, or maintaining contact between them and mounted retinues, but doubtless these were among their principal tasks. Edward, when advancing from Northampton to London in 1471, always left 'behind him in his journey a good band of spears and archers, his behind-riders, to counter, if it had needed, such of the Earl's [Warwick's] party as, peradventure, he should have sent to have troubled him on the back half if he so had done'.[121] As we have seen, on the march from Nottingham to Leicester in 1485, Richard covered the flanks of his army with wings of horsemen.[122] Thus the wars may have stimulated the development of light cavalry in England, and of expertise in its scouting roles.

The question arises whether, despite the heavy weight of assertions that the English habitually fought as infantry in set-piece battles, companies of horse were on occasion remaining mounted in the field. According to the author of *Knyghthode and Bataile*, horsemen were normally set in battle at each 'horn' or 'wing', covering the flanks of archers and other footmen.[123] But he is paraphrasing Vegetius. The frequent deployment, in the wars, of artillery and large numbers of sometimes ill-equipped and unreliable infantry suggests that there were flanking roles for cavalry. There are some tantalizing scraps of information hinting at cavalry actions. At Towton, according to Waurin, Edward concentrated his horsemen on a wing (*sus hesle*): they were put to flight early in the battle and pursued by the Lancastrian vanguard, presumably also mounted.[124] Though Commynes says that the battle of Barnet, ten years later, was fought on foot, Vergil, who had circumstantial, if not wholly accurate, information about it, recounts that Warwick arrayed his 'battles' 'with part of the horsemen in the left wing'. When his men were under heavy pressure, he 'relieved them who fought in the first front with a troop of light horsemen, and caused the enemy somewhat to give ground'.[125] According to the *Arrivall*, at

Tewkesbury Edward feared that the Lancastrians might place horsemen in ambush in a park on their right flank. Therefore he detached 200 spears, setting them in a 'plump' nearly a quarter of a mile from the field to watch the wood. But the Lancastrian command, lacking his tactical insight, failed to exploit the park. The Yorkist plump-commander, realizing this, used his initiative boldly by making a surprise charge against the flank of the Lancastrian vanguard, whilst it was heavily engaged with Edward's 'middleward'.[126] At Bosworth Richard led a charge against Henry Tudor: he 'struck his horse with the spurs, and runneth out of the one side without the vanward against him'.[127] Though the tactical circumstances were different, at both Tewkesbury and Bosworth we find Yorkist cavalry being used in an attempt to sway the balance when opposing infantry were heavily engaged. The Wars of the Roses probably produced a revival of English cavalry fighting, as well as of scouting.

Do contemporary manuscript illuminations and chivalrous romances throw any light on this? Indulgence in artistic and literary licence makes their evidence suspect, but it deserves some consideration, as a reflection of contemporary ideals. A manuscript of the French version of the *Arrivall* has miniatures depicting the battles of Barnet and Tewkesbury.[128] At Barnet the principal engagement is shown as taking place between heavily armoured cavalrymen fighting with swords and couched lances, whilst in the foreground a much smaller number of fully armoured men-at-arms fight on foot with sword and lance. At Tewkesbury the Lancastrians are shown in flight from Edward in a cavalry engagement, whilst in the foreground his more numerous archers gain the ascendancy in a shoot-out with their Lancastrian counterparts. Clearly the artist has taken considerable licence with his text, reversing the preponderance indicated in it of footmen over horsemen at Tewkesbury, depicting the horsemen as uniformly heavily armed, and suggesting that the battles were primarily cavalry engagements.

The series of drawings executed between 1485 and 1490 to illustrate the life of a chivalrous hero, Richard Beauchamp, earl of Warwick (d. 1439), besides being of much higher artistic quality, display a more detailed knowledge of arms and armour than the miniatures in the manuscript of the *Arrivall*. The drawings of the rout of Glyn Dŵr's forces show pursuing English spearmen charging on horseback accompanied by foot archers. Some of the horsemen are fully armoured, but others lack plates on their arms, and have helmets which do not cover the neck or the whole face. Perhaps the latter are wearing the equipment of the light cavalry which played such essential roles in the Wars of the Roses.[129]

The principal English literary work of the period concerned with fighting is Sir Thomas Malory's redaction into the vernacular of Arthurian romances, completed in 1469–70. The battles which Malory recounts, fascinatedly describing individual combats, commence as cavalry engagements, though knights perforce conclude struggles on foot sometimes. Malory echoed the traditional horse-fighting conventions of his sources. Having probably fought in France in the retinue of Richard Beauchamp, earl of Warwick, he was well aware of conventional English infantry methods. His opinion that mounted troops were more useful than foot soldiers was compatible with these as well as with the romance idiom. His King Lot exclaimed, 'ye may see what people we have lost and what good men we lose because we wait always on these footmen; and ever in saving of one of these footmen we lose ten horsemen for him'. Malory's descriptions of campaigns reveal an old soldier's eye. He was nervous about the need for good scouting. Merlin sends forth 'foreriders to skim the country' who encounter the northern army's foreriders and force them to reveal its line of approach. He mentions the scout watch in camp, and an army commander's shame at the destruction of his vaward before he could bring up his main force. Characteristically, Malory valued the military worth of gentlefolk above that of others.[130]

What Malory was particularly interested in applying to his delineation of Arthurian warfare was the methods and conventions of the contemporary tournament. 'A more jolier jousting was never seen on earth' is the comment on one battle. He may have been eager, as Caxton was to be, to promote among gentlefolk admiration for and the desire to emulate the cavalry skills and 'noble' qualities learnt in jousting on horseback.[131] Indeed, the need for cavalry in the Wars of the Roses may have given tournament techniques of controlling a horse in combat renewed practical relevance. There was a revival of interest in tournaments at Edward IV's court, which perhaps can be seen in this context as well as that of courtly splendour. The most famous combats at the Yorkist court were those held before the king at Smithfield on 11–12 June 1467, when his brother-in-law Lord Scales met the challenge of the Bastard of Burgundy. On the first day mounted combats were held – running at large, and tourneying with the sword. On the second day there were foot combats with axes and daggers.[132] It was this chivalrous sporting background which inspired Malory's battle scenes and those illustrated in so many contemporary manuscripts. The decorator of the *Arrivall* was seemingly adding another propaganda slant to the narrative by decking out some of Edward's grim triumphs in 1471 with a Burgundian chivalrous aura. Artistic and literary evidence therefore provide uncertain guides to the realities of the contemporary battlefield. But the impression so often conveyed by contemporary chroniclers, of struggles between dismounted hosts of men-at-arms and archers, also needs to be scrutinized hard and sceptically. In reality, infantry, cavalry and artillery were used in conjunction in the field, probably in increasingly sophisticated combinations which foreshadowed the tactical manoeuvring of early sixteenth-century armies.

The Wars of the Roses have the appearance of wars of movement, in which most commanders sought a speedy decision, if necessary by risking all in battle, rather than attempting to maintain a static defence in fixed fortifications. The traditional view of the relative insignificance of siege warfare in the struggles is implicit in A. Emery's statement: 'apart from the activities of Queen Margaret's troops in the north between 1461 and 1464, and the seizure of the rebel castles in Wales by Herbert, few castles were besieged'.[133] This absence of sieges cannot be attributed entirely to the lack of adequate fortifications. Generally, indeed, England and Wales did not have the density of fortification found in most neighbouring Continental provinces. One reason was that there were comparatively fewer cities than in northern France and the Low Countries. By the early fourteenth century London may have had approaching 50,000 inhabitants; in 1524 not more than fifteen other English towns exceeded 5,000. The typical town, of which there were hundreds, was what we would consider to be a large village, with a range of 500–1,500 inhabitants.[134] But as many as 108 English towns had walls built in the Middle Ages, and others had ditches and embankments, with wooden barriers and palisades.[135] Many of these fortifications are likely to have been in disrepair by the mid-fifteenth century, and were in any case constructed on too small a scale and in too old-fashioned or basic a manner to cater for majority military needs in the wars. The duke of York at Ludlow in 1459 and Henry VI at Northampton in 1460 did not use town walls as part of their defences, but constructed independent ones.

Nevertheless, a number of towns, particularly ports, and those near the sea or potentially hostile Marches, continued to repair and improve their defences. London, the greatest urban prize in Britain, had imposing fortifications, which the commons of Kent were unable to take by assault in 1450. The problems involved in mounting a siege of the city gave its governors power to bargain with the commanders of approaching armies on occasion.[136] Coventry had a particularly fine set of walls, which Warwick manned effectively in 1471. Edward IV and his brothers, unable to provoke the earl to sally forth, decamped, 'not thinking it behoveful to assail, nor to tarry for the assieging thereof; as well for the avoidance of great slaughters that should thereby ensue, and for that it was thought more expedient to them to draw towards London'.[137]

Though in the first half of the fifteenth century foreign threats and domestic discord were not sufficiently serious and prolonged to provide general stimulants to the improvement of English fortifications, the evolution of artillery and the consequently increasing vulnerability of defences provided some added incentive for work on them. The crown spent heavily, if intermittently, on its castles in the Anglo-Scottish Borders, and considerable sums were laid out on repairing castles in the principality of Wales damaged by Glyn Dŵr's rebellion. From 1399 onwards there was continuous building activity at some of the fine castles of the Lancastrian inheritance which Henry IV joined to the crown – at Bolingbroke, Lancaster, Leicester, Pontefract and Tutbury. This activity continued well into the reign of Henry VI at Bolingbroke, Pontefract and Tutbury. But, according to H. H. Colvin, 'with the exception of Nottingham, Windsor and Wallingford, few of the old royal castles in the midlands and south were now maintained in a defensible – or even in a habitable – condition'.[138] Colvin detects a decline in the tempo of work on royal fortifications under Henry VI. Available money was swallowed up by defence works on the perennially disturbed Anglo-Scottish Marches, on works in Normandy, and by the enormous cost of harbour works and repairs to fortifications necessitated by erosion at Calais. The long domestic peace of Henry VI's minority provided little inducement to reverse habitual neglect of ancient royal castles of the interior, though officials of the principality of Wales and the duchies of Cornwall and Lancaster strove conscientiously to maintain castles for which they were responsible.[139]

Nevertheless, there are a few indications that in the 1450s some efforts were made to strengthen royal castles, perhaps with the growing political tensions in mind. Ideas of fortifying them were certainly in the air: in 1450 the duke of Suffolk, constable of Wallingford castle, was accused in parliament of fortifying the castle for his own nefarious ends, and Jack Cade, withdrawing from London later in the year, contemplated barricading himself in Queenborough castle.[140] At Halton castle (Cheshire), in a region where Queen Margaret was soon to display particular diligence in rallying loyalties to its lord, her son, a new gatehouse was built at the main entrance in 1450–7.[141] At Tutbury castle (Staffs.), which she acquired as part of her jointure in 1446, she completed the new South Tower by 1450 and built the North Tower, completed in 1461.[142] At the Lancastrian castle of Bolingbroke (Lincs.), the entrance bridge was rebuilt and walls were repaired in 1457–9, and at Dunstanburgh (Northumberland), another duchy of Lancaster castle, a new tower was built in 1458 and the fortifications were strengthened in 1459.[143] Repairs were done at Newcastle (1458); and Pontefract – occupied by York's opponents in the 1460 campaign – had a lot of attention in Henry's last years.[144] In 1460 the royal council meeting at Coventry decided to make the well-maintained

Lancastrian castle at Kenilworth (Warwicks.) – exceptional in area and in the strength of its water defences – into the king's principal base: 'they determined to fortify . . . [it], and the king rode there and sent for all the guns and armaments in the Tower of London and filled up from these forty carts and transported them to Kenilworth and so armed that castle very strongly'.[145] The king's capture at Northampton after the complete rout of his army prevented the defences of Kenilworth from being put to the test. The laborious effort made to fortify it, to so little effect, suggests some of the reasons why strategy in the Wars of the Roses was not based mainly on the defence of fortifications. The long-term planning and large expenses required to set up and maintain a major base with victuals, batteries and ammunition were deterrents to such a strategy. Kings and nobles were not used to shouldering these burdens for domestic contingencies. Their familiarity with the great costs of maintaining the realm's frontier castles (e.g. at Roxburgh, Berwick, Calais and Guines) was likely to increase their reluctance. Moreover, a strong castle might in an emergency turn out to be strategically irrelevant: in 1460 the king's army moved away from Kenilworth, probably denuding it of artillery. There was a preference for settling domestic issues in short, sharp fights, which were relatively cheap and less annoying to the inhabitants than the tedious presence of soldiers inherent in static warfare. But castles certainly had important strategic roles in these wars of movement. They provided breathing spaces, into which king or magnate might dodge like a *banderillero*, to rally levies in comparative security, wait for allies to come to the rescue, and (not least) negotiate pardons from a position of vantage, or, if they were not forthcoming, a promise of sparing life and limb.

Yet, according to Colvin, by Henry VI's reign there was in some regions a dangerous imbalance between royal and private fortifications: 'The Midlands and the north were studded with private fortresses built and maintained by the over-mighty subjects into whose quarrels the Crown was soon to be drawn. The king still had castles in these areas, but they were no longer the largest, the strongest, or those that were most up-to-date in their defensive contrivances.'[146] There had indeed been some notable private castle-building in the later fourteenth century, particularly in the north to provide defences against Scottish incursions. The Percies' building works at Alnwick and Warkworth are notable examples of this.[147] William Worcester remarks on two magnates who had notably improved castles, though unfortunately he does not usually make clear how far their works were military or domestic. Ralph Neville, earl of Westmorland (d. 1425), he says, built or re-edified (*fundauit, edificauit*) the Yorkshire castles of Guiseley, Sheriff Hutton and Middleham, and the castles of Raby and Brancepeth in the bishopric of Durham.[148] The earl of Warwick (d. 1439) 'rebuilt (*de nouo renouauit*) the south side of Warwick castle, with a splendid new tower and various domestic offices'; he also renovated the castles of Hanley and Elmley (Worcs.), Baginton (Warwicks.) and Hanslope (Bucks.).[149] However, Emery's judgment that there was a marked decline in purely military building in England in the first half of the fifteenth century is surely correct, and should be applied as much to private as to urban and royal fortification.[150] Impressive remains survive of three notable private castles built early in Henry VI's reign. In the early 1430s Sir John Fastolf and Ralph Lord Cromwell, respectively, commenced major projects at Caister (Norfolk) and Tattershall (Lincs.), and in 1440 Roger Fiennes received a licence to crenellate his house at Hurstmonceux (Sussex). None of these castles, though provided with gunports, appear to have been built to withstand bombardment by heavy siege cannon.[151] Caister was in fact besieged from 21 August to 27 September 1469 by a force of 3,000, in a quarrel between the Paston family and the duke of Norfolk, guns being used in defence and assault. The castle was badly damaged by bombardment.[152] Most of the licences to crenellate granted to private individuals in the fifteenth century seem to have been intended for fortifications on a small scale, or of a relatively flimsy nature. They were erected by lords and gentlefolk who wanted to impress their neighbours, and guard against the dispossessions and mayhem endemic in shire society with an imposing tower or elaborately parapeted walls and gatehouse.[153] It is, indeed, difficult to detect any imbalance between royal and noble castles proving dangerous to the crown in the wars.

Control of castles became a major problem for the Lancastrian government after its victory at Ludford Bridge in 1459. There was the fear that the Yorkist lords might invade the realm and seize bases. At the start of December, Judde, master of the king's ordnance, was commissioned to visit all castles, fortified towns and fortalices in the realm, survey their ordnance and have it repaired.[154] Henry VI appointed his half-brother Pembroke constable of York's forfeited Marcher castle of Denbigh; but when the earl tried to take possession, entry was refused. On 16 February 1460 Henry referred to a recent letter from his brother requesting money and ordnance for the siege: the following month the defenders were still defiant.[155] The major siege of 1460 occurred after the Yorkist invasion in June, however. Royal supporters held out in the Tower of London, so as to deny the Yorkists full control of the capital. Lord Scales conducted a vigorous defence, firing his guns at the Yorkist army on its arrival in London.[156] The earl of Salisbury took command of the besieging force, a large part of which probably consisted of civic militia.[157] Scales's gunners continued to show their mettle: they 'cast wild fire into the city, and shot in small guns, and burnt and hurt men and women and children in the streets'.[158] The Yorkist batteries replied effectively: 'they of London laid great bombards on the further side of the Thames against the Tower and crazed the walls thereof in divers places'.[159] Scarcity of victuals, fading hopes of relief, and the distress of ladies sheltering in the Tower were among the factors which soon induced Scales to negotiate surrender,[160] but the intensity of the siege bears witness to the strategic importance of the Tower. Had the Yorkists not won so decisively at Northampton, Scales's continued pressure on the Londoners might have undermined Salisbury's ability to hold them in line.

After their victory, the Yorkist lords feared that their opponents in Wales, reluctant to give up York's forfeited properties, would garrison castles, opposing him on his return from Ireland. On 9 August the keeper of the privy seal was instructed to dispatch letters to the constables of Beaumaris, Conway, Flint, Hawarden, Holt and Ruthin castles. They were to be told to keep the castles securely, not allowing anyone to enter and fortify them. Jasper Tudor, earl of Pembroke, and his deputy at Denbigh castle, Roger Puleston, esquire, were ordered to surrender it to York's deputy.[161] Just over a week later Henry wrote to the Marcher Yorkists Sir William Herbert, Walter Devereux and Roger Vaughan, saying that reportedly certain persons 'usurp and take upon them to victual and fortify divers castles, places and strengths in our country of Wales'. The king enjoined them to take and keep these places securely on his behalf.[162] York's opponents were not able to obstruct his reinstatement, but the need for his presence in parliament in October and in the north in December left him little opportunity to reassert his ascendancy in Wales. The fact that the queen sought refuge in a castle there, that York dispatched his eldest son to the Welsh Marches, and that the latter had to fight a large-scale battle to retain them in February 1461 showed that the council's forebodings the previous August had substance.[163] The defiance of the Yorkists in Wales after Northampton started that prolonged resistance to Edward's rule there, and to the concomitant ascendancy of the Herberts and Vaughans, in which the seizure of some of the fine local baronial and 'Edwardian' castles figured prominently.

No siege played a decisive role in the bitter struggles of 1461 for the crown. But the northern army's advance and Edward's conquests probably led to the most widespread manning of fortifications in the wars. In January, to deal with the queen's threat, the council ordered the aldermen and burgesses of Stamford to have the town's defences manned, and the bailiffs of Shrewsbury to have theirs repaired and manned. Commissioners in Norfolk and adjacent shires were to deal with the disaffected who had fortified castles and fortalices.[164] On 3 February Nicholas Morley and John Bensted, esquires, were commissioned to array the lieges of Hertfordshire, Cambridgeshire and

Huntingdonshire as garrisons for castles and towns.[165] Many landowners, like William Grey, bishop of Ely, probably looked to their own defences: he garrisoned the Isle of Ely and Wisbech castle with men summoned from all his manors in Essex, Norfolk, Suffolk and Cambridgeshire, stiffened by thirty-five Burgundians armed with guns and crossbows.[166] However, the fortifications which turned out to be important in the queen's campaign were those of London, for her army's inability to threaten them negated her victory at St Albans.[167] Edward's victory at Towton, on the other hand, so disrupted the Lancastrian army that York and Newcastle could not be held against him. But the defeated party – as after Ludford Bridge or Northampton – tried hard to retain as toe-holds castles on the periphery of the realm.[168] For a time the Lancastrians may have even maintained a garrison in Northamptonshire. On 31 March William Lee, joiner, was empowered to find carriage, carters, horses and oxen to take three 'great bombards' which Edward IV had ordered to be sent for the siege of Thorpe Waterville castle – where the garrison may have held out since the Lancastrian retreat from St Albans. The siege commander was Sir John Wenlock, who had aided the siege of the Tower in 1460.[169]

Edward's government long remained apprehensive that the Lancastrians would seize castles. At the end of May 1461 Geoffrey Gate was ordered to safeguard Carisbrooke castle and the Isle of Wight.[170] But not until October 1462 were the Lancastrians able to reverse dramatically the defeat of their attempts to keep castles.[171] After the surrender of Bamburgh castle in June 1464, however, there remained only one substantial, menacing pillar of their 'castle-strategy' of the early 1460s. David ap Jevan ap Eynyon, whose levying activities as constable of Harlech castle for King Henry harmed Yorkist loyalists in North Wales in 1461, clung for years to this remote, forbidding fortress, a refuge for Lancastrian adherents. 'Gregory' wrote that 'that castle is so strong that men said that it was impossible to get it'. In the autumn of 1464 Lord Herbert, granted its constableship, commenced a serious siege. He was allowed £2,000 for costs by the crown, and was supplied with 'divers habilments of war' by the master of the king's ordnance. To no avail: David held out. In 1468, when Jasper Tudor was once more stirring in Wales, Herbert made another strenuous attempt against Harlech. This time, in August, he managed to negotiate terms of surrender.[172]

On the outbreak of 'Robin of Redesdale's' rising in 1469, Edward's favourites sought refuge in castles in Norfolk and Wales, but Earl Rivers and his son Sir John Wydeville, ensconced in Herbert's castle at Chepstow, had to surrender.[173] The fall of the Herberts encouraged rebelliousness in South Wales. In December 1469 Gloucester was granted full power to subdue the royal castles of Carmarthen and

Cardigan, which the rebellious gentlemen Morgan and Henry ap Thomas ap Griffith had seized, and from which they were raiding.[174] When Clarence and Warwick invaded England in September 1470, Edward's queen, Elizabeth Wydeville, then in an advanced state of pregnancy, 'well victualled and fortified' the Tower of London, and retired there. Her husband's flight made resistance futile, however. She went into sanctuary at Westminster, and the Tower was eventually surrendered to the mayor and aldermen of London, and to Warwick's man Sir Geoffrey Gate, who thus secured an important prize – King Henry, long a prisoner there.[175]

In 1471 Warwick garrisoned Coventry strongly and effectively, but erred gravely in failing to ensure that London was held on his behalf in sufficient strength.[176] The western Lancastrian army of 1471 was to gain an advantage by its uncontested admittance to Bristol. But a major factor in its defeat was the captain at Gloucester's refusal to surrender the castle and town.[177] Despite the débâcle at Tewkesbury, the irrepressible Jasper Tudor tried to hold South Welsh castles and fortified towns. He retreated with his retinue to Chepstow. After foiling Roger Vaughan's attempt against him there, he withdrew westwards to Pembroke castle. He was besieged by Morgan Thomas, 'and kept in with ditch and trench that he might not escape', but, just over a week later, was rescued by David Thomas. Nevertheless, Jasper had to give up Pembroke, and with his young nephew Henry Tudor he fled from Tenby to France.[178] But there may yet have been a Lancastrian attempt to revive the saga of Harlech: on 11 September 1471 the chief justice of North Wales, the earl of Shrewsbury, was empowered to give grace to any lieges within the castle.[179]

The previous May there had occurred the one major siege in the warfare of 1469–71, the only considerable assault on urban fortifications in the wars. This was the siege of London by the deceased Warwick's former sailors and their allies from Kent and Essex, led by his kinsman the Bastard of Fauconberg. He arrived on the Surrey bank of the Thames on 12 May. Denied entry to the city by the mayor and aldermen, he led his men up-river to cross Kingston bridge, intending to seize, and threatening to plunder, Westminster and the extensive London suburb between it and the walls. Such an attack might have induced the citizens to commit their forces rashly outside their gates, or to negotiate; but the Bastard speedily abandoned this bold strategy, which would have left his forces exposed to a royal advance from the west, with vulnerable lines of communication across the Thames. Warkworth condemned the Bastard's folly for not striking westwards directly at Edward, who 'by possibility could not by power have resisted the Bastard'. The latter's return to Southwark, not far from his ships, committed him to an assault on the city at its strongest points, after a display of indecision likely to hearten the defence. When he had guns brought from the ships and lined in battery to bombard the city from the south bank, the city gunners returned such accurate fire that the batteries could not hold position. The Bastard had to resort to assaults. One force tried in vain to burst across London Bridge after it and the houses on it had been fired. The author of the *Arrivall* considered this a hopeless attempt, because the defenders had such strong ordnance commanding the causeway. More worrying attacks were made by 3,000 troops ferried across to St Katherine's, near the Tower. They divided into two companies to assault Aldgate and Bishopsgate, shooting guns and arrows into the city with some effect and firing the gates. But the defences were well ordered by the earl of Essex, who stiffened the civic levies by mixing them with gentlefolk whom he had under arms. The rebels at the gates had a serious disadvantage: their line of communications was menaced by the Tower garrison, commanded by a spirited soldier, Earl Rivers. In one sally from a postern with 400–500 men, he drove the rebels from their position at Aldgate to the waterside. The assaults on the gates were finally repulsed when the defenders sallied out, routed the besiegers and drove them to their ships. Regrouping on the south bank, the Bastard's men made an orderly retreat to Blackheath, but held on there only from 16 to 18 May before dispersing, fearful of the king's approach.[180]

In the remaining desultory campaigns of the wars there occurred one memorable siege. About Michaelmas 1473 the Lancastrian earl of Oxford, who had fled abroad from the field of Barnet, sailed into Mount's Bay, Cornwall, and seized the fortified monastery on St Michael's Mount there, as a base from which to rally West Country loyalties. He had embarked at Dieppe with twelve ships equipped at Louis XI's expense, and had hovered for some time off English coasts. Warkworth remarked that the Mount was 'a strong place and a mighty, and cannot be got if it be well victualled with a few men to keep it; for twenty men may keep it against all the world'. He says that Oxford had 397 men to hold it, Worcester that he had only 80. Among his companions were his three brothers and two members of families which had suffered by supporting the Lancastrians, William Beaumont and Thomas Clifford. King and council commissioned Henry Bodrugan, 'chief ruler of Cornwall', to lay siege. He did not press the matter, being content to parley, and apparently even allowed the Mount to be victualled – perhaps running with the tide of local opinion. For when the earl and his men had seized the Mount, they reconnoitred the countryside 'and had right good cheer of the commons'. By 7 December news of these jaunts reached the court: they are alluded to in a commission appointing to the command of the siege, besides the slack Bodrugan, John Fortescue, squire of the king's body, and Sir John

Croker. Fortescue had 200 soldiers under his command. John Wode, master of the king's ordnance, organized the transport of cannon from the Tower. Operations may have been hampered by the enmity between Fortescue and Bodrugan, but the siege took a more serious turn, with daily skirmishes punctuated by brief truces.[181] The arrival of the reinforcements authorized by the king in December probably effectively cut Oxford off from any hope of Cornish support. The blockade commenced on 3 February 1474 by the king's ship *le Caricou*, with 260 soldiers and mariners aboard captained by William Fetherston, probably made surrender inevitable.[182] Warkworth was convinced that Oxford was eventually compelled to surrender because king and council had suborned his men with offers of pardons and rewards: 'and so in conclusion the Earl had not passing eight or nine men that would hold with him; the which was the undoing of the Earl'. It was, Warkworth concluded with unaccustomed joviality, a classic case of the proverb that 'a castle that speaketh, and a woman that will hear, they will be gotten both'.[183] For Oxford, the worst effect of the desertions was that they lessened his ability to bargain for good personal terms of surrender. His life was spared, but he was clapped into prison, and there he remained for the rest of Edward's reign.

A few attempts to hold and overcome fortifications in the later campaigns are to be noticed. In the 1483 rebellion Bodiam castle (Sussex) was held against Richard III, possibly by its owner, Sir Thomas Lewknor, who was attainted as a rebel.[184] Perhaps the object of holding it was to provide a base near the coast, in case Henry Tudor, sailing from Brittany, decided to land nearby and rally his Kentish supporters for an attack on London. His ally Buckingham's original base in the rising, Brecon castle, was successfully attacked by Sir Thomas Vaughan and his brothers Roger and Watkin.[185] In 1484 the earl of Oxford, imprisoned at Hammes castle in the March of Calais, suborned its captain, Sir James Blount. The pair fled to Henry Tudor in France, leaving a garrison in the castle. Perhaps they hoped to use Hammes as a base from which to win over the March and launch an attack through Kent. But the garrison at Calais remained loyal: a large part of it besieged Hammes in the winter of 1484-5. Oxford arrived nearby with a relieving force, and stiffened the garrison's resistance by passing to them a reinforcement of thirty men under Thomas Brandon. The royal commander (probably Lord Dinham), menaced by Oxford's proximity, allowed the Hammes garrison to march out, as the earl had hoped. He then withdrew with them from English territory. Considerable amounts of 'stuff' had been brought up during the siege, including stones for serpentines, powder for arquebuses, and scaling-ladders. The seriousness of the threat to Richard's rule posed by this Tudor attempt to gain the March has perhaps been underestimated.[186]

In 1496 James IV of Scotland, in support of the Yorkist claimant Warbeck, sacked peel towers in the Till valley, a characteristic activity in Border warfare.[187] When Warbeck landed in Cornwall in 1497, one of his aims was 'to capture wherever he went fortified places which might usefully serve in his defence', according to Vergil. He took and held St Michael's Mount, as Oxford had done.[188] The earl of Devon's retreat to Exeter may have given him hopes that he could occupy the city, as the Cornishmen had done earlier in the year, despite his lack of siege equipment.[189] We are fortunate in possessing an account of the first day of siege (17 September) written by Henry VII on the 20th, which almost certainly retails information contained in a letter to him from the commander, Devon, sent on the actual day. A letter from Devon to Henry dated 18 September survives, recounting that day's events.[190] According to Henry, the earl was well supported by the gentlefolk of Devon and Cornwall.[191] The rebels arrived at Exeter at about one o'clock on the 17th, 'and there ranged themselves in the manner of a battle, by the space of two hours'. Warbeck's request for the surrender of the city was refused by Devon. His men then assaulted the East Gate and the North Gate – both of which were in good repair.[192] They were driven off with losses of between 300 and 400. On the following day, Devon says, they once again assaulted the gates, concentrating on the North Gate. The defence was maintained strongly there, and the besiegers sustained heavy casualties, especially from gunfire. They requested a truce in order to regroup and withdraw from the city. This was granted, as the garrison, wearied and depleted by casualties, was not strong enough to attack. At about eleven o'clock in the morning the rebels withdrew: 'thanked be God [wrote the earl] there is none of your true subjects about this business slain, but divers be hurt. And doubt not again, one of yours is hurt, there is twenty of theirs hurt and many slain.' Gallantry forbade him from saying that he was one of those hurt: he was wounded by an arrow in the arm.[193] Vergil remarks on the fierceness of the fighting, and the martial conduct of the citizens. When the rebels fired the gates, the defenders, unable to extinguish the blaze, banked it up to drive them back. They dug ditches within the gates to provide new defences and repulsed attempts to scale the walls.[194]

The Wars of the Roses stimulated the strengthening of fortifications. Kings recognized the need to have some strategically placed interior castles in defensible condition. At the Tower of London Edward constructed c. 1480 the brick outwork on Tower Hill known as 'the Bulwark', perhaps an artillery emplacement.[195] In 1474 Richard Patyn had been commissioned to arrange the carriage of ordnance to Nottingham castle. Several months later he received a life grant of 4d. a day from a nearby mill and meadow: perhaps he was responsible for the custody of artillery there.[196] Between 1476 and 1480 Edward spent over £3,000 on the castle: a new tower was finished, but the works were apparently primarily residential.[197] Richard III planned and partially built impressive new defence works at Warwick castle where, like Henry VII, he probably kept artillery.[198] To strengthen his northern power-base, Richard also embarked in 1484 on a complete reconstruction of York castle: in 1478 Edward had already made clear his intention of repairing it. Events had shown the need for a royal stronghold there to overawe the citizens and the turbulent Yorkshire baronage.[199]

Urban corporations had an incentive to strengthen their defences, and the crown a reason to encourage them. Worcester's walls had apparently not been strong enough to prevent the rebel lords of 1459 from occupying the city. Soon afterwards, in November, the town received a royal grant of stones, including broken ones from the castle walls, for the repair of walls, bridge and gates. This was in response to the citizens' petition that the fortifications were so ruinous that 'a few ill-disposed persons could freely enter and have so done in the days last past'.[200] London was probably the city most frequently in fear of assault in the wars. The most thorough repairs of London Wall were initiated by Ralph Jocelyn (mayor 1476–7): 'and or his year came to an end he had made a good part of that which is new made, beside provision of lime and Brick' for further repairs. Traces of these brick repairs can be seen in surviving fragments.[201]

Since dynastic strife tended to increase the characteristic insecurities of landowners, there were incentives for them to maintain and improve fortifications. Newly rich and powerful gentlefolk built to impress neighbours and provide a refuge from their enemies. The most spectacular surviving example is Raglan castle (Monmouthshire), with its great gatehouse and its hexagonal moated keep, the 'Yellow Tower of Gwent'. The castle reflects the new and much-resented power of Edward IV's 'supremo' in South Wales, William Herbert, earl of Pembroke.[202] Another recently elevated servant of Edward, William Lord Hastings, gave expression to the influence which he had gained in Leicestershire by adding a keep to the old castle at Ashby de la Zouch (1474–83), and commencing in 1480 the building of an impressive castle at Kirby Muxloe.[203]

Though concerned to maintain the defences of the realm, Henry VII does not seem to have shared Edward's and Richard's determination markedly to improve royal strongpoints in the interior of the country. The projected works at York and Warwick castles lapsed, and during Henry's reign many royal castles entered what was to be a lasting phase of neglect and decay.[204] Perhaps youthful experience made him wary of putting his trust in castles. He had seen his guardian, Herbert, fall in

1469, without being able to rely on Raglan's splendid defences. In 1471 Henry had probably had to flee from Chepstow and Pembroke castles.[205] His invasions of the realm in 1483 and 1485 had taught him that men's loyalties were its keys. He may have felt safe in not building up royal fortifications because so many of the best private ones – such as the fine castles of the Nevilles – came to him by escheat or forfeiture. With some exaggeration, the Venetian commentator of 1498 asserted that fortresses, apart from those of the bishopric of Durham, were in royal hands.[206] Since, after 1486–7, dynastic revolt attracted little domestic support, magnates may have been glad of the excuse not to spend money on maintaining fortifications. Lord Hastings's son failed to complete his father's new buildings at Kirby Muxloe. Thus the petering-out of the Wars of the Roses in Henry's reign ended the recent revival of interest in developing fortifications in the interior of the country, and led to a resumption of the neglect generally characteristic of the first half of the fifteenth century. But the Anglo-Scottish Border region remained exceptional. There, frontier tensions intensified, exacerbated by the accession of the anglophobe James IV in 1488. In 1491 Henry VII showed interest in acquiring from the dissident earl of Angus the grim castle of Hermitage in Liddesdale, which would have given him an advanced base from which to control the troublesome local reivers. James's invasion of 1496 is likely to have made northern English landowners look to their defences. In 1497 the king of Scots besieged and bombarded Norham, Bishop Fox of Durham's exposed fortress on the Tweed, necessitating major repairs.[207]

The conditions and aims of warfare in the domestic conflicts certainly did not encourage prime reliance on fortifications. Yet there were some crucial sieges and many brief occupations of castles. Those which figure prominently are mostly the ones in regions where they were generally well maintained – in the far north, Wales, and the March of Calais. Castles and fortified towns were usually occupied briefly, as bases for the rallying of support, or as refuges from which to bar pursuers. However, our knowledge of siege warfare in the wars may be particularly defective. Except when London or a leading town was threatened with assault, or the siege of a castle attained peculiar fame, chroniclers were little interested. They concentrated on the decisive battle, the *iudicium Dei*. There are a number of sieges which we know about only because of casual mention in a record source. If the *Arrivall*, a detailed and expert account of Edward's campaigns in 1471, had not survived, we would not know about the importance of Gloucester castle, however brief, in the western campaign. Our knowledge of the defence of Chepstow and Pembroke in 1471 and Hammes in 1484–5 stems mainly from Polydore Vergil's particular interest in and sources of information about the early life and struggles of his patron Henry VII. In the local bickering which was a concomitant of the grand campaigns of the wars, there may have been considerable fighting around fortifications, even if on a relatively small and brief scale. At times this may have been an influence on the general outcome which is hidden from us. For instance, we may speculate that in February 1461 many men in the East Midlands, East Anglia and the south-east were, like the bishop of Ely, looking to the defence of their properties against the dreaded advent of Queen Margaret's northerners. If so, their static local defences may have been a factor in the odd outcome of the main campaign, in which both sides suffered defeat. Warwick's army may have lacked reliable levies (*pace* the choleric 'Gregory') because many men stayed at home at their masters' behest. The queen's precipitate and lengthy withdrawal, after her failure to secure London, may have been hastened by embattled manor-houses and townships along her line of communications, whose inhabitants were desperate to prevent their beasts from being herded off and their meagre winter food stocks from being seized.

It is difficult to be sure that the Vegetian advice given by the author of *Knyghthode and Bataile* about complex tactical formations and manoeuvres was more than a literary fancy, as far as the Wars of the Roses were concerned.[208] Probably masses of hastily arrayed contingents, often brought into battle within days of assembling, could only be expected to line up for a frontal assault or defence with their traditional weapons, bow and bill. But these very limitations may have stimulated commanders' use of elite bodies of specialist troops, often foreign mercenaries: there are references to the deployment of ordnance and flanking cavalry in the field, in conjunction with bowmen and billmen. The distinctive equipment and roles of light and heavy cavalry may have been well understood, for besides frequent references to the scouting and protecting roles for cavalry, there is Vergil's description of a cavalry charge against a main body of troops at Bosworth. Forewards often operated separately from the mass of troops: perhaps there was a trend to concentrate in them more experienced and manoeuvrable companies. Unfortunately few writers were interested in analysing tactical organization or assessing how responsive to sophisticated commands individual and grouped companies were. Vergil, whose military interests were based on the study of classical authorities, got veterans of Bosworth to explain tactics with unusual precision. He gives a Vegetian account of the formation and deployment of the forewards, which with other tactical details suggests a degree of professional expertise in captains and soldiers hardly hinted at by the customarily more pedestrian accounts of the wars. Vergil's Bosworth is anything but a formless slogging match between old-fashioned forces commanded by bull-headed traditionalists.[209]

Therefore the blending of traditional and innovatory methods in early Tudor armies was probably a development of precedents from the Wars of the Roses, not a completely new one. Why then has there been a tendency to dismiss the skills displayed in the wars as relics of the Hundred Years War? Perhaps it derives in no small measure from the judgments of a penetrating contemporary commentator, Philippe de Commynes. As we have seen, he admired traditional English skills in infantry fighting, particularly in archery, and appreciated their influence on Burgundian practice.[210] The one substantial English army which he personally observed was that with which Edward IV invaded France in 1475: 'never before had an English king brought across such a powerful army at one time . . . nor one so well prepared to fight'. The men-at-arms were 'very well equipped and accompanied'.[211] The army had good camping gear and a large number of scourers.[212] But Commynes also emphasized the English soldiery's deficiencies – significantly, in order to stress the lack of judgment of Edward's ally, Charles of Burgundy: 'these were not the Englishmen of his father's day and the former wars of France. They were inexperienced and raw soldiers, ignorant of French ways.'[213] Commynes watched them from Amiens with his master Louis XI, as they approached to encamp for the conclusion of the Anglo-French truce: 'I tell no lie when I say that Edward's troops seemed to be very inexperienced and new to action in the field as they rode in very poor order.' Soon afterwards he formed a low opinion of their discipline when sent to mop up their drunken disorders in Amiens.[214]

Perhaps Commynes's unfavourable impressions were somewhat harsh, and should not be taken as his considered judgment on English military methods. He was struck by Edward's fortunate experience of war in his domestic conflicts. In 1475 many of Edward's retinue commanders and soldiers were also highly experienced. But such a large army must have included raw arrayed men too. The invasion of France probably presented the English command with unaccustomed logistic problems. Armies of the Wars of the Roses are unlikely to have transported so much ordnance and equipment as the 1475 expedition, or to have been used to coping with victualling problems in a country where town gates were firmly shut against them and the ground had been rigorously scorched. Such conditions may have produced unimpressively sluggish progress, which a wealth of tactical expertise could not improve. Moreover, Commynes may not have realized that English infantry were not so used to having mounts as in earlier French campaigns. Molinet remarked more sagely that Edward's army was 'poorly mounted and little used to going on horseback'.[215] The consequent poor riding and bad order in his 'battles' on the move may have given Commynes a misleading impression of their tactical capabilities which his political stance made him eager to emphasize. Moreover, he observed the English army at a time when the news had probably penetrated to the ranks that there would be no fighting. English troops relaxing abroad, having a party on the local wine, have often given foreigners a misleadingly low impression of their military capabilities. In battle they could be transformed. Thus the chronicler Bernaldez recounted how, at the siege of Loja in Granada in 1486, Sir Edward Wydeville dismounted according to English custom (*a uso de suo tierra*), to fight with his 300 men on foot, devastatingly wielding their battleaxes against the Moors.[216]

Chapter 9

The Wars and Society

Contemporary annalists – mainly London chroniclers – on whom we rely heavily for accounts of the Wars of the Roses, dwell mainly on the wars' immediate political causes and effects. Their more general comments are focused on abuses of kingship and on the dynastic issue, with occasional reflections on the times being out of joint. They largely lacked the hindsight and historiographical concepts which enabled Tudor writers to view the wars as an integral episode or at least as a connected sequence of events, and predisposed them to moralize about the evils they inflicted on society.[1] There were, indeed, some contemporary writers who considered the wars more generally. The first continuator of the Crowland abbey chronicle, a Benedictine monk who chronicled events up to January 1470, wrote that the dissensions which had sprung up between Henry VI and Richard of York 'were only to be atoned for by the deaths of nearly all the nobles of the realm'. He alleged that divisions had spread within a variety of social organizations: 'And not only among princes and people had such a spirit of contention arisen, but even in every society, whether chapter, college, or convent, had this unhappy plague of division effected an entrance.' He summarized the dire results in a passage which has earned him the denigration of modern historians: 'the slaughter of men was immense: for besides the dukes, earls, barons, and distinguished warriors who were cruelly slain, multitudes almost innumerable of the common people died of their wounds. Such was the state of the kingdom for nearly ten years.'[2]

The chronicler Warkworth, ruminating on the reasons why Edward IV lost his crown in 1470, takes a perspective back to the start of his reign, and fixes on the miseries caused by continued warfare as the cause of subjects' alienation from him. He was probably referring principally to the costs of the Northumbrian campaigns (1461–4):

when King Edward IVth reigned, the people looked after all the foresaid prosperities and peace, but it came not; but one battle after another, and much trouble and great loss of goods among the common people; as first, the 15th of all their goods, and then an whole 15th, at yet at every battle to come far out their countries at their own cost.[3]

Warkworth also gives an illuminating description of how a region might suffer through the indiscriminate extortion of fines for pardons after rebellion. He describes how, after the suppression of the Bastard of Fauconberg's rising, royal commissioners sat on

all Kent, Sussex, and Essex, that were at the Blackheath, and upon many others that were not there; for some men paid 200 marks, some a £100, and some more and some less, so that it cost the poorest man 7s. which was not worth so much, but was fain to sell such clotheing as they had, and borrowed the remnant, and laboured for it afterwards; and so the King [Edward IV] had out of Kent much goods and little love. Lo, what mischief grows after insurrection, etc.![4]

This kind of comment on the regional consequences of rebellion is largely lacking in London chronicles, the principal literary source for later accounts. Their authors were unlikely to be concerned about the reduction of provincials to beggary, especially troublesome Kentishmen. Sporadic concern about the latter's designs on the city's wealth is one of the few signs of war nervousness shared by London chroniclers. Their general lack of a sense of civic and personal involvement is a valuable indication of wealthy Londoners' experience of the wars, but cannot be taken as a pattern of Englishmen's experience generally.[5]

To explore the latter, the comments of the Crowland monk and Warkworth respectively about heavy casualties and impoverishment through exactions provide a surer starting-point. It may be significant, however, that they do not picture widespread devastation and general social upheaval as consequences of the wars, unlike French polemicists, notably Alain Chartier and Thomas Basin, lamenting the effects of the Hundred Years War in France. One Englishman certainly argued that domestic strife had generally increased lawlessness in England. He had a partisan aim in doing so, for he was a royal official arguing before the Commons in 1474 to persuade them to grant a subsidy for the proposed royal expedition to France, on the grounds that war against the realm's 'outward' enemies would draw off disorderly elements.[6] What he said is in fact a valuable indication of people's feelings about the effects of the wars, for to be effective his arguments had to ring true for shire knights and burgesses. Dissension and discord, he said, had led to poverty and desolation, and Englishmen had generally suffered ills because of the civil wars: 'every man of this land that is of reasonable age hath known what trouble this realm hath suffered, and it is to suppose that none hath escaped but at one time or other his part hath be therein'. Though general acceptance of Edward's title had stilled dissension

> yet is there many a great sore, many a perilous wound left unhealed, the multitude of riotous people which have at all times kindled the fire of this great division is so spread over all and every coast of this realm, committing extortions, oppressions, robberies, and other great mischiefs.

Accounts of England written by foreigners in the later fifteenth century do not attribute evils to domestic warfare in the manner of the Crowland monk and Warkworth. In 1466 a Bohemian noble, Leo of Rozmital, landed at Sandwich and travelled via Canterbury to London, thence to Windsor and Salisbury, re-embarking at Poole. Two members of his retinue, his standard-bearer Schasek and Gabriel Tetzel of Nuremberg, wrote accounts of his travels.[7] They certainly do not give the impression that London and south-east England were lacking in prosperity. Perhaps Tetzel's account of what he considered the exceptional magnificence of Edward's court and the extraordinary reverence shown to the king and queen by kinsfolk and magnates reflects a style deliberately emphasized to assert the regal dignity of the new dynasty. Schasek remarked how Edward's sailors 'when they saw the King's letters, they all fell to their knees and kissed the letters. For they have the custom that when they hear the King's name or see his letters, they show their respect for them thus.'[8] Such obeisance seems over-elaborate, artificial, but perhaps prudent in a realm the title to which was in dispute.

The Venetian envoy Trevisan had written for him in 1498 by a fellow Italian a brief description of England and English affairs. The writer's personal knowledge of the realm seems to have been confined to London and the south – on this limited observation he was highly impressed with the wealth of the realm, particularly that of the London merchants who had entertained him. But he believed that the nobility had suffered as a result of domestic faction. He says that the peers ('li Signori honorati di Titolo') had patronized many clients, with whose support they had terrorized the crown and their own localities, and on whose account they were at last all executed.[9] This is indeed garbled stuff, but it cannot be entirely dismissed: it is a valuable if tantalizingly distorted echo of some Englishmen's notions that there had been an upheaval in their society. Enigmatic judgments of English government and society in the period are implicit in a famous treatise – *The*

Governance of England, by Sir John Fortescue, former chief justice of the King's Bench and chancellor to the exiled Henry VI. This short work, distilling a lifetime's bureaucratic and political experience near the centres of power, was finalized sometime between Fortescue's transference of his allegiance to Edward after Tewkesbury field in 1471 and his death *c.* 1479. In the *Governance* he defined what he considered to be the historic nature of the English polity, and diagnosed and prescribed for the crown's recent problems, clearly recalling his personal experience, particularly of those in Henry VI's majority. Fortescue distinguished the realm as being free from the arbitrary exercise of the royal will, but subject to 'Jus polliticum et regale', which entitled subjects to participate in law-making and settling grants of subsidy. He attributed the commons' prosperity and military strength to the effects of this 'mixed' rule, and Frenchmen's lack-lustre poverty to the authoritarian government burdening them. He argued that the English crown could recover its strength, and reduce the influence of 'overmighty' subjects clogging its institutions, by a vigorous implementation of what were in fact traditionally prescribed remedies for its better financial endowment, and for the appointment of a more effective council.

Fortescue's diagnosis is hard-hitting, but one wonders whether his conservative prescriptions and praise of English institutions cloak a deep anxiety about the possible political and constitutional consequences of recurrent domestic strife and disorder. He may have been arguing against advocates of harsh exercises of royal will as a remedy for instability: the king's representative in the 1474 parliament whose speech to the Commons survives projected 'outward' war as an alternative to stiff government. Though Fortescue had not lived under Edward's allegiance in the 1460s, he may have believed, like Warkworth, that Edward's heavy demands to suppress risings had alienated his subjects, so that the 'overmighty' could threaten his rule. Rebellion was begetting rebellion. Perhaps Fortescue was expressing a pious hope about Edward's restored rule rather than a considered judgment of it when he wrote:

> He hath done more for us, than ever did king of England, or might have done before him. The harms that hath fallen in getting of his Realm, be now by him turned into the good and profit of all of us. We shall now more enjoy our own goods, and live under justice, which we have not done of long time, God knoweth.[10]

On the other hand, this may be a sincere retraction: looking back, he may now have felt that the extinction of domestic strife mattered more than the perpetuation of the Lancastrians, and that the war of 1471 had given Edward an unrivalled opportunity to restore lasting peace and sound rule.

Literary comments do not provide much indication of the extent to which different social groups participated in the wars. The group likely to be involved most heavily was the secular peerage, because of close personal ties with the crown and dependence on court favour. But there were considerable variations in the extent of peers' participation, as individuals and as a group. Edward's Neville kinsmen were habitual participants, but his brother-in-law Suffolk stayed at home as much as possible. Dr Richmond has calculated that there were sixty secular peers in September 1459, joined by ten more between then and March 1461, and that fifty-six out of the seventy participated in the fighting of 1459–61.[11] The high active proportion indicates that this was the period of greatest peerage participation. At St Albans in 1455 eighteen secular peers were present, and at least sixteen were probably active in the campaign of 1459. The number rose to thirty-two in 1460, thirty-three in 1461 and reached thirty-eight, the highest point in the wars, in December 1462, when Edward took an exceptional number of peers northwards.[12] In the peripheral Lancastrian campaigns of 1463–4 and the Neville revolt against Edward in 1469 little more than a handful of peers were engaged. As the crisis of Yorkist rule intensified, more peers were drawn in – twelve in 1470, thirty-one in 1471. But totals as high as those of 1460–2 and 1471 were probably never approached again. In 1483 at least twelve peers were in the field, in 1485 ten, in 1487 thirteen or fourteen, and in 1497 four. Dr Richmond remarks that the low figure for Bosworth demonstrates the growing passivity of the nobility.[13] Other factors too may have lain behind these small numbers. The peerage was depleted by natural wastage – only thirty-eight peers were summoned to the 1484 parliament.[14] Changes in military method may have lessened royal reliance on a levy of peers – against rebels Richard III and Henry VII depended particularly on the military support of a few trusted peers and on that of their own retainers; they were anxious to nip rebellion in the bud rather than wait about for more distant, sluggish or hesitant nobles.[15]

The extent of participation by most other social groups, and the factors determining it, are harder to discern. Among gentlefolk – knights, esquires and gentlemen – it is likely that those closely linked by clientage to kings and participating nobles were most active. Chroniclers sometimes relate how men in receipt of fees were prominent in fighting and, as we have seen, kings and nobles tried to secure their active support.[16] Even kinds of retainers who would not normally be expected to fight were sometimes caught up in battle. Among the Lancastrians captured at Hexham (1464) was John Nayler, *cursarius* of chancery.[17]

Gentlefolk, like peers, were probably particularly active in the years

1459–63 and 1471. In January 1463, when Edward had assembled so many peers in the north, there was present in his army 'almost the whole English knighthood (*milicie*)'.[18] In regions on which risings were based, or on which special reliance was placed to oppose them, a higher percentage of gentlefolk is likely to have been recruited. Cheshire gentlefolk rallying to the young prince of Wales suffered high casualties at Blore Heath in 1459.[19] Where gentlefolk had become especially used to forming networks of clientage and political alliances, in order to support or oppose controversial magnate hegemonies – as in the north and Wales – they were more prone to joining in or indeed generating revolt. William Worcester's lists of recruits to the Tudor and Mortimer armies before Mortimer's Cross in 1461 suggest that Welsh and Herefordshire gentlefolk had flocked *en masse* to the respective standards. In the Edgcote campaign (1469), the Herberts had a large retinue of Welsh gentry.[20] Knights and esquires from the north-western shires figured prominently among the opponents of Henry VII's rule, expressing actively the regret felt by many northern gentlefolk at the destruction of the Neville hegemony cultivated by Richard of Gloucester, and their dislike of the Tudor, Stanley and Percy influence which had replaced it.[21]

It must not be too readily assumed that gentry participation in the last campaigns – for which information about participants is sparse – was negligible. The lists of those attainted for their part in the 1483 rebellion suggest a widespread involvement by south-eastern gentry.[22] Vergil names over sixty gentlemen in the king's army in 1487, and a selection of thirty-nine campaigning for him in the West Country in 1497.[23]

Clergy and burgesses were, by virtue of their avocations, generally regarded as exempt from military summons for personal service. But in the north, clergy as well as laity were customarily obliged to array against the Scots. In the early 1460s, Edward IV and Warwick dispatched mandates to Archbishop Booth of York for the array of the provincial clergy against threatened invasion in support of King Henry.[24] Clerics were also more generally present in armies acting as councillors, secretaries and chaplains. The future cardinal Morton, a steadfast servant of Henry VI, shared the privations of Lancastrian forces in Northumberland in the 1460s, and was captured at Tewkesbury in 1471. Earlier in the year William Dudley (later promoted to the see of Durham) had joined Edward at Doncaster at the head of 160 men.[25] But it is unlikely that such as Morton or Dudley had the inclination or skill to act the combatant as much as the friar who loosed off guns all night after Blore Heath.[26]

As landed magnates, bishops may have been expected to provide military contingents. When the bishop of Winchester took leave of

Henry VII at Coventry before the Stoke campaign, he left the 'substance of his company' to serve under the standard of his kinsman the earl of Devon; the archbishop of Canterbury departed at Loughborough, leaving his folk under his nephew Robert Morton's command, to be put under Oxford's standard in the foreward. The main clerical involvement was political and financial. Dr Knecht has shown how the aristocratic links of Henry VI's bishops generated episcopal partisanship.[27] The Crowland monk wrote with feeling of how the dissensions rippled through corporate bodies of ecclesiastics.[28] Henry VII, despite the papal sanction of 1486 for excommunication of plotters against his rule, suffered from clerical dissentients. Richard Symonds, Simnel's priestly *éminence grise*, presumably hoped that rebellion would lead him to high office. Among those convicted of treason in 1495 were some prominent and well-reputed ecclesiastics.[29] Specifically clerical grievances, exacerbated by the wars, may have contributed to clerical dissent, besides dynastic, familial and patronal ties. The convocation of Canterbury's grant in 1463 of an exceptional subsidy of 13s. 4d. from every priest with a minimum annual income of ten marks is alleged to have caused bitter complaints.[30] The curtailment under Henry VII of the recognition of rights of sanctuary for fugitive traitors at common law may have provoked clerical misgivings.[31] In 1497 Warbeck accused Henry and his adherents of 'great and execrable offences daily committed . . . in breaking the liberties and franchises of our Mother Holy Church, to the high displeasure of Almighty God'.[32]

Citizens and burgesses were obliged to don armour and head the defence in person when their town was threatened by rebel advances. There were numerous occasions in the wars when they prepared to do so, but few actual urban sieges. Town dwellers probably assisted in defending Carlisle against assault in 1461, and York in 1487: the burgesses of Exeter manned their gates and walls with spirit in 1497. The London mercer John Harowe helped to besiege the Tower in June 1460.[33] In 1471 London burgesses helped to repel the Bastard of Fauconberg's attacks: leading citizens were knighted by Edward IV for their steadfastness.[34] But on occasion burgesses and other townsmen ventured to fight outside their walls, enrolling as captains or soldiers in the summoned urban contingents, in order to fulfil obligations of clientage, or in search of adventure, or for pay and reward.[35] Harowe died fighting for Richard of York at Wakefield in December 1460, and the account in *Gregory's Chronicle* of the second battle of St Albans strongly suggests that the writer (a Londoner) was present as a soldier in Warwick's army.[36] 'Master Hervy, the recorder of Bristol' was killed on the Lancastrian side at Tewkesbury.[37] Nicholas Faunt, mayor of Canterbury, was a principal abettor of the Bastard of Fauconberg's rising, and, as Dr Richmond has shown, over 200 men from the city were involved in it.[38]

Evidence of urban participation in particular suggests that many of the campaigns were more than clashes between aristocrats and their rural clients and tenants. This is contrary to the impression often given by chroniclers, who in their accounts of battles tended to concentrate on the actions of the principals, and were hardly concerned to analyse the composition of armies, to indicate the relative strengths of noble retinues, shire levies and town companies. A poem on the battle of Towton uniquely celebrates the participation of urban as well as noble contingents – no other literary source mentions the presence of the former there.[39]

Chroniclers, moreover, concentrated on the forces which fought in major battles. But it is clear that many others were in arms, whose less decisive activities are shadowy. Forces were raised to guard towns and coasts which were never engaged: in 1461, many places in southern England were guarded against the northern men. The speed with which the issue was sometimes settled in battle precluded the involvement of some contingents. In 1455 the numbers engaged at St Albans may indeed have been surpassed by those under arms who did not arrive in time or were deliberately withheld.[40] In all three major campaigns of 1469 and 1470 the armies commanded by Warwick and Clarence remained on the sidelines, since the issue was settled by the actions of supporters commanding subordinate and separate forces. In 1471 sizeable Lancastrian forces were raised in Wales and the north about which nothing is known, since they were disbanded after Edward's victory at Tewkesbury. In 1483 there was clearly a large-scale rebellion in the south-east, but, because it petered out after Buckingham's débâcle, it is ill documented.

London chroniclers, writing for an elite especially sensitive about the city's corporate and individual relations with kings and magnates, emphasized their decisive clashes in the wars. Another sensitive interest was the often threatening behaviour of the amorphous, ambiguously termed 'commons' – hence an emphasis on their resort to arms with minimal encouragement or support from nobles and gentlefolk, categorized as being inspired by righteous indignation at misgovernment or malignant, covetous turbulence. As McFarlane indicated, commoners certainly expressed violent opinions about the matters at issue between lords, and communities were rent by resulting quarrels at a popular as well as at elite levels. The passage of Lancastrian lords through Nottingham in October 1459 provoked divisions in the town, as depositions soon after in the borough court show.[41] Two men deposed that Thomas Bolton had said that there were traitors to the earl of Northumberland and Lord Egremont in the town, 'and owed them no good will, and that he would make good and fight, and waged his glove, because he was born and fostered on their ground'. Bolton himself deposed that he had heard John Whitele say that 'there rode many strong thieves with my Lord of Northumberland and my Lord of Westmorland through the town' and that he had argued against the baker Robert Shirwood's assertions in favour of the earl of Salisbury. Thus the quarrels of lords might widen the cracks underlying laboriously maintained urban unity and peace, besides threatening that a town might give offence to a lord. External demands for financial support in the wars might also have the same effects. Early in Edward's reign, at a Nottingham peace session, John Michell accused Thomas Skrymshire of having spoken treasonably:

> [when] John asked if he would go with the King in his journey northward, Thomas said 'Nay, his money should go, but he would not go himself, and it was nought that they went about, for the King was not king, but that he was made King by the Kentishmen, and the very right King and the Prince were in Scotland'.[42]

Commoners often behaved, in the context of the wars, with a violence which their superiors found difficult to control. In 1460 the Yorkist lords at Calais were anxious that the captured Rivers and his son should not enter the town till the evening, 'pour doubte du commun qui ne les amoit point'.[43] In London, to their chagrin, their sailors lynched Lord Scales after his submission.[44] Allegedly the earl of Salisbury might have been ransomed after his capture at Wakefield, had not the common people of the region violently extricated him from Pontefract castle and beheaded him.[45] In 1461, when the queen's army was threatening London, 'communes civitatis' disrupted the pact between her and the city government, seizing victuals which the aldermen had ordered to be dispatched for her to Barnet, and threatening her knights Baldwin Fulford and Alexander Hody at Westminster.[46] In 1463, when the former Lancastrian duke of Somerset rode through Northampton with Edward IV, the commons thereabouts rose up to kill the duke despite the royal presence.[47] Soon after the battle of Edgcote in 1469 the commons at Bridgwater (Somerset) captured an erstwhile leader of the royal army, Humphrey Stafford, earl of Devon: there he was beheaded.[48] It is no wonder that, as Fortescue says, 'Some men have said that it were good for the king, that the commons of England were made poor, as be the commons of France. For then they would not rebel, as now they do oftentimes.'[49]

The commons' interest in expressing opinions about what was at issue in the wars and in participating – even on occasion initiating risings – was facilitated and stimulated by the continuing failure of magnates to resolve the political rifts which deepened between them from the 1440s onwards, and their desire, when resort was made to arms, to widen the basis of support. In what other period has a leading Yorkshire landowner, in order to gain popular support, assumed the nickname of a heroic mythical lawbreaker? Sir John Conyers's apparent assumption of the pseudonym 'Robin of Redesdale' echoed the recent use of the name Robin by leaders of popular protest in Yorkshire[50] – an allusion to Robin Hood. In 1485 northern rebel leaders allegedly had the names of Robin of Redesdale, Jack Straw (a leader of the Peasants' Revolt in Kent in 1381), and Master Mendall (recalling the Robin Mend-All of 1469).[51] The Yorkshire rebels of 1489 summoned support 'in the name of Master Hobbe Hyrste, Robin Goodfellow's brother he is, as I trow'.[52]

Southern popular revolt lacked a vague, but powerfully emotive, unitary symbol such as that provided in Yorkshire by the ballad images of Robin Hood. But it relied perhaps more on relatively sophisticated rallying-points – political manifestos, and allusions to noble causes. The south-eastern rebels of 1450 drew up elaborate petitions and their leader, Jack Cade, used the politically charged, aristocratic pseudonym of Mortimer. The rioters in the London suburbs in May 1486 displayed homely 'Ploughs Rokkes Clowtes Shoes and Wolsakkes', but also two standards blazoning the ragged staff (badge of the imprisoned earl of Warwick) and the Yorkist badge of the white rose.[53]

Why were the common folk often willing participants in the wars? Many, especially those who had suffered financial and judicial hardships, may have been convinced by propaganda denouncing court favourites, such as was disseminated by the Yorkists and later by Clarence and Warwick. As the Peasants' Revolt and Cade's rebellion had strikingly demonstrated, there was a firm connection in the popular mind between evil counsel given to kings and the financial and judicial oppressions and default of royal redress suffered by the 'poorest he'. Moreover, even the lowliest may have felt concern about the dynastic issue. The usurper was a hideous crack in the chain of nature, *ipso facto* incapable of fulfilling his royal functions as mediator between God and his subjects, consequently visiting them with wrath divine and human. In a period when all ranks of society were concerned with the rightful inheritance of property, and when the economic factors stimulating exceptional tensions between landlords and peasants early in the century had declined, one must not underestimate the force of conviction among commons that they should be ruled by the noble as well as royal families who had customarily done so.[54] Practical as well as numinous benefits flowed from rightful tenure – the true inheritor was trusted to mediate, like his forbears, between the men in his lordship and the royal power. When Sir Robert Welles, supported by other local gentlefolk, told the Lincolnshire commons that they could not mitigate the royal wrath in 1470, he appears to have been unhesitatingly believed and widely followed in rebellion. The previous year, there had been a revolt in Yorkshire in favour of restoring the young Henry Percy to the earldom of Northumberland forfeited by his father in 1461, in place of the 'usurping' John Neville.[55] In 1471, soon after Percy was restored and Neville demoted to Marquess Montague, the latter's influence had shrunk in Yorkshire, and the former was all-powerful, simply because he was the Percy, not as a result of his personality and policy: 'great part of [the] noble men and commons in those parts were towards the Earl of Northumberland, and would not stir with any lord or noble man other than with the said Earl, or at least by his commandment'.[56] Later in the year Westcountrymen reputedly joined the Lancastrian invaders because they considered Edmund Beaufort, duke of Somerset, and John Courtenay, earl of Devon, as 'old inheritors of that country'.[57]

Recurrent forfeitures by magnates and gentlefolk therefore often created conditions in the localities which provoked revolt. 'New men', and sometimes the newly restored, found it hard to assert authority and gain trust. Their efforts to do so might exacerbate hostile feelings; they were easily defamed. Few English fingers were lifted in defence of Edward's newly aggrandized favourites, an easy target for noble incitement, in 1469. According to a Gloucester abbey annalist, the Kentishmen and northerners rose in arms to crush the recently elevated earl of Pembroke, William Herbert, 'since he was a cruel man prepared for any crime, and, it was said, he plotted to subdue the realm of England and totally plunder it'.[58]

Bereft of trusted protectors, commons were easily persuaded to take up arms to restore them, or to defend themselves against royal 'oppressions' or anticipated punishment. Thus in 1486 Yorkshiremen, fearful of the imminent arrival of a probably hostile Henry VII, and lacking confidence in the recently imprisoned earl of Northumberland's ability to moderate royal anger, flocked to Lovell's Yorkist standard. In 1497 Westcountrymen clearly did not rate Edward Courtenay, granted the earldom of Devon by Henry VII, as capable of modifying royal subsidy demands or, subsequently, protecting them against punishment for their revolt. The extraordinary trust which Warwick the Kingmaker had widely and tenaciously inspired as a champion of popular grievances, making him such a formidable threat to Edward, may have been enhanced because many men's ties with their traditional lords had been weakened as a result of the vicissitudes of the wars.

Such were among the local factors determining the commons' willingness to participate. But the imprecision of the sources makes it difficult to be specific about the parts played by commons' grievances over landlords' and urban oligarchies' policies, royal taxation, and about the effects of economic depression and competitiveness. There are hints in London chronicles that economic tensions between the city and its hinterlands helped to provoke rural rebellion. The Kentish supporters of Warwick who in September 1470 'Robbed and despoiled divers Dutchmen and their beer houses' in the London suburbs, were intent on undermining competition to their ale-brewing for the London markets.[59] A Londoner scornfully described how Essex peasants joined the Bastard of Fauconberg's rising:

> The faint husbands cast from them their sharp Scythes and armed them with their wives' smocks cheese cloths and old sheets and weaponed them with heavy and great Clubs and long pitchforks and ashen staves, and so In all haste sped them toward London, making their avaunt as they went that they would be Revenged upon the mayor for setting of so easy pennyworths of their Butter, Cheese, Eggs, pigs and all other victual, and so Joined them unto the Kentishmen.[60]

Kentishmen took a major part in risings in 1460, 1469, 1470, 1471 and 1483. Their rebellious tendencies seem to have been widely recognized – Richard of York in 1452, Warbeck in 1495 and the Cornishmen in 1497 assumed too readily that they would give armed support. These Kentish tendencies may have been fostered by political, military and economic factors hinging on the shire's proximity to London, and its domination of vital commercial and strategic routes from London to Calais. The shire's prosperous gentry and yeomen – uncontrolled by any one great secular lord – looked to the court for patronage and to London markets for agrarian profits. They were consequently sensitive to currents of opinion in court and city – and to those circulating among merchants (many of them Londoners) and soldiers at Calais, the other main external centre for Kentish trade. Kentish gentlefolk and commons were financially vulnerable to the effects of failures to keep the narrow seas safe for commerce, and of crises over pay between the crown and the Calais garrison. They were geographically vulnerable to the implementation of harsh royal fiscal and judicial policies. Kentish commons, in defence of their interests, may have cherished the example set by the saint in their midst, Thomas of Canterbury, of defence of liberties against tyranny, and may have cherished, too, memories of how they and their forbears had occupied London in 1450 and 1381 to save the realm from treason.[61] Some of the Kentish elites may have looked kindly on these sentiments. The fact that many Kentishmen could afford good military equipment, and that they were accustomed to arraying because of their long coastline, contributed to their military weight.

In parts of Yorkshire, too, the commons repeatedly joined in rebellions or instigated them in our period. One origin of these tendencies lay in the struggle for dominance over the shire in the early

1450s between the Percies and the Nevilles, into which gentlefolk, townsmen and commons were drawn. The force with which the Percies ambushed the Nevilles at Heworth (Yorks.) in 1453 included more than a hundred citizens of York, about a third of whom were either merchants or else engaged in the cloth and leather trades.[62] Susceptibility in York – and its hinterland – to noble patronage may have been increased by the city's economic decline.[63] Moreover, the continued instability of noble power in Yorkshire – except during Richard of Gloucester's hegemony – was an incitement for men to take up arms for gain or to air their grievances. The strategic importance of the Yorkshire plain as a launching-pad from which to invade the northeast or the Midlands probably brought upon the region – as upon more prosperous Kent – particularly burdensome financial levies and arrays in the wars. The heavy casualties which Yorkshire Lancastrians suffered in the campaign there in 1461 were bitterly remembered a decade later by gentlemen and others:

> having in their fresh remembrance, how that the King [Edward], at the first entry-winning of his right to the Realm and Crown of England, had and won a great battle in those same parts, where their Master, the Earl's [Northumberland's] father, was slain, many of their fathers, their sons, their brethren, and kinsmen, and other many of their neighbours.[64]

Such weighty testimony to a heavy casualty rate in the wars is exceptional, and gives some support to contemporaries' assertions that the numbers involved in the Towton campaign, and the casualties suffered, were unusually large. Soon afterwards Bishop Beauchamp had written: 'There consequently perished an amount of men nearly . . . hitherto unheard of in our country, and estimated by the heralds at 28,000, besides the wounded and those who were drowned.'[65]

The related questions of the numbers involved and the size of casualties in the wars are vexed and insoluble ones, because of the lack of documentary evidence for the total size of most armies, and the tendency of some chroniclers to repeat uncritically the conflated figures often circulating. One contemporary observer certainly felt acutely embarrassed by these. Prospero di Camulio wrote to Francesco Sforza from Ghent in March 1460 about the St Albans campaign: 'My Lord, I am ashamed to speak of so many thousands, which resemble the figures of bakers, yet everyone affirms that on that day there were 300,000 men under arms, and indeed the whole of England was stirred, so that some even speak of larger numbers.'[66] Nevertheless, chroniclers make it clear that forces engaged in some famous battles were small, or briefly engaged – in these cases casualties were relatively light. Armies were small at St Albans (1455) and at Hedgeley Moor and Hexham (1464).

At Ludford Bridge (1459) only skirmishing took place; Northampton (1460) and Losecoat Field (1470), though bloody, were brief. Before Northampton the Yorkist lords proclaimed that no one was to 'lay hand upon' king or commons, only on lords, knights and esquires. The rule that only the commons should be allowed quarter was a frequent convention in the Wars of the Roses.[67] Nevertheless, there were large-scale routs in which many common soldiers were doubtless put to the sword – Blore Heath (1459), St Albans and Towton (1461), Edgcote (1469), Barnet and Tewkesbury (1471), Bosworth (1485) and Stoke (1487). William Worcester says that about 168 'validioribus gentibus Wallie' were killed at Edgcote.[68] Casualty rates may have tended to be higher than average for English (and Anglo-Welsh) armies because skilled longbowmen were often deployed on both sides.

The convention of executing gentlefolk captured on or near the field became general after Wakefield, but was not always rigorously observed. According to *Gregory's Chronicle*, forty-two Lancastrian knights were executed after Towton.[69] Apart from the leading protagonists, gentlefolk who evaded capture by the opposing army were generally safe: John Paston, on the losing side at Barnet, fled and lay low without mortal anxiety, waiting for a pardon to be sued out.[70] K. B. McFarlane demonstrated that the wars were not responsible for the wholesale destruction of the 'old nobility': the percentages of failures in the male line of peers for the last two quarters of the fifteenth century were in fact below average.[71] Nevertheless, there was a large-scale slaughter of peers in the wars. In the period 1455–87 at least thirty-eight adult peers were killed in battle, or afterwards because of their participation: of these, eighteen were killed in the years 1460–1, and only four after 1471. The deaths in domestic warfare of so many peers, unparalleled in scale in any recent period (and the deaths of some of their kinsfolk and faithful servants besides) is likely to have had profound psychological effects on the nobility. Chroniclers' singling out of the demise in battle of sprigs of nobility hints that this was especially galling.[72] For losers and their families there were many possible vicissitudes. Professor Lander has calculated that between 1453 and 1504, 397 people (excluding members of the houses of Lancaster and York) were condemned for treason. At least 256 of these (about 64 per cent) had their attainders reversed.[73] But years might elapse before a reversal: in the meantime families might be in at least relative poverty, and see their court and local influence decline swiftly – on Hastings's execution in 1483, his servants speedily entered Buckingham's service.[74] Participants risked personal privations: as plotters, fugitives or exiles they sometimes discovered, painfully, the life of a penurious, despised commoner. Sir William Tailboys, hiding from the Yorkists near Newcastle in 1464, experienced life in a coalpit.[75] Commynes saw the exiled duke of Exeter 'begging his livelihood from house to house without revealing his identity'.[76] As a fugitive in 1483 Buckingham lived in a cottage, and may have been discovered because of his inability to adjust his life-style: suspicion was aroused 'in consequence of a greater quantity of provisions than usual being carried thither'.[77] To keep his son and heir, Henry Stafford, safe from search, Dame Elizabeth Delabeare had the boy's head shaved and dressed him in girl's clothes. When searchers were near, she took him in her lap, waded a brook and sat for four hours in a park till they had gone. Later she took him to Hereford, dressed as a gentlewoman, riding pillion behind a faithful servant.[78] There were worse vicissitudes. After Barnet field, Exeter, 'greatly despoiled and wounded', was left for dead.[79] The earl of Oxford's leap from the walls of Hammes castle, where he had been imprisoned for over five years, was widely interpreted as a suicide attempt.[80]

Civil war affected the lives of noble ladies too. In 1461 the aldermen of London sent the duchesses of Bedford and Buckingham to the queen 'pro gratia et pace civitatis habenda'.[81] The sisters of Edward IV and Clarence helped in their reconciliation in 1471.[82] In 1483 Elizabeth Wydeville (who had had some grim political experiences) and Margaret Beaufort were prime movers in the plot to revive their families' fortunes. Many ladies suffered privations as a result of the wars. In October 1459 the duchess of York probably witnessed the pillage of her residence at Ludlow, and was subsequently 'kept full strict and many a great rebuke' in her brother-in-law Buckingham's household.[83] Her sister-in-law the countess of Salisbury had the experience – unusual for a woman – of being attainted.[84] In January 1460 Rivers's wife, the duchess of Bedford, was taken off with him to Calais by Dinham's raiders.[85] Other court ladies, including the duchess of Exeter, endured short commons and hot bombardment in the Tower the following June, and begged the commander to surrender.[86] In 1467 Eleanor Dacre, widow of an attainted Lancastrian, received a royal grant of one of his forfeited manors: 'she has been despoiled of her goods by the Scots and other rebels and has no means of support'.[87] After the collapse of the rebellions instigated by Warwick and Clarence in April 1470, their wives took flight with them. The pregnant duchess of Clarence, whose ship was not allowed to dock at Calais, gave birth at sea to a baby which soon died.[88] In 1488 a royal grant was made for the sustenance of the attainted Lord Zouche's wife and children, in consideration of their 'poverty and wretchedness'.[89]

Bitter mutual feelings about deaths, privations, and insults to ladies are likely to have helped prolong plots and risings after Edward's victories in 1461. The nobility's lack of solidarity facilitated the intrigues of aspiring claimants and kingmakers. But, in the long run, may not there have been a significant noble revulsion against participation in domestic strife? We are handicapped by a dearth of surviving expressions of feeling. Margaret Lady Hungerford, in her will of 1476, referred to heavy debts incurred, 'caused by necessity of fortune, and misadventure that hath happened in this seasons of troubled time last past'.[90] The family fortunes had been blasted by the French ransom of her son Robert Lord Moleyns, and his persistent attachment to the Lancastrian cause, leading to attainder and death. Lady Hungerford's solution was to make her bequests to her grandsons contingent on their continued allegiance to Edward IV and his heirs.

Another noble exasperated by the wars, despite the eminence which he attained as a result of them, was Edward's brother-in-law Anthony Wydeville, Earl Rivers. In the prologue he wrote to his translation *The Dictes or Sayengis of the Philosophres*, published by Caxton in 1477, he says that he had endured perplexity because of worldly adversities and, when released from them by divine grace, had set off on pilgrimage abroad.[91] Rivers had indeed experienced adversities. As a youthful knight he was ignominiously captured with his father in 1460 and was again captured at Towton in 1461.[92] In 1469 he was lucky to escape death, unlike his father and brother. In 1470–1 he shared Edward's hazardous escape abroad, his precarious exile and hard-fought recovery of the crown. With Edward re-established, and despite the king's tart expression of irritation, Rivers determined to escape further politic cares by going on pilgrimage abroad. He wanted to absorb himself in the world of shrines and scholarship, but his nearness in blood to the crown was eventually to shatter his retreat from the violence that had filled his youth.[93]

Some magnates certainly seem to have displayed caution and a reluctance to take up arms when their interests were eclipsed. Henry Percy, whose father and grandfather had died defending King Henry and opposing the Neville challenge to their northern interests, failed to show similar determination – above all, it is likely, he wanted to keep his earldom and avoid the pains of treason. He acquiesced in the limitation of his northern influence by Richard duke of Gloucester in the last decade of Edward's reign. He failed to play the kingmaker when opportunities arose in 1471, 1485, 1486 and 1487.

After the earl of Lincoln's death at Stoke in 1487, his family, the de la Poles, eschewed treason and the promotion of their claim to the throne till 1500, when Lincoln's brother Edmund earl of Suffolk fled abroad after discrediting himself. He and his father, John duke of Suffolk, had acquiesced in the 1480s in the eclipse of their influence in East Anglia by that of Henry VII's favourite, Oxford. When John died in 1491, Edmund peaceably accepted the humiliating royal admonition that he should succeed to an earldom rather than a duchy. It was to be alleged that in 1497 Lord Abergavenny tried to tempt him to put himself at the head of the Cornish rebels. According to the story, Suffolk was shocked by the suggestion and speedily dissociated himself from the rebellion, riding off wearing Abergavenny's shoes, presumably to stop him from following.[94] Another magnate who learnt caution was Thomas Howard, earl of Surrey. His lengthy funeral inscription, formerly at Norwich, is likely to have been based on his own reminiscences of his experiences in the wars.[95] It emphasized his faithfulness to Edward IV in the vicissitudes of 1469–71, his support for him at Edgcote and Losecoat Field, and when the king was 'taken by the Earl of Warwick at Warwick'. After Edward's flight to Flanders, Howard, unable to get abroad, took sanctuary at Colchester, and rejoined the king on his return. At Barnet he was 'sore hurt' and he was wounded and captured at Bosworth. But he prudently passed up an opportunity to escape from his prison in the Tower during the Stoke campaign, and after release from an imprisonment of over three years, worked hard and loyally to maintain Henry VII's interests in the north, despite Oxford's predominant political interest in his native 'country' and Henry's failure to restore to him his father's duchy of Norfolk.

For many lesser participants the experience of the wars was uncomfortable and expensive. Thomas Denyes claimed that, fighting for Warwick at St Albans in 1461, 'there lost I £20 worth horse, harness, and money, and was hurt in divers places'.[96] John Paston, probably in hiding a fortnight after his flight from Barnet, had exhausted his credit, as he wrote to his mother:

> I beseech you, and ye may spare any money, that ye will do your alms on me and send me some in as hasty wise as is possible; for by my troth my leech craft and physic, and rewards to them that have kept me and conducted me to London, hath cost me since Easter Day [the date of the battle] more than £5, and now I have neither meat, drink, clothes, leechcraft, nor money but upon borrowing; and I have assayed my friends so far, that they begin to fail now in my greatest need that ever I was in.

He requested that two of his shirts, three long gowns, two doublets, a jacket of 'plonket chamlett' and a murray bonnet should be sent to him.[97] Such experiences may have increased the reluctance to participate of those with anything to lose. Commentators on some of the later campaigns note this reluctance. According to the official account, though many Kentishmen eagerly joined the Bastard of Fauconberg, others 'would right fain have sat still at home, and not to have run into the danger of such rebellion'.[98] According to Vergil, Warbeck found the Kentishmen reluctant to revolt in 1495: 'they recalled that all their recent revolts had always fallen out badly for themselves and they decided to remain obedient'.[99] He says that the Cornishmen at Blackheath found them in a similar frame of mind, 'remembering only too well that their elders had often paid the penalty for similar rashness'.[100]

How did the wars in general affect non-participants? The fact that Englishmen became so divided, and spilt each other's blood so freely, depressed the reflective, inducing gloomy clerical rhetoric, notably that of Abbot Whethamstede of St Albans, witness to savage killings, and of the first Crowland continuator. The unhappy events led to theorizing even by the unreflective about the unstable temperament of the English. Recounting Sir Mordred's usurpation, which resulted in the destruction of King Arthur's realm, Sir Thomas Malory exclaimed (*c.* 1470):

> Lo, ye all Englishmen, see ye not what a mischief here was? For he that was the most king and noblest knight of the world . . . yet might not these Englishmen hold them content with him. Lo thus was the old custom and usage of this land, and men say that we of this land have not yet lost that custom. Alas! this is a great default of us Englishmen, for there may no thing us please no term.[101]

In 1490, in his prologue to *Eneydos*, Caxton commented on the instability of the English: Vergil's elaborate theory of how their nourishment on faction had been subdued by Edward IV and revived by the example of his brother Richard may have been derived from the discourse of the early Tudor elite.[102] Vergil's views, as we have seen, were to influence heavily those of subsequent sixteenth-century historians. But the long-lasting nervousness about faction and rebellion which was so conspicuous in sixteenth-century politics was nourished by more than literary tradition. It was founded on living folk-memories, as John Smyth's seventeenth-century record of village recollections of the battle at Nibley Green (Gloucs.) in 1470 shows: 'And the blood now spilt was not clearly dried up till the seventh year of King James, as after in many places of these relations appeareth.'[103]

But it is necessary to inquire whether the understandable and long-remembered gloom of contemporaries reflected widespread experience of losses by non-participants – and whether, indeed, the wars had significant material effects on society and the economy in general. Professor Dunham has emphasized the brevity of campaigns:

> Actual fighting probably occupied less than 12 weeks between 1450 and 1485; and the battles, seldom lasting longer than an eight-hour day, were well dispersed among the English counties. So there was really no physical disruption of normal life for over 95% of the people for about 97% of the time.[104]

Professor Lander has underlined these points: 'These almost miniature campaigns bear no comparison with the scale of warfare in the rest of Europe.. . . The English suffered hardly at all compared with the damage which they had inflicted on many of the provinces of France during the Hundred Years' War.'[105] In the Appendix an attempt has been made to calculate the total number of days' campaigning (not fighting) in the wars between 1455 and 1485. Sieges and manoeuvres which were of local importance, and desultory land and naval warfare such as that centring on Calais and Sandwich in the winter of 1459–60, have been omitted. The Northumbrian campaign of 1462–3 has been included because, although localized, it involved major efforts by both sides. The length of campaigns has been calculated from the date when the first army in the field set out on the march till the date when the last one was dismissed. As initial and terminal dates are often unknown, on this definition the lengths calculated err on the short side. Some companies clearly had earlier starting or finishing dates. The conclusion is that there were at least sixty-one weeks' campaigning, and that there were major campaigns in ten out of the thirty years. There were, indeed, few actual days of fighting, and the battles seldom lasted more than eight hours, but this was characteristic of medieval warfare. Some of the campaigns were short even by short medieval standards.

Most of the campaigns in the wars are likely to have had far-flung effects, since armies often travelled long distances, sometimes splitting on to different roads, or traversing the same one in different groups. Most parts of the realm experienced the movement of armies, and the people of the Cinque Ports, London, Leicester, Nottingham, York and Newcastle, and those living along the routes between them, at various times became particularly familiar with their movement. The main regions which saw practically no fighting were parts of the north-west, East Anglia and some of the southern shires along the Channel coast.

Commanders in the wars sometimes countenanced the harrying of opponents' estates and servants, as deterrent or punishment. But they were mostly anxious to abate plundering, in order to avoid damage to opponents' estates which they and their followers coveted, but more generally in order to keep and win friends and open town gates. Englishmen's fear and hatred of suffering the ravages which they had often inflicted abroad was the most effective deterrent to plundering in the wars. Until the wars escalated, most English folk were unused to large-scale military operations within the realm. The London writer of *Gregory's Chronicle* remarked in shocked wonder that Cade's encampment at Blackheath in 1450 was fortified 'as it [had] been in the land of war'.[106] It behoved captains to prevent their soldiers from behaving as if they were in such a land. In 1465 (?) Margaret Paston (?) alluded to the force of public opinion about military unruliness in Norfolk: 'for and your soldiers be of such disposition that they will take that they may get it, shall no worship be to you, nor profit in time to come'.[107]

Consequently commanders ordered their soldiers to behave, and promised that they would enforce discipline, while their opponents alleged that they had given licence to plunder. York requested the citizens of Shrewsbury in 1452

> that such strait appointment and ordinance be made, that the people which shall come into your fellowship, or be sent unto me by your agreement, be demeaned in such wise, by the way, that they do no offence, nor robbery, nor oppression upon the people, in lesion of justice.[108]

In 1460 the corporation of London admitted the Yorkist lords on condition that their men did not misbehave and, Warwick in person diligently attempted to enforce this in the difficult conditions created by the siege and surrender of the Tower.[109] A Yorkist partisan alleged that about this time proclamations made in Lancashire and Cheshire in Henry VI's name promised that the king's soldier should be able to 'take what he might and make havoc' in Kent, Essex, Middlesex, Surrey, Sussex, Hampshire and Wiltshire.[110] As the queen concerted resistance that autumn in Yorkshire, Yorkist propaganda played on southern fears that men from poor, remote parts of the realm were being promised that they could plunder southern wealth. The prince of Wales wrote denying this allegation.[111] But denials were in vain. According to Clement Paston, 'the people in the north rob and steal, and [have] been appointed to pillage all this country, and give away men's goods and livelihoods in all the south country, and that will ask a mischief'.[112] The conduct of the queen's army seemed to confirm Yorkist propaganda. Abbot Whethamstede of St Albans prevailed on Henry VI to make proclamation against pillage in the aftermath of the battle there, but, he says, to no avail: 'For they were all at liberty and licenced, as they asserted, by the Queen and Northern lords, to plunder and seize anything they could find anywhere on this side of the Trent, by way of remuneration and recompense for their services.'[113] In a vain attempt to reassure the Londoners, the queen withdrew her army to Dunstable – to protect the goods of the Londoners, according to the author of the *Annales*, who thought this was a calamitous decision for the Lancastrian cause: 'Et hoc fuit destructio regis Henrici et reginae suae.'[114] In September 1470, by proclamation, Warwick forbade his soldiers to loot and rape, and at the start of the 1487 campaign Henry VII issued detailed ordinances designed to protect civilians' rights from outrage by his army. In 1487 Lincoln and Lovell seem to have made a great effort to discipline their foreign troops after their difficult march across the Pennines – 'Edward VI' wrote to the citizens of York promising to pay for victuals, and Vergil noted that Lincoln entered Yorkshire 'offering no harm to the local inhabitants, for he hoped some of the people would rally to his side'.[115] In 1489, playing on memories of the northern invasion of 1461, Henry VII proclaimed that the Yorkshire rebels intended 'to rob, despoil, and destroy all the south parts of this his realm, and to subdue and bring to captivity the people of the same'.[116] When Warbeck invaded Northumberland with James IV, he was upset by the Scots' impolitic plundering: he 'besought the king to harry his [Warbeck's] people no further and to damage his native land with no more flames'.[117]

Whatever the good intentions of commanders, it must have been difficult for them to prevent their men from oppressing non-participants – especially difficult if pay was in arrears or not controlled by them, or if troops were poor and ill equipped. Commanders' difficulties in accumulating victuals made them acquiesce in their men's procuring of crops, beasts, ale. When harvests had been poor, or when, as in 1460–1 and 1462–3, campaigning continued in winter, foraging doubtless caused regional hardships. Moreover, after battles and sieges, it was hard, as it always has been, to control troops whose blood was up, and to prevent the injuries to non-participants which Abbot Whethamstede recounted with horror. Two documents perhaps reflect the anxiety of commanders to protect individuals from their soldiers' depredations. March, Warwick and Salisbury issued a safe-conduct under their signets, dated London, 24 August 1460, to the Bridgwater merchant John Davy to protect his goods from pillage.[118] Possibly during the campaigns of 1469–71, Clarence issued letters of protection forbidding on pain of death the spoliation of Lord Mountjoy's manors of Barton and Elveston (Derbyshire) or of any of his servants, farmers or tenants there or elsewhere.[119]

There are numerous allusions to losses inflicted by land and sea. The Yorkist lords at Ludlow complained to Henry VI in October 1459 that 'our lordships and tenants [have] been of high violence robbed and spoiled'.[120] The town of Warwick may have been one of the places alluded to.[121] After the Yorkist lords' flight, a partisan chronicler alleged that York's town of Ludlow 'was robbed to the bare walls'.[122] Waurin says that the devastation of the Yorkist lords' lands was general.[123] The versifying parson of Calais, unable to reach his benefice because of the Yorkist lords' presence there, alleged that they plundered by land and sea: Warwick certainly seized merchant ships on his voyage thence to Ireland.[124] Late in 1460 the queen's army in Yorkshire plundered the duke of York's and the earl of Salisbury's tenants: York's manor of Sandal suffered losses and no herons nested in the park that year.[125] But Professor Lander's suggestion that 'rumours and tradition seem to have exaggerated' the horrors of her army's advance southwards may well be right.[126] Though the chroniclers who recounted the plundering were mostly Yorkist in sympathy, they reflected the widespread southern belief that her soldiers were exceptionally ill behaved – and beliefs can be as potent in their effects as deeds. Southern reactions may have been decisive for the dynastic conflict. The conviction that the Lancastrian cause was associated with northern threats to south-eastern prosperity, and that Edward and Warwick were sure shields against them, may have persuaded many people in some of the wealthiest parts of the realm reluctantly to reject their traditional allegiance and accept a usurper.

In the years following 1461 it was the extremities of the realm which endured depredations. Property in Carlisle suffered damage as a result of the Lancastrian siege in 1461.[127] In 1463 Edward IV granted £100 to Alnwick abbey, in recompense for its losses in goods at the hands of French and Scots, and of the Yorkist force which had besieged Alnwick castle.[128] An inventory from Durham priory recorded that in 1464 the value of the priory's properties in Norhamshire and Islandshire (now part of Northumberland) was reduced by the depredations of the Lancastrian rebels, particularly by the occupation of Sir Ralph Percy's and Sir Ralph Grey's men.[129] In 1468 the bailiffs and burgesses of Bamburgh were allowed by the crown remissions in their fee farm 'on account of the losses which they have sustained from the king's enemies of France and the rebels, who held the town and castle as a refuge' in 1462–4.[130] The Welsh too suffered in the 1460s. In verses addressed to Lord Herbert, the poet Guto'r Glyn refers to the 'total war and slaughter' which Herbert's expedition against Lancastrian rebels loosed in Gwynedd. In fact the poet pleaded with Herbert to moderate vengeance: 'be not Savage, loosing fire on men'.[131]

The outbreaks of domestic conflict in England in 1469–71 once more posed threats to communities which had been free from them for ten years. In 1470 the Kentishmen committed depredations in Southwark.[132] The next year, under the Bastard's indulgent leadership, they were once more swarming over the London suburbs in search of pickings. Kentishmen and shipmen led away fifty of the hundred oxen which the London butcher William Gould was grazing in a meadow by the Tower – their meat, intended for Elizabeth Wydeville's household, presumably graced the rebels' tables.[133] The recent West Country operations had also involved some depredations. The Lancastrian army sacked the bishop's palace at Wells (Somerset), and Edward's army, after its deprivations and victory, entered town and monastery at Tewkesbury with violence, despoiling many people and stealing monastic goods.[134]

The later risings and invasions of the 1480s and '90s probably caused only desultory damage. In 1483 the Kentish rebels were reported as saying that they intended to rob London.[135] Henry VII, a conscientious man not hardened in warfare, in 1485 authorized the disbursement of £72. 2s. 4d. to townships whose harvests had been seized by him and his army on the way to Bosworth field, and the following month the abbot of Merevale, near Atherstone (Warwicks.), was granted 100 marks for his house's losses resulting from the army's march.[136]

There is, however, a dearth of evidence about the general economic effects of campaigns, which has led to the frequent assumption that the effects were negligible. The assumption is supported by evidence of the continued normal functioning of royal administration – but this may not have always been the case. In April 1470 Thomas Flemmyng, esquire, former escheator of Surrey and Sussex, was pardoned debts owed to the king: 'owing to rebellions and insurrections in divers parts of England' he dared not carry out his office.[137] In 1472 debts were pardoned to Thomas Tempest owed for the shrievalty of Lincoln by his late brother Sir Richard, who 'lost a great part of the profits which should have accrued to him in office and was hindered from exercising it by an insurrection in that county' and was removed from office by the rebels.[138] Robert Throckmarton, appointed sheriff of Warwickshire and Leicestershire soon after the battle of Bosworth, was pardoned arrears of account in February 1486 on his petition that, in the period of about a month in which he had occupied the office, he could not execute it to the king's profit, 'in which time of [his] occupation was within this your realm such rebellion and trouble, and your laws not established'.[139]

Dr Reynolds has written that the wars' effects on trade and urban life 'look fairly limited'; overseas trade may have been especially vulnerable to disruption.[140] The royal embargo on trade with Calais during the winter of 1459–60, and the Readeption government's war with Burgundy, threatened the main arteries of English trade, which were particularly dominated by London merchants.[141] Overseas trade probably suffered also by the impressment of ships into royal service to assist against rebellion and threats of invasion: the support that the Lancastrians received from Bristol in 1471 may have been stimulated partly by exasperation at Edward's shipping demands in the 1460s.[142]

The passage of armies may, in varying circumstances, have stimulated sales, reduced potential profits, or caused food shortages.[143] Rumours about their lines of march may have disrupted trade more than their actual destructiveness. The Shrewsbury bailiff's account for 1458–9 graphically reflects tensions among the townsmen during the 1459 rebellion. They were threatened with possible sack, or loss of privileges and patronage, if they backed the losing side, as they may have done in 1452 in response to York's summons. Men were dispatched in 1459 to negotiate with the king and others at Nottingham, and to reply to a royal letter; as the campaign developed, others were dispatched to ascertain the truth about reports of Salisbury's victory at Blore Heath, about the route he was taking and the situation between the king and the opposing lords at Worcester, and to take a letter to the duke of York and receive his reply. Watches were set at gates and bridges, and a banner was bought for the day watch in the tower of St Mary's church.[144]

It is unlikely that in these circumstances the normal flow of commerce continued through Shrewsbury – circumstances paralleled in many other towns during the wars. Shrewsbury was to feel threatened again. In January 1461 the burgesses were probably apprehensive about the advance of the forces of the earls of Pembroke and Wiltshire from Wales. In 1468 they feared assault by the Welsh Lancastrians. In 1485 the Welsh and their foreign allies at last stood at the gates; the townsmen put up a token resistance of twenty-four hours, probably in the hope of escaping Richard III's wrath and of negotiating guarantees of good conduct by Henry Tudor's dubious army.[145]

For Shrewsbury in 1459 – and for other towns – escape from physical involvement still entailed expense: repairs to defences had to be made, arms had to be bought, guards, spies and messengers paid. A commission was appointed in February 1471, on petition in parliament, by the burgesses and inhabitants of Great Yarmouth for pardon of a great part of their fee farm owed to the crown, because of the port's decline. Among other expenses Yarmouth men listed 'watches for defence against the king's enemies, the repair of the walls of the town and the cleansing of the moats, bombards and powder for the defence of the town'.[146]

Moreover, since ready supplies of money were concentrated in towns and soldiers could be quickly recruited there, townsmen probably contributed disproportionately to the costs of warfare. The surviving evidence suggests that leading towns were obliged to provide large numbers of paid-up companies for the campaigns of 1460–3. Royal demands for such – and for financial and material aid – were frequent in the wars (the Coventry and Norwich archives contain particularly full records of war taxation). But, since the evidence for contributions in urban archives is generally patchy, it remains unclear whether such demands were repeatedly wide, and whether they imposed a significant burden on many towns. K. J. Allison's analysis of war expenses incurred by Hull shows that the conflict 'had seriously depleted Hull's financial resources and the chamberlains in 1460–1 ended their year in office with a huge deficit'. In the years 1461–4 the inhabitants had to make heavy contributions in victuals, shipping, money and soldiers for the king's forces in the north. In 1468–9 they sent twelve soldiers; in

1470 thirty-two, to support the king. Not surprisingly, Hull refused to admit the suppliant Edward in 1471.[147]

When Edward IV was at Durham in the winter of 1462, the prior handed him a bill petitioning for compensation for the 400 marks that Margaret of Anjou had forcibly borrowed from the house, and for the total of £66. 9s. 4d. which the earl of Northumberland and other Lancastrians had borrowed. The prior also wrote to Lady FitzHugh (Warwick's sister), among others, complaining about the money which Margaret 'had of me, utterly against my will, through dread and fear of her and other lords of her counsel, at that time having rule of these North parties'.[148] The Lancastrians had wrung out the wealth of Durham priory, and its experience is unlikely to have been unique. There was a price to be paid for non-participants' relative immunity from sack and disruption in the Wars of the Roses: they had to find much of the war finance. Chroniclers' comments imply that men thought they were having to shoulder a heavy burden of war taxation in the early 1460s.[149] Much has been written in recent years about the relative wealth of Englishmen in the fifteenth century, and the optimism of their elites, with the Wars of the Roses as puffs of cloud on the horizon. But for many non-participants, the strife involved heavy financial burdens: the fact that recurrent demands were for hated internecine strife, not glorious war against foreigners, probably soured feelings further.

Moreover, it would be misleading to see the violence of the wars as more or less satisfactorily contained between the combatants, with a minimal spillage into the lives of non-participants. For the origin of the wars themselves lay in Henry VI's inability in the 1440s to contain the spread of local faction and violence, inherent in the elites' concern for property, office and influence. The outbreak of major revolts from the 1450s onwards and the relative political weakness of novel rulers, both kings and magnates, increased existing social tensions and gave opportunities for the violent pursuit of quarrels and for haphazard mayhem.

Fear of sack in London in 1461, like the passage of soldiers through Nottingham in 1459, provoked individual quarrels.[150] Governors and commons in London sometimes differed sharply in their attitudes to approaching armies.[151] Scores were settled under the cloak of general conflict. John Stafford, who loved Sir William Lucy's wife, had him killed in the confusion at the end of the battle of Northampton.[152] John Paston the youngest described how Norfolk misdoers exploited the dynastic struggles of 1460–1:

> there was a certain person forthwith after the journey at Wakefield, gathered fellowship to have murdered John Damme, as is said; and

also there is at the Castle of Rising, and in other two places, made great gathering of people, and hiring of harness, and it is well understood they be not to the King ward, but rather the contrary, and for to rob. . . . my brother has ridden to Yarmouth for to let [prevent] bribers that would have robbed a ship under colour of my Lord of Warwick, and belong nothing to him ward [are unconnected with him].[153]

Humphrey Neville of Brancepeth's 'Lancastrian' revolts of the 1460s may have been basically the pursuit of his feud with Durham priory, whose prior wrote in October 1461 to the chancellor George Neville (Warwick's brother) that Humphrey had been 'a cummerouse man to me and my house, and if he come again to our country to have liberty and rule, as he had afore, I dread that I and my brethren shall not rejoice our goods in peace'.[154] Soon after Edward's restoration in 1471, a defendant before the mayor of London's court alleged that a property had been wrongfully occupied in the recent 'troublous season' and that the occupier 'menaced him to flee and also openly noised him that he was a false traitor to Henry late called King of England the sixth'.[155] The wars had emboldened and hardened misdoers, according to one commentator, author of the speech drafted for the 1474 parliament, who alluded to 'the multitude of the misdoers, the readiness of them to mischievous and adventurous deeds by custom had and taken therein during the time of this long trouble and dissension'.[156] The proclamation which Henry VII made immediately after the battle of Bosworth vividly suggests how misdoers were accustomed to exploit uncertain and disordered situations after battles:

upon pain of death, that no manner of man rob or spoil no manner of commons coming from the field; but suffer them to pass home to their countries and dwelling-places, with their horse and harness. And, moreover, that no manner of man take upon him to go to no gentleman's place, neither in the country, nor within cities nor boroughs, nor pick no quarrels for old or for new matters; but keep the king's peace, upon pain of hanging etc.[157]

Gentlefolk were quick to take advantage of the disturbed conditions in the realm by defiantly holding and besieging castles, even by fighting private battles, to gain advantages in their quarrels. In November 1460 two esquires, John and William Knyvet, occupied Buckenham castle (Norfolk), despite its being in the king's hands. When Sir Gilbert Debenham and other royal commissioners entered the outer ward of the castle to remove them, in February 1461, they could get no further than the foot of the raised drawbridge over the moat surrounding the inner ward. This was being held in defensive array by a garrison of about fifty, for whom John Knyvet's wife Alice spoke defiantly from a little tower over the inner foot of the drawbridge: 'if ye begin to break the peace or make any war to get the place of me I shall defend me, for liever I had in such wise to die than to be slain when my husband cometh home, for he charged me to keep it'. The royal commissioners were nonplussed by this.[158]

In August 1469, just after the battle of Edgcote had given Warwick shaky control of the realm, the duke of Norfolk commenced a regular siege of Caister castle (Norfolk), in which he and the defender, John Paston the younger, used cannon. Paston was eventually forced to capitulate.[159] In March 1470, when Edward was defending his crown in the north, Viscount Lisle and Lord Berkeley arranged through their heralds to fight a pitched battle at Nibley Green (Gloucs.); in the bloody little conflict Lisle was killed.[160]

Historians of the Hundred Years War have been particularly concerned to trace gains as well as losses, and to assess their general social effects.[161] Some of the Hundred Years War's characteristic avenues of profit — ravaging, and ransoming noble prisoners — were partly barred in the Wars of the Roses, because of their particular political character. Nevertheless, forfeitures for treason and dynastic changes provided opportunities to gain estates, offices, annuities and chattels. The rise in status of some participants — not always sustained — was due in part or wholly to their military services. Fauconberg's elevation to the earldom of Kent in 1462 is probably a case in point.[162] Warwick's brother John Neville is said to have been granted the earldom of Northumberland as a reward for his victories in 1464, and Herbert the earldom of Pembroke for capturing Harlech castle.[163]

The Hundred Years War, if it did not create the English professional soldier, mightily advanced his sphere of opportunities. The Wars of the Roses helped to maintain the profession, threatened with unemployment by the dramatic loss of most of its French stamping-grounds in the 1440s and '50s.[164] Urgent demands for soldiers in the domestic emergencies tended to drive wage rates up. In November 1459 the crown was arranging to pay Somerset's and Rivers's 1,000 men 6d. a day, the rate granted by Norwich to its company in January 1461.[165] But in 1461–2 Nottingham hired ten men to fight in the north for two months at 8d. a day, and in 1469 Coventry, recruiting to support the king against Robin of Redesdale, 'could get no soldier under xd. a day, and so they were paid'.[166] In April 1470 Coventry made a levy to pay forty soldiers to accompany the king southwards against Clarence and Warwick, waged for a month at 12d. a day.[167] This was the rate which Rivers's horsemen received for their service to the crown in Kent in 1471, and which the city of York contracted to give eighty men for ten days in 1485, to support Richard III.[168]

A glimpse of the hiring of professional soldiers is provided by a letter of 1468 from Sir John Paston to his brother, giving an account of the four he was providing to help safeguard Caister castle against the duke of Norfolk's menaces:

> they be proved men, and cunning in the war, and in feats of arms, and they can well shoot both guns and crossbows and amend and string them, and devise bulwarks, or any things that should be a strength to the place; and they will, as need is, keep watch and ward. They be sad and well advised men, saving one of them, which is bald, and called William Peny, which is as good a man as goeth on the earth, saving a little he will, as I understand, be a little copschotyn [high-crested], but yet he is no brawler, but full of courtesy.[169]

Sir John may have been able to hire good men with comparative ease because there was then little domestic military employment − in such periods English soldiers tended to go abroad into Burgundian service.[170] Those who stayed were probably often seen (as has frequently been the case in England) as a disruptive burden, brawlers and beggars. The author of the 1474 speech in parliament argued that one benefit of war with France would be that 'the men of war, that had none other purveyance' would 'be set in garrisons and live by their wages, which else were like to continue the mischief in this land that they now do'.[171] Unemployed English soldiers, at home and on the Continent, prepared for desperate ventures in the hope of gain, may have formed a pool of support for dynastic pretenders in the 1480s and '90s. The brevity of the English invasions of France in 1475 and 1492 and of Scotland in 1482 must have been sorely disappointing to professionals. One can glimpse some of them on the crusade of Granada in May 1486, distinguishing themselves at the siege of Loja, where Sir Edward Wydeville led a company of 300 Englishmen. In 1488 men flocked to Southampton to join Wydeville's expedition to Brittany. When it was countermanded, 200 of them set off without royal licence in a Breton ship to try their fortunes. Next year Henry VII's occupation of Breton ports in defence of the duchess Anne against the French crown seemed to be reopening a traditional field of English military activity, but the French victory at St Aubin-du-Cormier, where the English were allowed no quarter, dashed such hopes.[172]

Though non-combatants paid heavily towards the costs of the Wars of the Roses, some profited. During most major campaigns, when well-disciplined armies passed through towns, their markets doubtless boomed, sucking in the hinterland's produce. London, Coventry, Nottingham, Newcastle and York were among the principal beneficiaries. When Henry VII visited York it was 'drunk dry'.[173]

Cloth production was stimulated by the demand for uniforms, 'bends', etc.[174] There was need for weapons and armour. In 1472 the crown commissioned two specialists from as far afield as Ecclesfield and Sheffield to take smiths for the manufacture of arrowheads in Yorkshire.[175] Arms and armour were often imported, particularly from Brabant. In 1482 Harry Bryan at Calais wrote to George Cely at Bruges: 'I must within this eight days send you word to pray you to lay out money for six hor[se] harness for my lord of Buckingham.'[176]

English 'merchant venturers' – particularly Londoners – probably profited from entrepreneurial roles in importing war *matériel* or purchasing it from native manufacturers. On 28 September 1459 Henry Waver, citizen and draper of London, appeared in the mayor's court and declared that his enemies had charged him in the king's household and elsewhere with having 'contrary to the king's most dreadful commandment now of late . . . sold furnished and stuffed for the earl of Warwick divers harness and armour'. He deposed that the previous month he had possessed 29 'harneys of milen [Milan] touche', which on 2 September he had sold in London to William Eliot, citizen and mercer, for twenty-nine 'buttes of red rommeney', and denied the sale of any harness or armour for Warwick's use.[177] In 1467 reference was made to the purchase by the master of the king's ordnance, John Wode, of gunpowder to the value of £559. 10s. 8d. from the London grocer John Nicolle.[178]

England has often been depicted as a realm which in the fifteenth and sixteenth centuries was becoming more unified on several levels – in economic development, political organization, and national sentiment. How may the Wars of the Roses have affected such developments? As regards the economy, it seems unlikely that they caused general falls of production and shortages. They may indeed have provided local stimuli, particularly helpful to the commercial dominance of leading towns of the eastern seaboard and Midlands. In politics, they were the major cause of that revival and development of royal authority whose consequences are reflected so strikingly in Edmund Dudley's treatise, *The Tree of Commonwealth*.[179]

It is easy to fall into anachronistic traps when discussing 'national sentiment' in the later Middle Ages. Nevertheless, it does seem that the Hundred Years War and the involvement of natives in economic competition with aliens developed a common sense of national identity, on occasion expressed by 'the commons', as well as by the elites of gentlefolk and merchants among whom it was strongest.[180] But, as the second Crowland continuator and other chroniclers bewailed, the Wars of the Roses were internecine struggles. The terms in which armies are often described make it clear that they might be distinguished as the levies of a particular shire or group of shires. The attack at St Albans in

1455 of the 'marchmen' – from the Marches towards Scotland – was remarked on; at Blore Heath northerners battered a force from Cheshire and Shropshire.[181] The Yorkist lords marched on Northampton in 1460 'with much other people of Kent, Sussex, and Essex'.[182] A poem celebrated the lord's victory there, accompanied by 'the true commoners of Kent'.[183] Chroniclers assert that the queen's army which invaded the south in 1461 was mainly a northern one. She was opposed by a great army drawn from Kent, Essex, Norfolk and Suffolk,[184] and soon afterwards March and Warwick entered London with an army of 'Western men and Welshmen, Kents men and Essex men together'.[185] Predominantly northern armies stood against predominantly southern ones at Ferrybridge and Towton. In 1469 there were distinct northern, western, Kentish (and Welsh) forces in the field; in 1470 a Lincolnshire army operated on its own, and in 1471 so did armies from East Anglia and neighbouring counties, the West Country, and Kent and Essex.

But men often fought against their neighbours, and often forged ties with allied arrays from distant shires. Despite the antagonism of Kentishmen and northerners in 1460–1, in 1469 'communitas de Kente, et communitas ex boriale parte Anglie' rose separately with a common aim.[186] Nevertheless, frequent clashes between levies from unfamiliar shires are likely to have hardened natural antipathies. So was the passage of strangers through communities, not only Welshmen, Cornishmen and others whose native tongue was not English, but Englishmen whose speech seemed thick to the inhabitants. As we have seen, a Nottingham man was moved in 1459 to doubt the honesty of passing northern soldiers. A few years later, another Nottingham man viewed Edward as the Kentishmen's king. One shire's pride in reforming the realm may have sometimes seemed a humiliating imposition to other shires.

On the whole the wars probably increased local patriotism at the expense of an embryonic sense of English nationality. London chroniclers recounting the campaigns of 1460–1 were indignant at what one of them termed 'the malice of the Northermen'.[187] When, in January 1461, the northerners' approach southward was rumoured, Clement Paston described the southern levies' eagerness to attack them: 'My Lords that be here have as much as they may do to keep down all this country more than four or five shires, for they would be up on the men in north, for it is for the weal of all the south.'[188] Abbot Whethamstede of St Albans harped on the warlike, penurious and plundering nature of the northerners, and saw the conflict from Wakefield to Towton as a revolt by them against the south.[189] The endurance of such attitudes is perhaps reflected in Henry VII's proclamation of 1489 asserting that the Yorkshire rebels intended the destruction of the south.[190] But the view of northerners current in East Anglia, the East Midlands and the south-east was not necessarily shared elsewhere. A monk of Crowland abbey in Lincolnshire saw them as deliverers of the English in 1469 from invasion by the Welsh, so puffed up that they thought to gain the mastery of England.[191] A Gloucester monk, more frightened by the Welsh than the northerners, was similarly relieved by the Welsh defeat.[192]

Generally the effects of the wars may have been to stiffen shire communities' resolve to rely on their own military strength and that of their neighbours, and to hesitate over relying on co-operation with strangers, or on moving far from their own 'countries' to combat them. In 1469 the western men apparently deserted their Welsh allies, and the Kentishmen gave minimal aid to their Yorkshire ones. In 1470 the Lincolnshiremen fought on their own in defence of their shire. In 1471 Yorkshire, East Anglian, Midlands, West Country, Welsh, northern and south-eastern opponents of Edward gave him victory against the odds as a result of failures to co-ordinate. In 1483 the southern English rebels seem to have moved timidly: south-eastern and south-western groups failed to link up. The débâcles can be explained in terms of the personal deficiencies of magnate leaders: perhaps the limited horizons of shire communities were more of a constraint on their strategy than has been recognized.

Memories of inter-provincial antagonisms, which had sharpened particularly in the campaigns of 1459–61 and 1469–71, may have increased the difficulty of launching national military efforts. In 1489 Yorkshiremen jibbed at helping to finance a Breton war that was of concern to southern coastal communities; in 1497 Westcountrymen felt similarly about financing a war with Scotland in aid of Marcher security. Provincial movements against Henry VII in 1486, 1487, 1489 and 1497 failed to widen the scope of their appeal. One legacy of the Wars of the Roses which helped to strengthen royal authority against rebellion was a tradition of inter-regional distrust, demonstrated in the resolutely provincial character of Tudor rebellions.

Appendix

Campaigning Periods, 1455–85

The totals given are the minimum numbers of mostly continuous days on which one or more major forces were in arms. The sum total suggests that there was an equivalent in the period of at least sixty-one weeks' domestic campaigning. The majority of campaigns appear to have lasted not much more than three weeks. The most prolonged and intensive were those of 1462–3 and 1471; in 1460, 1461 and 1470 there was prolonged campaigning but more sporadic fighting. The length given for Edward IV's first royal campaign, in 1461, may appear excessive: it includes the time after Towton when he and some of his forces remained on a war footing in the north to consolidate his position there.

Number of days

1455
18 May: Yorkist lords in arms (Armstrong, 17).
22 May: first battle of St Albans.   5

1459
Henry VI in the field 'thirty days or thereabouts' (*Rot. Parl.*,
   V, 348).   30

1460
26 June: Yorkist lords in arms in Kent (Stone, 79).
10 July: battle of Northampton.
19 July: surrender of the Tower of London (*Benet's Chron.*,
   227n).   24
9 December (or several days earlier): Yorkist lords go north
   (*ibid.*, 228 and n).
30 December: battle of Wakefield.   22

Number of days

1461

2 or 3 February: battle of Mortimer's Cross (*ibid.*, 229 and n).

17 February: second battle of St Albans.

26 February: Yorkist lords enter London (*ibid.*, 229 and n).   24

13 March: Edward IV sets out northwards (*ibid.*, 230 and n).

29 March: battle of Towton.

1 May: Edward enters Newcastle (Scofield, I, 175).   50

1462–3

25 October: Lancastrian invasion of Northumberland (Ross, *Edward IV*, 50).

6 January: Scottish raid on Alnwick (*Chronicles of London*, 178).   74

1469

5 July: Edward reaches Stamford in arms (Ross, *Edward IV*, 129).

26 July: battle of Edgcote.   22

1470

6 March: Edward sets out from London – assembly date for Lincolnshire levies (*ibid.*, 140).

14 April: Edward reaches Exeter (*ibid.*, 145).   40

13 September: Warwick's invasion (Scofield, I, 536).

6 October: Warwick enters London (*ibid.*, 541–2).   24

1471

14 March: Edward lands at Ravenspur (*Arrivall*, 2).

27 May: Bastard of Fauconberg submits (Richmond, 'Fauconberg's Kentish rising of May 1471', 682).   75

1483

18 October: various risings (*Rot. Parl.*, VI, 244ff.).

8 November: Richard III at Exeter (Chrimes, 26n).   22

1485

7 August: landing of Henry Tudor (*ibid.*, 40).

22 August: battle of Bosworth.   16

Total number of days   428

Glossary

aforerider	see *forerider*
avant coureur	see *scourer*
battle	main or large body of soldiers
bend	riband, band or strap often worn to display allegiance
bombard	cannon throwing very large shot
brigandine	body armour composed of iron rings or small thin iron plates, sewn on canvas, linen or leather, and covered over with similar materials
caltrop	spiked iron ball used to obstruct cavalry; snare to trap feet and hooves
covey	type of gun
crapaud	type of gun
culverin	type of cannon
forerider	scout; one who rides ahead of an army or as part of its vanguard
foreward	first line or 'battle' of an army; vanguard
fowler	type of light cannon
harbinger	one sent ahead of an army to secure lodgings; advanced company sent out to prepare camping ground
middleward	middle body or 'battle' of an army
mortar	short type of ordnance with large bore and steep trajectory
pavis	shield large enough to cover the whole body
šallet	light globular helmet, either with or without a vizor, but lacking a crest
scourer, scurrier	scout; one sent out to reconnoitre
serpentine	type of cannon
ward	one of the three main divisions of an army — the van, middle and rear wards or 'battles'

Abbreviations

BIHR	*Bulletin of the Institute of Historical Research*
CCR	*Calendar of Close Rolls*
CDS	*Calendar of Documents Relating to Scotland*
CP	*The Complete Peerage*
CPR	*Calendar of Patent Rolls*
CSP	*Calendar of State Papers*
EETS	Early English Text Society
EHR	*English Historical Review*
HMC	*Royal Commission on Historical Manuscripts*
PRO	Public Record Office
Rot. Parl.	*Rotuli Parliamentorum*
TRHS	*Transactions of the Royal Historical Society*
VCH	*Victoria History of the Counties of England*

Notes

Introduction

1 S. Anglo, *Spectacle, Pageantry and Early Tudor Policy* (Oxford 1969), 36n. For popular references to York and March as a rose in 1460–1, C. L. Kingsford, *English History in Contemporary Poetry*, II (London 1913), 40–1; 'Gregory', 215. In 1460 York had displayed his livery of the fetterlock ('Gregory', 208); in 1556–7 Edward Courtenay, earl of Devon, was described in a list of Paduan students as 'Curtinek nob. anglus ex regia Albae Rosae britannorum familia' (A. Goodman, *A History of England from Edward II to James I* (London 1977), 300, 333).

2 Anglo, 36–7, 36n.

3 See some of the political verses in *Historical Poems of the XIVth and XVth Centuries*, ed. R. H. Robbins (New York 1959).

4 See below, pp. 151, 203.

5 *Rot. Parl.*, V, 463–4.

6 For what follows on Henry's career, S. B. Chrimes, *Henry VII* (London 1972); for the interpretation of Henry's view of English history, A. Goodman, 'Henry VII and Christian renewal', *Religion and Humanism. Studies in Church History*, 17, Ecclesiastical History Society (Oxford 1980).

7 Anglo, 44–5; *Historiae Croylandensis Continuatio*, ed. W. Fulman (Oxford 1684), 542–3.

8 Bouchard, *Les croniques Annales des pays dangleterre et Bretaigne* (Paris 1581), especially fols li *seq.*; cf. Goodman, 'Henry VII and Christian renewal'.

9 P. S. Lewis, 'Two pieces of fifteenth-century political iconography', *Journal of the Warburg and Courtauld Institutes*, 27 (1964), 319–20; Dominic Mancini, *The Usurpation of Richard III*, ed. C. A. J. Armstrong (Oxford 1969), 24–5; Goodman, 'Henry VII and Christian renewal'.

10 Bernard André, *De vita atque gestis Henrici septimi . . . historia*, in *Memorials of King Henry the Seventh*, ed. J. Gairdner (Rolls ser. 1858), 9–11, 13–14, 68.

11 *Memorials*, lvi ff; Edinburgh, National Library of Scotland, Adv. MS 33. 2. 24 (Ogilvie's address); cf. Goodman, 'Henry VII and Christian renewal'.

12 Goodman, 'Henry VII and Christian renewal'.

13 D. Hay, *Polydore Vergil* (Oxford 1952), 141ff; M. McKisack, *Medieval History in the Tudor Age* (Oxford 1971), 105ff; J. R. Lander, *Crown and Nobility 1450–1509* (London 1976), 57 and n; M. Aston, 'Richard II and the Wars of the Roses', in *The Reign of Richard II*, ed. F. R. H. Du Boulay and C. M. Barron (London 1971), 280ff.

14 D. Hume, *The History of England*, III (London 1834), 307–8; first published in 1762.

15 Sir John Fortescue, *The Governance of England*, ed. Charles Plummer (Oxford 1885), 127–30.

16 *Ibid.*, 14ff.

17 K. B. McFarlane, 'Parliament and "bastard feudalism" ', *TRHS*, 4th ser., 26 (1944); 'Bastard feudalism', *BIHR*, 20 (1947). The Ford Lectures were published in McFarlane, *The Nobility of Later Medieval England* (Oxford 1973).

18 K. B. McFarlane, 'The Wars of the Roses', *Proceedings of the British Academy*, 50 (1964), 95ff. Dr J. A. F. Thomson has suggested that dynastic loyalties may have been a stronger political motive among nobles and gentry than McFarlane allowed ('The Courtenay Family in the Yorkist Period', *BIHR*, 45 (1972), 244–5).

19 R. L. Storey, *The End of the House of Lancaster* (London 1966); C. Ross, *Edward IV* (London 1974); see also Lander, *Crown and Nobility*, and D. A. L. Morgan, 'The King's Affinity in the Polity of Yorkist England', *TRHS*, 5th ser., 23 (1973).

20 C. Ross, *The Wars of the Roses* (London 1976).

21 Storey, *End of the House of Lancaster*; R. A. Griffiths, 'Local rivalries and national politics: the Percies, the Nevilles, and the Duke of Exeter, 1452–1455', *Speculum*, 43 (1968); cf. also M. A. Hicks, 'Dynastic Change and Northern Society: the Career of the Fourth Earl of Northumberland, 1470–89', *Northern History*, 14 (1978).

22 Some of the battles were briskly reconstructed by the late Lt.-Col. A. H. Burne in *The Battlefields of England* (London 1950) and *More Battlefields of England* (London 1952).

23 Storey, *End of the House of Lancaster*, 98ff.

24 Whethamstede in *Registra quorundam Abbatum Monasterii S. Albani*, ed. H. T. Riley, I (Rolls ser. 1872); C. L. Kingsford, *English Historical Literature in the Fifteenth Century* (Oxford 1913), 151–4.

25 *Historiae Croylandensis Continuatio*, ed. Fulman; translated by H. T.

Riley in *Ingulph's Chronicle* (etc.) (London 1854); see A. Hanham, *Richard III and His Early Historians* (Oxford 1975), 74ff.

26 *John Benet's Chronicle for the years 1400 to 1462*, ed. G. L. Harriss and M. A. Harriss, in *Camden Miscellany*, vol. XXIV (London 1972), 151ff.

27 *Annales rerum anglicanum* (henceforth referred to as *Annales*) in *Letters and Papers Illustrative of the Wars of the English in France*, ed. J. Stevenson, II, pt 2 (Rolls ser. 1864); K. B. McFarlane, 'William Worcester, A Preliminary Survey', in *Studies Presented to Sir Hilary Jenkinson*, ed. J. Conway Davies (London 1957), 206–7; William Worcestre, *Itineraries*, ed. and trans. J. H. Harvey (Oxford 1969).

28 *The Anglica Historia of Polydore Vergil A.D. 1485–1537*, trans. D. Hay (Camden ser. 1950); *Three Books of Polydore Vergil's English History . . . from an early translation*, ed. Sir Henry Ellis (Camden Soc. 1844); cf. Hay, *Polydore Vergil*.

29 Kingsford, *English Historical Literature*, 70ff.

30 *An English Chronicle from 1377 to 1461*, ed. J. S. Davies (Camden Soc. 1856); see Kingsford, *English Historical Literature*, 127–9.

31 Printed in *The Historical Collections of a London Citizen in the Fifteenth Century*, ed. J. Gairdner (Camden Soc. 1876) and referred to henceforth as 'Gregory'. Cf. Kingsford, *English Historical Literature*, 96–8, and J. A. F. Thomson, 'The Continuation of "Gregory's Chronicle" – A Possible Author?', *British Museum Quarterly*, 36 (1971–2), 92ff.

32 Warkworth, *A Chronicle of the First Thirteen Years of the Reign of King Edward the Fourth*, ed. J. O. Halliwell (Camden Soc. 1839); Kingsford, *English Historical Literature*, 171–2; Lander, *Crown and Nobility*, 259–61 and 260n.

33 *Chronicle of the Rebellion in Lincolnshire, 1470*, ed. J. G. Nichols (Camden Soc. 1847).

34 *Historie of the Arrivall of King Edward IV, A.D. 1471*, ed. J. Bruce (Camden Soc. 1838); cf. J. A. F. Thomson, ' "The Arrivall of Edward IV" – The Development of the Text', *Speculum*, 46 (1971).

35 A. Goodman and A. MacKay, 'A Castilian report on English affairs, 1486', *EHR*, 88 (1973), 92ff.

36 *The Paston Letters 1422–1509*, 3 vols, ed. J. Gairdner (Edinburgh 1910). Two volumes of Professor N. Davies's definitive edition, *Paston Letters and Papers of the Fifteenth Century* (Oxford 1971–6) have been published. In this book the 1910 edition by Gairdner has been used.

37 *Plumpton Correspondence*, ed. T. Stapleton (Camden Soc. 1839); *The Stonor Letters and Papers 1290–1483*, ed. C. L. Kingsford, 2 vols (Camden ser. 1919); J. Taylor, 'The Plumpton Letters, 1416–1552', *Northern Hist.*, 10 (1975).

38 Basin, *Histoire de Louis XI*, ed. C. Samaran and M.-C. Garand, I–II (Paris 1963–6).

39 Commynes, *Memoirs*, editions by J. Calmette, III (Paris 1925); M. Jones (London 1972); S. Kinser and I. Cazeaux, II (Columbia, S. Carolina 1973).

40 Chastellain, *Chronique*, in *Oeuvres*, IV–V, ed. K. de Lettenhove (Brussels 1864); *Chronique de Jean Molinet*, ed. G. Doutrepont and O. Jodogne, I–II (Brussels 1935).

41 Waurin, *Recuiel des Croniques et Anchiennes Istories de la Grant Bretagne, à present nommé Engleterre*, 5 vols, ed. W. Hardy and E. L. C. P. Hardy (Rolls ser. 1864–91); cf. Kingsford, *English Historical Literature*, 136–7.

Chapter 1 : Yorkist Rebellions, 1452–60

1 Storey, *End of the House of Lancaster*, 94.

2 Text in *Paston Letters*, ed. Gairdner, introductory vol., p. cxi.

3 Storey, 98.

4 Text in *Paston Letters*, ed. Gairdner, introductory vol., pp. cxii–cxiii. For York's appeals to other towns, see Storey, 98. Shrewsbury sent a contingent (*HMC, Fifteenth Report, Appendix, part x, The MSS of Shrewsbury Corporation*, 1899, 29; H. Owen and J. B. Blakeway, *A History of Shrewsbury*, I (London 1825), 223n).

5 Storey, 98–9.

6 *Benet's Chron.*, 206; *Chronicles of London*, 163; *Arundel MS 19*, 297; *John Piggot's Memoranda*, 372–3.

7 *Proceedings and Ordinances of the Privy Council*, VI, 116. By then the council was well informed about the ramifications of the rebellion in south-east England (Storey, 98).

8 *Piggot's Memoranda*, 373; *Benet's Chron.*, 206; *English Chron.*, 69–70; *Arundel MS 19*, 297. Bourchier was referred to by the author of *Benet's Chron.*, as occasionally by other chroniclers, as count of Eu, his Norman title.

9 Storey, 99.

10 *English Chron.*, 69–70; *Arundel MS 19*, 297; *Benet's Chron.*, 206. The Yorkist army may have advanced through the Thames valley via Oxford, which was one of the towns to which the duke was alleged to have written inciting rebellion (Storey, 98).

11 *Benet's Chron.*, 206; *A Yorkist Collection*, 367–8.

12 *Piggot's Memoranda*, 373; *Benet's Chron.*, 206–7; *English Chron.*, 70; *Arundel MS 19*, 298; Whethamstede, I, 161ff; *Yorkist Collection*, 367–8. The author of *Benet's Chron.* thought that, at the climax of the campaign, the royal army was larger than the duke's, 24,000 to 20,000.

13 *Benet's Chron.*, 206–7; *Arundel MS 19*, 298; *Yorkist Collection*, 368;

Piggot's Memoranda, 373; *English Chron.*, 70; Whethamstede, I, 161ff; Waurin, V, 265–6. Out of the seven towns to whom (the council learnt on 17 February) York had sent letters allegedly inciting rebellion, three (Canterbury, Maidstone and Sandwich) were in Kent, and one (Winchelsea) was nearby in Sussex (Storey, 98).

14 See below, pp. 164–5.

15 'Gregory', 198. My account is heavily indebted to C. A. J. Armstrong's thorough article, 'Politics and the Battle of St Albans, 1455', *BIHR*, 33 (1960), 1ff.

16 Their lateness may indeed have been deliberate. In view of Stanley's behaviour near the fields of Blore Heath in 1459 and Bosworth in 1485, it is doubtful whether he would have given Henry more than fair words (see below, pp. 27–8, 92ff).

17 Lord Clinton was with them, and so was Richard Grey of Powis, first summoned to parliament just after the battle. Viscount Bourchier and Lord Cobham may have been with them too. (Armstrong, 27; *Benet's Chron.*, 213 and n).

18 *Chronicles of London*, 165; *Paston Letters*, I, no. 240; cf. Whethamstede, I, 171. Ogle had been one of the leaders of a raiding-party which burnt Dunbar in 1448 (*The Auchinleck Chron.*, ed. T. Thomson (1819), 39).

19 Cf. *Benet's Chron.*, 213.

20 *English Chron.*, 72.

21 *Fastolf Relation*, 67.

22 *Ibid.*, 65; *Paston Letters*, I, no. 239; *English Chron.*, 72; *Dijon Relation*, 63–4.

23 *Paston Letters*, I, no. 239.

24 *Ibid.*, no. 240.

25 Royal Commission on Historical Monuments (England), *An Inventory of the Historical Monuments in Hertfordshire* (London 1911), 188.

26 Whethamstede, I, 168; *English Chron.*, 72; *Paston Letters*, I, no. 240; *Dijon Relation*, 64; 'Gregory', 198.

27 *Benet's Chron.*, 214; cf. Armstrong, 49–50.

28 *Fastolf Relation*, 66–7.

29 *Bale's Chron.*, 148; cf. M. H. Keen, *The Laws of War in the Late Middle Ages* (London 1965), 107–8.

30 See below, p. 169.

31 For York's second protectorate, see Lander, *Crown and Nobility*, 74ff; Ross, *Edward IV*, 18–20.

32 *Benet's Chron.*, 223. Among the absentees were Thomas Bourchier, archbishop of Canterbury; Salisbury and Warwick; William Grey, bishop of Ely; Warwick's brother George Neville, bishop of Exeter; the earl of Arundel; and the archbishop's brother Viscount Bourchier.

33 *Rot. Parl.*, V, 348.

34 *English Chron.*, 80.

35 *Benet's Chron.*, 223–4; 'Gregory', 204–5; *Bale's Chron.*, 147–8; Waurin, V, 274. Warwick's presence at Coleshill is difficult to account for: perhaps he was attempting a solitary stroke against the king or his supporters.

36 *Rot. Parl.*, V, 348, 369.

37 *Ibid.*, 369; 'Gregory', 204; *Benet's Chron.*, 224; *English Chron.*, 79–80. Whethamstede (I, 338) says that 'totam quasi militiam' of Shropshire as well as Cheshire was to fight against Salisbury.

38 *Rot. Parl.*, V, 348, 369–70; *English Chron.*, 80; 'Gregory', 204.

39 F. R.Twemlow, using expert topographical knowledge and relying heavily on Waurin's inaccurate accounts of the battle, attempted a detailed but highly speculative reconstruction of it (*The Battle of Bloreheath*, 1912).

40 *Benet's Chron.*, 224; *Chronicles of London*, 169; 'Gregory', 204. Waurin thought that Salisbury had 400 against 6,000–8,000 (V, 269); the author of *Benet's Chron.* that he had 3,000 against 8,000; Whethamstede (I, 338) that he had at most 3,000 against almost 10,000; the author of *Bale's Chron.*, 148, 3,000 against 12,000; the author of *Short English Chron.*, 72, 4,000 against 14,000. The official account put his force at '5,000 persons and more' (*Rot. Parl.*, V, 348).

41 *Rot. Parl.* V, 348; cf. Whethamstede, I, 338; *Benet's Chron.*, 224; *Chronicles of London*, 169; *English Chron.*, 80; *Bale's Chron.*, 148; Waurin, V, 269. According to *Benet's Chron.*, 2,000 of the royal army were killed or captured.

42 *Rot. Parl.*, V, 369; 'Gregory', 204; *Benet's Chron.*, 224; *Chronicles of London*, 169; C. L. Scofield, *The Life and Reign of Edward the Fourth* (London 1923), I, 33n.

43 'Gregory', 204.

44 *Rot. Parl.*, V, 369–70.

45 'Gregory', 204.

46 For the nobles who probably participated in the Ludford campaign, see below, p. 237 n. 57.

47 See above, p. 26.

48 *Records of the Borough of Nottingham*, II, 1399–1485 (London 1883), 368–9.

49 *Benet's Chron.*, 224.

50 *English Chron.*, 80–1; *Benet's Chron.*, 224.

51 '. . . coepit revolvere res gestas varias, annaliaque multa, praecipue tamen, inter alia, illud quod sententiat Vegetius in Libro suo "De Dogmatibus Rei Militaris" ' (etc.) (Whethamstede, I, 338–9). This probably refers to Vegetius, I, i. For the interest of Henry and his supporter Beaumont in Vegetius' *Epitoma Rei Militaris*, see below, p. 124.

52 Whethamstede, I, 338–41; *Benet's Chron.*, 224.

53 For the Yorkist leaders' resentment at being proclaimed traitors and at the

plundering of their estates, see their letter of 10 October to the king (*English Chron.*, 81–3).

54 Scofield, I, 35; *English Chron.*, 81–3.

55 *Rot. Parl.*, V, 348; Whethamstede, I, 341ff.

56 According to Whethamstede, the king had almost 60,000 men before he reached Worcester (I, 338); according to *Short English Chron.*, 72, he had 50,000 at Ludlow; according to *Benet's Chron.*, 224, 40,000 to York's 25,000; according to *Bale's Chron.*, 148, 50,000 to York's 20,000. 'Gregory', 205, said that the king had 30,000 'harnessed' men, besides 'naked' men, and that York was 'over weak'.

57 Salisbury's brother Lord Fauconberg, in the king's retinue at St Albans, safeguarded Calais for Warwick during the 1459 campaign (Waurin, V, 278; Whethamstede, I, 368). Dr Richmond has listed the peers who in the months after the encounter received rewards for service against the rebels, and who may therefore have served at Ludford Bridge. They were the dukes of Buckingham and Exeter, the earls of Arundel, Devon, Northumberland, Shrewsbury and Wiltshire, Viscount Beaumont, and at least ten barons of parliament ('The Nobility and the Wars of the Roses, 1459–61', *Nottingham Mediaeval Studies*, 21 (1977), 74). For glimpses of military movements in the weeks before Ludford Bridge by Somerset, Shrewsbury's fellowship, Westmorland, Northumberland and Egremont, see above, pp. 26, 28.

58 The most circumstantial account is that of Waurin (V, 276–7), who says that Trollope was won over by a secret message from Somerset. If he had indeed been given command of the *avantgard* by Warwick, as Waurin says, his desertion is likely to have made the Yorkists particularly vulnerable. Waurin says that Trollope's men attacked the Yorkist lords as they withdrew.

59 Keen, 108.

60 *Rot. Parl.*, V, 348–9; Whethamstede, I, 342ff, 368; Waurin, V, 276–7; *Chronicles of London*, 169–70. Grey of Powis, Walter Devereux, esquire, and Sir Henry Retford were among those who submitted and were granted their lives at Ludford (*Rot. Parl.*, V, 349).

61 *Knyghthode and Bataile*, ed. R. Dyboski and Z. M. Arend, EETS, 1935; cf. D. Bornstein, 'Military Manuals in Fifteenth-Century England', *Mediaeval Studies*, 37 (1975), 472. I do not think that the editors' discussion of the date of the poem's composition is conclusive.

62 Commissions of array to resist the rebellion of the attainted lords were issued, dated 21 December 1459 (*CPR, 1452–61*, 557ff). For the fixing in February 1460 of Coventry's contingent of forty soldiers to support the king if they landed, *Coventry Leet Book*, 308–10; cf. *Paston Letters*, I, no. 346.

63 *Wars of the English in France*, ed. Stevenson, II, pt 1, 512; *Chronicles of London*, 170; Scofield, I, 50–1. Two of Somerset's leading

supporters, Lord Audley and Humphrey Stafford, esquire, were captured; another, Lord Roos, had returned to England by 28 January 1460 (Whethamstede, I, 369–70; *Benet's Chron.*, 224; Waurin, V, 284; *English Chron.*, 84; *Paston Letters*, I, no. 346; Scofield, I, 62).

64 *Annales*, 772; Waurin, V, 281–2; 'Gregory', 206.

65 *English Chron.*, 84–5; *Annales*, 771–2; Waurin, V, 282–4; Scofield, I, 50ff. Ships under guard at Sandwich belonging to Warwick were also seized and taken to Calais. For a commission of 6 December 1459 to take measures for their safeguard, especially in the spring tides, *CPR, 1452–61*, 525; cf. *ibid.*, 526. For Lydd's contribution of soldiers to Rivers at Sandwich, *HMC, Fifth Report*, I, *MSS of the Corporation of Lydd*, 522.

66 *Knyghthode and Bataile*, 103ff.

67 Scofield, I, 53–4, 59–61.

68 *Annales*, 772.

69 *Benet's Chron.*, 225; *Annales*, 772; *English Chron.*, 85; Waurin, V, 287ff; *Chronicles of London*, 170–1; *HMC, Fifth Report*, I, *MSS of the Corporation of Rye*, 492; Scofield, I, 64–5. For the raising of 4,000 marks in loans by the end of March, to pay for Exeter's and Fulford's naval expedition, *Wars of the English in France*, ed. Stevenson, II, pt 2, 515–16. For Wiltshire's abortive naval measures, Scofield, I, 70.

70 *English Chron.*, 85–6; *Annales*, 772; Whethamstede, I, 370–1; *Paston Letters*, I, no. 181; *Knyghthode and Bataile*, 19; Scofield, I, 63–5.

71 C. Rawcliffe, *The Staffords, Earls of Stafford and Dukes of Buckingham 1394–1521* (Cambridge 1978), 26.

72 Scofield, I, 71ff.

73 Waurin, V, 286–7, 290–1.

74 P. Clark, *English Provincial Society from the Reformation to the Revolution: Religion, Politics and Society in Kent 1500–1640* (Hassocks, Sussex 1977), 11.

75 'Gregory', 206.

76 *English Chron.*, 86–90.

77 *Ibid.*, 94; 'Gregory', 207; *Bale's Chron.*, 149; *Short English Chron.*, 73; *Annales*, 772; Scofield, I, 76. The legate Coppini wrote on 4 July that the lords crossed the Channel on 26 June. He apparently accompanied them to London (*CSP Milan*, I, pp. 23ff, no. 37; *Annales*, 772).

78 John Stone, *Chronicle*, ed. W. G. Searle (Cambridge 1902), 79; *Short English Chron.*, 73; *English Chron.*, 95; Waurin, V, 292–3. Horne, Scot and Fogge had been appointed on a commission of array in Kent in February, in which Abergavenny was second-named after Buckingham, but from which Cobham was prudently excluded (*CPR, 1452–61*, 561). Horne and Fogge had certainly been active in the royal interest, for the men of Lydd sent a deputation to Canterbury to them to intercede for

March's imprisoned men (*HMC, MSS of the Corporation of Lydd*, 523). But they and Scot joined the Yorkists: royal letters dated 28 January 1461 ordered them (with Cobham, Abergavenny and others) to lead the Kentish array to the king for service against the northern army (*Proceedings and Ordinances of the Privy Council*, VI, 307–8).

79 *HMC, MSS of the Corporation of Rye*, 492. The Rye and Winchelsea officials appear to have gone off to join the Yorkists. A Lydd contingent may have gone too, and fought at Northampton (*HMC, MSS of the Corporation of Lydd*, 523).

80 Stone, 79–80; *Short English Chron.*, 73–4; *English Chron.*, 94–5; Waurin, V, 293–5; *Bale's Chron.*, 149–50; *Annales*, 772; Scofield, I, 77ff. The author of the *Annales* put the size of the Yorkist army when it arrived at 20,000; the author of a pro-Yorkist London chronicle and Whethamstede mentioned the figure 40,000 as their nearest approximation (*Annales*, 772; *English Chron.*, 73; Whethamstede, I, 372).

81 *Bale's Chron.*, 150–1.

82 *Short English Chron.*, 73; *English Chron.*, 95–6; *Annales*, 772.

83 *English Chron.*, 94.

84 *Short English Chron.*, 73.

85 *English Chron.*, 94–5. Bourchier may have fought for York in 1455, Clinton did then and in 1459 (see above, p. 235 n.17, p. 30).

86 *CSP Milan*, I, pp. 23ff, no. 37.

87 *Annales*, 773.

88 *Benet's Chron.*, 225 and n; *Foedera*, XI, 454–6. Royal letters were dated at Coventry on 5, 11 and 26 June (*ibid.*, 454–6).

89 *Foedera*, XI, 444–6; commissions to the earl of Pembroke and prince of Wales. Cf. below, p. 184.

90 As late as 5 June Somerset was empowered to grant pardons to the rebels at Calais (*ibid.*, 454).

91 *English Chron.*, 95; *Benet's Chron.*, 225–6.

92 For the siege, see below, pp. 184–5.

93 Stone, 80; *HMC, MSS of Shrewsbury Corporation*, 29; G. Poulson, *Beverlac*, I (London 1829), 226ff. The Beverley governors' account for 1460–1 raises doubts as to whether the town contingent got to Northampton in time.

94 *CSP Milan*, I, p. 27, no. 38.

95 *Bale's Chron.*, 150–1.

96 *Benet's Chron.*, 226.

97 See below, pp. 184–5.

98 Waurin, V, 295–6. According to *Bale's Chron.*, 150–1, one part of the army was routed through St Albans, the other through Ware – the latter intended to forestall any move by the king to the Isle of Ely. If so, the wait at Dunstable may have been to allow the Ware force to catch up.

99 Waurin, V, 299–300. Hunsbury Hill, an ancient encampment, may have been the *montagne* which, according to Waurin, Warwick used as an observation post.

100 Stone, 80; *Benet's Chron.*, 226; *Short English Chron.*, 74; Scofield, I, 86 and n.

101 Whethamstede, I, 372–3; Waurin, V, 296ff; *English Chron.*, 95–7; *Short English Chron.*, 74. The chroniclers mention as being with the Yorkists, besides the legate and archbishop, the prior of St John's and the bishops of Exeter, Ely, Salisbury and Rochester. See also *Benet's Chron.*, 226; *CSP Milan*, I, p. 27, no. 38.

102 For Buckingham's family connections with Shrewsbury and Beaumont, see Rawcliffe, 21 and n.

103 *Knyghthode and Bataile*, 43. The author probably had in mind the oaths of the Yorkist leaders at Worcester in 1459. They probably swore on the Sacrament in St Paul's before Northampton (see above, p. 36).

104 'Gregory', 207.

105 *English Chron.*, 95; *Short English Chron.*, 74; Waurin, V, 296; Richmond, 'The Nobility and the Wars of the Roses, 1459–61', 74. Scrope was one of the two captains whom, according to Waurin, V, 299, Warwick had put in charge of the vanguard until the army had completely assembled near Northampton.

106 Sources used for the battle are Whethamstede, I, 373–5; Waurin, V, 299–300; *English Chron.*, 97–8; *Benet's Chron.*, 226; 'Gregory', 207; *Short English Chron.*, 74; Stone, 80. A succinct account is in R. Ian Jack, 'A Quincentenary: the Battle of Northampton, July 10th, 1460', *Northamptonshire Past and Present*, 3 (1960).

107 Whethamstede I, 372, says that the Yorkists had an 'infinite number of commons', in the region of 160,000; *Bale's Chron.*, 151, attribute to them a superiority of 160,000 to 20,000; Waurin, V, 299, of 80,000 to between 40,000 and 50,000; *Benet's Chron.*, 226, 60,000 to 20,000.

108 *Historical Poems of the XIVth and XVth Centuries*, ed. R. H. Robbins (New York 1959), 210ff.

109 Stone, 80. *Benet's Chron.*, 226, says that about 400 royal troops were killed, the *Annales*, 773, that 300 of them were killed and others drowned, *Bale's Chron.*, 151, that 50 of them were killed.

110 *English Chron.*, 97; 'Gregory', 207.

111 See below, pp. 184–5.

112 Grey had gained royal favour in the Coventry parliament, perhaps after allaying suspicions that he was pro-Yorkist. An observer wrote that Warwick's brother Bishop Neville and Grey 'have declared them full worshipfully to the King's great pleasure' (*Paston Letters*, I, no. 342). For Grey's motives for treason, J. S. Roskell, *The Commons in the Parliament of 1422* (Manchester 1954), 176–7.

113 For a recent assessment of Buckingham's role in the conflicts, and

particularly the impact he made on them in 1459–60, see Rawcliffe, 24ff.
114 For entrenched camps, see also below, pp. 170–1.

Chapter 2 : The War of Succession, 1460–1

1 This was how it was seen by Whethamstede, who personally experienced its ferocity (I, 386ff); cf. 'The Battle of Towton', Robbins, 215ff.
2 *Annales*, 773.
3 'Gregory', 208–10; Waurin, V, 324–5; *Annales*, 774–5; Scofield, I, 114. Hull may have been chosen as a base because of the opportunities which it provided for victualling by river and sea (cf. below, pp. 156–7, 219–20).
4 R. R. Sharpe, *London and the Kingdom*, I (London 1894), 118. On 2 December, a few days before the loan was granted, common council had received letters from the queen, the prince of Wales and Pembroke: no reply was sent.
5 *Bale's Chron.*, 152; *Chronicles of London*, 172; *Benet's Chron.*, 228; 'Gregory', 210; *English Chron.*, 106; Whethamstede, I, 381; *Annales*, 775. According to *English Chron.*, the Yorkist lords lodged at Sandal castle and Wakefield; according to *Annales*, at Sandal castle, where they kept Christmas, whilst Somerset and Northumberland were at Pontefract castle.
6 *English Chron.*, 106–7; *Brief Notes*, 154. Greystoke had been appointed on the Yorkist commission in Yorkshire in August.
7 Richmond, 'The Nobility and the Wars of the Roses, 1459–61', 75.
8 Waurin, V, 325–6.
9 C. 20,000 Lancastrians and 12,000 Yorkists (*Benet's Chron.*, 228); 15,000 Lancastrians and, on the Yorkist side, 'great people' ('Gregory', 210); 800 with Somerset and Devon, 8,000 with Neville and, on the Yorkist side, 'a few persons' (*English Chron.*, 106); 'a great army' on the Lancastrian side and 6,000 Yorkists (*Annales*, 775).
10 *CSP Milan*, I, pp. 42–3, no. 54.
11 Whethamstede, I, 381–2; cf. *Annales*, 775.
12 *Annales*, 775; *English Chron.*, 106–7; Whethamstede, I, 382. Whethamstede (I, 386–7) put the Yorkist death-toll at 700; the author of *Benet's Chron.* at about 1,000; the author of *Annales* at about 2,000; the author of *English Chron.* at 2,200; 'Gregory', who says that the queen's party lost 200, at 2,500.
13 *CSP Milan*, I, p. 39, no. 52.
14 Whethamstede, I, 381.
15 *Annales*, 774.
16 'Gregory', 212; *English Chron.*, 107.
17 See below, p. 215; cf. the bishop of Terni's and Antonio della Torre's

letters of 9 January, *CSP Milan*, I, pp. 37ff, nos 52, 54.

18 Sharpe, I, 128; cf. 119.

19 *The Records of the City of Norwich*, ed. W. H. Hudson and J. C. Tingey, I (Norwich 1906), 405–6.

20 *CPR, 1452–61*, 657.

21 *Paston Letters*, I, no. 367.

22 *Proceedings and Ordinances of the Privy Council*, VI, 307ff.

23 *CPR, 1452–61*, 658.

24 *HMC, MSS of the Corporation of King's Lynn*, 167.

25 *Henley Borough Records. Assembly Books i–iv, 1395–1543*, ed. P. M. Briers, 63.

26 *Rot. Parl.*, V, 477–8. These included five esquires and a grocer from London, an esquire from Southwark, one from Lambeth, and an esquire and yeoman from Westminster. Some others attainted, whose residence was not stated, such as Sir Edmund Mountfort and Sir Edmund Hampden, were from regions in Yorkist control.

27 *CPR, 1452–61*, 657–9.

28 *Ibid.*, 658–9; cf. below, p. 156.

29 *Ibid.*, 658.

30 *Paston Letters*, II, no. 384.

31 *Ibid.*, I, nos 83, 172, 260, 319.

32 *Ibid.*, nos 53, 56.

33 *Ibid.*, nos 68, 96.

34 *Ibid.*, no. 172.

35 *Ibid.*, III, no. 997.

36 *Rot. Parl.*, V, 477–8; *Paston Letters*, II, no. 486.

37 Poulson, I, 234.

38 Whethamstede, I, 388ff; *Brief Notes*, 154–5; 'Gregory', 212; *Annales*, 776. For the fight at Dunstable, see below, p. 126.

39 *Benet's Chron.*, 229 and n; cf. *CSP Milan*, I, p. 48, no. 63, and Waurin, V, 328.

40 See below, p. 177; cf. *English Chron.*, 107. On 14 February an Italian reported from London that the northerners did not seem to have got past Northampton (*CSP Milan*, I, p. 48, no. 63).

41 'Gregory', 212–13.

42 *Brief Notes*, 154–5; *Benet's Chron.*, 229; *English Chron.*, 107; 'The Battle of Towton', Robbins, 216.

43 *CSP Milan*, I, p. 43, no. 63.

44 The more experienced Bourchier, Bonville and Fauconberg were also with Warwick (Richmond, 'The Nobility and the Wars of the Roses, 1459–61', 75).

45 *Annales*, 776; cf. Richmond, 'The Nobility and the Wars of the Roses, 1459–61', 75.

46 Whethamstede, I, 390ff.

47 *Brief Notes*, 155, puts the total killed in the battle at 7,500; *Benet's Chron.*, 229, at about 4,000; 'Gregory', 212, at over 3,500; George Neville at nearly 3,000 (*CSP Venice*, I, p. 99, no. 370); *Annales*, 776, at 2,000; *English Chron.*, 108, at 1,916.

48 'Gregory', 212ff; see below, pp. 177, 171–2.

49 *English Chron.*, 107–8; Waurin, V, 328ff, 334.

50 *CSP Milan*, I, pp. 48–9, no. 64.

51 One explanation for this may be that Lovelace had kept them out of the battle.

52 *CSP Milan*, I, p. 54, no. 71.

53 *English Chron.*, 108; *Annales*, 776; *CSP Venice*, I, p. 99, no. 370. Bonville's switch to the Yorkist side was regarded with particular indignation – he was speedily executed.

54 'Gregory', 212. According to *Annales*, 776, the queen's army was 80,000 strong.

55 *Paston Letters*, III, no. 997.

56 On 12 February, March was commissioned by the Council, as Edward duke of York, to array the lieges of Bristol, Staffordshire, Shropshire, Herefordshire, Gloucestershire, Worcestershire, Somerset and Dorset to go with him against the king's enemies (*CPR, 1452–61, 659*). Two days after the battle of St Albans he was reputed in London to be in the Cotswolds (*CSP Milan*, I, p. 49, no. 64).

57 See below, p. 77.

58 'The Battle of Towton', Robbins, 216.

59 *CSP Venice*, I, p. 101, no. 371.

60 See below, pp. 156, 204, 215.

61 *Annales*, 775.

62 *Ibid.*, 775ff; *Short English Chron.*, 76–7; *Chronicles of London*, 172; 'Gregory', 211; *English Chron.*, 110; *Benet's Chron.*, 229; Worcestre, *Itineraries*, ed. J. Harvey, 202ff; H. T. Evans, *Wales and the Wars of the Roses* (Cambridge 1915), 139. According to *Annales*, March had 50,000 men and Pembroke 8,000; according to *Short English Chron.*, March raised 30,000. *English Chron.* says that his opponents were slain to the number of 4,000.

63 *Paston Letters*, I, no. 239; 'Gregory', 198; *English Chron.*, 90.

64 *Coventry Leet Book*, 313.

65 *Ibid.*, 314.

66 *Chronicles of the White Rose of York*, ed. J. A. Giles (1845), 8, henceforth cited as *White Rose*.

67 *Ibid.*, 8; *Chronicles of London*, 175; *CSP Venice*, I, pp. 99ff, nos 370–1. A commission of array dated 8 March empowered Warwick to raise levies from Northamptonshire, Warwickshire, Leicestershire, Staffordshire, Worcestershire, Gloucestershire, Shropshire, Nottinghamshire, Derbyshire, and Yorkshire (*CPR, 1461–7, 31*).

68 Waurin, V, 335–6; Scofield, I, 162.
69 *Coventry Leet Book*, 314–16; 'The Battle of Towton', Robbins, 215ff.
70 Waurin, V, 336–7; *Benet's Chron.*, 230. The latter says that Edward passed through Newark, as one might expect from his previous route, and does not mention his presence at Nottingham.
71 Waurin, V, 336–7; cf, *White Rose*, 8; *Benet's Chron.*, 230; 'Gregory', 216; *Annales*, 777. The author of *Hearne's Fragment*'s chronology of the battles of Ferrybridge and Towton differs from that of other sources (*White Rose*, 8). The fact that the battles were fought on successive days confused some chroniclers, who failed to distinguish them (*Short English Chron.*, 77; *Chronicles of London*, 175; Stone, 83). Even Warwick's brother George, in his account, fails to make the distinction clear (*CSP Venice*, I, pp. 99–100, no. 370).
72 *CSP Venice*, I, pp. 99–100, no. 370; Waurin, V, 337–8.
73 'Gregory', 216.
74 Waurin, V, 338.
75 *Benet's Chron.*, 230.
76 The duke of Norfolk, the earl of Warwick, Viscount Bourchier, Lords Clinton, Dacre (Richard Fiennes), Fauconberg, Grey of Ruthin, and Scrope of Bolton (Richmond, 'The Nobility and the Wars of the Roses, 1459–61', 75).
77 The dukes of Exeter and Somerset; the earls of Devon, Northumberland, and Shrewsbury; Viscount Beaumont; Lords Clifford, Randolph Dacre, de la Warre, FitzHugh, Grey of Codnor, Lovell, Neville, Rivers, Roos, Rugemont-Grey, Scales, Welles, and Willoughby (*ibid.*).
78 Bishop Beauchamp and the author of *Benet's Chron.* both thought that the army which Edward took north reached around the 200,000 mark (*CSP Venice*, I, p. 102, no. 371; *Benet's Chron.*, 230). According to William Paston and Thomas Playter, immediately after the battle Edward believed there were about 20,000 Lancastrian dead. Beauchamp wrote that the total death-toll on both sides, as estimated by the heralds, came to 28,000; they had not counted drowned or wounded. The heralds' estimate was given by other writers (*Paston Letters*, II, no. 385; *Chronicles of London*, 175). But some went much higher (*White Rose*, 8; *Short English Chron.*, 77). It is not clear whether Ferrybridge casualties were included in the totals. *Annales*, 778, is exceptional in putting the total deaths for all these engagements merely at over 9,000. Bishop O'Flanagan wrote on 8 April that 800 of Edward's troops were killed (*CSP Venice*, I, p. 103, no. 372).
79 *York Civic Records*, I, 135.
80 Waurin, V, 339ff.
81 *CSP Venice*, I, p. 100, no. 370.
82 Richmond, 'The Nobility and the Wars of the Roses, 1459–61', 75.
83 *CSP Venice*, I, p. 102, no. 371; *White Rose*, 8. For an interesting

news-letter about the battle and its aftermath, written from Bruges on 11 April, see J. Calmette and G. Périnelle, *Louis XI et l'Angleterre* (Paris 1930), 273–4.

84 *Chronicles of London*, 175; *Short English Chron.*, 77; 'Gregory', 217.

85 *White Rose*, 8; *Chronicles of London*, 175; *CSP Venice*, I, p. 100, no. 370; *Benet's Chron.*, 230–1; 'Gregory', 217–18; Poulson I, 239ff; Scofield, I, 174ff.

86 See below, p. 123.

87 *Oeuvres de Georges Chastellain*, ed. K. de Lettenhove, IV, 66.

88 'Gregory', 206.

89 *Annales*, 781.

90 *Brief Notes*, 154–5.

91 'Gregory', 214; cf. below, p. 127.

Chapter 3: Lancastrian Risings and Invasions, 1461–4

1 The meeting of Margaret and her son with James II's widow Mary of Guelders at Lincluden in the winter of 1460–1 laid the foundations of subsequent close Lancastrian–Stewart relations (A. I. Dunlop, *The Life and Times of James Kennedy, Bishop of St Andrews* (Edinburgh 1950), 215ff).

2 For Lancastrian disturbances in many parts of England and Yorkist fears of an invasion supported by the French in 1461 and 1462, Ross, *Edward IV*, 42ff.

3 Scofield, I, 205 and n; *Paston Letters*, II, no. 416. Whetehill received the surrender of Guines castle before 25 February 1462 (F. Devon (ed.), *Issues of the Exchequer*, I (London 1837), 486–7).

4 *Paston Letters*, II, no. 386.

5 *Ibid.*, nos 385, 387; John Major, *A History of Greater Britain*, trans. and ed. A. Constable (Scottish Hist. Soc., Edinburgh 1892), 387. Berwick was ceded on 25 April (Dunlop, 221).

6 *Rot. Parl.*, V, 478; Scofield, I, 180.

7 *The Priory of Hexham*, I (Surtees Soc. 1864), p. c; *Coventry Leet Book*, 317–19. The Coventry contingent served till 29 July.

8 *Paston Letters*, II, no. 391; Scofield, I, 180. The initiative of Richard Salkeld, esquire, probably helped to save Carlisle from capitulating before Montague's relief. In 1467 he was said to have seized the city and castle and successfully defended them against Scots and English (*CPR, 1467–77*, 25).

9 *Rot. Parl.*, V, 478; Scofield, I, 186. On 30 June Prior Burnby of Durham wrote from there to the earl of Warwick asking for grace and good lordship for his poor kinsman Richard Billingham who had adhered to and accompanied Humphrey Neville (*Priory of Hexham*, I, p. ci). On

31 July the earl was appointed warden of the East and West Marches (Ross, *Edward IV*, 31).

10 *CSP Venice*, I, pp. 110–11, no. 384.

11 Scofield, I, 204. For Edward's garrisons at Newcastle and Tynemouth, *ibid.*, 204n.

12 *Oeuvres de Georges Chastellain*, ed. K. de Lettenhove, IV, 64ff; *Paston Letters*, II, nos 413, 416; Scofield, I, 187ff; Calmette and Périnelle, 6ff and 6n. For references to preparations for Edward's Welsh expedition in July and August, see, besides Scofield, *Paston Letters*, II, nos 409–10, 413. For the commission of 8 July 1461 to Ferrers, Herbert and James Baskerville to array in Herefordshire, Gloucestershire and Shropshire for defence against enemies in France and Scotland, and Lancastrians, *CPR, 1461–7*, 36.

13 *CSP Venice*, I, pp. 110–12, nos 384–5.

14 H. T. Evans, *Wales and the Wars of the Roses* (Cambridge 1915), 135ff; Scofield, I, 201–2; *Rot. Parl.*, VI, 29–30.

15 *Paston Letters*, II, no. 416. For Jasper's determination to hold Denbigh castle, Evans, 140. Thomas Cornwall, constable of Radnor castle, probably held it for a while for King Henry (Scofield, I, 197).

16 *Rot. Parl.*, V, 478.

17 *King's Works*, II, 602.

18 *CSP Milan*, I, pp. 106ff, no. 125; *Annales*, 779; Scofield, I, 230ff. Other leading conspirators were Oxford's eldest son, Aubrey de Vere, and Henry VI's former keeper of the wardrobe and treasurer of the household, Sir Thomas Tuddenham of Oxborough (Norfolk). According to *Brief Latin Chron.*, 175, the Veres had prepared for a landing in Essex by Somerset. For the release of the duke and his companions from arrest in France, Calmette and Périnelle, 8–9.

19 *Annales*, 779; Scofield, I, 241ff. For diplomatic and shipping movements on the Continent, helping to produce the alarm felt by Edward particularly in March 1462, Calmette and Périnelle, 15–17.

20 *Brief Notes*, 159.

21 *Annales*, 779–80; *Paston Letters*, II, nos 452, 458–9; Scofield, I, 246ff; Calmette and Périnelle, 18ff; Dunlop, 227–9. For the activities of Dacre and Tailboys in 1461, see above, p. 57. Warwick had already met Mary of Guelders at Dumfries in April (Dunlop, 227–8).

22 A. F. Pollard, *The Reign of Henry VII from Contemporary Sources*, I (London 1913), 137ff; cf. below, p. 111.

23 See below, p. 112.

24 For the powers conferred on William Herbert and his brothers in Wales after Towton, Evans, 135ff.

25 'Gregory', 218; Warkworth, 2; *Annales*, 780; Waurin, V, 431; Scofield, I, 261. The chronicler Thomas Basin denounced the meagreness of Louis' aid (*Histoire de Louis XI*, ed. Samaran, I, 80ff). Calmette and

Périnelle, 25ff, discuss the Lancastrian preparations at Honfleur and the reasons for an embarkation late in the year. They date it on 9 October and estimate the size of the expedition as 2,000, the figure given in *Annales* and by Waurin.

26 Warkworth, 2; cf. *Short English Chron.*, 79; *Annales*, 780. Any soldiers they placed in Warkworth castle were probably soon withdrawn to nearby Alnwick, as there is no mention of a Yorkist siege of Warkworth.

27 Warkworth, 2; *Brief Notes*, 157–8; *Paston Letters*, II, no. 460. In August the city of London had agreed to lend the crown £1,000, in response to a request by the earl of Worcester and others of the royal council for a loan of £3,400 to protect Calais from attack, and in October the city lent a further 2,000 marks (Sharpe, I, 308). In October a possible invasion of Scotland by the earl of Douglas was being envisaged (*CDS*, IV, no. 1332).

28 *Short English Chron.*, 79; cf. Scofield, I, 262 and n.

29 Scofield, I, 262.

30 *Chronicles of London*, 177–8; *Annales*, 780; *Brief Latin Chron.*, 175–6; 'Gregory', 218–19; *White Rose*, 13; *Priory of Hexham*, I, pp. cviii–cix; Scofield, I, 262–3. For the connection between the Ogle and Manners of Etal families, R. B. Dobson, *Durham Cathedral Priory 1400–1450* (Cambridge 1973), 197ff.

31 Scofield, I, 263–4. Sir John Clay commenced his attendance on the king for the expedition on 2 November (*CDS*, IV, no. 1342). According to *Annales*, Edward departed on 3 November.

32 *Brief Notes*, 157–8.

33 Scofield, I, 264.

34 *Brief Notes*, 158–9; *Annales*, 780; 'Gregory', 219; Scofield, I, 264ff.

35 *Paston Letters*, II, no. 464. According to *Brief Notes*, 158–9, Warwick, Kent, Grey of Powis, Greystoke and Cromwell besieged Alnwick; Wenlock and Hastings were at Dunstanburgh; and Worcester, Arundel, Ogle and Montague were at Bamburgh.

36 *Brief Latin Chron.*, 176; 'Gregory', 219; *Annales*, 780; Scofield, I, 265.

37 Warkworth, 2; cf. Scofield, I, 265–6.

38 *Priory of Hexham*, I, p. cvii.

39 Major, 388.

40 *Brief Latin Chron.*, 176; Warkworth, 2; 'Gregory', 220; *Annales*, 780–1; Major, 388; Waurin, V, 433. Major says that Angus reached Alnwick castle at noon, implying a less impressive achievement than the night crossing of the Border implicit in his arrival there, according to 'Gregory', at dawn.

41 *Brief Latin Chron.*, 176; *Chronicles of London*, 178; Scofield, I, 266ff.

42 *Annales*, 781–2; *Brief Latin Chron.*, 176; 'Gregory', 220; *Rot. Parl.*, V, 511; Scofield, I, 274, 287–8. Montague received powers as warden

general of the East March on 1 June (*Foedera*, XI, 550ff).

43 *Priory of Hexham*, I, pp. cvii–cviii.

44 'Gregory', 220–1; *Annales*, 781; Waurin, V, 431–3; Thomas Basin, *Histoire de Louis XI*, I, ed. Samaran, 82ff; Chastellain, IV, 278–9; Scofield, I, 293–4, 300; Dunlop, 236–7.

45 'Gregory', 220; Basin, I, 84ff; Chastellain, IV, 279ff; Scofield, I, 301, 306, 308ff; Calmette and Périnelle, 38–9, 38n, 40ff; Dunlop, 238ff.

46 *Rot. Parl.*, V, 511; 'Gregory', 221ff; Scofield, I, 312–13.

47 *Paston Letters*, II, no. 486; Scofield, I, 318–19.

48 *Brief Latin Chron.*, 178–9. According to this, Norham castle was also captured – but the Lancastrians cannot have held it long.

49 *Rot. Parl.*, V, 511.

50 'Gregory', 223–4; *Brief Latin Chron.*, 178; Waurin, V, 440–1; *Priory of Hexham*, I, p. cix and n; Scofield, I, 329–30.

51 *Annales*, 782; 'Gregory', 224–6; *Brief Latin Chron.*, 178–9; *Priory of Hexham*, I, pp. cix–cx; Scofield, I, 333–4. For a discussion of the site of the battle, Charlesworth, 'The Battle of Hexham, 1464', *Archaeologia Aeliana*, 4th ser., 30 (1952), 63ff.

52 *Brief Latin Chron.*, 179.

53 *Annales*, 782.

54 *Rot. Parl.*, V, 511.

55 College of Arms MS, in Warkworth, 37–9; *Annales*, 782–3; Scofield, I, 336ff.

Chapter 4: Local Revolts and Nobles' Struggles to Control the Crown, 1469–71

1 Scofield, I, 380ff, 478.

2 *White Rose*, 18–20; Scofield, I, 384–5.

3 *HMC, MSS of Shrewsbury Corporation*, 30.

4 *CSP Milan*, I, p. 121, nos 154, 162; Ross, *Edward IV*, 114, 120; *CPR, 1467–77*, 103. For the siege of Harlech, see below, p. 186.

5 Scofield, I, 480ff; Ross, *Edward IV*, 122ff. For the accusations against a rich draper, former mayor of London, M. A. Hicks, 'The case of Sir Thomas Cook', *EHR*, 93 (1978).

6 *Brief Latin Chron.*, 183. The risings and the sources for them are thoroughly discussed by Ross, *Edward IV*, 126ff and Appendix IV (439–40).

7 *Hist. Croylandensis Continuatio*, 542–3; Warkworth, 6; Waurin, V, 548; Worcestre, *Itineraries*, 340–1; *White Rose*, 24; *Coventry Leet Book*, 341–3; Scofield, I, 488–9, 491–3; Ross, *Edward IV*, 127ff. According to Warkworth, the northern rebels were 20,000 strong; according to the first Crowland continuator, about 60,000.

8 Warkworth, 6, 46ff; *Hist. Croylandensis Continuatio*, 542–3; Waurin, V, 579; Stone, 110–11; Scofield, I, 493ff; Ross, *Edward IV*, 129ff. Cf. Warwick's disingenuous requests to Coventry for military support (*Coventry Leet Book*, 341–2).

9 Waurin, V, 581–3; Warkworth, 6–7; *White Rose*, 24; *Hist. Croylandensis Continuatio*, 543, 551; *Gloucester Annals*, 356–7; Scofield, I, 496–8; Ross, *Edward IV*, 130ff. Warkworth says that Pembroke had 43,000 men and Devon 7,000; *Hearne's Fragment* (in *White Rose*) that Pembroke had 7,000–8,000 and Devon 4,000–5,000; Waurin, that Devon had 7,000–8,000. The first Crowland continuator says that allegedly 4,000 were killed on both sides, Warkworth that 2,000 Welshmen were slain. Worcester lists 24 Welshmen killed or executed, and says that about 168 others of the wealthier persons of Wales were killed. He puts the northerners' alleged death-toll at 1,500, including the sons of Lords Latimer, FitzHugh and Dudley (*Itineraries*, 338ff).

10 *Priory of Hexham*, I, p. cx; Warkworth, 7; *Hist. Croylandensis Continuatio*, 551–2; Scofield, I, 501ff; Ross, *Edward IV*, 134–5. In 1469 Shrewsbury paid 10s. to a messenger sent to York 'ad scrutandum de rumoribus domini Regis' (*HMC, MSS of Shrewsbury Corporation*, 30).

11 Warkworth, 8; Scofield, I, 509ff; Ross, *Edward IV*, 138ff. For Burgh's career, see R. L. Storey, 'Lincolnshire and the Wars of the Roses', *Nottingham Mediaeval Studies*, 14 (1970), 71ff.

12 *Lincolnshire Rebellion*, 5ff; *Chronicles of London*, 180; Waurin, V, 587ff; *Foedera*, XI, 652–3; Scofield, I, 510ff. On 9 February, by signet letter, Edward commanded Coventry to send him an armed contingent, to meet him at Grantham on 12 March. He asserted that 'we be ascertained that our rebels and outward enemies intend in haste time to arrive in this our Realm', to be joined by domestic adherents (*Coventry Leet Book*, 353–4). Reference to the threat from external enemies in his commission to Clarence and Warwick also suggests that he may have thought the disturbances were Lancastrian-inspired.

13 *Lincolnshire Rebellion*, 6ff; Waurin, V, 589ff.

14 *Lincolnshire Rebellion*, 9ff; Waurin, V, 592–3; *Chronicles of London*, 180–1. Waurin says that the Lincolnshiremen were more than 30,000 strong, and that most of them would have been killed had not Edward taken pains to stop the slaughter.

15 *Lincolnshire Rebellion*, 10–11, 21ff; Waurin, V, 593–4; Warkworth, 53ff. The proclamation forbidding arrays which Edward dispatched from Stamford to Warwickshire and Leicestershire the day after his victory reflects but does not specify his suspicions (Warkworth, 52–3). De la Launde and John Neille, 'a great captain', were executed at Grantham on 15 March, Welles and another great captain were at Doncaster on the 19th (*Paston Letters*, II, no. 638).

16 *Lincolnshire Rebellion*, 10ff; Waurin, V, 593ff, 602–3; Warkworth, 53ff; *Paston Letters*, II, no. 638. Edward was probably joined at Grantham by the Coventry contingent sent in response to his February request (*Coventry Leet Book*, 353–5).

17 Warkworth, 53ff; Waurin, V, 595, 600ff; *Foedera*, XI, 655–6; cf. *ibid.*, 654–5.

18 Scofield, I, 518–20; Ross, *Edward IV*, 145–6. A royal proclamation dated Nottingham, 31 March, declared Clarence and Warwick traitors, since they had not submitted. The confessions made at York were cited as evidence of their further treasons (Warkworth, 56ff). For the levy at Coventry for the soldiers 'that went with the king into the south country', *Coventry Leet Book*, 355–6. Gifts, notably of wine, to the duke of Norfolk and Lords Dinham and Scales, recorded in the Bridport cofferers' account for 1469–70, may reflect their presence in the royal army in the West Country (Dorset County Record Office, B3/M6).

19 Scofield, I, 523ff; Ross, *Edward IV*, 146–7.

20 *CPR, 1467–77*, 220.

21 *CSP Milan*, I, pp. 141–2, nos 192, 194.

22 *Paston Letters*, II, no. 648.

23 Waurin, V, 606–7; T. Basin, *Histoire de Louis XI*, ed. C. Samaran and M.-C. Garand, II, 20ff; *Oeuvres de Georges Chastellain*, ed. K. de Lettenhove, V, *Chronique*, 468.

24 Waurin, V, 606–7; *White Rose*, 28–9; *Paston Letters*, III, no. 648; *Coventry Leet Book*, 356–7; Ross, *Edward IV*, 150ff. Professor Ross discusses pro-Neville assemblies centring on Carlisle. Also this summer Oxford fled to Normandy to join Clarence and Warwick, but a conspiracy by Sir Geoffrey Gate and Clapham to pass over from Southampton was foiled by the earl of Worcester and Lord Howard (*White Rose*, 28–9).

25 Warkworth, 10; *Brief Latin Chron.*, 183; *Chronicles of London*, 181; *CSP Milan*, p. 142, no. 195; Basin, II, 48ff; Chastellain, *Oeuvres*, V, 468–9; *Coventry Leet Book*, 358; Scofield, I, 536; Ross, *Edward IV*, 151–2; Calmette and Périnelle, 118–19.

26 Scofield, I, 538.

27 *Coventry Leet Book*, 358.

28 Warkworth, 10–11; *Hist. Croylandensis Continuatio*, 553–4; *Chronicles of London*, 181; *Coventry Leet Book*, 358–9; Scofield, I, 538–9; Ross, *Edward IV*, 152–4. Chastellain says that Edward had granted command of his *avant-garde* to Montague (*Oeuvres*, V, 499ff).

29 *Coventry Leet Book*, 359; *Chronicles of London*, 182; Sharpe, I, 311–12; Scofield, I, 541–2. Shrewsbury and Stanley had probably joined the rebels with companies in the Midlands. Jasper Tudor had gone to Wales to rally support (Scofield, I, 538).

30 *Arrivall*, 1–2; Warkworth, 13; Scofield, I, 567–8. Warwick wrote on 25 March that Edward had landed with Flemings, 'Esterlinges'

(= Germans ?) and Danes, and that his company did not number more than 2,000 (*HMC, Rutland MSS*, I, 3–4). For Warwick's preparations, Ross, *Edward IV*, 160.

31 *Arrivall*, 2; Warkworth, 13; *Paston Letters*, II, no. 663; Scofield, I, 568–9.

32 *Arrivall*, 2ff; Warkworth, 13–14; *York Civic Records*, I, 136; Scofield, I, 569ff. According to one source, Edward reached the Trent on 25 March (J. A. F. Thomson, ' "The Arrivall of Edward IV" – The Development of the Text', *Speculum*, 46 (1971), 91. Sir William Par and Sir James Harington joined him at Nottingham with two well-arrayed 'bands' totalling 600 (*Arrivall*, 7). According to Warkworth, 14, Sir William Stanley, Sir William Norys and men and tenants of Lord Hastings came in there, bringing Edward's force to over 2,000. The author of the *Arrivall*, 8–9, says that Hastings's supporters joined up at Leicester, to the number of 3,000.

33 *Arrivall*, 7–8; *Paston Letters*, II, no. 664.

34 *Arrivall*, 8; *HMC, Rutland MSS*, I, 3–4; Basin, II, 80–1.

35 *Arrivall*, 8–9, 12; Basin, II, 66–7; Warkworth, 14; Malory, *Works*, II, 621–2; Scofield, I, 571–2. The author of the *Arrivall* says that Warwick had 6,000–7,000 soldiers in Coventry. According to Basin, Edward heard that Oxford, Beaumont and many others were coming to reinforce Warwick, and sent against them, at Leicester, part of his forces, which on 3 April defeated Oxford and his men (Basin, II, 68–9; cf. Thomson, ' "The Arrivall of Edward IV" ', 91).

36 *Arrivall*, 10–11. For Clarence's movements, see his letters to Vernon, *HMC, Rutland MSS*, I, 2–4.

37 *Arrivall*, 9ff; Scofield, I, 573–4. On 27 March a commission had been issued to the prince of Wales (still in France) granting him powers to array and make proclamations throughout the realm (*Foedera*, XI, 706–7).

38 *Arrivall*, 12ff; Warkworth, 15; Scofield, I, 574–5.

39 *Arrivall*, 15–17; Warkworth, 15; *CSP Milan*, I, p. 153, no. 213; Scofield, I, 574ff.

40 *Paston Letters*, III, no. 668; *Arrivall*, 19ff; Warkworth, 16–17; Scofield, I, 578ff.

41 *CSP Milan*, I, p. 153, no. 213; *Arrivall*, 20–1; Warkworth, 15.

42 *Arrivall*, 19ff; Warkworth, 16–17; *Paston Letters*, III, no. 668; Scofield, I, 578ff. Warkworth says that 4,000 were killed on both sides.

43 *Arrivall*, 22ff; Warkworth, 17–18; Hist. *Croylandensis Continuatio*, 555.

44 For Edward's preparations, Ross, *Edward IV*, 169–70. Coventry sent 'new soldiers' to him at London, having just probably contributed a company to Warwick's army which fought at Barnet (*Coventry Leet Book*, 364–6, 369).

45 *Arrivall*, 24–5; Basin, II, 80–1.

46 *Arrivall*, 25. By 28 April Edward received at Abingdon a letter addressed by the prince of Wales to the civic governors of Coventry, dated Chard, 18 April (*Coventry Leet Book*, 366–7). It is difficult to surmise how Edward would have interpreted the prince's presence at Chard. The prudent Coventry citizens probably sent the letter to him promptly because of the support they had given Warwick at Barnet (*ibid.*, 364–6).

47 *The Little Red Book of Bristol*, ed. F. B. Bickley, II, 130–1.

48 *Arrivall*, 25–6.

49 *Ibid.*, 25–6; Basin, II, 80–1.

50 *Arrivall*, 26–8; Basin, II, 82–3.

51 *Arrivall*, 28ff; Warkworth, 18–19; *Paston Letters*, III, no. 671. For a discussion of Somerset's attack, see below, pp. 178–9. According to *MS Tanner 2*, in *Six Town Chronicles*, 168, Wenlock 'proditor pugni a suis in vestigio occisus est'.

52 *HMC, Rutland MSS*, I, 4–6; *Arrivall*, 31–3.

53 *Arrivall*, 33ff; *Hist. Croylandensis Continuatio*, 555–6; Warkworth, 19–20; Basin, II, 84ff; *Yorkist Notes*, 374–5. For the Bastard's siege of London, see below, pp. 187–8.

54 *Arrivall*, 38ff; Stone, 116; Richmond, 'Fauconberg's Kentish Rising of May 1471', 681–3. The earl of Essex and Lord Dinham led a force into Essex to pursue the rebels from that shire who had rebelled with the Bastard.

55 *CSP Venice*, I, p. 129, no. 437; Calmette and Périnelle, 145; *CPR, 1467–77*, 289, 281. For Oxford's 1473 invasion, see below, pp. 188–9.

Chapter 5 : The Later Risings, 1483–97

1 This account is based on Polydore Vergil, *English Hist.*, 192ff; *Hist. Croylandensis Continuatio*, 567; *Chronicles of London*, 191–2. For a recent account of the rebellion, A. Hanham, *Richard III and His Early Historians 1483–1535* (Oxford 1975), 14ff.

2 For Henry Tudor's early life, see S. B. Chrimes, *Henry VII* (London 1972).

3 For a discussion of Peter Courtenay's possible motives for joining the rebellion, J. A. F. Thomson, 'The Courtenay Family in the Yorkist Period', *BIHR*, 45 (1972), 241–2.

4 For a recent discussion of Buckingham's motives, and his role in the 1483 rebellion, Rawcliffe, 30ff.

5 *Letters and Papers illustrative of the reigns of Richard III and Henry VII*, I, ed. J. Gairdner (Rolls ser., 1861), 54–5, for reference by the duke of Brittany on 22 November 1483 to 10,000 crowns delivered as a loan to the 'sire de Richemont' (Henry Tudor). For Margaret's raising of

loans to support the rebellion in the city of London and elsewhere, Chrimes, 329.

6 *Paston Letters*, III, no. 876.

7 *Stonor Letters and Papers*, II, no. 333.

8 P. Tudor-Craig, *Richard III* (Ipswich 1977), 78–9.

9 *HMC, MSS of Southampton Corporation*, 31.

10 *CPR, 1476–85*, 370. Commissions of array dated Leicester, 23 October, were issued to various counties and towns (*ibid.*, 371).

11 According to a rebel proclamation, Buckingham had repented of his past conduct (*Hist. Croylandensis Continuatio*, 568). For a hostile reaction to his attempts to raise revolt, see Edward Plumpton's letter of 18 October (*Plumpton Letters*, no. vi). There were suspicions current that the duke really wanted the throne for himself (Vergil, *English Hist.*, 195).

12 Chrimes, 328–9.

13 Cf. Owen and Blakeway, 241; Rawcliffe, 32ff.

14 *CPR, 1476–85*, 370. For the wine payment, Dorset County Record Office, Bridport Borough Records, B3/M6, Cofferer's Account, 1483–4. I owe this reference to the kindness of the Rev. E. B. Short.

15 There were rebels at Rochester on 20 October, Gravesend on 22nd, and Guildford on 25th (Chrimes, 328).

16 For the connections of St Leger's daughter the duchess of Exeter with the marquess of Dorset, Bishop Courtenay and possibly Buckingham, see *Grants, Etc. from the Crown during the Reign of Edward the Fifth*, ed. J. G. Nichols (Camden Soc., 1854), pp. lxv–vi.

17 Chrimes, 26–7 and 26n.

18 *Plumpton Letters*, no. vi.

19 *CPR, 1476–85*, 370–1.

20 *Ibid.*, 427–8, 433, 479.

21 Others were Sir Robert Willoughby, Sir Giles Daubeney, Thomas Arundel, John Cheyney, William Brandon and Richard Edgecombe (Vergil, *English Hist.*, 200; *Paston Letters*, III, no. 883). For a list of Henry's companions in exile, Chrimes, 327.

22 For Richard's subversion of Dorset, Chrimes, 38.

23 *Paston Letters*, III, no. 883; Hanham, 19–20. In June the city of London advanced £2,000 to assist the king against the rebels, daily expected to land, and precautions were taken to safeguard the city (Sharpe, I, 326).

24 A. Goodman and A. MacKay, 'A Castilian report on English affairs, 1486', *EHR*, 88, 92ff; for the text of Valera's letter, Tudor-Craig, 67–8, and Hanham, 54ff. Valera also says that Henry had with him 3,000 Englishmen who had fled from Richard. Vergil says that he had a total of 2,000 men, Molinet that Charles provided him with 1,800 soldiers and 60,000 francs, Commynes that he raised 3,000 men of low fighting quality in Normandy (Vergil, *English Hist.*, 216; Molinet, I,

434; *The Memoirs of Philippe de Commynes*, ed. and trans. Kinser and Cazeaux, II, 414–15; cf. Chrimes, 40 and n). John Major (393) says that Charles gave Henry the aid of 5,000 men, including 1,000 Scots captained by John Haddington.

25 The account of the campaign is based mainly on those of Vergil (*English Hist.*, 216ff) and the second Crowland continuator (*Hist. Croylandensis Continuatio*, 573ff). For a recent account, Chrimes, 40ff.

26 *Hist. Croylandensis Continuatio*, 572–3.

27 For Oxford's command and for Chandée, Bernard André, *De vita atque gestis Henrici septimi ... historia*, 25, 27, 29; cf. Goodman and MacKay, 94–5.

28 Cf. Chrimes, 42ff and 42n.

29 Pollard, I, 14–15; Owen and Blakeway, 245ff, 247n; H. L. Turner, *Town Defences in England and Wales* (London 1971), 208. For Richard Crompe's part in the surrender of Shrewsbury, *Materials for a History of the Reign of Henry VII*, I, p. 156.

30 Chrimes, 45.

31 *Ibid.*, 46.

32 Cf. *ibid.*, 63 and n. Norfolk had intended to rally his company at Bury St Edmunds (Suffolk) on 16 August, the day on which he expected the king to set forth (*Paston Letters*, III, no. 884). Richard had been joined by Brackenbury's force, though on the way, at Stony Stratford, Sir Thomas Bourchier and Sir Walter Hungerford deserted it to join the rebels.

33 For the topography of the battlefield, J. Gairdner, 'The Battle of Bosworth', *Archaeologia*, 55 (1896), 159ff; A. H. Burne, *The Battlefields of England* (London 1950), 140–1.

34 *Materials*, I, 188; cf. 201.

35 Gairdner's argument that Richard had no artillery (an exceptional situation for a royal army in the period) is contradicted by Molinet's mention of his 'grande quantité d'engiens volans' and by the roll of Henry's first parliament ('The Battle of Bosworth', 169; Molinet, *Chronique*, I, 434; *Rot. Parl.*, VI, 276).

36 Salaçar, Archduke Maximilian's renowned Spanish captain who fought for Richard, may have had a mercenary company (cf. Goodman and MacKay, 95 and n; Hanham, 54n). For the Salazar family, see Commynes, *Mémoires*, ed. Calmette, III, 148 and n, and P. Contamine, *Guerre, état et société à la fin du moyen âge* (Paris 1972), 446.

37 According to Commynes, Charles VIII furnished Henry with artillery. Cannonballs have been dug up on the brow of Ambien Hill, presumably fired by Henry's men at the royal army there (Gairdner, 'The Battle of Bosworth', 167ff). For finds of cannonballs fired at Bosworth, Burne, *Battlefields of England*, 151; Tudor-Craig, 73.

38 These knights were to distinguish themselves in warfare after 1485. According to Vergil, Savage, Brian Sandford and Simon Digby joined

Henry with a 'choice band' late in the afternoon of 21 August. Sir John Savage the younger described as 'eminent in arms as in character and counsel' was rewarded for his service to Henry at Bosworth 'with a multitude of his brothers, kinsmen, servants and friends' (*CPR, 1485–94*, 101–2).

39 For Brackenbury's command, Molinet, *Chronique* I, 434–5.

40 Pollard, I, 16.

41 Vegetius, *Epitoma Rei Militaris*, III, 20, 14.

42 Molinet, *Chronique*, I, 434.

43 Vergil, *Anglica Historia*, 96–7.

44 Molinet says (*Chronique*, I, 435) that Northumberland and his retinue failed to charge Henry's Frenchmen as they should have done, but did nothing and fled, because the earl had an understanding with Henry. For other reflections on Northumberland's conduct and a discussion of his motives, Goodman and MacKay, 95ff. Valera says that 'my lord Tamorlant', commanding Richard's left wing, circled with a large number of soldiers to fight against the king's vanguard, in front of Henry's men (*ibid.*, 92). For the tentative identification of 'Tamorlant' with Northumberland, see below, p. 96 and n. 55.

45 Goodman and MacKay, 92; cf. Vergil, *English Hist.*, 225–6.

46 Molinet, *Chronique*, I, 435. The story that the crown was found abandoned on a hawthorn bush has been rejected by modern scholarship (Chrimes, 49n). Molinet says that another Welshman took the royal corpse, laid 'like a sheep' on horseback with the hair hanging down. Is it not possible that the killer of an anointed king was frightened by what he had done, and removed and abandoned the crown before having the corpse presented, so that it was not clear that he had known what he was doing?

47 Chrimes, 51; Gairdner, 'The Battle of Bosworth', 177. Richard's putative place of death, north-west of Ambien Hill, may have a bearing on the positions of Henry's main 'battle' and the Stanleys' forces.

48 Richard's standard now evocatively hangs at the place.

49 According to Molinet (*Chronique*, I, 435), the royal van was attacked in flight by Lord Stanley.

50 Molinet says that only 300 were killed on both sides in the battle (*Chronique*, I, 436).

51 According to his funeral inscription, in J. Weever, *Ancient Funerall Monuments* (etc.) (London 1631), 835.

52 Pollard, I, 17; cf. *ibid.*, 17n, for John Payntor's remark in 1491 that the earl of Northumberland had betrayed the king.

53 On the day after Bosworth, York city council recorded that Richard 'was piteously slain and murdered, to the great heaviness of this City' (Pollard, I, 17). For Richard's relations with northern society, R. R. Reid, *The King's Council in the North* (London 1921), 42ff; A. J. Pollard, 'The Tyranny of Richard III', *Journal of Medieval Hist.*, 3 (1977); M. A.

Hicks, 'Dynastic Change and Northern Society: the Career of the Fourth Earl of Northumberland, 1470–89', *Northern Hist.*, 14 (1978).

54 Vergil, *Anglica Historia*, 2–3.

55 Goodman and MacKay, 93, 95ff; Pollard, I, 28–9; Hanham, 55–6; but cf. Tudor-Craig, 69.

56 Pollard, I, 19–20. Henry commissioned John de la Pole, duke of Suffolk, to lead the lieges of Suffolk and Norfolk to attend on the king, and suppress 'certain his rebels associate to his old enemies of Scotland' (Suffolk to the sheriff, John Paston, 20 October, Pollard, I, 21–2).

57 *Ibid.*, 21.

58 *Tudor Royal Proclamations*, I, ed. P. L. Hughes and J. F. Larkin, no. 4, p. 5.

59 Pollard, I, 31–2.

60 Goodman and MacKay, 96 and n; Hicks, 92ff.

61 Pollard, I, 34–5.

62 Vergil, *Anglica Historia*, 10–11. Lovell and Stafford had been among Richard's adherents attainted in the 1485 parliament (Pollard, I, 32). The party which had taken sanctuary at Colchester after Bosworth was a large one, and included Stafford's brother Thomas (Vergil, *English Hist.*, 225).

63 Pollard, I, 45; *CPR, 1485–94*, 89, 156, 94–5, 115. The account of the 1486 rebellion is based mainly on Vergil, *Anglica Historia*, 10–13, and C. H. Williams, 'The Rebellion of Humphrey Stafford in 1486', *EHR*, 43 (1928), 181ff.

64 Stafford was forcibly extracted from sanctuary, condemned and executed; his brother Thomas was pardoned. General pardons were granted in 1487 to John Griffith, late of Worcester, and Simon Mawditt, late constable of Worcester castle (*CPR, 1485–94*, 155–6).

65 *Ibid.*, 112.

66 *Tudor Royal Proclamations*, I, p. 10, no. 8. Broughton was a feedman of the earl of Northumberland in 1483–4 (Cockermouth Castle MSS, Carlisle Record Office, Receiver's Account Roll, 1–2 Richard III, D/Lec/29/8). Sir John Hudleston senior had received a fee from the estates of the Kingmaker's uncle Lord Latimer in 1462 and 1465–6 (Cockermouth Castle MSS, Account Rolls of the receiver of the Latimer estates in Cumberland and Westmorland, D/Lec/28/28–9).

67 *CPR, 1485–94*, 119.

68 *Ibid.*, 133; Pollard, I, 32. Sir Robert Harington and Sir Robert Middleton received general pardons and reversals of attainder dated 17 August (*CPR, 1485–94*, 119).

69 *VCH, Lancs.*, VIII, 402–3.

70 I. Grimble, *The Harington Family* (London 1957), 48, 53–4; *CCR, 1468–76*, no. 136; *CPR, 1467–77*, 426–7; *CPR, 1485–94*, 130; Pollard, I, 32.

71 *CPR, 1485–94*, 169; Waurin, V, 344–5; Scofield, I, 381 and n; Grimble, 53–4; *VCH, Lancs.*, VIII, 232–3.
72 Grimble, 44ff; *CCR, 1468–76*, no. 136; *VCH, Lancs.*, VIII, 191ff.
73 Grimble, 54–5; *CCR, 1468–76*, no. 136.
74 *Foedera*, XI, 699.
75 *Arrivall*, 7; Warkworth, 14.
76 *CPR, 1467–77*, 426–7; Grimble, 55ff.
77 Pollard, I, 52–3.
78 Vergil, *Anglica Historia*, 12ff; André, 49ff; Molinet, I, 562ff; Pollard, I, 51–2 and 3, 246–7, 261–3; *York Civic Records*, II, 6–7. For the reasons for Irish support of the Yorkist cause in Henry's reign, Chrimes, 73ff.
79 Hearne, *Collectanea*, IV, 209; Vergil, *Anglica Historia*, 20–1; *York Civic Records*, II, 10–13.
80 *York Civic Records*, II, 13–14, 16; Hearne, 209–10; Pollard, I, 47.
81 *Paston Letters*, III, no. 895.
82 Vergil, *Anglica Historia*, 20–3; Molinet, I, 562–3; Pollard, III, 262–3, 265–6; *York Civic Records*, II, 20; F. Redlich, *The German Military Enterpriser and his Work Force*, I (Wiesbaden 1964), 107–8; *VCH, Lancs.*, VIII, 287, 309, 402–3; Hearne, 210.
83 Hearne, 209–14; *York Civic Records*, II, 22–3; Vergil, *Anglica Historia*, 22ff; Molinet, I, 563.
84 *York Civic Records*, II, 3ff.
85 Pollard, I, 52–4.
86 *York Civic Records*, II, 22; *CP*, XI, 544–5, 569–70; *Testamenta Vetusta* ed. N. H. Nicholas, 2 vols (London 1826), II, 587; Hicks, 89, 97–8. The York records say that the Scropes made their assault on the city 'constrained as it was said by their folks'; perhaps by an appearance of half-heartedness they secured the gentle treatment which Henry gave them (*CPR, 1485–94*, 190, 199, 238, 264). Scrope of Bolton's half-heartedness in rebellion in 1470 had turned out to his advantage. He was a councillor of Richard III (*CPR, 1476–85*, 501–1).
87 For northern gentlefolk who joined Henry, Vergil, *Anglica Historia*, 23n.
88 *York Civic Records*, II, 4–6, 16, 20–22. Molinet says that the invaders passed over great mountains to 'Scanfort', where many local lords came into the Yorkist obedience (*Chronique*, I, 563). Perhaps he meant Carnforth.
89 *York Civic Records*, II, 22–3. On 23 June Northumberland was at Richmond (Yorks.) (Pollard, I, 54).
90 Molinet, I, 563–4.
91 This account of the movements of Henry's army is based on the anonymous account printed by Hearne.
92 For an impressive list of Henry's supporters, Vergil, *Anglica Historia*, 22n. For agreements by the community of Henley (Oxon.) to finance

soldiers on 25 May and on 8 and 10 June, 'pro domino rege intendente transmeare versus partes boreales', *Henley Borough Records. Assembly Books i–iv*, 94–5.

93 Vergil, *Anglica Historia*, 22–3; *The Place-Names of Nottinghamshire*, ed. J. E. B. Gover, Allen Mawer and F. M. Stenton (Cambridge 1940), 245.

94 Vergil, *Anglica Historia*, 24–7; Pollard, I, 53; Hearne, 213–14; *York Civic Records*, II, 22–3; Molinet, I, 564–5.

95 Vergil, *Anglica Historia*, 20–1; Hearne, 209.

96 Vergil, *Anglica Historia*, 24–7; Pollard, III, 263–4; *York Civic Records*, II, 23ff.

97 *York Civic Records*, II, 28–9. For the expedition under Sir Richard Edgecombe which reasserted Henry's authority at Dublin, Chrimes, 78–9.

98 Molinet, I, 563–4; *Letters and Papers*, I, 94–5.

99 Pollard, I, 51.

100 Weever, 835.

101 Some southerners were attainted for rebellion in 1487 – four of the Mallary family from Northamptonshire and Robert Mannyng of Dunstable, Beds. (Pollard, I, 52–3).

102 Vergil, *Anglica Historia*, 38–9.

103 *Plumpton Correspondence*, letter XXV, p. 61.

104 Vergil, *Anglica Historia*, 38–9; M. E. James, 'The Murder at Cocklodge', *Durham Univ. Jnl*, n.s., 26 (1964–5), 80ff; Hicks, 78ff.

105 Pollard, I, 72ff; Hicks, 79–80, 100.

106 *Paston Letters*, III, no. 916; cf. no. 915.

107 Hicks, 78; Vergil, *Anglica Historia*, 38–9; James, 85.

108 Pollard, I, 80; James, 86n.

109 *Paston Letters*, III, no. 915.

110 Vergil, *Anglica Historia*, 38–9; Pollard, I, 79–81; James, 86–7. Henry was in Yorkshire by 22 May, but departed before the end of the first week in June (*ibid.*, 87n).

111 Pollard, I, 81 and n. For Surrey's return to favour, see M. J. Tucker, *The Life of Thomas Howard Earl of Surrey and Second Duke of Norfolk 1443–1524* (The Hague 1964), 48ff.

112 R. L. Storey, *The Reign of Henry VII* (London 1968), 148–9, 144–5.

113 A. Conway, *Henry VII's Relations with Scotland and Ireland 1485–1498* (Cambridge 1932), 39–40, 48ff. Henry wrote in 1493 that at first in Ireland Warbeck claimed to be an illegitimate son of Richard III, and later claimed to be Warwick, but was at present claiming to be Edward IV's younger son, Richard duke of York – the claim on which he finally settled (Pollard, I, 93–4). For an official Tudor account of Warbeck's intrigues and invasions, André, 65ff.

114 Pollard, I, 93–5. For Henry's naval preparations, Conway, 41.

115 Vergil, *Anglica Historia*, 70ff; Pollard, I, 100–3, 109ff. FitzWalter was only executed in 1496 after plotting to escape from his prison in Guines castle (*ibid.*, 144).

116 Vergil, *Anglica Historia*, 80–3; Molinet, II, 421–2; Pollard, I, 103ff, 111–12; *Chronicles of London*, 206–7, for captured foreigners. It was reported in London that 500–600 invaders landed and that the fourteen ships which remained at sea probably carried up to 800 more. The Kentish force was 140–160 strong; it captured 169 invaders, killed 2, and others were drowned (*ibid.*, 105). Albon wrote that 140 rebels were slain or captured, de Puebla that 150 were killed and 80 captured, Molinet that 300 landed and suffered about 150 casualties (Pollard, I, 105, 107; Molinet, II, 421–2).

117 Pollard, I, 105ff. For the capture of the captains 'Jennot', 'Quentin' and 'Beld', *Memorials of King Henry the Seventh*, 147–8.

118 Vergil, *Anglica Historia*, 82–5. For Anglo-Scottish relations, Conway, *passim*; Chrimes, 86ff. See also R. L. Mackie, *King James IV of Scotland* (Edinburgh 1958), 78ff; R. Nicholson, *Scotland. The Later Middle Ages* (Edinburgh 1974), 549ff. Warbeck had been in correspondence with James in March 1492 (Conway, 39).

119 Conway, 84–6, 99; Pollard, III, 278–9. Waterford had defied the Yorkist rebels in 1487 (*ibid.*, 265–6).

120 Pollard, I, 136–7. Bothwell was also certain that Northumberland men were showing disloyal tendencies at 'march days' and secret meetings with Scots, and facilitating the escape of 'vagabonds' to join Warbeck.

121 Pollard, I, 137ff. Bothwell reports Lalain as referring to 'Richard IV' as 'Perkin' in his remarks to James, in Perkin's presence (*ibid.*, 142). Both Neville and Lalain were to serve the Yorkist pretender Edmund de la Pole (*Letters and Papers*, I, 276–8).

122 *Accounts of the Lord High Treasurer of Scotland*, I, cxxxix ff, 296ff; Mackie, 81ff. Warbeck's movements on 21 September were mysterious: he seems to have been returning to Scotland from James in England. For their quarrel, see below, p. 216.

123 Pollard, I, 143.

124 Vergil, *Anglica Historia*, 86ff. In 1497 Henry's envoy to James, Bishop Fox of Durham, was instructed to claim compensation for the destruction of castles and fortalices in the previous year's invasion, as a condition of peace (*Letters and Papers*, I, 107).

125 *Accounts of the Lord High Treasurer*, I, 297.

126 *Ibid.*, 296.

127 Nicholson, 551–2, 600ff.

128 Vergil, *Anglica Historia*, 90ff; *Tudor Royal Proclamations*, I, 39–40, no. 35; *Letters and Papers*, I, 232; Sharpe, I, 331–2; Chrimes, 90.

129 Vergil, *Anglica Historia*, 94–5; *Select Cases in the Council of Henry VII*, ed. C. G. Bayne and W. H. Dunham Jr (Selden Soc. vol. 75,

London 1958), xxix–xxx; *Letters and Papers*, I, 263ff.
130 *CPR, 1494–1509*, 117, 115.
131 Conway, 110–11; Chrimes, 90–1.
132 Pollard, I, 162–3.
133 *Ibid.*, 163ff.
134 Vergil, *Anglica Historia*, 104–5, 108–9; Pollard, I, 166–8. For the siege of Exeter, see below, p. 190.
135 Pollard, I, 167–8; Sharpe, I, 333.
136 Pollard, I, 168–9; Vergil, *Anglica Historia*, 106–7.
137 Molinet, II, 439–40; *MS Tanner 2*, in *Six Town Chronicles*, 173; Sharpe, I, 333; Vergil, *Anglica Historia*, 106ff. According to the official London version, Warbeck went from Taunton to 'Mynet' with fewer than sixty adherents. But Minehead, on the Bristol Channel, is in the opposite direction from the one Warbeck is known to have taken. He may have gone to Minehead first, and found that Henry's fleet made escape thence impossible.
138 Vergil, *Anglica Historia*, 106ff.
139 See M. Levine, *Tudor Dynastic Problems, 1460–1571* (London 1973).

Chapter 6: Military Convention and Recruitment

1 *Rot. Parl.*, V, 348.
2 *Knyghthode and Bataile*, 74.
3 Whethamstede, I, 392. Henry knighted his son, one of his opponents, after the battle (*Annales*, 776).
4 Quoted in C. T. Allmand (ed.), *Society at War* (Edinburgh 1973), 17.
5 F. H. Russell, *The Just War in the Middle Ages* (Cambridge 1975), 298; cf. *ibid.*, *passim*, and M. H. Keen, *The Laws of War in the Late Middle Ages* (London 1965), 63ff.
6 Keen, 106ff.
7 Armstrong, 36.
8 *Rot. Parl.*, V, 280–2; Armstrong.
9 See above, pp. 29–30, 34ff.
10 *Records of the Borough of Nottingham*, II, 369.
11 *English Chron.*, 81–2.
12 *Rot. Parl.*, V, 348. According to *Bale's Chron.*, 148, Henry was in the foreward at Ludford Bridge, where he would have been more vulnerable to shot.
13 See above, pp. 72, 97. The opposing sides in Yorkshire had made a brief truce in December 1460: its rupture by the Lancastrians probably prejudiced the chances of negotiation in 1461.
14 *Foedera*, II, 709–11.

15 Valera, cited in Goodman and MacKay, 92; Vergil, *English Hist.*, 225–6.
16 See above, pp. 105, 108, 115.
17 See above, pp. 57ff.
18 *HMC, Rutland MSS*, I, 3–4; cf. *Arrivall*, 17, 20.
19 See below, p. 205.
20 Richmond, 'Fauconberg's Kentish rising of May 1471', 676.
21 'Tunc rex constituit sui certaminis constabularium et principalem actorem ducem Bokyngamiae' (Armstrong, 23 and n).
22 G. D. Squibb, *The High Court of Chivalry* (Oxford 1959), 1ff; Keen, 27ff; cf. *Tudor Royal Proclamations*, I, no. 13, p. 15.
23 *Annales*, 782; Warkworth, 38–9. For the placing of prisoners in the constable's ward by King Arthur, Malory, I, 211.
24 *CPR, 1494–1509*, 34, 115. These knights were holding the offices as deputies (cf. Squibb, 228ff). For the commission, including Digby, to execute the offices on the rebel Lord Audley in 1497, *CPR, 1494–1509*, 115. At York in 1487 Sir John Turberville, knight marshal, had judged recent rebels for treason (*York Civic Records*, II, 28).
25 Squibb, 1ff.
26 *Knyghthode and Bataile*, 32–3, 44–5.
27 Pollard, I, 67–9.
28 *Tudor Royal Proclamations*, I, no. 213, pp. 14–15. For earlier proclamations on discipline in the wars, see below, p. 215.
29 Whethamstede, I, 394ff; Malory, I, 243.
30 Waurin, V, 325.
31 *Knyghthode and Bataile*, 58–9.
32 Hearne, *Collectanea*, IV, 209–10; Armstrong, 23–4; *Arrivall*, 3; *Hist. Croylandensis Continuatio*, 555. For Oxford's proposed arrangements to consult with his council and three or four Norfolk gentlemen over defence measures in 1471, *Paston Letters*, II, no. 663.
33 Waurin, V, 290–1, 293, 295–7, 299, 306, 325–6, 337.
34 See above, pp. 84–5, 87ff.
35 See above, p. 37.
36 Whethamstede, I, 338; *Knyghthode and Bataile*, 1ff.
37 Cf. *Knyghthode and Bataile*, 11, 32.
38 K. Fowler, *The Age of Plantagenet and Valois* (London 1967), 125–6; cf. Powicke, 'Lancastrian Captains', 371ff.
39 *Rot. Parl.*, V, 369; Hearne, *Collectanea*, IV, 209–10.
40 Malory, I, 232–3, 235.
41 See above, pp. 120, 75.
42 *Short English Chron.*, 75.
43 Fowler, *Age of Plantagenet and Valois*, 125–6; K. Fowler (ed.), *The Hundred Years War* (London 1971), 10; cf. Powicke, 'Lancastrian Captains', *passim*. For Harowe, below, p. 202.

44　*Annales*, 776; *Short English Chron.*, 77; Worcestre, *Itineraries*, 203.
45　*Brief Latin Chron.*, 178.
46　Vergil, *English Hist.*, 200.
47　*Coventry Leet Book*, 282–3.
48　*Records of the City of Norwich*, I, 406. For Rokewode, *Paston Letters*, I, nos 174, 201.
49　Chamberlain's Account, 1463–4, in *Records of the Borough of Nottingham*, II, 377.
50　'Gregory', 212–13.
51　Warkworth, 13–14; *Arrivall*, 3–4.
52　Vergil, *Anglica Historia*, 90ff.
53　'Gregory', 193; *English Chron.*, 64, 66; *Paston Letters*, I, p. 133n.
54　Waurin, V, 334.
55　*Bale's Chron.*, 151; *English Chron.*, 107–8. Cade had a certain 'Lovelase' in his service at Southwark in 1450 (*Paston Letters*, I, no. 99).
56　'Gregory', 214.
57　*Ibid.*, 205.
58　Waurin, V, 273, 276, 278–9, 306, 325–6; cf. *Paston Letters*, I, no. 357.
59　For some documentary illustrations, Allmand (ed.), *Society at War*, 57ff.
60　J. W. Sherborne, 'Indentured retinues and English expeditions to France, 1369–1380', *EHR*, 79 (1964); A. Goodman, 'The military subcontracts of Sir Hugh Hastings, 1380', *EHR*, 95 (1980).
61　For examples of fourteenth-century life indentures, see N. B. Lewis, 'Indentures of Retinue with John of Gaunt, duke of Lancaster' (etc.), *Camden Miscellany*, XXII (1964). For the effects of legal limitations on the grant of liveries, and a sceptical view of the importance of retaining in constituting the first duke of Buckingham's military companies, Rawcliffe, 72ff.
62　*CDS*, IV, nos 1387, 1466.
63　Allmand (ed.), *Society at War*, 74–6; *Wars of the English in France*, ed. Stevenson, II, 512–15; *English Chron.*, 85; Scofield, I, 53–4.
64　See, for example, *Foedera*, XI, 444.
65　*Rot. Parl.*, V, 348.
66　'Gregory', 226.
67　Vergil, *English Hist.*, 215–16.
68　*Paston Letters*, III, no. 874.
69　*Plumpton Correspondence*, p. 96n.
70　*Letters and Papers*, I, 112. To encourage a good response to such summonses, it was enacted in 1495 that no person attending in response to a royal summons for military service was to be liable for that cause to conviction or attaint of high treason or for any other offences (*Statutes of the Realm*, II, 568).
71　*CDS*, IV, no. 1342.

72 W. H. Dunham, Jr, *Lord Hastings' Indentured Retainers 1461–1483* (New Haven, Conn., 1955), 25.
73 See above, pp. 127, 165.
74 E.g., *CCR, 1454–61*, 408, 410, 415.
75 *Annales*, 780.
76 *Hist. Croylandensis Continuatio*, 568.
77 Lander, *Crown and Nobility*, 143 and n; *Statutes of the Realm*, II, 568 (1495 c. I).
78 For Lancastrian contracting of mercenaries in 1462, Calmette and Périnelle, 282.
79 W. Fraser, *The Douglas Book*, III (Edinburgh 1885), 92–3.
80 *English Chron.*, 79–80; 'Gregory', 204.
81 'Gregory', 212. He may have been referring to the Lancastrian magnates' servants as well as the queen's.
82 *Short English Chron.*, 78.
83 They were the queen's servant John Marfyn, Henry's purser Roger Water, the queen's yeoman Thomas Hunte, Henry's porter Robert Wattys. Also executed were Sir Thomas Fynderne, king's knight and former lieutenant of Guines (*CPR, 1452–61*, 22), and John Gosse, Somerset's carver (*Short English Chron.*, 79–80; 'Gregory', 225–6).
84 *CPR, 1452–61*, 323.
85 *Paston Letters*, I, no. 357; 'Gregory', 214; *Paston Letters*, II, no. 413.
86 *CPR, 1452–61*, 18, 335, 338; D. A. L. Morgan, 'The King's Affinity in the Polity of Yorkist England', *TRHS*, 5th ser., 23 (1973), 7–8.
87 *Paston Letters*, II, no. 463; Warkworth, 3.
88 Morgan, 7–8 and 8n; *CPR, 1467–77*, 227.
89 Morgan, 1 off.
90 *Coventry Leet Book*, 353–4. Pluralists were to send a man for each office they held.
91 *Paston Letters*, II, no. 648.
92 *Arrivall*, 7–9, 20; Warkworth, 14; Morgan, 11.
93 Morgan, 16–17; cf. below, pp. 188–9.
94 *Epístolas y otros varios tratados de Mosén Diego de Valera*, ed. J. A. de Balenchana (Madrid 1878), 91ff.
95 Vergil, *Anglica Historia*, 6–7, 10–11.
96 *Italian Relation*, 39.
97 *Statutes of the Realm*, II, 582.
98 *Ibid.*, 648–9.
99 *Arrivall*, 31–2.
100 *Plumpton Correspondence*, no. I.
101 *Stonor Letters and Papers*, I, no. 112.
102 *Paston Letters*, II, no. 653.
103 *HMC, Rutland MSS*, I, 4–5.
104 *Ibid.*, 7–8; *Household Books of John Duke of Norfolk* (etc.), 480ff.

105 *HMC, Rutland MSS*, I, 8; *Plumpton Letters*, p. 96n. Henry's summons to Vernon is dated London, 17 October. The editor thought the year was 1485, but the contents appear to refer to the Yorkshire rebellion of 1489.
106 Pollard, I, 93–5; cf. his summons to Talbot in 1497, *ibid.*, 162–3.
107 *Statutes of the Realm*, II, 426.
108 Dunham, 26ff.
109 A recent study of the first duke of Buckingham's 'affinity' has been made by Dr Rawcliffe (72ff); cf. A. J. Pollard, 'The Northern Retainers of Richard Nevill, Earl of Salisbury', *Northern Hist.*, 11 (1976), 52ff.
110 Cf. Morgan, 16 and n, 19 and n.
111 *HMC, Rutland MSS*, I, 2.
112 *Ibid.*, 3ff.
113 *Stonor Letters and Papers*, II, no. 333.
114 *Paston Letters*, III, no. 876.
115 *Ibid.*, no. 884.
116 *Ibid.*, no. 887.
117 *CPR, 1452–61*, 552–3.
118 This and the following paragraphs on commissions of array are based on M. R. Powicke, *Military Obligation in Medieval England* (Oxford 1962), *passim*, and H. J. Hewitt, *The Organization of War under Edward III, 1338–62* (Manchester 1966), 36–43.
119 Numbers were usually specified only for contingents going abroad.
120 Mounts came to be required for expeditions abroad.
121 The customary weapons were bow and arrows, sword and knife.
122 *CPR, 1452–61*, 557ff.
123 *Paston Letters*, I, no. 346. Paston added that commissions were certainly made out for various shires 'that every man be ready in his best array to come when the King send for them' – perhaps referring to the commissions of December 1459.
124 *Arrivall*, 23.
125 *Coventry Leet Book*, 341ff.
126 *Foedera*, XI, 444–5.
127 *CPR, 1452–61*, 557ff.
128 *Ibid.*, 659. 'Gregory', 211, says that March 'mustered his men without the town walls [of Hereford] in a marsh that is called Wyg mersche. And over him men saw . . . three suns shining' – perhaps the origin of the Yorkist 'sunburst' badge.
129 *Paston Letters*, II, no. 664.
130 *Ibid.*, III, no. 887. The proclamation was to say that the arrayed men were to be 'ordered according to the last commission afore this'. Frequency and continuity of summons enabled arrayers to expect that the organization would work efficiently.
131 See above, p. 42.
132 *Coventry Leet Book*, 342–3.

133 Warkworth, 53–4; cf. Edward's proclamation of 31 March, *ibid.*, 56–7.
134 *Ibid.*, 52–3.
135 See above, p. 75.
136 *Paston Letters*, III, no. 894; cf. no. 895. For confusion in 1483 caused by opponents' attempts to raise soldiers in the same region, *Plumpton Correspondence*, no. vi.
137 *Foedera*, XI, 501–2.
138 *Ibid.*, 523–4.
139 *Ibid.*, 624. The Norfolk and Suffolk array commissioned in October 1485 was to have hobelars and archers (*Paston Letters*, III, no. 887).
140 *Foedera*, XI, 680–1.
141 *Tudor Royal Proclamations*, I, no. 28, pp. 30–1.
142 *Ibid.*, no. 61, pp. 83–4.
143 *Arrivall*, 33; cf. Richmond, 'Fauconberg's Kentish rising of May 1471', 676. For the Bastard's supporters, *ibid.*, 684ff.
144 *Foedera*, XI, 523–4.
145 *Arrivall*, 8.
146 *Foedera*, XI, 706–7.
147 *Hist. Croylandensis Continuatio*, 573.
148 See pp. 145–6.
149 *Paston Letters*, II, no. 384.
150 Warkworth, 12. The Kentish and Sussex forces arrayed in 1492 for service on Henry VII's French expedition were to receive the king's wages: no such stipulation was made in the commissions to array for war with the Scots in 1497 (*Tudor Royal Proclamations*, I, pp. 30–1, 40–1). Warbeck promised recompense for arrayed service in 1497 (Pollard, I, 155).
151 Bridport Muster Roll, 1457, Dorset County Record Office, B3/FG3; *CPR, 1452–61*, 406–10.
152 *Stonor Letters and Papers*, II, no. 258; for Oxford's 1487 arrays, *Household Books of John Duke of Norfolk* (etc.), 501–3, 493ff; cf. M. J. Tucker, 'Household Accounts 1490–1491 of John de Vere, earl of Oxford', *EHR*, 75 (1960). Kingsford dated the Stonor muster as ?c. 1480.
153 *Coventry Leet Book*, 282–3.
154 Hudson and Tingey, I, 405–6.
155 *Records of the Borough of Nottingham*, II, 377.
156 Dominic Mancini, *The Usurpation of Richard III*, ed. C. A. J. Armstrong (Oxford 1969), 98–9, 132–3.
157 Quoted in J. Cornwall, *Revolt of the Peasantry 1549* (London 1977), 21.
158 'Gregory', 204–5, 212; *English Chron.*, 107–8.
159 *Hist. Croylandensis Continuatio*, 542.
160 *Ibid.*, 552; cf. the author of the *Arrivall*'s remarks on the poor service

which Yorkshiremen would have given if the earl of Northumberland had raised them in Edward's interest after his landing in 1471 (*Arrivall*, 6–7).

161 *Coventry Leet Book*, 308.

162 For Bridport's hire of a man to purchase gunpowder at Abbotsbury in 1465–6, Bailiffs' Account, Dorset CRO, B3/M6; for 'The harness belonging to the town' of Reading in 1488, *Reading Records*, I, 1431–1602, ed. J. M. Guilding (1892), 85. For towns' possession of guns, Turner, 84.

163 *Paston Letters*, III, no. 908.

164 *Paston Letters*, II, no. 638.

165 *Hist. Croylandensis Continuatio*, 582.

166 Cf. Commynes, *Memoirs*, ed. and trans. Jones, 81.

167 *Paston Letters*, II, no. 384.

168 'Gregory', 215.

169 Alternatively, many of the levies who had won at Wakefield may have had to be dismissed when their pay ran out, and replaced by new, perhaps less experienced and poorly financed levies.

170 *Paston Letters*, II, no. 464; cf. above, pp. 61–2.

171 *Arrivall*, 24.

172 *Ibid.*, 32.

173 Warkworth, 20.

174 *English Chron.*, 87.

175 Sir John Fortescue, *The Governance of England*, ed. C. Plummer (Oxford 1885), 137ff.

176 See J. J. Goring, 'The general proscription of 1522', *EHR*, 86 (1971), 681ff; A. C. Chibnall (ed.), *The Certificate of Musters for Buckinghamshire in 1522* (HMC 1973).

Chapter 7: Supply, Billets and Ordnance

1 Pollard, III, 44; *Italian Relation*, 23.

2 Malory, *Works*, I, 235.

3 Sir John Fortescue, *De Laudibus Legum Angliae*, trans. Grigor, 60; cf. H. J. Hewitt, *The Organization of War under Edward III, 1338–62*, 52ff; C. G. Cruickshank, *Army Royal. Henry VIII's Invasion of France 1513* (Oxford 1969), 60ff.

4 *Foedera*, XI, 449.

5 *Knyghthode and Bataile*, 41–2, 58, 85.

6 Malory, *Works*, I, 24, 228.

7 Poulson, I, 227–8.

8 *Coventry Leet Book*, 356–7.

9 *Knyghthode and Bataile*, 22–3.

10 'Gregory', 214.

11 *Arrivall*, 28. In 1484 the duke of Norfolk had made prior arrangements for the provision of horse fodder in the event of an expedition. Sir Harry Rosse and two others had undertaken 'to get my Lord's grass of his servants and tenants' (*Household Books of John Duke of Norfolk* (etc.), 492).

12 See p. 218.

13 Fortescue, *De Laudibus Legum Angliae*, trans. Grigor, 56–7.

14 See below, p. 218.

15 *Tudor Royal Proclamations*, I, no. 12, p. 13.

16 *Ibid.*, no. 13, p. 14.

17 Pollard, I, 50; *York Civic Records*, II, 25–6. Henry's 'knight herbingers' sent a copy of the royal ordinances of war to the mayor to be published through the city, prior to the royal arrival (*ibid.*, 26–7).

18 *Annales*, 775; see above, p. 43.

19 *Short English Chron.*, 76; *Brief Notes*, 155; 'Gregory', 214; *Annales*, 776–7; *York Civic Records*, I, 135.

20 *CPR, 1452–61*, 658–9.

21 *VCH Yorks., East Riding*, I, 24. For Lynn, see above, p. 44.

22 *CSP Milan*, I, p. 54, no. 71.

23 Waurin, V, 335; cf. the remarks of Bishop Beauchamp, *CSP Venice*, I, pp. 101–2, no. 371.

24 *HMC, Fifth Report*, part I, 523.

25 *Henry the Sixth. A Reprint of John Blacman's Memoir*, ed. and trans. M. R. James (Cambridge 1919), 20, 43; *Paston Letters*, II, no. 464.

26 *VCH Yorks., East Riding*, I, 25.

27 *Lincolnshire Rebellion*, 16–17; Warkworth, 54; cf. above, pp. 72–3.

28 *Lincolnshire Rebellion*, 17.

29 *Arrivall*, 31–2; see above, pp. 77, 83. The Beverley governors' account of 1460–1 contains expenses incurred as a result of the Yorkist occupation after Towton, which may have been harsh because the town had sent men to the losing side (Poulson, I, 238ff).

30 Warkworth, 6; see above, pp. 68–9.

31 *Knyghthode and Bataile*, 30.

32 *Arrivall*, 26.

33 *Tudor Royal Proclamations*, I, no. 13, p. 14; Hearne, 212.

34 Fortescue, *De Laudibus Legum Angliae*, trans. Grigor, 60.

35 Malory, *Works*, I, 172–3.

36 See above, p. 31.

37 *Arrivall*, 18, 25–6.

38 Vergil, *Anglica Historia*, 22ff.

39 *Household Books of John Duke of Norfolk* (etc.), 33, 47, 50, 67.

40 O. F. G. Hogg, *The Royal Arsenal*, I (Oxford 1963), 8ff; H. L. Blackmore, *The Armouries of the Tower of London*, I, *Ordnance* (London 1976), 1ff.

41 For fortifications, see below, pp. 181ff.

42 Hogg, 32–3.

43 Devon, 482. For the cost of transporting guns to Kenilworth the previous year, *ibid.*, 481.

44 *Short English Chron.*, 73.

45 *Wars of the English in France*, ed. Stevenson, II, pt 2, 512; Scofield, I, 50.

46 Blackmore, 3; J. R. Hooker, 'Notes on the Organization and Supply of the Tudor Military under Henry VII' *Huntington Library Quarterly*, 23 (1959–60), 26ff.

47 Blackmore, 3. Foreigners were heavily involved in the provision of firearms in England. Motte was reappointed with two subordinates by Henry VII in December 1485 (*CPR, 1485–94*, 48). In Henry's reign Nele supervised the iron foundries making royal munitions in Ashdown Forest, Sussex (Hooker, 27–8).

48 *CPR, 1485–94*, 18, 77–8.

49 *Memorials of King Henry the Seventh*, 303; 'To the City of London', in *A Choice of Scottish Verse*, ed. J. and W. MacQueen (London 1972), 33, cf. 202; *The Pylgrymage of Sir Richard Guylforde*, ed. Sir Henry Ellis (Camden Soc. 1851), 7–8.

Chapter 8: Methods of Warfare

1 For the techniques of the *chevauchée*, see Hewitt, *The Black Prince's Expedition of 1355–1357*, 46ff.

2 The terms used in the early sixteenth century were 'foreward', 'middleward' and 'rearward' (Cruickshank, *passim*). The 'battles' in which soldiers fought were not necessarily identical with those in which they had ridden: considerable regrouping often took place when an action was anticipated (Fowler, *Age of Plantagenet and Valois*, 100–1).

3 Fowler, 101, 107–8.

4 Powicke, 'Lancastrian Captains', 371.

5 Commynes, *Memoirs*, ed. and trans. Jones, 72.

6 Fowler, 59ff, 79.

7 M. Mallett, *Mercenaries and their Masters* (London 1974), 37.

8 Commynes, *Memoirs*, ed. and trans. Jones, 71; cf. 73, 76, 101, 124.

9 B. H. St J. O'Neil, *Castles and Cannon* (Oxford 1960), *passim*; Turner, 65–6.

10 *King's Works*, I, 448–9. In 1451 the south-east corner of Sandwich was fortified with the two-storey 'Bulwark', armed with guns: this may have been 'le bollewert' captured by assault by the French in 1457 (Turner, 165; Waurin, V, 385ff). For the development of gun emplacements, M. G. A. Vale, 'New Techniques and Old Ideals: The Impact of Artillery on

War and Chivalry at the End of the Hundred Years War', in *War, Literature and Politics in the Late Middle Ages*, ed. C. T. Allmand (Liverpool 1976), 61ff.

11 Cited in Bornstein, 470.

12 Fowler, 109ff; P. E. Russell, introduction to O'Neil, xiv ff; Mallett, 160ff; Hooker, 28–9; Cruickshank, 72ff; Vale, 57ff; *Knyghthode and Bataile*, 68. For *Mons Meg*, Blackmore, 108.

13 Mallett, 156ff; cf. Vale, 62ff.

14 *Paston Letters*, I, no. 67. Gairdner's tentative dating of the letter is 1449.

15 Mallett, 160–1.

16 Vale, 65ff; Basin, *Histoire des règnes de Charles VII et de Louis XI*, ed. J. Quicherat, I, 263–8, trans. by C. T. Allmand in *Society at War*, 111–13.

17 See below, p. 172.

18 Powicke, 'Lancastrian Captains', 376, 379; Fowler, 110; *CP*, II, 388; J. S. Roskell, *The Commons in the Parliament of 1422* (Manchester 1954), 153.

19 *CP*, VI, 619 and n.

20 *Ibid.*, XI, 504ff; *English Chron.*, 98.

21 *CP*, V, 281ff; *English Chron.*, 93; *CPR, 1452–61*, 243; *Wars of the English in France*, ed. Stevenson, I, 519–20.

22 *CP*, V, 284. Fauconberg was acting as lieutenant at Calais on 31 January 1461 (*CSP Milan*, I, p. 47, no. 61).

23 Other veterans who fought in the Wars of the Roses were John Bourchier, earl of Essex (d. 1483), who had been comte of Eu, William Herbert, earl of Pembroke (d. 1469), Richard Wydeville, earl Rivers (d. 1469), James Butler, earl of Wiltshire (d. 1461), Viscount Beaumont (d. 1460), who had been comte of Boulogne, Lords Audley (d. 1459), Clinton (d. 1464), de la Warr (d. 1476), Roos (d. 1461), Sudeley (d. 1473) and Wenlock (d. 1471) (*CP, passim*).

24 *Paston Letters*, I, no. 99.

25 See K. B. McFarlane, 'William Worcester, a Preliminary Survey', in *Studies presented to Sir Hilary Jenkinson*, ed. J. C. Davies (London 1957).

26 Worcestre, *Itineraries*, 204–5. Worcester also noted the French service of Welshmen who were killed at Edgcote in 1469 (*ibid.*, 338–41).

27 See above, p. 30.

28 Worcestre, *Itineraries*, 352–3; *CPR, 1452–61*, 553. For Trollope, see also pp. 52–3, 127. Another highly regarded veteran who fought in the wars was Sir Thomas Kyriel, whose experience of command in France went back at least to 1429. He was summarily executed by the queen's party after being captured at St Albans in 1461 (*English Chron.*, 108, 205; Waurin, V, 329–30).

29 See above, p. 124.

30 William Caxton, *The Book of the Fayttes of Armes and of Chyualrye*, ed. A. T. P. Byles (EETS 1937), 291.

31 'Gregory', 213–14.

32 Whethamstede, I, 162; *Cely Letters*, ed. Hanham, no. 178. Guto'r Glyn, describing Lord Herbert's invasion of Gwynedd in the 1460s, says that 'Three warbands went into Wales' (*Medieval Welsh Lyrics*, ed. and trans. Clancy (London 1965), 207).

33 Molinet, II, 332; Pollard, I, 92; Cruickshank, 29ff.

34 *Bale's Chron.*, 150–1; *Benet's Chron.*, 226, 229–30; Waurin, V, 336–7; see also above, p. 37. These complexities may be an illusion created by chroniclers' muddles.

35 *CSP Venice*, I, p. 99, no. 370.

36 Vergil, *English Hist.*, 219–20; Vergil, *Anglicae Historiae libri* ... (1555), 561.

37 *Arrivall*, 28.

38 Vergil, *Anglica Historia*, 24–5.

39 Molinet, I, 564. According to *Bale's Chron.*, 151, the Yorkist army at Northampton was divided into four 'battles', but Whethamstede, I, 373, says it was divided into three.

40 *Knyghthode and Bataile*, 39–40.

41 See above, pp. 37, 46, 50.

42 See above, pp. 71, 83.

43 Vergil, *English Hist.*, 222ff.

44 Vergil, *Anglica Historia*, 10–11; see above, p. 97.

45 *Ibid.*, 24–5.

46 Pollard, I, 80–1; see above, p. 108.

47 See above, p. 114.

48 See above, p. 115.

49 See above, p. 82.

50 Vergil, *English Hist.*, 223; Molinet, I, 564; Pollard, I, 80–1.

51 Vergil, *English Hist.*, 145, 223.

52 See p. 24.

53 Warkworth, 6–7; see above, pp. 68–9.

54 *Arrivall*, 29.

55 Vergil, *English Hist.*, 223.

56 See above, pp. 92–3.

57 Molinet, I, 564.

58 See above, p. 165.

59 Mallett, 160–1.

60 Commynes, *Memoirs*, ed. and trans. Jones, 94ff.

61 Contamine, *Guerre, état et société à la fin du moyen âge* (Paris 1972), 299–300.

62 Commynes, *Memoirs*, ed. and trans. Jones, 65.

63 *Ibid.*, 77, 87, 101.

64 *Benet's Chron.*, 206; Whethamstede, I, 161; see above, pp. 20–1. Jack Cade's men had 'dyked and staked well about' their camp at Blackheath in 1450 ('Gregory', 190).

65 *Rot. Parl.*, V, 347; see above, pp. 22–3. At St Albans buildings and possibly parts of the town ditch provided some protection.

66 'Gregory', 204; see above, pp. 27–8.

67 'Gregory', 205; Whethamstede, I, 341–2; *Rot. Parl.*, V, 348.

68 *Knyghthode and Bataile*, 19–21, 55ff. But, being a cleric, not a soldier, he was unable to link this with advice about the deployment of guns.

69 *English Chron.*, 96–7; Waurin, V, 295, 297; Whethamstede, I, 373–4.

70 *English Chron.*, 97. Guns were fired in the brief battle, for Sir William Lucy heard them ('Gregory', 207). The Yorkists had gone to Northampton 'with great ordnance' (*Short English Chron.*, 74). For the rainy weather in the days preceding the battle, Waurin, V, 296; Whethamstede, I, 374.

71 *Short English Chron.*, 73. For Judde, see above, p. 160.

72 Scofield, I, 118–19; Whethamstede, I, 381–2; Waurin, V, 325ff.

73 Scofield, I, 262 and n.

74 'Gregory', 213–14. According to one London chronicle, there were 500 Burgundians, and 18 of them were burned and killed by their own fire (*Brief Notes*, 155). The 'wild fire' may have been naphtha, the 'Greek fire' long familiar in medieval warfare. The gunners' defences sound like a sophisticated adaptation of the *champ de guerre* principle.

75 Waurin, V, 335: 'grant plente de charriotz et charrettes chargies de vivres et artilleries'.

76 Scofield, I, 197.

77 *Paston Letters*, II, no. 464.

78 Probably in preparation for his campaign against Robin of Redesdale, on 20 June 1469 the king commissioned a group including his master of the ordnance, John Wode, to impress wheelwrights, cartwrights and other carpenters, stone-cutters, smiths, plumbers and other workmen for the works of the royal ordnance on various types of guns and other armaments (*CPR, 1467–77*, 163).

79 Warkworth, 8. On 3 March, three days before Edward set out from London, he issued an ordnance commission similar to that of June 1469 (*CPR, 1467–77*, 163).

80 Warkworth, 13. According to *Chronicles of London*, 183, Edward had 500 Englishmen and as many 'Dutchmen'. For estimates of his invasion force, see above, p. 75 and n. 30.

81 *Arrivall*, 18–19. Warkworth, 16, gives a different account of the night bombardment.

82 *Arrivall*, 24, 29. A week before the king set out from Windsor commissioners were appointed to impress workmen for the work of the royal ordnance (*CPR, 1467–77*, 259).

83 Molinet, I, 434-5; cf. above, p. 93. In his 'Yorkist' invasion of 1496, James IV brought an artillery train, but Warbeck had no siege guns with which to assault Exeter the following year (below, p. 190). Fifty gunners received wages for their service against the Cornishmen at Blackheath in 1497 (Hooker, 26n).

84 J. Smyth, *The Berkeley Manuscripts. The Lives of the Berkeleys*, ed. J. Maclean (Gloucester 1884), II, 109.

85 Allmand (ed.), *Society at War*, 66; Calmette and Périnelle, 183-4, 358-61.

86 For the royal ordnance, see above, pp. 160-1.

87 Calmette and Périnelle, 358-9.

88 Armstrong, 41.

89 Vergil, *English Hist.*, 107.

90 *Benet's Chron.*, 230; Waurin, V, 340. George Neville's account of the fight for the Aire crossing implies infantry fighting (*CSP Venice*, I, pp. 99-100, no. 370).

91 Warkworth, 16.

92 Commynes, *Memoirs*, ed. and trans. Jones, 181; cf. 195. Which nine battles was Commynes referring to? I count seven major ones in which Edward was one of the victorious commanders − Northampton, Mortimer's Cross, Ferrybridge, Towton, Losecoat Field, Barnet and Tewkesbury. He was a mere boy at St Albans in 1455.

93 Mancini, 98-101; cf. below, p. 194.

94 Poulson, I, 228; cf. above, p. 38.

95 *Knyghthode and Bataile*, 50-2, 57, 70ff.

96 'Gregory', 205.

97 *Bale's Chron.*, 149.

98 Waurin, V, 296.

99 *MS Tanner 2*, 167.

100 'Gregory', 214.

101 *Chronicles of London*, 175. For a distinction between his horsemen and footmen, *Benet's Chron.*, 229-30.

102 'Gregory', 217.

103 *Lincolnshire Rebellion*, 15, 11-12.

104 *Coventry Leet Book*, 366.

105 *Arrivall*, 27-8. After the Bastard of Fauconberg's retreat from London, Rivers led a retinue of thirty horsemen and forty footmen into Kent (Devon, I, 494).

106 *Chronicles of London*, 217; Vergil, *Anglica Historia*, 106ff.

107 *Knyghthode and Bataile*, 50-2. Cf. *ibid.*, 57-8, for the roles of horsemen in protecting those fortifying a camp, and in scouring from a camp.

108 Armstrong, 23-4.

109 'Gregory', 204-5.

110 See above, pp. 26–7.

111 See above, pp. 42–3.

112 'Gregory', 213.

113 Waurin, V, 336ff. But in the 1469 campaign Edward's intelligence network seems to have failed him badly (see above, pp. 67ff). In the 1470 campaigns it was his political rather than his military intelligence which was at fault.

114 *Arrivall*, 7–8.

115 *Ibid.*, 18.

116 *Ibid.*, 28.

117 Vergil, *English Hist.*, 216–17, 219; Hearne, *Collectanea*, IV, 210.

118 *Arrivall*, 24–5.

119 Cf. above, p. 106.

120 Vergil, *English Hist.*, 225.

121 *Arrivall*, 14.

122 Vergil, *English Hist.*, 219–20.

123 *Knyghthode and Bataile*, 70ff.

124 Waurin, V, 337–8.

125 Commynes, *Memoirs*, ed. and trans. Jones, 195; Vergil, *English Hist.*, 145–6.

126 *Arrivall*, 29–30.

127 Vergil, *English Hist.*, 224.

128 C. Ross, *The Wars of the Roses*, 108, 127.

129 *Pageant of the Birth, Life and Death of Richard Beauchamp Earl of Warwick K. G. 1389–1439*, ed. Viscount Dillon and W. H. St John Hope, plates VII and XL.

130 Malory, *Works*, I, xix ff, 19, 25ff, 35, 75–6, 235; cf. *ibid.*, 212–13, 243.

131 *Ibid.*, 238; *The Prologues and Epilogues of William Caxton*, ed. W. J. B. Crotch (EETS 1928), 82ff; cf. *The Great Tournament Roll of Westminster*, ed. S. Anglo, 19ff.

132 Scofield, I, 374–5, 414ff; Anglo (ed.), 33 and n.

133 A. Emery, 'The Development of Raglan Castle and Keeps in Late Medieval England', *Archaeological Journal*, 132 (for 1975), 185.

134 Goodman, *A History of England from Edward II to James I*, 39.

135 Turner, 13.

136 For London's defences, see p. 191. For other town defences in the fifteenth century, see Turner, *passim*, and esp. 80. In 1471 the citizens of Hull, within their sturdy walls, refused Edward admission; those of York, similarly protected, were only slightly more obliging to him (*Arrivall*, 4–5). York was to man its defences against the Scropes' assault in 1487 (see above, pp. 103–4).

137 *Arrivall*, 12–13. Turner, 118–19, for frequent repairs to Coventry's walls in the fifteenth century.

138 *King's Works*, I, 238. The Tower of London was of course well maintained (*ibid.*, 2, 728–9).

139 *Ibid.*, 238ff.

140 *Rot. Parl.*, V, 177; *English Chron.*, 67.

141 *King's Works*, II, 667; cf. above, p. 26.

142 *Ibid.*, II, 848–9.

143 *Ibid.*, I, 572, 642.

144 *Ibid.*, II, 782.

145 *Benet's Chron.*, 225; *King's Works*, II, 684–5. The author of *Knyghthode and Bataile*, 83ff, had a lot of advice for Henry VI *c.* 1460 on defending and assaulting fortifications. But he stuck to Roman methods and had nothing to say about the employment of artillery.

146 *King's Works*, I, 240.

147 Worcestre, *Itineraries*, 344–5. Alnwick even built a town wall in the fifteenth century: the first murage grant was made in 1434, and work was still incomplete in 1474 (Turner, 50).

148 Worcestre, *Itineraries*, 342–5.

149 *Ibid.*, 218–19.

150 Emery, 'The Development of Raglan Castle', 182.

151 See brief descriptions in J. Evans, *English Art 1307–1461* (Oxford 1949), 126ff.

152 Worcestre, *Itineraries*, 186–91; *Paston Letters*, II, nos 592, 641.

153 The best recent account of private castles is Emery's article, 'The Development of Raglan Castle'.

154 *CPR, 1452–61*, 527.

155 *Ibid.*, 534, 550; *Foedera*, XI, 444–6; Scofield, I, 56. For the struggle between Warwick and Somerset, based on their castles at Calais and Guines, see above, pp. 31–2.

156 *Brief Notes*, 153.

157 Waurin, V, 295.

158 *English Chron.*, 96; *Benet's Chron.*, 226–7; *Brief Latin Chron.*, 169.

159 *English Chron.*, 96. Lord Cobham and the sheriffs of London laid 'great ordnance' against the Tower on the city side; Sir John Wenlock and Harowe, mercer, 'kept on' St Katherine's side (*Short English Chron.*, 74).

160 *English Chron.*, 96, 98; Waurin, V, 302ff; *Benet's Chron.*, 226–7. *Benet's Chron.* says that the siege lasted for four weeks.

161 *Proceedings and Ordinances of the Privy Council*, VI, 302ff. Denbigh was to be delivered to 'Edward Bou . . .'., probably 'Bourchier'. Richard Grey, lord of Powis, was ordered to deliver York's castle at Montgomery to 'Wal . . . squyer', possibly Walter Devereux.

162 *Ibid.*, 304–5.

163 For York, the queen and March in this period, see above, pp. 41, 49.

164 *CPR, 1452–61*, 657. For the defence of Lynn and Castle Rising, see above, pp. 44–5.

165 *Ibid.*, 659.
166 *Brief Notes*, 155.
167 See above, pp. 48–9.
168 See above, pp. 56ff.
169 *CPR, 1461–7*, 28; cf. above, pp. 184–5.
170 *CPR, 1461–7*, 38.
171 See above, pp. 59–60. In 1461 the island of Jersey and its castle of Gorey (or Mount Orgueil) were surrendered to the French by the Lancastrian warden. They were recovered in 1468 after a long siege of the castle by a force commanded by Richard Harleston and Edmund Weston, aided by the Jerseymen (*King's Works*, II, 606; Scofield, I, 478–80).
172 *Rot. Parl.*, V, 486, 512; 'Gregory', 237; Warkworth, 3; *Chronicles of London*, 179; Scofield, I, 338–9, 458–9. The castle had been repaired in 1417–19, and its 'great bridge' had been repaired or rebuilt in 1458–9 (*King's Works*, I, 365). The castle's defenders probably used firearms (Worcestre, *Itineraries*, 204–5).
173 *Hist. Croylandensis Continuatio*, 542; J. C. Perks, *Chepstow Castle* (London 1967), 10–11.
174 *CPR, 1467–77*, 180–1; Scofield, I, 505.
175 Warkworth, 13; *Chronicles of London*, 182; Scofield, I, 540–1.
176 *Arrivall*, 8ff; Warkworth, 14–15.
177 *Arrivall*, 25–7. Considerable sums had been spent on the royal castle at Gloucester under the Lancastrians (*King's Works*, II, 656). For a plan showing the castle site and its relation to the town's fortifications, *ibid.*, 653.
178 Vergil, *English Hist.*, 154–5.
179 *CPR, 1467–77*, 293.
180 *Arrivall*, 33ff; *Brief Latin Chron.*, 184–5; Warkworth, 19–20; *Hist. Croylandensis Continuatio*, 555–6; cf. Richmond, 'Fauconberg's Kentish rising of May 1471', 677ff.
181 Warkworth, 26–7; Worcestre, *Itineraries*, 102–3; *CPR, 1467–77*, 418, 412; *CDS*, IV, no. 1412. For Fortescue, cf. Morgan, 17.
182 *CDS*, IV, no. 1413.
183 Warkworth, 27, who says that he surrendered on 15 February 1474. Worcester says that he left the Mount on 19 February (*Itineraries*, 102–3). On 20 February it was rumoured in London that Oxford had either sued for his pardon and was surrendering to the king, or that he had left the Mount well garrisoned (*Paston Letters*, III, no. 736). *Le Caricou* was at sea for six weeks after 3 February, perhaps to intercept any reinforcements for Oxford, who had not heard of his surrender.
184 G. N. Curzon, *Bodiam Castle, Sussex*, 31–3. Vergil says that, in preparation for the rising, the rebels 'held furnished fit places with force of men' (*English Hist.*, 198).
185 Owen and Blakeway, *A History of Shrewsbury*, I, 241; Rawcliffe, 34.
186 Vergil, *English Hist.*, 212–13; PRO, E.101/55/14. According to

Vergil, some Welsh castles were garrisoned against Henry's advance in 1485, but were quickly surrendered (*ibid.*, 217). In 1486 Viscount Lovell may have garrisoned Middleham castle as a centre of resistance to Henry VII (see above, p. 97).

187 See above, p. 112.

188 Vergil, *Anglica Historia*, 104–5, 108–9.

189 Raimondo de Soncino to duke of Milan, 30 September 1497, in Pollard, I, 169–70; Vergil, *Anglica Historia*, 105–6.

190 Pollard, I, 167–9.

191 Henry names as among the defenders Sir William Courtenay, Sir John Sapcotes, Sir Piers Edgecombe, Sir John Croker, Sir Walter Courtenay and Sir Humphrey Fulford.

192 Turner, 195; cf. *ibid.*, 196.

193 Pollard, I, 180–1.

194 Vergil, *Anglica Historia*, 104–5; cf. Pollard, I, 180–1 (text of *Chronicles of London*, 217); Molinet, II, 439–40. For expenditure by the city of Exeter resulting from the rebellion, including £17. 4s. 7d. spent on repairing the North Gate, Exeter City Receiver's Account Roll, 13–14 Henry VII, Devon Record Office; cf. for other repairs to the defences, *ibid.*, 14–15 Henry VII.

195 *King's Works*, II, 729.

196 *CPR, 1467–77*, 463, 470.

197 *King's Works*, I, 241, 2, 764–5.

198 Emery, 184; *CPR, 1485–94*, 64.

199 *King's Works*, II, 893–4.

200 *CPR, 1452–61*, 528. For a discussion of urban defences and the Wars of the Roses, Turner, 80.

201 *Chronicles of London*, 187–8; *Cal. of Plea and Memoranda Rolls*, 110–11 and 111n.

202 Emery, *passim*; cf. above, pp. 68–9, 186. There are no building accounts from which the Raglan works can be dated. Emery argues that, in the main, they are more likely to have been carried out by Herbert than by his father or son.

203 Emery, 180–1, 184; W. Douglas Simpson, ' "Bastard Feudalism" and the Later Castles', *Antiquaries Jnl*, 26 (1946). On 17 April 1471, just after Hastings's support of Edward's reconquest of the realm, he was licenced to crenellate houses at Ashby de la Zouch, Bagworth, Thornton and Kirby (Leics.) and at Slingesby (Yorks.) (Dunham, 23).

204 H. M. Colvin, 'Castles and government in Tudor England', *EHR*, 83 (1968).

205 See above, p. 187.

206 *Italian Relation*, 37–8.

207 C. H. Hunter Blair and H. L. Honeyman, *Norham Castle* (London 1966), 9, 12.

208 *Knyghthode and Bataile*, 22, 70ff.
209 See above, pp. 92ff.
210 See above, p. 163.
211 Commynes, *Memoirs*, ed. and trans. Jones, 226.
212 *Ibid.*, 241–2.
213 *Ibid.*, 229.
214 *Ibid.*, 252ff.
215 Molinet, I, 106.
216 A. Bernaldez, *Memorias del reinado de los Reyes Católicos*, ed. M. Gomez-Moreno and J. de M. Carriazo (Madrid 1962), 167–8; cf. E. Benito Ruano, 'La Participacion Extranjera en la Guerra de Granada', *Andalucia Medieval*, 2 (Cordoba 1978), 306–8, 318–19.

Chapter 9 : The Wars and Society

1 See above, pp. 2ff.
2 *Hist. Croylandensis Continuatio*, 529–30; translation from *Ingulph's Chron.*, trans. H. T. Riley (London 1854), 418–19.
3 Warkworth, 12. In 1463, he says, 'the people grudged sore' at the grant of a fifteenth and a half (p. 3); Edward's coinage debasement of 1464 was 'to the great harm of the common people' (p. 4); the fifteenth granted in 1469 'annoyed the people' because of their recent heavy payments (pp. 7–8). An anonymous chronicler also stresses the various exactions which Edward made in 1461–3 (*Brief Latin Chron.*, 173, 175, 177).
4 Warkworth, 21–2. For financial losses resulting from the wars, below, pp. 197, 216ff.
5 For the greater involvement of some Londoners, see p. 202.
6 *Literae Cantuarienses*, III, ed. J. B. Sheppard (Rolls ser., London 1889), no. 1079, pp. 274ff.
7 *The Travels of Leo of Rozmital*, ed. M. Letts (Cambridge 1957).
8 *Ibid.*, 45ff, 63.
9 *Italian Relation*, 28ff, 39; 'si facevano molti clientoli, e seguaci; con li quali poi infestavano la corona, et la propria patria, et in fine fra di loro medesimi, perchè in ultimo erano tutti decapitati'.
10 Fortescue, *Governance of England*, 155–6.
11 Richmond, 'The Nobility and the Wars of the Roses, 1459–61', 72–3, 78. These and subsequent figures given include attainted claimants to peerages.
12 All these figures must be regarded as approximations. Dr Richmond has listed participants in the campaigns of 1459–61 (*ibid.*, 74ff), and Professor Lander has listed participants from 1455 to 1485 (*Crown and Nobility*, Appendix A, 301–5).
13 Richmond, 'The Nobility and the Wars of the Roses, 1459–61', 83–4.

14 *Ibid.*, 84n.
15 See above, pp. 132ff.
16 See above, pp. 131ff.
17 *Annales*, 782.
18 *Brief Latin Chron.*, 176. Another source lists fifty-nine knights in his company (*Brief Notes*, 157–8).
19 See above, pp. 26–7.
20 Worcestre, *Itineraries*, 202ff, 338ff.
21 See above, pp. 97ff.
22 *Rot. Parl.*, VI, 244–9.
23 Vergil, *Anglica Historia*, 22n–23n, 106n–107n.
24 Cf. above, pp. 61–2. For arms and armour bequeathed by northern clergy in the 1470s, *Testamenta Eboracensia*, III, 202, 210, 235.
25 R. J. Knecht, 'The Episcopate and the Wars of the Roses', *Univ. of Birmingham Hist. Jnl*, 6 (1957–8), 118.
26 See above, p. 28.
27 Hearne, *Collectanea*, IV, 212; Knecht, 111ff.
28 See above, p. 196.
29 See above, p. 109. For references to the threat and use of excommunication against rebels, Goodman, 'Henry VII and Christian renewal'.
30 *Brief Latin Chron.*, 177.
31 I. D. Thornley, 'The Destruction of Sanctuary', in *Tudor Studies*, ed. R. W. Seton-Watson (London 1924), 198–200.
32 Pollard, I, 153–4.
33 *Short English Chron.*, 74.
34 *Arrivall*, 38.
35 For links between townsmen and nobles, R. B. Dobson, 'Urban Decline in late Medieval England', *TRHS*, 5th ser., 27 (1977), 14–16.
36 *Annales*, 775; 'Gregory', 211ff.
37 *Benet's Chron.*, 233.
38 Warkworth, 20; Richmond, 'Fauconberg's Kentish rising of May 1471', 684–5.
39 Robbins, 215–18. Warkworth's statement (1–2) that Edward 'for so much as he found in time of need great comfort in his commoners, he ratified and confirmed all the franchises given to cities and towns, etc. and granted to many cities and towns new franchises than was granted before' in his first parliament suggests Edward's appreciation of the urban support which he received in 1460–1.
40 See above, pp. 22–3.
41 *Records of the Borough of Nottingham*, II, 368–9. For commons' involvement in the wars, see McFarlane, 'The Wars of the Roses', 112–13.
42 *CDS*, IV, no. 1357.

43 Waurin, V, 284.

44 *Annales*, 773; *Short English Chron.*, 75.

45 *English Chron.*, 107.

46 *Annales*, 777; cf. *English Chron.*, 109. Warwick, meeting March at Burford about this time, told him that the commons were on his side ('Gregory', 215).

47 'Gregory', 221.

48 Warkworth, 7.

49 Fortescue, *Governance of England*, 137–8.

50 Ross, *Edward IV*, 126–8.

51 See above, p. 96. Allegedly, when Henry VII was in York in 1486 confronting rebellion which centred on Middleham, 'two fellows that dwelt about Middleham said [in York] that here is good gate for us to Robin of Redesdale over the walls' (*York Civic Records*, II, 5).

52 *Paston Letters*, III, no. 916.

53 Williams, 'The Rebellion of Humphrey Stafford in 1486', 188 and n. The standards which Warbeck was reputed to fly with his Cornish peasants in 1497 seem obscure in their symbolism (Pollard, I, 165).

54 For a discussion of peasants' relations with landlords in this period, and peasant revolts, see R. H. Hilton, *The English Peasantry in the Later Middle Ages* (Oxford 1975), 64ff.

55 See above, p. 67.

56 *Arrivall*, 6; Warkworth, 13–14. The invading Edward IV in these circumstances played on Yorkshiremen's respect for rightful inheritance by claiming he had only come to occupy the duchy of York, to which he was undoubted heir.

57 *Arrivall*, 23.

58 *Gloucester Annals*, 356; cf. *Brief Latin Chron.*'s verdict on Herbert (p. 183): 'a very grave oppressor and despoiler of priests and many others for many years'.

59 *Chronicles of London*, 181.

60 *The Great Chronicle of London*, ed. A. H. Thomas and I. D. Thornley (London 1938), 218.

61 For distant rebel Yorkshiremen's invocation of Becket's example, see above, pp. 107–8.

62 Griffiths, 'Local rivalries and national politics: the Percies, the Nevilles, and the Duke of Exeter, 1452–1455', 597ff.

63 *Ibid.*, 599; cf. Dobson, 'Urban Decline', 20.

64 *Arrivall*, 6–7; cf. above, p. 51.

65 *CSP Venice*, I, no. 371, p. 102.

66 *CSP Milan*, I, no. 71, pp. 55–6.

67 *English Chron.*, 97. Before the first battle of St Albans Henry VI allegedly included yeomen among those to be slain (*Paston Letters*, I, 239).

68 Worcestre, *Itineraries*, 340–1.

69 'Gregory', 216–17.
70 See below, p. 212.
71 McFarlane, *The Nobility of Later Medieval England*, 146ff.
72 *English Chron.*, 107; 'Gregory', 217; Warkworth, 7, 17; Worcestre, *Itineraries*, 340–1. For the numerous aristocratic casualties, see also McFarlane, 'The Wars of the Roses', 100.
73 Lander, *Crown and Nobility*, 129.
74 *Stonor Letters and Papers*, II, 161.
75 'Gregory', 226.
76 Commynes, *Memoirs*, ed. and trans. Jones, 180.
77 *Hist. Croylandensis Continuatio*, 568; *Ingulph's Chron.*, 492.
78 Owen and Blakeway, I, 241–2.
79 Warkworth, 16–17; *Arrivall*, 20.
80 *Paston Letters*, III, no. 821.
81 *Annales*, 776. *English Chron.*, 109, mentions the mediation only of the duchess of Buckingham.
82 *Arrivall*, 10.
83 'Gregory', 206–7; *Benet's Chron.*, 225.
84 Scofield, I, 38; cf. *ibid.*, 64.
85 'Gregory', 206.
86 *English Chron.*, 95–6; Waurin, V, 302.
87 *CPR, 1467–77*, 26. For the duchess of Somerset's plight, Scofield, I, 313.
88 Scofield, I, 518–19. The countess of Warwick took sanctuary after her husband's death in 1471 (*ibid.*, 582–3).
89 *CPR, 1485–94*, 222–3.
90 *Testamenta Vetusta*, I, 310ff; McFarlane, *The Nobility of Later Medieval England*, 29–30.
91 *The Prologues and Epilogues of William Caxton*, ed. W. J. B. Crotch (EETS 1928), 111–12. Bishop Beauchamp graphically expressed the terror that he among others felt after the Lancastrian victory at St Albans (*CSP Venice*, I, no. 371).
92 *Annales*, 771–2; *CP*, XI, 21.
93 See pp. 68–9, 75ff.
94 See above, p. 114.
95 J. Weever, *Ancient Funerall Monuments* (etc.) (London 1631), 834–5.
96 *Paston Letters*, II, no. 389.
97 *Ibid.*, III, no. 670.
98 *Arrivall*, 33.
99 Vergil, *Anglica Historia*, 82–3.
100 *Ibid.*, 94–5.
101 Malory, *Works*, III, 1229.
102 Caxton, *Prologues and Epilogues*, 108; Vergil, *Anglica Historia*, 12–13. In his epilogue to Book 2 of *The Recuyell of the Historyes of Troye*, written in 1471, Caxton had gloomily mentioned the great divisions in

England (*Prologues and Epilogues*, 6).

103 *The Berkeley Manuscripts. The Lives of the Berkeleys*, II, ed. Sir John Maclean (Gloucester 1883), 114–15.

104 Dunham, *Lord Hastings' Indentured Retainers 1461–1483*, 25.

105 Lander, *Crown and Nobility 1450–1509*, 61ff.

106 'Gregory', 190.

107 *Paston Letters*, II, no. 516.

108 Sir Henry Ellis, *Original Letters* (etc.), 2nd ser., I (London 1827), 11–13.

109 Waurin, V, 294; cf. above, p. 204 and n. 44.

110 *English Chron.*, 98.

111 Scofield, I, 136–7. His mother wrote in similar vein.

112 *Paston Letters*, I, no. 367; cf. above, pp. 44ff.

113 Whethamstede, I, 394–6.

114 *Annales*, 776. For a proclamation by Edward asserting that the Lancastrian lords had given their men licence to rob and forbidding his own men to do so, Scofield, I, 154–6.

115 Scofield, I, 537; *Tudor Royal Proclamations*, I, no. 13; Pollard, I, 50; Vergil, *Anglica Historia*, 22–3.

116 *Tudor Royal Proclamations*, I, no. 19.

117 Vergil, *Anglica Historia*, 88–9.

118 *Bridgwater Borough Accounts, 1445–1468*, p. 110, no. 815.

119 Ellis, *Original Letters*, 2nd ser., I, 139–40.

120 *English Chron.*, 82.

121 *Bale's Chron.*, 147–8.

122 *English Chron.*, 83; cf. Whethamstede, I, 344–5.

123 Waurin, I, 277.

124 *Knyghthode and Bataile*, 37; Scofield, I, 59.

125 *Annales*, 774. For Sandal, PRO, DL 29, no. 8899, m. I, cited in *The Wars of the Roses*, Catalogue of an Exhibition at the Public Record Office (1961), ed. R. L. Storey, no. 24.

126 Lander, *Conflict and Stability in Fifteenth-Century England* (3rd edn, London 1977), 85n. For alleged plundering at Totteridge (Middlesex) by the duke of Exeter's men, PRO, C I, bdle 31, no. 516, cited in Storey (ed.), *The Wars of the Roses*, no. 30.

127 *CPR, 1461–7*, 82, 87. For a theft by Welshmen (presumably Edward's soldiers) after Towton, *Testamenta Eboracensia*, III, 208–9.

128 *CDS*, IV, p. 271, no. 1333.

129 *Feodarium Prioratus Dunelmensis* (etc.) (Surtees Soc. 1871), 98–102.

130 *CPR, 1467–77*, 114.

131 *Medieval Welsh Lyrics*, ed. and trans. Clancy (London 1965), 207ff.

132 See above, p. 75.

133 Ellis, *Original Letters*, 2nd ser., I, 140–1.

134 Scofield, I, 583n; *Tewkesbury Chron.*, 376–7, in Kingsford, *English*

Historical Literature.

135 *Paston Letters*, III, no. 876.
136 *Materials*, I, 188, 201. For the sack of Tadcaster in 1487, *York Civic Records*, II, 22.
137 *CPR, 1467–77*, 208.
138 *Ibid.*, 360–1.
139 Pollard, I, 33.
140 S. Reynolds, *An Introduction to the History of English Medieval Towns* (Oxford 1977), 147.
141 For the Anglo-Burgundian war in 1471, Ross, *Edward IV*, 158–9.
142 A petition from Bristol to the earl of Warwick emphasized unemployment experienced there resulting from declining cloth manufacture, and outlined some of the burdens incurred to aid the crown – the city's waging of sixty soldiers for eleven months for the king, at a cost of £800, as well as earlier waging of men for service in the north and the cost of finding ships for operations in Wales and to convey Edward's envoys to Castile (*The Great Red Book of Bristol*, III, ed. E. W. W. Veale (Bristol Record Soc. 1951), 77–8). For Edward's impressment of Hull ships, K. J. Allison, 'Medieval Hull', *VCH Yorks., East Riding*, I, 25.
143 See above, pp. 154ff.
144 *HMC, MSS of Shrewsbury Corporation*, 29–30.
145 See above, p. 90.
146 *CPR, 1467–77*, 250.
147 Allison, 23ff; *Arrivall*, 4. In 1483 Hull sent a paid-up contingent to support Richard III against the rebels (Allison, 26).
148 *Priory of Hexham*, I, pp. cii–civ.
149 See above, pp. 196–7 and n. 3.
150 Scofield, I, 148.
151 See above, pp. 163–4.
152 'Gregory', 207; *Annales*, 773.
153 *Paston Letters*, II, no. 384.
154 *Priory of Hexham*, I, p. ci; cf. *ibid.*, pp. cxii–cxiii.
155 *Cal. of Plea and Memoranda Rolls, 1458–1482*, 57ff. For another case of the pursuit of private vengeance through opportunities provided by the dynastic conflict, PRO, C I, bdle 31, no. 485, cited in *The Wars of the Roses*, ed. Storey, no. 25.
156 *Literae Cantuarienses*, III, 276.
157 Pollard, I, 11–12.
158 *CPR, 1461–7*, 67.
159 See above, p. 184.
160 J. Blow, 'Nibley Green 1470', *English Society and Government in the Fifteenth Century*, ed. C. M. Crowder (Edinburgh 1967), 87ff.
161 Goodman, *History of England from Edward II to James I*, 258ff, 443.
162 See above, p. 165; for some examples of upward social mobility in the

Wars of the Roses, see pp. 125, 127.

163 *Annales*, 782, 791; cf. the terms of a grant to Hastings in 1467 (*CPR, 1467–77*, 26–7).

164 The garrison establishment at Calais in time of truce in the 1470s was about 780 (Lander, *Crown and Nobility*, 240n).

165 Stevenson, II, part 2, 512; *Records of the City of Norwich*, I, 406.

166 *Nottingham Borough Records*, III, 414–15; *Coventry Leet Book*, 343.

167 *Coventry Leet Book*, 355.

168 Devon, 494; *York Civic Records*, I, 118. Rivers's footmen received 8*d*. Henry VII contracted with Lord Hastings in 1492, for the French expedition, that Hastings's men-at-arms (including himself) should receive 18*d*. a day, his demi-lances 9*d*. and his archers 6*d*. (*HMC Report on the Manuscripts of R. R. Hastings*, I (1928), 306).

169 *Paston Letters*, II, no. 592.

170 Commynes, *Memoirs*, ed. and trans. Jones, 122–3, 225; *Coventry Leet Book*, 426–8.

171 *Literae Cantuarienses*, III, 282.

172 *Paston Letters*, III, nos 905, 913; Bernaldez, 167–8, 241.

173 Pollard, I, 66.

174 See above, pp. 145–6.

175 *CPR, 1467–77*, 362.

176 *Cely Letters*, ed. Hanham, no. 161. For the local purchase of 'harness' by the warden and community of Henley for the four soldiers whom they provided for the king in 1487, and the four in 1497, *Henley Borough Records ... 1395–1543*, 94, 118–19.

177 *Cal. of Plea and Memoranda Rolls ... 1458–1482*, 11–12. Eliot confirmed his account.

178 *CPR, 1467–77*, 25.

179 Edmund Dudley, *The Tree of Commonwealth*, ed. D. M. Brodie (Cambridge 1948).

180 Goodman, *A History of England from Edward II to James I*, 257–8.

181 See above, pp. 23, 26–7. The Marches comprised Cumberland, Westmorland and Northumberland.

182 *Short English Chron.*, 74.

183 Robbins, 213.

184 *Brief Notes*, 155.

185 *Short English Chron.*, 77.

186 *Gloucester Annals*, 356.

187 *English Chron.*, 106.

188 *Paston Letters*, I, no. 367.

189 Whethamstede, I, 171ff, 386ff.

190 See above, p. 216.

191 *Hist. Croylandensis Continuatio*, 542–3.

192 *Gloucester Annals*, 356.

Select Bibliography

Accounts of the Lord High Treasurer [of Scotland], ed. T. Dickson, I, 1473–1498 (Edinburgh 1877).

ALLISON, K. J., 'Medieval Hull', *VCH Yorks., East Riding*, I.

ALLMAND, C. T. (ed.), *Society at War* (Edinburgh 1973).

ANDRÉ, BERNARD, *De vita atque gestis Henrici septimi ... historia*, in *Memorials of King Henry the Seventh*.

ANGLO, S., *Spectacle, Pageantry and Early Tudor Policy* (Oxford 1969).

Annales [rerum anglicanum], in *Letters and Papers Illustrative of the Wars of the English in France*, II, pt 2.

ARMSTRONG, C. A. J., 'Politics and the Battle of St Albans, 1455', *BIHR*, 33 (1960).

Arrivall: Historie of the Arrivall of King Edward IV, A.D. 1471, ed. J. Bruce (Camden Soc. 1838).

Arundel MS 19, in Kingsford, *English Historical Literature*.

ASTON, M., 'Richard II and the Wars of the Roses', in *The Reign of Richard II*, ed. F. R. H. Du Boulay and C. M. Barron (London 1971).

Bale's Chronicle, in *Six Town Chronicles*.

BASIN, THOMAS, *Histoire de Louis XI*, I–II, ed. C. Samaran and M.-C. Garand (Paris 1963–6).

Benet's Chronicle: John Benet's Chronicle for the years 1400 to 1462, ed. G. L. Harriss and M. A. Harriss, in *Camden Miscellany*, vol. XXIV (London 1972).

BERNALDEZ, ANDRES, *Memorias del reinado de los Reyes Católicos*, ed. M. Gomez-Moreno and J. de M. Carriazo (Madrid 1962).

BLACKMORE, H. L., *The Armouries of the Tower of London*, I, *Ordnance* (London 1976).

BORNSTEIN, D., 'Military Manuals in Fifteenth-Century England', *Mediaeval Studies*, 37 (1975).

BRIDPORT COFFERERS' ACCOUNTS, 1469–70, 1483–4, Dorset County Record Office, B3/M6.

BRIDPORT MUSTER ROLL, 1457, Dorset County Record Office, B3/FG3.

Brief Latin Chronicle, in *Three Fifteenth-Century Chronicles*.

Brief Notes, in *Three Fifteenth-Century Chronicles*.

BURNE, A. H., *The Battlefields of England* (London 1950).

BURNE, A. H., *More Battlefields of England* (London 1952).

Calendar of Close Rolls: Henry VI, vol. VI, 1454–61; Edward IV, vols I–II, 1461–8, 1468–76; Edward IV – Edward V – Richard III, 1476–85; Henry VII, 1485–1500 (London 1949–67).

Calendar of Documents Relating to Scotland, ed. J. Bain, IV, 1357–1509 (London 1888).

Calendar of Patent Rolls, Henry VI, vol. VI, 1452–61; Edward IV, vols I–II, 1461–7, 1467–77; Edward IV – Edward V – Richard III, 1476–85; Henry VII, vols. I–II, 1485–94, 1494–1509 (London 1910–16).

Calendar of Plea and Memoranda Rolls . . . of the City of London, 1458–1482, ed. P. E. Jones (Cambridge 1961).

Calendar of State Papers and Manuscripts existing in the Archives and Collections of Milan, I, 1385–1618, ed. A. B. Hinds (London 1913).

Calendar of State Papers and Manuscripts relating to English Affairs, existing in the Archives and Collections of Venice (etc.), I, 1202–1509, ed. R. Brown (London 1864).

CALMETTE, J., and PÉRINELLE, G., *Louis XI et l'Angleterre* (Paris 1930).

CAXTON, WILLIAM, *Prologues and Epilogues*, ed. W. J. B. Crotch (EETS 1928).

CAXTON, WILLIAM, *The Book of the Fayttes of Armes and of Chyualrye*, ed. A. T. P. Byles (EETS 1937).

The Cely Letters 1472–1488, ed. A. Hanham (EETS 1975).

CHARLESWORTH, D., 'The battle of Hexham, 1464', *Archaeologia Aeliana*, 4th ser., 30 (1952).

CHARLESWORTH, D., 'Northumberland in the early years of Edward IV', *Archaeologia Aeliana*, 4th ser., 31 (1953).

CHASTELLAIN, GEORGES, *Chronique*, in *Oeuvres*, IV and V, ed. K. de Lettenhove (Brussels 1864).

CHRIMES, S. B., *Henry VII* (London 1972).

Chronicles of London, ed. C. L. Kingsford (Oxford 1905).

COCKERMOUTH CASTLE MSS, Carlisle Record Office, Receivers' Account Rolls, D/Lec/28/28–9 (Neville); D/Lec/29/8 (Percy).

COMMYNES, PHILIPPE DE, *Mémoires*, ed. J. Calmette, III (Paris 1925); ed. and trans. M. Jones (London 1972); ed. and trans. S. Kinser and I. Cazeaux, II (Columbia, S. Carolina, 1973).

The Complete Peerage of England, Scotland, Ireland and the U.K., ed. G. E. Cokayne, V. Gibbs, H. A. Doubleday and others, 13 vols (London 1910–59).

Conway, A., *Henry VII's Relations with Scotland and Ireland 1485–1498* (Cambridge 1932).

Coventry Leet Book, ed. M. D. Harris, 4 pts (EETS, Original Ser., 1907–13).
DEVON: *Issues of the Exchequer*, I, ed. F. Devon (London 1837).
Dijon Relation, in Armstrong, 'Politics and the Battle of St Albans, 1455'.
DUNHAM, W. H., JR, *Lord Hastings' Indentured Retainers 1461–1483* (New Haven, Conn., 1955).
DUNLOP, A. I., *The Life and Times of James Kennedy, Bishop of St Andrews* (Edinburgh 1950).
ELLIS, SIR HENRY, *Original Letters* (etc.), 2nd ser., I (London 1827).
EMERY, A., 'The Development of Raglan Castle and Keeps in Late Medieval England', *Archaeological Jnl*, 132 (1975).
[An] English Chron[icle of the reigns of Richard II, Henry IV, Henry V and Henry VI], ed. J. S. Davies (Camden Soc. 1856).
EVANS, H. T.,*Wales and the Wars of the Roses* (Cambridge 1915).
EXETER CITY RECEIVERS' ACCOUNT ROLLS, 13–14 and 14–15 Henry VII, Devon Record Office.
Fastolf Relation, in Armstrong, 'Politics and the Battle of St Albans, 1455'.
Feodarium Prioratus Dunelmensis (etc.), Surtees Soc., 58 (1871).
Foedera[, Literae . . . et Acta Publica] (etc.), I–XV (London 1704–13).
FORTESCUE, SIR JOHN, *De Laudibus Legum Angliae*, trans. F. Grigor (London 1917).
FORTESCUE, SIR JOHN, *The Governance of England*, ed. C. Plummer (Oxford 1885).
FOWLER, K., *The Age of Plantagenet and Valois* (London 1967).
FOWLER, K. (ed.), *The Hundred Years War* (London 1971).
GAIRDNER, J., 'The Battle of Bosworth', *Archaeologia*, 55 (1896).
Gloucester Annals, in Kingsford, *English Historical Literature*.
GOODMAN, A., *A History of England from Edward II to James I* (London 1977).
GOODMAN, A., 'Henry VII and Christian renewal', *Religion and Humanism. Studies in Church History*, 17, Ecclesiastical History Society (Oxford 1981).
GOODMAN, A., and MACKAY, A., 'A Castilian report on English affairs, 1486', *EHR*, 88 (1973).
'GREGORY': *The Historical Collections of a London Citizen in the Fifteenth Century*, ed. J. Gairdner (Camden Soc. 1876).
GRIFFITHS, R. A., 'Local rivalries and national politics: the Percies, the Nevilles, and the Duke of Exeter, 1452–1455', *Speculum*, 43 (1968).
GRIMBLE, I., *The Harington Family* (London 1957).
HANHAM, A., *Richard III and His Early Historians 1483–1535* (Oxford 1975).
HAWARD, W. I., 'Economic Aspects of the Wars of the Roses in East Anglia', *EHR*, 41 (1926).
HEARNE, T. (ed.), John Leland's *Collectanea*, IV (London 1770) – anonymous account of the Stoke campaign.
Henley Borough Records. Assembly Books i–iv, 1395–1543, ed. P. M. Briers (Oxford 1960).

HICKS, M. A., 'Dynastic Change and Northern Society: the Career of the Fourth Earl of Northumberland, 1470–89', *Northern Hist.*, 14 (1978).

Historiae Croylandensis Continuatio, in *Rerum Anglicarum Scriptorum Veterum*, I, ed. W. Fulman (Oxford 1684); trans. in *Ingulph's Chronicle* (etc.), by H. T. Riley (London 1854).

HOGG, O. F. G., *The Royal Arsenal*, I (Oxford 1963).

HOOKER, J. R., 'Notes on the Organization and Supply of the Tudor Military under Henry VII', *Huntington Library Quarterly*, 23 (1959–60).

Household Books of John Duke of Norfolk and Thomas Earl of Surrey 1481–1490, ed. J. Payne Collier (Roxburghe Club 1844).

Ingulph's Chronicle (etc.), trans. H. T. Riley (London 1854).

Italian Relation: A Relation, or rather a True Account, of the Island of England, ed. C. A. Sneyd (Camden Soc. 1847).

KEEN, M. H., *The Laws of War in the Late Middle Ages* (London 1965).

KINGSFORD, C. L., *English Historical Literature in the Fifteenth Century* (Oxford 1913).

King's Works: Brown, R. Allen, Colvin, H. M., and Taylor, A. J., *History of the King's Works*, 3 vols (London 1963).

KNECHT, R. J., 'The Episcopate and the Wars of the Roses', *Univ. of Birmingham Hist. Jnl*, 6 (1957).

Knyghthode and Bataile, ed. R. Dyboski and Z. M. Arend (EETS 1935).

LANDER, J. R., *The Wars of the Roses* (London 1965).

LANDER, J. R., *Crown and Nobility 1450–1509* (London 1976).

LANDER, J. R., *Conflict and Stability in Fifteenth-Century England* (3rd edn, London 1977).

Letters and Papers [illustrative of the reigns of Richard III and Henry VII], I, ed. J. Gairdner (Rolls ser. 1861).

Lincolnshire Rebellion: Chronicle of the Rebellion in Lincolnshire, 1470, ed. J. G. Nichols, in *Camden Miscellany*, 1847.

MCFARLANE, K. B., 'The Wars of the Roses', *Proc. of the British Academy*, 50 (1964).

MCFARLANE, K. B., *The Nobility of Later Medieval England* (Oxford 1973).

MCKISACK, M., *Medieval History in the Tudor Age* (Oxford 1971).

MAJOR, JOHN, *A History of Greater Britain*, trans. and ed. A. Constable (Scottish History Society, Edinburgh 1892).

MALLETT, M., *Mercenaries and their Masters. Warfare in Renaissance Italy* (London 1974).

MALORY, SIR THOMAS, *Works*, ed. E. Vinaver, 3 vols (Oxford 1967).

MANCINI, DOMINIC, *The Usurpation of Richard III*, ed. C. A. J. Armstrong (Oxford 1969).

Materials [for a History of the Reign of Henry VII], I, ed. W. Campbell (Rolls ser. 1873).

Memorials [of King Henry the Seventh], ed. J. Gairdner (Rolls ser. 1858).

MOLINET, JEAN DE, *Chronique*, ed. G. Doutrepont and O. Jodogne, I–II

(Brussels 1935).

MORGAN, D. A. L., 'The King's Affinity in the Polity of Yorkist England', *TRHS*, 5th ser., 23 (1973).

MS Tanner 2, in *Six Town Chronicles*.

O'NEIL, B. H. ST J., *Castles and Cannon* (Oxford 1960).

OWEN, H., and BLAKEWAY, J. B., *A History of Shrewsbury*, I (London 1825).

The Paston Letters 1422–1509, ed. J. Gairdner, 3 vols (Edinburgh 1910).

PIGGOT, JOHN, *Memoranda*, in Kingsford, *English Historical Literature*.

Plumpton Correspondence, ed. T. Stapleton (Camden Soc. 1839).

POLLARD, A. F., *The Reign of Henry VII from Contemporary Sources*, 3 vols (London 1913–14).

POLLARD, A. J., 'Lord FitzHugh's rising in 1470', *BIHR*, 52 (1979).

POULSON, G., *Beverlac*, I (London 1829).

POWICKE, M. R., *Military Obligation in Medieval England* (Oxford 1962).

POWICKE, M. R., 'Lancastrian Captains', in *Essays in Medieval History presented to Bertie Wilkinson*, ed. T. A. Sandquist and M. R. Powicke (Toronto 1969).

The Priory of Hexham, I (Surtees Soc. 1864).

Proceedings and Ordinances of the Privy Council of England, ed. Sir Harris Nicolas, VI (London 1837).

PUBLIC RECORD OFFICE, EXCHEQUER, VARIOUS ACCOUNTS, E. 101/55/14; ordnance received at Calais and other fortresses in France, *temp.* Edward IV–Henry VII.

RAWCLIFFE, C., *The Staffords, Earls of Stafford and Dukes of Buckingham 1394–1521* (Cambridge 1978).

Records of the Borough of Nottingham, II–III (London 1883–5).

The Records of the City of Norwich, ed. W. H. Hudson and J. C. Tingey, I (Norwich 1906).

RICHMOND, C., 'Fauconberg's Kentish rising of May 1471', *EHR*, 85 (1970).

RICHMOND, C., 'The Nobility and the Wars of the Roses, 1459–61', *Nottingham Mediaeval Studies*, 21 (1977).

ROBBINS: *Historical Poems of the XIVth and XVth Centuries*, ed. R. H. Robbins (New York 1959).

ROSS, C., *Edward IV* (London 1974).

ROSS, C., *The Wars of the Roses* (London 1976).

Rotuli Parliamentorum, ed. J. Strachey and others, 6 vols (London 1767–83).

The Royal Commission on Historical Manuscripts: Fifth Report, I, Rye, Lydd (1876); *Eleventh Report*, Appendix, part 3, Southampton and King's Lynn (1887); *Fifteenth Report*, Appendix, part 10, Shrewsbury (1899).

SCOFIELD, C. L., *The Life and Reign of Edward the Fourth*, 2 vols (London 1923).

SHARPE, R. R., *London and the Kingdom*, I (London 1894).

Short English Chronicle, in *Three Fifteenth-Century Chronicles*.

Six Town Chronicles of England, ed. R. Flenley (Oxford 1911).

The Statutes of the Realm, II (London 1816).

STONE, JOHN, *Chronicle*, ed. W. G. Searle (Cambridge 1902).

The Stonor Letters and Papers 1290–1483, ed. C. L. Kingsford, 2 vols (Camden ser. 1919).

STOREY, R. L., *The End of the House of Lancaster* (London 1966).

STOREY, R. L. (ed.), *The Wars of the Roses*. Exhibition of Records, Public Record Office, March–May, 1961 (Catalogue).

Testamenta Eboracensia, II and III (Surtees Soc. 1855–64).

THOMSON, J. A. F., ' "The Arrivall of Edward IV" – The Development of the Text', *Speculum*, 46 (1971).

THOMSON, J. A. F., 'The Courtenay Family in the Yorkist Period', *BIHR*, 45 (1972).

THOMSON, J. A. F., 'John de la Pole, Duke of Suffolk', *Speculum*, 54 (1979).

Three Fifteenth-Century Chronicles, ed. J. Gairdner (Camden Soc. 1880).

TUDOR-CRAIG, P., *Richard III* (Ipswich 1977).

Tudor Royal Proclamations, ed. P. L. Hughes and J. F. Larkin, I (New Haven, Conn., 1964).

TURNER, H. L., *Town Defences in England and Wales* (London 1971).

VALE, M. G. A., 'New Techniques and Old Ideals: The Impact of Artillery on War and Chivalry at the End of the Hundred Years War' in *War, Literature and Politics in the Late Middle Ages*, ed. C. T. Allmand (Liverpool 1976).

VERGIL, POLYDORE, *Anglicae Historiae libri viginti septem* (Basel 1555); *Three Books of Polydore Vergil's English History . . . from an early translation*, ed. Sir Henry Ellis (Camden Soc. 1844); *The Anglica Historia of Polydore Vergil A.D. 1485–1537*, trans. D. Hay (Camden ser. 1950).

WARKWORTH, JOHN, *A Chronicle of the First Thirteen Years of the Reign of King Edward the Fourth*, ed. J. O. Halliwell (Camden Soc. 1839).

Wars of The English in France: Letters and Papers Illustrative of the Wars of the English in France during the Reign of Henry VI, ed. J. Stevenson, 2 vols (Rolls ser. 1864).

WAURIN, JEHAN DE, *Recuiel des Croniques et Anchiennes Istories de la Grant Bretagne, à present nommé Engleterre*, V, ed. Sir William Hardy and E. L. C. P. Hardy (Rolls ser. 1891).

WEEVER, J., *Ancient Funerall Monuments* (etc.) (London 1631).

WHETHAMSTEDE, JOHN, *Register*, in *Registra quorundam Abbatum Monasterii S. Albani*, ed. H. T. Riley, I (Rolls ser. 1872).

White Rose: Chronicles of the White Rose of York, ed. J. A. Giles (1845).

WILLIAMS, C. H., 'The Rebellion of Humphrey Stafford in 1486', *EHR*, 43 (1928).

WORCESTRE, WILLIAM, *Itineraries*, ed. J. H. Harvey (Oxford 1969).

York Civic Records, I–II, ed. A. Raine (Yorkshire Archaeological Soc., Record Ser. 1939–41).

A Yorkist Collection, in Kingsford, *English Historical Literature*.

Yorkist Notes, in Kingsford, *English Historical Literature*.

Index